MMADD about the arts!
An Introduction to Primary Arts Education

Dedicated to my much-loved nieces
Heidi (1982–2002),
Erica (1984–) and
Bonnie (1989–) Hendriks
Through their active involvement in the arts from an early age
they developed into creative, sensitive and artistic young women!

MMADD about the arts!

An Introduction to Primary Arts Education

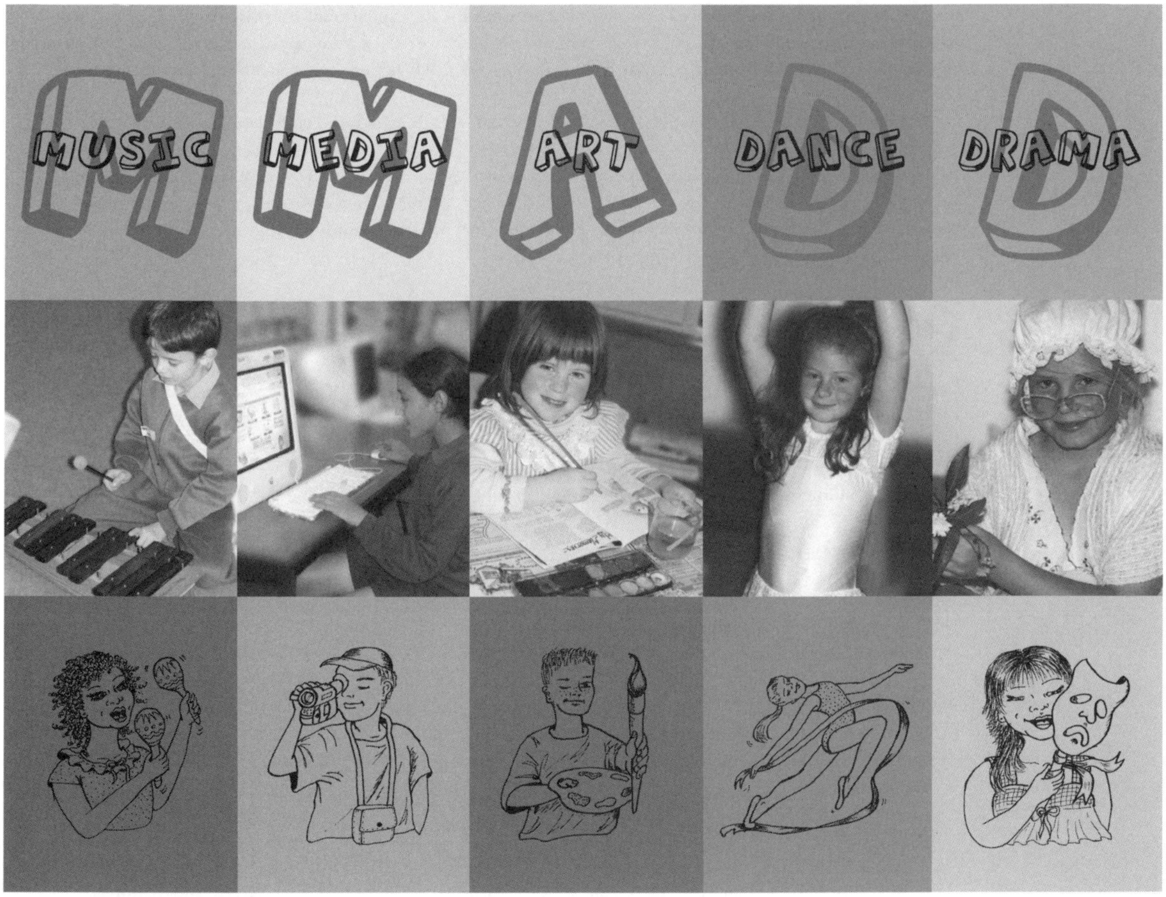
MUSIC
MEDIA
ART
DANCE
DRAMA

PEARSON
Prentice Hall

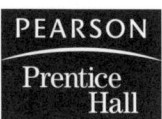

Deirdre Russell-Bowie

Copyright © Pearson Education Australia (a division of Pearson Australia Group Pty Ltd) 2006

Pearson Education Australia
Unit 4, Level 3
14 Aquatic Drive
Frenchs Forest NSW 2086

www.pearsoned.com.au

The *Copyright Act 1968* of Australia allows a maximum of one chapter or 10% of this book, whichever is the greater, to be copied by any educational institution for its educational purposes provided that that educational institution (or the body that administers it) has given a remuneration notice to Copyright Agency Limited (CAL) under the Act. For details of the CAL licence for educational institutions contact:
Copyright Agency Limited, telephone: (02) 9394 7600, email: info@copyright.com.au

All rights reserved. Except under the conditions described in the *Copyright Act 1968* of Australia and subsequent amendments, no part of this publication may be reproduced, stored in a retrieval system or transmitted in any form or by any means, electronic, mechanical, photocopying, recording or otherwise, without the prior permission of the copyright owner.

Senior Acquisitions Editor: Alison Green
Senior Project Editor: Kathryn Fairfax
Assistant Editor: Jill Gillies
Copy Editor: Valerie Marlborough
Proofreader: Annie Chandler
Indexer: Garry Cousins
Cover and internal design by Wideopen
Typeset by Midland Typesetters, Maryborough, Vic.

Printed in Malaysia (CTP - PP)

3 4 5 10 09 08 07 06
National Library of Australia
Cataloguing-in-Publication Data

Russell-Bowie, Deirdre
MMADD about arts: an introduction to primary arts education.

   Bibliography.
   Includes index.
   ISBN 1 74103 235 0.

   1. Art - Study and teaching - Australia. 2. Art - Study and teaching (Primary). 3. Performing arts - Study and teaching (Primary). 4. Music - Study and teaching (Primary). I. Title.

372.5044

Every effort has been made to trace and acknowledge copyright. However, should any infringement have occurred, the publishers tender their apologies and invite copyright owners to contact them.

An imprint of Pearson Education Australia
(a division of Pearson Australia Group Pty Ltd)

Contents

Preface	vii
About the author	ix
Acknowledgements	x

Chapter 1 The state of the arts — 1

Introduction	2
The arts in society	2
A brief history of primary arts education in Australia	5
Different ways of viewing arts education	11
Who should teach the arts? The generalist versus the specialist debate	13
Implementing a quality arts program	16
Springboards for discussion and application	18

Chapter 2 The creative arts classroom — 19

Introduction	20
The importance of the arts	20
Effective communication	24
Behaviour management strategies	29
Lesson planning in the arts	33
Assessment in arts education	38
Springboards for discussion and application	42

Chapter 3 Introduction to music education — 43

Introduction	44
Why teach music education?	44
Music in the primary classroom	45
Elements of music	46
Repertoire in music	48
Some musical terms explained	49
Making, performing and appreciating	54
Practical considerations	56
Five ways of learning music	57
Activities to introduce and teach the musical elements	66
Springboards for discussion and application	103

Chapter 4 Introduction to media education — 105

Introduction	106
Media and the child	106
Why teach media education?	108
Forms of media	109
Designing, making and appreciating media	110
Practical considerations	115

Activities to introduce and teach forms of media	117
Springboards for discussion and application	146

Chapter 5 Introduction to visual arts education — 147

Introduction	148
Designing, making and appreciating	148
Subject matter in visual arts	150
Composition and design in visual arts	155
Practical considerations	170
Brief overview of art history	171
Activities to introduce the different forms of visual arts	174
Springboards for discussion and application	187
Further reading	187

Chapter 6 Introduction to dance education — 189

Introduction	190
Learning *through* dance	190
Learning *in* dance: The elements of dance	192
Making, performing and appreciating dances	193
Practical considerations	196
Activities to introduce the elements of dance	203
Springboards for discussion and application	225

Chapter 7 Introduction to drama education — 226

Introduction	227
Drama in the classroom	227
Learning *through* drama	228
Learning *in* drama: The elements of drama	230
Types of drama	233
Practical considerations	239
Activities to introduce the elements of drama	244
Springboards for discussion and application	254

Chapter 8 Integration and the arts — 256

Introduction	257
To integrate or not to integrate, that is the question!	257
Various models of integration	258
Integrated arts programs, multiliteracies and Multiple Intelligences	262
Community Harmony Project: Real-life *syntegrated* creative arts project	262
How do the Multiple Intelligences relate to the classroom?	270
Four approaches using the Multiple Intelligences in the classroom	271
The arts, Multiple Intelligences and literacy	273
Syntegrating the arts and Multiple Intelligences to explore colour	276
Springboards for discussion and application	286
Useful websites	286

Chapter 9 Putting it all together: An introduction to programming in the arts — 288

Introduction	289
Programming in arts education	289
Making, performing, and appreciating	289
Purpose, content and teaching strategies	291
Summary of content in music, media, art, dance and drama	294
Sample integrated arts programs for four stages: Introduction	296
I Am Me	298
Wombat Stew	303
Transport	308
The Sea	313
Sounds Great!	318
'Advance Australia Fair!'	324
Springboards for discussion and application	333

Index — 335

Preface

So you want to teach music, media, art, dance and drama in the primary school? This book will give you the basics and get you started on this wonderfully rewarding and exciting journey you are beginning!

This book is aimed at preservice and beginning teachers who would like to teach the arts (music, media, art, dance and drama) in their classroom but do not feel they have sufficient skills or adequate knowledge to implement a quality arts program. As such, the book seeks to provide some introductory theory and practical suggestions for implementing creative arts lessons. Using this text, beginning teachers can gain confidence in teaching the arts and involve children in valuable arts processes and practices. When confident, they can then delve further into each art form, using the suggested references to create more challenging and in-depth arts experiences for their children.

Unsure where to start?

The songs and learning experiences in this book will provide support for preservice and beginning generalist teachers as the book contains a wealth of practical classroom ideas that can be adapted and used to suit the needs, interests, cultures and prior experiences of your children. The activities can be modified to be taught across all stages, and lend themselves to simplification or extension to suit younger or older children and those who are less or more experienced in the arts. Once you have gained some confidence in teaching the art forms, find and use other songs, poems, music, movement stimuli, dances, artworks and learning experiences to suit the interests, culture and experience of your class.

How does it fit my state syllabus?

Adapt and use the songs, activities and ideas to fit the framework of your state syllabus. Avoid using them as a shopping cart of gimmicks; rather, try to understand the theory, practice and philosophy behind your state syllabus and how these activities relate to this. You can then create your own sequential, developmental lessons and programs for your particular class. Don't be afraid of repeating activities across the

grades, using different content and challenging children to move deeper into their understanding and experience of the art form.

Brief overview

The first chapter puts the arts in perspective within the Australian setting, and discusses different ways of viewing and teaching the arts. The second chapter argues the importance of the inclusion of the arts in the primary curriculum and details effective classroom communication, assessment and management skills. The five central chapters introduce basic content for each of the art forms of music, media, visual arts, dance and drama. The last two chapters recognise that although each art form is a discrete entity in itself, children's learning and understanding of the arts can also be enhanced through integrating the art forms across the arts key learning area and across the curriculum using the Multiple Intelligences. Examples of integrated programs are suggested and a compact disc (CD) of simple introductory songs is included with cross-referencing to activities throughout the book.

Going further

In a book this size aimed at covering such a diverse collection of art forms, it is impossible to devote sufficient time and space to each or to all the different theories and practices related to teaching each of the art forms, to completely satisfy the confident arts student or specialist arts teacher. Further in-depth study of different theoretical approaches to each of the art forms and child development within each art form can be followed up using the reference books listed at the end of each chapter as well as books from your local or university library.

About the author

Associate Professor Deirdre Russell-Bowie, DipTeach, BEd, AssDipMusic, GradDipArts, Dalcroze Level II, MEd(Hons), PhD

Deirdre Russell-Bowie has been teaching, lecturing and researching in creative arts education in several countries for over 25 years and has published prolifically in journals, professional publications, national and international conference proceedings, and popular magazines. She was the president of the Creative and Practical Arts Association for ten years and during that time organised and presented at primary arts education conferences around New South Wales. As well as being in demand as a practitioner-researcher, Deirdre has produced over 30 creative arts resource books, cassettes and videos that have sold both nationally and internationally. Recently, she was awarded the 2001 Australian Award for University Teaching (Social Sciences) and in 2002 she received the University of Western Sydney Vice Chancellor's Award for Excellence. Deirdre is currently Associate Professor in Creative Arts Education at the University of Western Sydney.

Acknowledgements

This book has been written as a result of the inspiration, encouragement and enthusiasm of teachers, lecturers and children with whom I have worked over the years. While president of the Creative and Practical Arts Association, I was delighted to work with creative and inspiring colleagues and friends who encouraged me to extend my learning in all art forms; they include Verity Madsen, Nika Norman, Moira Gibson, Tania Chahoud, Laura Solomon and Nicki Graham. My university students have also been influential in keeping me in touch with the challenges and practicalities of teaching the arts in today's classrooms. Working with them in arts tutorials and on professional experience has been a rewarding and enjoyable experience. Another colleague and friend, Elsa Jara, created the wonderful drawings throughout the book, which often say more than many words — thank you for sharing your talent! Recently I have been honoured to work on a creative arts project with staff and children from Banksia Road Public School from whom I have learned so much. A special 'thank you' to Penny Lee and the Community Harmony project children, many of whose photos and artworks appear in the following chapters!

As this book was in the development stages I was grateful for the constructive and helpful feedback I received from reviewers, such as Margaret Baguley, Lee Emery, Maria Egan, Kate Donelan, Mary-Rose McLaren, Kath Grushka, Margery Hertzberg and Terry Mason. Thank you, also, to Judy Thistleton-Martin for collaborating with me on some of the literature-based visual arts and drama activities and to my research assistants, Lynne Murray and Richard Hodge, for their excellent work. Finally, I wish to gratefully acknowledge my husband, Vaughan, for his loving support and encouragement while I was writing this book and Ripley, our blue heeler, for making us take time out of our busy writing schedules to play and sit in the sun!

chapter one
The state of the arts

The best schools have the best arts programs. Excellence in education and excellence in the arts seem to go hand in hand.
(Fowler, 1999)

Learning outcomes
By the end of this chapter, students will be able to:
- briefly outline the history of primary arts education in Australia;
- list ways in which the arts are important in social and cultural contexts;
- discuss the pros and cons of having specialist or generalist teachers responsible for arts education in the primary school;
- identify key principles for implementing a quality arts program.

Introduction

The arts are an integral and important component of our everyday lives. As such, they need to be a vital part of our children's education. Every day we are surrounded in some way by music, media, dance, visual arts and drama, at home, at school, at work and in public places. We engage in the arts as we listen to music; attend concerts and plays; decorate our lounge rooms; doodle as we talk on the phone; choose products based on colour, line and shape; buy clothes to make us look good; express ourselves through voice, gesture and movement; celebrate birthdays, weddings and funerals with music, colour, rituals and movement; and are surrounded by advertisements which use all art forms to persuade us to become more ardent consumers.

Through the arts we gain information, sell products, enjoy leisure time, learn about different cultures and different times, express our innermost feelings and thoughts, and share in the dreams and experiences of others. Millions of dollars are spent on the arts every year in Australia, as the arts are used as vehicles for consumerism, teaching, pleasure, performance, self-expression, information sharing, earning a living, consciousness raising and many more significant end products. But where are the arts in our schools? Do they have the all-encompassing pervasiveness and prominence that is their place in society? And how can they be taught effectively in the primary school? This chapter will examine the place of the arts in society, explore the history of primary arts education, investigate different ways of viewing arts education, discuss the use of specialist and generalist teachers in relation to arts education in the primary school, and identify key factors of a quality arts program.

The arts in society

Communication and self-expression

Children engaged in the arts ... are engaged in a potentially profound form of communication. (Eisner, 2002)

Since the beginning of time, in all societies and cultures, human beings have used the arts to communicate and express themselves. Pictures were drawn on cave walls, songs accompanied by instruments from the environment were sung and acted out to tell of brave deeds, dances told of hunting expeditions and play-acting was used to teach children survival and life skills. For thousands of years, indigenous people across the world have understood that the arts are integral to life and vital to the rituals, routines, celebrations and continuation of tribal culture. Artworks for decoration and instruction cover the walls, ceilings and floors of places of worship; and music, dance and drama are often used in religious, sporting or entertainment rituals. Today, we use the arts as ways of knowing and communicating who we are, where we have come from and what we believe. Symbols have been developed to enhance communication and self-expression with each area of the arts, which has its own unique language to express and communicate meaning and identity.

Cultural heritage and social identity

The arts are intrinsic components of human culture, heritage and creativity. (Clay, Hertrich, Jones, Mills & Rose, 1998)

The arts have evolved within each society as a means of consolidating cultural and social identity and connecting past with future generations. The arts have been used to pass on rituals, values, stories, knowledge, beliefs and attitudes from one generation to the next, strengthen social identity and keep history and culture alive. In modern society some cultures sell their arts so others may learn more about them. Through studying and engaging in the arts of our own and other cultures and traditions, we deepen our knowledge and understanding of them.

As well as being used to preserve and transmit cultural traditions and stories through the generations, the arts can be used as dynamic agents of social change, challenging old perspectives and reinterpreting familiar ideas. Even in cultures and religions that do not celebrate all the art forms there is still a significant amount of their identity, culture and heritage expressed in the art forms in which they do participate. By understanding our past through the arts, we can gain an appreciation of our current culture and dream of the possibilities that can shape the future.

We use the arts as ways of knowing and communicating who we are.

Values and emotions

The value of the arts lies in their ability to depict and explore universal human experiences and emotions. (Clark, 1997)

The arts can be used to communicate values and emotions. We use the arts to formulate, clarify and critically reflect on our own ideas, beliefs and feelings and to construct and reinforce our values. Then we challenge and transform these as we interact with the values and emotions of others through the arts. They help us to understand the beliefs and feelings of other people, other cultures and other societies, as we 'walk in their shoes' by engaging with their artworks and participating in different reflections of reality. Because the arts can embody and communicate emotions, ideas, beliefs and values they can convey meaning through aesthetic forms and symbols and evoke emotive responses to life with or without words.

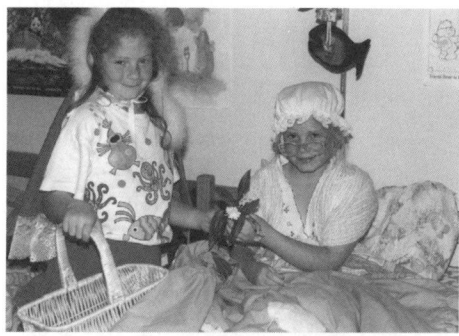

The arts can be used to preserve and transmit cultural traditions and stories through the generations.

Personal development

Engagement in the arts nurtures the development of cognitive, social and personal competencies. (Fiske, 1999)

The arts are fundamental to the development of emotional, social and cultural skills and also make a significant contribution to our

The arts help develop creativity and self-expression.

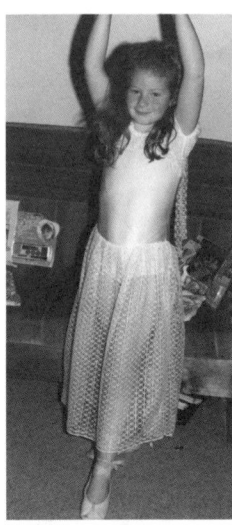

The arts develop our fine and gross motor skills.

spiritual, physical and cognitive growth. They are unique in their ability to combine intellect with emotion, left-brain with right-brain thinking, formal training with free expression, rigid personal self-discipline with creative, free-flowing interactive experiences, and divergent with convergent thinking. The arts develop our verbal, sensory and literacy skills, our critical and intuitive thinking skills, our fine and gross motor skills, and our interpersonal and emotional skills. They reach into our very souls and touch the deepest parts of our lives, tapping into previously unknown wells of creativity and self-expression, and releasing a wealth of new ideas, initiatives and innovations to expand our world view and deepen our experience of life.

Creativity and life skills

Without the arts we would lose the fabric of creativity, expression of the self, and ultimately civilisation. **(Penny, Ford, Price & Young, 2002)**

The arts are a vital component in the development of creativity in children and provide us with meaningful explorations of our own personal creativity. They stimulate our imagination and bring us into other times, places and cultures to assist in our understanding of other people. Creativity does not just belong to the arts — it can be seen in many aspects of life — but the arts are crucial in developing and nurturing this innate creative urge which sets us apart from any other being on this earth. The arts develop in us life skills that are sought after in the workplace and in social settings — skills such as planning, experimenting, problem solving, decision making, leadership and teamwork. Through involvement in the arts we can develop self-esteem, trust, cooperation, critical thinking skills, social skills, self-discipline and creativity. All of these skills developed through active engagement in the arts are essential for effective participation in the workforce and in adult life.

The arts help develop children's social skills such as leadership, teamwork and problem solving.

Industry and vocation

Arts education is important not only to train the next generation of professional artists but also to raise the next generation of artistic consumers. **(SERCARC, 1995)**

The arts are a multimillion dollar industry of significant importance to the economy. In Australia the 'cultural industries' have been described as similar in economic importance to the electricity, transport and banking industries; greater than the building, motor vehicle, pharmaceutical or alcohol industries; and much greater than the sheep, wheat, wool and beef industries. They have grown substantially each year and continue to contribute significantly to the Australian economy (SERCARC, 1995). However, although this can give some credibility to the arts in an economic rationalist environment, this should not be the reason for engaging in the arts as it ignores their fundamental contribution to the spiritual, cultural, creative, aesthetic and human side of life. But it does raise the issue that, for such an impressive industry, major funding should be released to educate the next generation of arts consumers, and to identify, nurture, train and mentor future artists in each of the different art forms to ensure the arts industry continues to grow and thrive.

Quality of life

Arts learning can enhance the sense of accomplishment and well-being among our young people. **(Fiske, 1999)**

Engagement in the arts plays an important role in enhancing our quality of life, giving us opportunity to relax, create, communicate and explore what it means to be 'me'. Most people experience some forms of the arts every day, either as spectators (through television, radio, films, CDs, concerts, plays, advertising and so on), or as active participants engaging creatively in making, performing and appreciating one or more art forms. Through these experiences, we find that the arts offer us enjoyment, satisfaction and meaning in life. In a society where technology and economics play such a major role in everyday life the arts bring a humanising influence to our sense of being and identity and touch deep into our psyche, giving us a rich quality of life that consumerism and materialism cannot begin to fill.

The next generation of artists needs to be nurtured, mentored and trained.

A brief history of primary arts education in Australia

Pre-1770

The Indigenous people of Australia saw the arts as an integrated part of their life. The arts were passed down from parent to child, and from elder to initiate, and were experienced throughout their lives as part of their identity and culture. Children's involvement in the arts from birth formed a major part of the spiritual, relationship, social and entertainment life of the community.

1880s

Since colonial times the arts have been present in Australian education systems in some form or other. As Australia was a British colony, it was natural that the Australian system of education came from that which was practised in 19th-century Britain. Music, drawing and painting were valued as part of a refined education, and in some vocational courses mechanical drawing or perspective was taught. Singing was seen to have a humanising and civilising influence on the lower classes;

It is vital to bring this wellspring of creativity into our children's lives at an early age.

it was taught to improve the quality of worship in the churches and to ensure that the workers were industrious, loyal and religious. If listening lessons were included, high art music was used and 'proper' upper class young ladies learned to play an instrument. Music was not taught for its own sake and there was no thought of children composing or moving creatively to music.

In the mid-1800s, singing and drawing masters visited the primary schools as specialist teachers, taking children for lessons that focused specifically on these two subjects. However, this became too costly to continue and in the 1860s music and drawing were moved out of the school curriculum and became extracurricular

subjects for which parents needed to pay a fee if they wanted their children to learn these skills. The concept of free and compulsory education for primary schoolchildren was introduced in the early 1870s, and singing and drawing were once again included in the core curriculum. However, with the economic depression of the 1890s government systems could no longer afford specialist teachers in these areas. This resulted in the generalist teachers, who were often untrained and ill-equipped to teach these subjects, becoming responsible for all subjects in their classroom, resulting in singing and drawing becoming almost non-existent in the primary school.

1900s

In the early 20th century, each state responded to this situation with its own policy of generalists and/or specialists teaching the arts subjects. Music education consisted of mainly singing and visual arts was predominantly drawing. Dance and drama were rarely seen as separate subjects or as an important part of the primary curriculum. If included at all, dance was part of physical education, and drama was covered in English. Media studies in the primary classroom were non-existent and only in preschool education were the arts seen as part of the core curriculum. By the mid-1920s, although there were singing and drawing classes in independent schools and private lessons in dance, piano and theory outside of school, there were no music or art specialists in Australian state schools apart from a few advisors in New South Wales and Victoria. Over the next 40 years, these state policies changed, depending on how strongly or otherwise the political leaders valued the arts in education.

1950s

In the 1950s dramatic changes were introduced in the area of arts education, as new theories of children's creativity were explored. Art education began to move away from the formal whole-class step-by-step textbook teaching that pervaded the other subjects in the curriculum and children were being given materials, stimuli and assistance to create their own artworks through discovery and creativity. In music education, recorders along with tuned and untuned percussion instruments were introduced into the classroom and in some schools percussion bands were developed. However, drama and music still tended to consist of formal study of the subject, singing songs and presenting plays, and movement and dance were restricted mainly to young children.

1960s

As a reflection of the emphasis on the formal study of the arts, arts curricula were generally developed and prepared by experts in the particular arts areas until the 1960s. This was based on the presumption that every primary schoolteacher was literate within that area and so could implement the highly prescriptive activities presented in the syllabus. Curriculum development procedures were characterised by certain traditions which included centralisation, lack of independence for teachers and schools in relation to curriculum decision making, and syllabuses being firmly locked into a content and age–grade approach. Few teachers were involved in the revision and content of the syllabus, and inspectors and principals were expected to act as the change agents, disseminating information to the teachers about the new syllabus. Thus the teacher was seen as a curriculum-content implementer and had no input into the actual development of the curriculum. The arts syllabuses of this era usually focused on music, art and craft, with a fairly formal approach to drama being included in the language arts syllabus and formal movement and folk dance strands included in the physical education syllabus.

1970s

In the early 1970s the heady optimism of the new federal Labor Government resulted in an abundance of resources being made available to schools and government departments on an educational and social, rather than an economic, basis. The Whitlam Government introduced large-scale changes that led to a rapid growth of resources in the educational arena. New trends, processes, structures and programs began to appear on the Australian education scene. These provided opportunities for educational innovations to be approved and funded by the state departments of education who made the decisions and allocated the resources within the state systems.

Significant changes influencing curriculum development

The 1970s also brought the emergence of other significant factors that created a profound shift in curriculum development. These factors included this greater availability of resources for innovative activity in schools, increasing migration which was changing the nature of Australian society, substantial advances in the understanding of ways in which children develop and learn, the extension of teacher-training programs and the development of more participative ways of decision making in many areas of public life. All of these affected curriculum development within arts education and other curriculum areas.

Since World War II, there has been a significant increase in the number of people coming from other countries and settling in Australia. As the demographics of Australia changed, so did the values and content in relation to arts education. Until then, Australian arts education had been focusing on Anglo-European content; however, with incoming migrants this narrow view was being questioned. A more multicultural approach was promulgated, and content and policy reflected this change. As well, Aboriginal communities became increasingly recognised and vocal, and this had a significant impact on the school and curriculum planners in relation to the arts. These influences resulted in multicultural and Aboriginal artists, music, artworks and culture being incorporated into the Australian arts curricula to give children a broader, more inclusive experience within the arts.

However, arts education was still given a minor role in most educational institutions. Within the arts, there was still a pecking order of subject importance, with music, art and craft being fairly widely accepted, drama being seen as part of English and not as a subject in its own right, and dance mainly being taught at the preschool level or as part of physical education.

1977 research project: *Education and the arts*

At this stage in the history of arts education, two federal government bodies (the Schools Commission and Australia Council, 1977) combined to research the state of arts education in Australia. Within this project, *Education and the arts*, the arts

were defined as visual arts, craft, music, drama, dance, film, television and radio as well as creative writing. This joint project was the first national study of its kind in relation to arts education and as such it confirmed what arts educators have always known: that the arts are an important and recognised part of the curriculum. Findings from this extensive report indicated that although the arts were seen to have value in a child's education, many primary-aged children did not have access to a quality, developmental arts program in their schooling and few children had the opportunity to engage in significant experiences in the art forms. The report recommended a substantial shift in approach to arts education in order to emphasise the learning involved in quality engagement within the arts instead of focusing just on the skills that could be developed. It advanced national objectives and strategies for arts education programs to ensure that all young persons were able to actively engage in quality arts experiences in every year of their schooling at least until mid-secondary school and continue their involvement in the arts throughout their lives.

1980s

As a result of the 1977 *Education and the arts* project, which indicated clearly that arts education had been inadequately supported in the past, the federal government set up a taskforce to recommend Commonwealth strategies and initiatives in education and arts.

1985 Taskforce — *Action: Education and the arts*

The 1985 report from this taskforce, *Action: Education and the arts* (Commonwealth Department of Education, 1985), noted the inadequacies of arts education in the present systems and emphasised the need for a concerted effort to promote and develop arts education in and out of schools. It put forward 34 recommendations for action and linked these with specified funding to ensure the outcomes would be achieved by Australia's Bicentennial Year (1988) and consolidated over the next few years. Various national and state committees were set up to monitor and facilitate the implementation of these recommendations which aimed to significantly improve the quality of arts education in schools and the community.

The 1980s also heralded another influence on arts education: the influx of new technologies available to teachers and the arrival of computers in classrooms and libraries around the country. If their remote communities had the appropriate infrastructure, this allowed rural and isolated schools to reduce their disadvantage by networking with other schools throughout the country and overseas, as well as having a multiplicity of arts resources literally at their fingertips. It allowed teachers and children to access artworks from museums and galleries around the world; listen to music, compose their own music and print it out professionally; record, critique and store their dance, music and drama performances; critically analyse and use a variety of media; learn about the arts interactively; and in many ways change the way the arts had previously been conceived and taught. There were, of course, continuing debates about using such technology within an arts education program, and each teacher and school needed to work out how they would use this technology as a tool to create the best quality arts program that was possible within their context.

1988 Dawkins Green Paper: *Strengthening Australia's schools*

Within the political arena in 1988 the federal government published the Dawkins Green Paper *Strengthening Australia's schools* as an attempt to bring about improvement in literacy, numeracy and critical thinking skills. This paper proposed that the content and focus of schools should be restructured with an emphasis on literacy, mathematics, science and technology; however, no mention of the arts was included as part of the basic skills for Australian children. This marginalised the arts further as the policies and philosophies of this paper placed national educational decisions within the context of economic rationalist principles, which viewed artistic expressions and arts education as merely a marketable commodity, being valued as training for employment and not in its own right. As a result, state educational systems followed the Green Paper's priorities and channelled their focus and resources into literacy, mathematics, science and technology.

1989: National goals for Australian schooling

Dawkins also recommended the creation of a national curriculum and in 1989 the Australian Education Council (AEC) published the *Common and agreed national goals for Australian schooling* which outlined eight key learning areas: English, mathematics, science, studies of society, health, languages other than English (LOTE), environment and technology, and the arts (which included music, media, visual arts, dance and drama).

1990s

In the early 1990s the Finn and Mayer reports (Finn, 1991; Mayer Committee, 1992) recommended certain generic competencies that employers required of school leavers. These key competencies were specific to the areas of language and communication, mathematics, scientific and technological understanding, cultural understanding, problem solving, and personal and interpersonal skills, again with no specific reference to the arts. This led to the recommendation that a national standards framework be developed which described clearly each of the competencies at a range of different levels of performance. These standards were to be instrumental in the development of future curriculum and assessment procedures for the last years of schooling.

1994: National curriculum statements and profiles

As a result of the agreed national goals for schooling in Australia and the resulting national standards framework, a series of statements and profiles for schools were developed in relation to each of the eight key learning areas. The *statements* provided a framework for curriculum development by education systems and schools, and the *profiles* were developed to improve learning and teaching in schools and to provide benchmarks and a common language for reporting student achievement. The profiles described the typical learning progress of children in each of the arts areas throughout the compulsory years of schooling, and arranged these in eight levels across four bands of schooling.

Based on these statements and profiles, each state developed its own syllabuses based on the eight key learning areas. Some states, such as Victoria, kept their syllabuses very close to the statements and profiles while other states, such as New

South Wales, developed their own syllabuses, which were only loosely based on the statements and profiles. For example, in New South Wales primary schools there are six key learning areas and not eight: English, maths, science and technology, PDHPE, human society and its environment and the arts, which include music, dance, drama and visual arts, but not media. Thus individual arts subject syllabuses were no longer used, and the more general arts syllabuses formed part of the new curriculum for primary schools across Australia.

This rationalisation of subjects into key learning areas and the placing of music, dance, drama, visual arts and sometimes media into the one key learning area called the arts has been also a trend across many countries such as South Africa, the United States, Canada, England, Scotland, Ireland and New Zealand. These countries all have new arts syllabuses, recently written and implemented, and no longer follow individual subject syllabuses such as they had previously for music and visual arts.

1995: Senate inquiry into arts education

In the midst of these curriculum changes, the Commonwealth Government commissioned an inquiry (SERCARC, 1995) into the state of arts education in relation to practices, policies and programs across Australia in all educational institutions. Findings from this report indicated that little had changed in primary arts education since the 1977 report: the arts were still being marginalised and, for systemic reasons, teachers still lacked confidence, skills, adequate training and resources. It also indicated that the situation had been compounded by many generalist teachers having to provide children with experiences in music, visual arts, craft, dance, movement, drama and media studies. The report reiterated the importance of the arts in children's lives, especially in the primary school, and made 25 recommendations that included a high priority for primary arts education both at the preservice training level and as professional development for practising teachers. No strategies were developed or funding assigned to respond to the recommendations so very few of them have been implemented.

2000s

In February 2003 a motion was passed by the House of Representatives, confirming the importance of music education in the lives of children and calling for music to be recognised as a core subject, enjoying similar priorities to English and mathematics, and for quality music education to be accessible for every student in every Australian school. In the same year, key national music organisations embarked on a project to identify what provisions were being made for music education across the country. The main recommendation arising from this project was that a comprehensive national survey of music education in Australian schools should be developed.

2004–05: National review of art and music education

The next year, partly as a result of this, and in recognition of the importance of arts education for all children, the federal minister for education launched a national review of both school music and visual arts education as he had noted significant deficiencies in these areas. One would hope that the findings from these reviews would produce key recommendations with significant funding and practical strategies to implement them, to ensure a quality arts education for all children in our schools.

Despite continued changes in policies and rhetoric in classrooms all over Australia, many teachers and schools are continuing to implement innovative, quality arts programs with their children despite their lack of training, resources and support. Preservice teachers are receiving less and less training in arts education but some still learn the skills to teach carefully planned, quality lessons and programs and inspire and motivate the children in their professional experience classrooms. Practising teachers are attending and benefiting from professional development in the arts and proving that confidence can be developed through experience, skills can be learned, adequate time can be allocated to the arts, attitudes can be changed, relevant resources can be collected and generalist teachers can implement quality arts programs. The obstacles to this are great and can be daunting, but a firm belief in the value of arts education for all children, a positive attitude, basic knowledge and an enthusiastic approach can go a long way to overcoming these obstacles and giving children the opportunity they deserve to engage in authentic, effective arts programs.

But how are quality arts programs implemented? What sort of arts lessons are appropriate and who should teach the arts? Should the untrained generalist teacher be responsible for arts education in the primary school, or should arts specialists take on this important role? The next sections examine different views of the arts, the role specialist and generalist teachers can have in arts education and guidelines for implementing a quality arts program.

Different ways of viewing arts education

When looking at how the arts are taught in different classrooms and schools across the country and overseas, at least five different ways of viewing the teaching of arts education can be identified. The first four rarely occur in a quality developmental arts education program and teachers should aim to use the fifth approach in their planning and teaching of the arts. The five different approaches are as follows:

1. Time-filler activity: *Let's do art to fill in time*

The arts are often seen as an easy Friday afternoon activity, when children can relax and unwind by colouring in a stencilled card for Mothers' Day or colouring in pretty pictures for the front of their workbooks. In this approach, the arts are used to fill in time, for example in the five minutes between lessons or before the bell. When used this way, little value is placed on the arts as an important part of the curriculum and often the activities are spontaneous and not part of a developmental, sequential arts program, so few significant educational outcomes are achieved.

2. Closed activities: *We've done the theme, now colour the picture*

This approach views the arts as a closed activity, which may relate, but not contribute, to the understanding of a theme in another key learning area and is not part of a developmental, sequential arts program. For example, children may perform the *Nutbush* dance if they are involved in a theme on plants or colour a

MMADD about the arts

picture red if they are 'doing' the red theme. In this approach, there are right and wrong answers, there is little allowance for imagination or creativity, and all children are doing the same activity that is often a one-off learning experience and may not relate to any other art form.

3. Open-ended activities: *Here are the materials, let's make something*

This view of arts education is very open-ended, with the teacher saying, 'Here is some plasticine, make some farm animals' or 'Here is a CD, make up a dance to it'. This approach may encourage some creativity, but there are few if any scaffolding activities to develop relevant skills and knowledge; so children use what they already know and are not extended in their understanding of the art form. It can be very child-directed with little assistance or facilitation by the teacher, and although it may achieve some arts outcomes it is not generally part of a quality, developmental arts program.

4. Product-oriented activities: *Let's put on a show*

This product-oriented approach is a very popular view of arts education as it produces an obvious outcome and can be used to showcase the school at performing arts festivals, shopping centres and education week. There is a strong focus, for example a musical production, an art exhibition or a dance festival item, and the *product* is generally more important than the *process*. There is a major emphasis on convergent thinking, with one way of doing the arts; children have to 'get it right and make it perfect' so the activity or experience is repeated many times in rehearsal. Many children are involved, though often it is only the talented ones who are included. Some educational and arts outcomes can be achieved, but these may not be part of a sequential, developmental program. This view of the arts can be very teacher-directed with little opportunity for input by the children or for creativity and imagination. It may be a one-off experience with no more arts experiences after the presentation, and principals and teachers may see the performance as their having 'done' the arts for that year, even though not every child had been involved.

5. Process-oriented activities: *Let's learn the arts and be creative*

This approach is the most authentic way of implementing quality arts education programs. In this process-oriented approach there is generally a balance between teacher- and child-directed activities, with opportunities for action and reflection and for individual and group work. The regular and relevant learning experiences are stimulating and are integrated across the curriculum, and they use quality resources, artworks and activities. Every child is involved and it is

In process-oriented activities, every child is involved.

inclusive of all children: the English as a second language (ESL) students, those with special needs, the gifted and talented, and literacy- or numeracy-challenged children. All can feel challenged and successful. It takes into consideration children's needs, interests, cultures, past experiences, knowledge and previously developed skills. This approach focuses on divergent thinking which is flexible, with few right or wrong ways of doing the arts and it allows for tangential developments as appropriate. It is part of a sequential, developmental program and, as such, develops significant educational and personal outcomes for the children within each of the art forms as well as across other key learning areas. It is a challenging but very rewarding way to teach the arts. And it also leads to the question of who should teach the arts in the primary classroom?

Who should teach the arts? The generalist versus the specialist debate

If primary classroom teachers have very little training, confidence, resources and skills, are they actually the best people to teach the arts? The specialist versus generalist debate has been argued long and hard for many years with no resolution, but often the issue is a rhetorical one, as in some states there are policies which specifically advocate that either the specialist or the classroom teacher is responsible for the children's arts education. Some states provide art and music specialist teachers but expect the generalists to teach drama and dance. But even in these states where policies provide for specialist arts teachers, often funding cuts and other priorities see the use of specialists decreasing and the responsibility for arts education being moved more to the generalist teacher. Basically, there are two conflicting avenues of thought:

1. The best music teacher a child could have is a highly skilled professional artist or performer with suitable and relevant training in primary teacher education.
2. The child's best music teacher is the classroom teacher because he/she knows the children well and can integrate music within the classroom, and children can see music as part of their whole curriculum, not separated from the reality of day-to-day school work.

The specialist teaching the arts

The main arguments of those who advocate the first position (having specialist teachers teaching the arts) are as follows:

- Often the arts are not taught effectively in primary schools by the generalist classroom teachers as they don't have the confidence, resources or time to teach them.
- If specialist teachers are hired, this ensures that a certain time is allocated within the school day for

Who should teach the arts: the generalist or the specialist?

arts lessons; without specialist teachers the arts are often dropped out of the crowded curriculum through lack of time and priority.
- Few generalist teachers have the knowledge, skills and interest to implement each of the art forms effectively, so children will be disadvantaged in those areas in which their teachers are not confident or do not have sufficient expertise.
- Specialist arts teachers are more able to develop a relevant whole-school arts program so that all children receive sequential, developmental arts education throughout their primary schooling.

The generalist teaching the arts

Those who advocate for the classroom teacher as being the most appropriate person to teach the arts put forward the following arguments:
- Throughout the year primary schoolchildren develop a rapport and trust for their classroom teacher who provides them with the nurturing and pastoral care that they require at this stage in their lives.
- The classroom teacher knows each of their children's interests, backgrounds and abilities and can develop arts programs to meet their specific educational needs.
- Because the classroom teacher programs and teaches all the other subjects throughout the day they are better able to integrate arts education learning experiences throughout the curriculum in a meaningful way, to enhance learning in other subjects and to teach relevant arts education skills, knowledge and attitudes.
- If specialists were hired for the arts subjects, there would also be strong arguments that they should also be hired for science, physical education, maths and every other subject in the curriculum. This could disrupt meaningful and relevant integration of the curriculum and would not give children the pastoral care and sense of identification with one teacher.
- The use of specialist teachers in the arts could lead children to view arts education as elitist and irrelevant to day-to-day life, as they are withdrawn from their regular classroom and taught by a different teacher, with little reference to, or integration with the rest of their learning experiences throughout the week.

Specialist *or* generalist?

These opposing views have been argued incessantly in relation to arts education, since the first singing teachers were employed in the mid-1800s. Although the specialist/generalist debate has been most fierce within the music education arena, it still applies to the other arts areas. By the late 19th century, it was observed that the standard of singing was very poor if taught by the classroom teachers but in schools where the singing master paid regular visits, the singing was, on the whole, satisfactory. However, from 1872 onwards some state policies required classroom teachers to teach music instead of specialists, and from then on music specialists generally had little formal role in the public education system.

In the states that use classroom teachers to teach all subjects, including the arts, the presumption is that every generalist teacher is able to sing; has access to and can use musical instruments as resources; is able to move confidently in response to music; can develop relevant and meaningful drama experiences for children; can integrate media studies throughout the curriculum; can understand arts symbols, terminology and languages, as well as the underlying principles of art, dance, drama, media and music; and can confidently use these to implement a quality, developmental arts program within their classroom.

Specialist *and* generalist

However, many teachers indicate clearly that this is not the case. Classroom teachers often indicate that they do not feel that they have the artistic skills, knowledge, resources or confidence to provide their children with an adequate arts education program. Some principals also say that the arts are taught well only when specialist arts teachers are involved in their school. With the structural changes in some state school systems resulting in decentralisation of power and accountability to regions and to schools, principals may now have the flexibility to advertise for teachers with specialist skills in particular subjects. Thus principals seeking to improve the arts education situation are now in a position to appoint one or more suitable advisory teachers who could work with staff to produce a more effective arts program throughout the school. So a compromise could be developed whereby schools hire and use classroom teachers who have a strength in one or more of the arts areas, to act in an advisory role to assist and support teachers in the implementation of the arts syllabus within the school. This would require some reorganisation of staffing to allow these teachers to work alongside other classroom teachers, developing their skills and confidence in each of the arts areas, but the long-term rewards would be well worth the effort and cost.

Research indicates that arts lessons are taken more often and produce more effective results in the lower primary years than in the upper primary. Therefore, the role of these arts advisory teachers could be to work in conjunction with lower primary teachers, assisting them where necessary in planning, implementing and assessing their arts programs. However, in the middle and upper primary grades, where children need more than the basic musical concepts and skills which can be taught by teachers with little or no arts background, and where often little quality arts education takes place at present, the advisory teachers could be used to take each class for arts subjects at regular intervals throughout the term, after working with the classroom teacher to determine, for example, the theme and content of these lessons and how they would fit into the overall class program. As well as planning lessons with the advisory teacher, the classroom teacher could also observe the lessons taken by the advisory teacher and follow these up with their own lessons from the program developed together. This professional development role would allow for a classroom teacher's arts education expertise and confidence to grow through demonstration and practice. Resources would be readily available to them through the advisory teacher, and the children would be receiving a well-planned arts program. In this way children would be encouraged to see these arts lessons as part of their core curriculum and the teacher would receive professional development in these areas.

Such a solution would appear to be a viable compromise in the specialist/generalist debate in that advisory teachers could work in a supportive role in the lower grades, where children are in the greatest need of pastoral care and where

integration of subjects tends to occur more frequently. They could then be used in a semi-replacement role for the teaching of the upper grades, which would seem appropriate for children of this age group and which would also provide professional development to the classroom teachers. Give the importance and significance of quality arts education in children's development, each school needs to decide, within its arts education policy, how it can best provide for the children's sequential and developmental engagement in quality arts education from their first to their last days in primary school and so provide them with a holistic and meaningful education.

Implementing a quality arts program

Whatever the state and/or school policy declares in relation to the use of specialist, generalist and advisory arts teachers, there are certain key principles, attitudes, attributes and understandings to be considered in order to implement a quality arts program. For this to happen effectively, teachers need particular knowledge, skills and attitudes.

Knowledge

Teachers need:

- to understand clearly the syllabus outcomes expected of children in each of the art forms;
- to understand the key developmental concepts or elements of each of the art forms;
- to understand and be able to use the vocabulary and language of the arts;
- to know their children, their needs, interests and past experiences in the arts, their cultural backgrounds and their preferred intelligences and learning styles;
- to develop a working knowledge of relevant and useful resources and equipment for teaching each of the art forms.

Skills

Teachers need:

- to develop skills in teaching each of the art forms;
- to be able to plan individual lessons as well as integrated programs of work which include outcomes for each of the art forms and other key learning areas;
- to be able to engage their children in a wide range of relevant and authentic learning experiences which will help them develop a sound understanding of the elements, knowledge, skills and attitudes relevant to the arts;
- to be able to act as a facilitator of learning in the arts for their children;
- to be able to give their children adequate time to learn new skills, be creative and express themselves;
- to provide children with a safe environment in which to experiment and take risks and develop their creativity;
- to know how to effectively assess their children in the area of arts education;
- to build networks with other teachers for mutual support.

Attitudes

Teachers need:

- to value the arts and understand the importance of the arts in education;
- to give the arts equal priority and time as the other areas of the curriculum;
- to be enthusiastic about teaching the arts and make them interesting so children want to engage in the arts;
- to be able to take risks and try new teaching strategies;
- to be willing to be involved in professional development in arts education;
- to have the positive support of their principal.

This book aims to equip preservice and in-service teachers with the ability to implement quality arts education programs in their classrooms, and covers the above principles, knowledge, skills and values in detail over the next eight chapters.

MMADD about the arts

SPRINGBOARDS FOR DISCUSSION AND APPLICATION

1. List the key developments in the history of primary arts education in Australia and then, based on these, present two scenarios describing the possible future for primary arts education in the 21st century.
2. Take a day of your life and list all the ways in which you are actively or passively involved in the arts; categorise them under the seven headings under 'The arts in society' as discussed in this chapter, adding your own headings if necessary.
3. Pretend you are a primary school principal. Describe how you would develop an effective whole-school arts education policy and practice in your school and state the rationale behind your decision.
4. Brainstorm different ways you have seen arts education presented in schools. Discuss the pros and cons of these different approaches.
5. Select a preferred grade and outline key principles of implementing a quality arts program for that grade. Avoid focusing on the content and subject matter, but rather describe the key factors that would help you implement an arts program.

FURTHER READING

Commonwealth of Australia (1994), *Creative nation — Commonwealth cultural policy*, Author, Canberra.

Comte, M. (1988), 'The arts in Australia schools: The past fifty years', *International Journal for Music Education*, no. 1, pp. 102–120.

Curriculum Corporation (1994), *National curriculum and statement on the arts for Australian schools*, Author, Melbourne.

Curriculum Corporation (1994), *The arts — A curriculum profile of Australian schools*, Author, Melbourne.

REFERENCES

Clark, V. (1997), 'Using the arts to explore issues of loss, death and bereavement', in D. Holt (ed.), *Primary arts education*, Falmer Press, London.

Clay, G., Hertrich, J., Jones, P., Mills, J. and Rose, J. (1998), *The Arts Inspected*, Heinemann, London.

Commonwealth Department of Education (1985), *Action: Education and the arts*, Australian Government Publishing Service, Canberra.

Eisner, E. (2002), *The arts and the creation of mind*, Yale University Press, Connecticut.

Finn, B. (1991), *Young people's participation in post-compulsory education and training*, Australian Education Council, Melbourne.

Fiske, E. (1999), *Champions of change: The impact of the arts on learning*, The Arts Education Partnership, Washington, DC.

Fowler, C. (1999), 'Strong arts, strong schools', *ArtsEdNet*, <http://artsednet.getty.edu/ArtsEdNet/Advocacy/strong.html>.

Mayer Committee (1992), *Putting education to work: The key competencies report*, Australian Education Council/Ministerial Council of Vocational Education, Employment and Training, Melbourne.

Penny, S., Ford, R., Price, L. and Young, S. (2002), *Achieving QTS: Teaching arts in primary schools*, Learning Matters Ltd, Exeter.

Schools Commission and Australia Council (1977), *Education and the arts*, Author, Canberra.

SERCARC (Senate Environment, Recreation, Communication and the Arts Reference Committee) (1995), *Arts education*, Commonwealth of Australia, Canberra.

chapter two
The creative arts classroom

Teaching arts everyday in the core curriculum of primary schools is the single, most powerful tool presently available to educators to motivate students, enhance learning and develop higher order thinking skills. (Oddliefson, 1994)

Learning outcomes
By the end of this chapter, students will be able to:
- argue the importance for including the arts in the core primary curriculum;
- demonstrate effective communication skills;
- prepare an arts lesson with appropriate assessment strategies;
- list at least five effective behaviour management strategies.

Introduction

The arts are crucial to children's education and to their overall development. Quality arts programs need to become an integral part of the school curriculum. Children should be given the opportunity to engage in all the art forms regularly so that they can develop their full potential as human beings and future leaders and adults in the 21st century. A key component for the arts to be taught effectively in primary schools is adequate and careful preparation of each lesson with consideration being given to effective communication, behaviour management strategies, thoughtful lesson planning and appropriate assessment techniques. This chapter documents the importance of children being involved in a quality arts education program, and then provides preservice and in-service teachers with practical tools for quality planning and implementation of arts lessons and programs.

The importance of the arts

The arts constitute one of the most powerful, and possibly most overlooked, resources available to us to intensify learning and to tangibly enrich the study of many other disciplines. (Ultan, 1989)

Learning the arts for arts sake is vitally important. Children need to experience and understand the complexity and beauty of the world of music, drama, dance, visual arts and media for themselves. Being involved in the arts gives children the tools for lifelong learning within the arts so they have the opportunity for pleasure and for self-development, and for creativity and self-expression, opening up a vista of new and exciting experiences and opportunities they may have never realised existed. However, quality arts programs also have far-reaching tangential effects that influence every aspect of children's lives, both inside and outside school, that enhance their social, cognitive, spiritual, physical, emotional and creative development and give them a deeper understanding of themselves and others.

But the arts are messy: they can be noisy, they often need extra space and resources, and children need time to work through the creative processes to produce both tangible and intangible outcomes. Some teachers feel they cannot teach the arts effectively and some schools do not value the arts as an important part of the school curriculum for every child. However, it is imperative that these barriers are overcome so that all children can experience the aesthetic wonder and creativity, the feelings of success, the improvement in academic performance, the development of higher order thinking skills and the many ways of knowing and communicating that engagement in the arts offer them. Without involvement in a quality arts program, children will not receive a well-rounded education and may not reach their fullest potential. The arts enhance children's *Academic achievement*, develop *Respect* for themselves and others, give them *Training for life* and provide them with valid ways for *Self-expression*.

The importance of the arts

Academic achievement

Respect for self and others

Training for life

Self-expression

Academic achievement

At the same time that educators are searching for tools to revitalise student performances and teach kids how to think creatively, legislators and school administrators across the country are annihilating one of the most vital sources for teaching those skills: the creative arts. **(Combs, 1991)**

Involvement in the arts can help children engage actively in learning, understand the concepts being taught, develop deep understandings in whatever subject is being taught and be able to express their understandings in different ways. The arts can enhance the process of learning and contribute to intellectual development. Regular involvement in the arts develops the higher order skills of analysis, synthesis and evaluation, as well as critical-thinking, problem-solving and decision-making skills. The arts present children with multiple ways of thinking, knowing, creating and learning and act as points of entry of understanding and learning for other curriculum areas through integration. Using the arts gives children a multifaceted approach to learning and improves their learning environment, so all children are given the opportunity to learn using their preferred intelligences and learning styles and are challenged to move from the concrete to the abstract.

Learning can be *explicit*, where children are reading, writing, talking, listening to the teacher, and watching videos and visual aids, or it can be *implicit*, where children are involved in hands-on experiences such as role-playing, singing, dancing and playing instruments — this is experiential, active and discovery learning. With implicit learning the effects are far greater and last longer than those achieved through explicit learning, children find it easier to learn this way and learning is not correlated with children's intelligence quotient (IQ) or dependent on their cognitive abilities. The arts, more than any other subjects, provide the environment for the hands-on experiences of implicit, deep learning (Jensen, 2001).

Much research has been undertaken relating to the effects that studying the arts has on academic achievement, and there are clear indications that involvement in quality arts programs improves children's academic performance in mathematics and literacy as well as developing multiple skills and abilities across all subjects. In the ground-breaking work *Champions of change: The impact of the arts on learning* Fiske (1999) and his team of researchers confirmed through extensive research that in relation to academic achievement, students with high levels of arts participation outperformed their peers who had little involvement in the arts, by every measure in a range of comprehensive tests, even in the low socioeconomic areas, which are traditionally poor achievement areas. This report concluded that, when well taught, the arts provide young people with real, authentic learning experiences which reach students who previously have been failing, connect students to themselves and others, transform the learning environment, provide new

Students with high levels of arts participation outperformed their peers who had little involvement in the arts.

challenges for successful students and create real-world learning experiences (Fiske, 1999). Surely this is what quality teaching is all about!

Respect for self and others

An education in the arts benefits society because students of the arts gain powerful tools for understanding human experiences both past and present. (Mahlmann, no date)

Art making is an activity that is unique to humankind and which has been in existence as long as people have been able to hold a twig to paint, sing a song, play a simple instrument, dance and act out their stories. The arts are an expression of culture and, as such, being involved in the arts can create a sharing of cross-cultural heritages and a pride in one's own heritage. Through involvement in quality arts programs, children are able to connect and empathise with others as they understand and appreciate their cultures, traditions and symbols. The arts are a way of changing perceptions and stereotypes of people who are different from them, as children are exposed to different societies and cultures through their arts, learn their dances, appreciate their artworks, read and act out their plays and listen to, sing and play their music. They learn to respect and appreciate the differences and become more tolerant of other people, as well as accepting and respecting their own culture.

As children are involved in the arts, they learn that there are different ways of knowing and different ways of understanding about themselves and the world in which they live. As well as learning to accept differences in cultures, they learn to accept physical, mental and emotional differences within the classroom and see each person as deserving of respect and understanding. The arts give a voice to the special-needs children, the children from non-English speaking backgrounds, the 'non-achieving' children, the 'regular children', and the gifted and talented children, allowing them self-expression and success, challenging them to extend themselves and to take further risks. Through this process the arts enhance their self-respect, giving them joy and fulfilment, as a sense of wonder, creation and the satisfaction of achievement.

The arts enhance their self-respect, giving them joy and fulfilment.

Training for life

Arts are a necessity in the curriculum, not a frill. To cut the arts is to deny students a whole avenue of learning — one that specifically promotes not only individual development but also the development of the kind of citizens the future will require. (Perrin, 1994)

What are the skills required by future employers? The Finn (1991) and Mayer Committee (1992) reports suggest that to succeed in the workplace in the 21st century, young people need to be able to collect, analyse and organise information, communicate ideas and information, plan and organise activities, work with others in a team, use mathematical ideas and techniques, solve problems and use technology. Within a quality arts program each of these skills is developed and so, by involvement in the arts, children, as tomorrow's leaders, are being comprehensively prepared for the competitive and creative arena of the world of work. They learn self-discipline, delayed gratification, social, problem-solving and communication skills, teamwork and risk taking, and they develop a realistic self-concept.

The arts not only prepare children for the general world of work, but also give them the opportunity to discover their talents and develop these to become visual artists, actors, dancers, media personnel and musicians. The arts develop and prepare audiences for these artists and so contribute to the multimillion dollar arts industry. They give children the tools to enjoy the arts in their leisure time, as a hobby, for relaxation and for lifelong learning. In the fast-paced life of the 21st century, the arts give them permission to stop in the midst of the busyness of stressful day-to-day interactions, pressures and deadlines and provide a place of peace and creativity in the middle of a world which seems at times to be out of control. The arts provide them with the opportunity to centre themselves in reality, to step out of the time-centred world and to refresh and renew themselves through self-expression and creativity. Such anti-stress strategies can bring about changes in health. Although the arts might not solve health problems, they could improve the quality of life and help us deal with the pain intrinsic to human life (Smith, 2002). The arts can be a positive and life-changing force, impacting the whole child, inside and outside school, in the present and in the future.

By involvement in the arts, children are being prepared for the competitive world of work.

Self-expression

The arts ... are intrinsic components of human culture, heritage and creativity. They mirror the whole repertoire of human experience, and are worthy of study in their own right. It is difficult to imagine a world without the arts, with no drawing, music or painting for example. Few if any cultures are without these elements. (Mills, 1998)

To create an artwork is to make oneself vulnerable and to reflect one's inner self. Children draw upon their knowledge, skills and attitudes learned within an arts program and use these, combined with their knowledge of themselves and others, to express their thoughts and feelings through paintings, drawings and sculptures, as well as in compositions and improvisations in dance, music, media and drama. The arts stimulate children's imagination and creative life, which is fundamental to their being human beings. Through self-expression in the arts, children learn focus, self-discipline, innovation, creativity and emotional expression as well as verbal and non-verbal communication skills. They learn to use a variety of media to express themselves and communicate using multiliteracies. They learn to use movements, symbols, visuals and sounds as well as words to convey meaning. They discover new ways of knowing, thinking and being, and learn to pay

The arts stimulate children's imagination and creative life.

MMADD about the arts

attention to detail as well as seeing the big picture. They learn to get in touch with their own feelings and those of others. When they create or observe a work of art they respond emotionally, they feel good about themselves, and they learn that there is more to life than what can be assessed by quantitative measures. A quality arts program is one of the greatest gifts a teacher can give to their children.

To present a quality arts program so that children can develop academic outcomes, respect, training for life and self-expression, there are basic requirements of teachers. Firstly, teachers need to be able to communicate effectively, and then they need to plan, implement and assess quality learning experiences within each of the arts for their children. This next section presents practical information about communication and lesson planning within the classroom.

Effective communication

How effectively do you communicate? What sort of a SPEAKER are you? How confident are you when you stand in front of a class of children, peers or adults? Can you communicate effectively, through your words, gestures, resources and attitudes? As teachers you will be required to act professionally and confidently in many situations where you will be addressing children, parents and other teachers. When teaching arts lessons you need to communicate enthusiasm, confidence, instructions, skills and explanations using your body, voice, posture, visual aids, artworks and other resources.

Ralph Waldo Emerson wrote: 'Who you are speaks so loudly, that I can't hear what you are saying!' Good communicators realise that 65% of spoken communication has nothing to do with words. Our body expresses 45% of the message we are giving, our tone of voice expresses 20% and what we actually say expresses 35% of the message. Try saying something really positive and helpful to a friend in an angry tone of voice, while frowning and shaking your fist. What is the main message being communicated? Yes, anger! Marshall McLuhan, a great American communicator said, 'The Medium is the message'. *How* you say it is often more important than *what* you say.

Here are some practical guidelines to help you communicate confidently and effectively as a teacher. They are based on the mnemonic SPEAKER to help you remember them. If you are already a teacher, skim through them as a reminder to help you be an even better communicator!

Effective communication

Self-confidence

Posture

Enthusiasm

Aids

Know your subject

Engage your students

Review for feedback

Self-confidence

- **Breathing.** Breathing is the basis for confident speech. Learn to breathe deeply from the diaphragm and avoid small top-up breaths from the top of your lungs.
- **Relaxation.** Tension in the body can constrict your breathing, your voice production when you speak and your confidence. Stand still and mentally examine each part of your body for tension, relaxing any part that seems tense.

- **Self-talk: I *can* do it!** If you are well prepared and know your subject and those you are addressing, you can confidently tell yourself that you *can* do it! Employ a behaviour modification technique and 'fake it until you make it!' Your positive attitude is a key component of your self-confidence — choose to be confident!
- **Look good!** If you think you look good, you feel good! Clothes can impart an aura of confidence, so think carefully about what you will wear. Make sure your clothes are professional, fit in with the dress code of the rest of the school and imply respect and authority.
- **Check first impressions.** Most people will make a snap judgement about how confident and believable you are in the first 15 seconds of meeting you. No matter what you say, your looks and voice will speak more loudly.
- **Self-confidence.** To give yourself confidence before starting to speak, remain silent, stand straight and solid on your feet, and breathe calmly and deeply. Take three seconds to look left, right and centre to cover the entire room with your eyes and focus your thoughts.

Posture

How you stand will influence people's perceptions of your confidence and believability.

- **Balance.** Stand comfortably and balance forward on the balls of both feet, keeping your heels on the ground. Pretend you have a golden thread attached from the crown of your head to the ceiling; feel it pulling the back of your head up and your spine straight. Relax your shoulders.
- **Free hands and arms.** Keep your hands away from your back, your pockets or inside your clothing so that you are free to use gestures.
- **Take possession of your space.** Different cultures have different amounts of personal space in which they feel comfortable with others. If someone enters our personal space we may feel comfortable if we know the person well, or uncomfortable if it is not appropriate that the person comes so close. Be confident in moving in your own personal space, but also be aware of, and respect, other people's personal space.
- **Body language (SO FINE).** Do you rush into the classroom, frantically looking for the electric power point for the CD player, the paintbrushes or the CD? Or do you stand in front of the class, nervously pulling at your clothes, avoiding any eye contact with the children, lacking in confidence? Or perhaps you stand calmly and confidently, fully prepared, looking at the children. Whatever your body language, it speaks louder than anything you can say! When you next have to speak to a group of children or adults, check your body language; use the mnemonic of SO FINE to help you remember the important points.
    - **Smile!** People respond to a smile and it conveys your confidence and goodwill. However, sometimes a smile

> **Body language**
>
> **S**mile!
>
> **O**pen stance
>
> **F**orward lean and movement
>
> **I**nitiate touch
>
> **N**od your head
>
> **E**ye contact

may not be appropriate, such as when you are reprimanding a child or the class. Think about how you use your facial expressions and remember that your face communicates so much!
- **Open stance.** An open stance with the arms relaxed gives the impression of your being welcoming, trusting and accepting. With stiff, crossed arms and raised shoulders, the opposite seems true. Hands on hips can look aggressive but holding your hands in front of you can look inviting.
- **Forward lean and movement.** Lean forward slightly, balancing on the balls of your feet but keeping your heels on the ground, to ensure you have a relaxed posture. Make your movements minimal, deliberate and controlled and know why and how you move.
- **Initiate touch.** Use touch, only if appropriate, on a shoulder, arm or head to convey warmth and encouragement.
- **Nod your head.** If someone is talking with you, nod your head and give other verbal and non-verbal cues to show that you are interested and listening.
- **Eye contact.** Keep your eyes on the children as much as possible. This will help with behaviour management and feedback as well as helping you to look confident.

Enthusiasm

Attitudes are caught and not taught! If you want your children to be enthusiastic about the arts, be enthusiastic yourself! How can you communicate this enthusiasm? By using your voice and body language.

- **Voice.** Your voice needs to be firm, enthusiastic and confident, not weak and diffident. Tape yourself talking and consider if you need to change the pitch, clarity, volume, pace, intonation or emphasis, or your use of pauses, silences or colloquialisms.
- **Gestures.** Non-verbal gestures and body movements can be a very powerful way of communicating your enthusiasm and what you want to teach in an arts lesson. Use gestures to clarify and support your words. Make gestures natural, convincing, smooth, well timed and spontaneous.

Aids

Effective communication can be achieved by using relevant and attractive resources, artworks and visual aids.

- **Yourself.** Remember that your body is an important visual aid! Use your voice, face, gestures and body language to aid your communication.
- **Teaching resources.** These can be as simple as the blackboard or whiteboard. They can also include paper, pens, posters, artefacts, cassettes, CDs, slides, photocopier, artworks, overhead projectors, PowerPoint presentations, videos, TV, computers and cameras. Teaching resources can be pivotal to some lessons, and they can add interest and variety, simplify and clarify the message, and aid better comprehension in others (especially for ESL, special-needs children, and visual and kinaesthetic learners).

Know your subject

Preparation builds self-confidence. If you are really well prepared your lesson will generally go well. Sometimes you may teach a good lesson with very little preparation but imagine how much better it would have been with more preparation! For effective communication and preparation you need to know:

> ## Know your subject
> *Who?* Yourself and your children
> *Where?* Classroom
> *Why?* Purpose of lesson
> *What?* Content of lesson
> *How?* Aids and resources

- *Who?* **Yourself and your children.** Know your ability to communicate through voice, gesture and body language. Know you are confident and well prepared. Know your children's needs, interests, abilities, cultural background, prior learning experiences in the subject and how they learn best. Understand what is behind a student's actions and you will understand your students better.
- *Where?* **Classroom.** Know the environment in which you will be teaching, how much space you need and have, how the chairs and desks will be organised, where the children will be at each stage of the lesson, how they will move from one place to another, how they will clean up after the lesson, and so on.
- *Why?* **Purpose of lesson.** Know why you are teaching the lesson and what you want the children to achieve by the end of the lesson. Know how you will assess their learning both throughout and at the end of the lesson.
- *What?* **Content of lesson.** Know how you will begin the lesson and motivate the children, how you will develop the body of the lesson so the children will understand and learn what you want to teach them, and how you will create an effective closure.
- *How?* **Aids and resources.** Know what resources you are going to use, where they are, how they work and how you will use them effectively throughout the lesson.

Remember that in many instances, a good lesson is 75% preparation and 25% presentation. Successful teaching and effective communication in arts and other lessons depends on thorough planning.

Engage your students

The arts can be very practical subjects and activities are often interactive and hands-on. To learn effectively, children need to be engaged and interested in learning, and the arts often engage students who have been otherwise disengaged in learning. You can assist their engagement in the learning experiences by communicating the activities, skills and concepts clearly.

- **Communicate with every child.** Children learn in different ways and have preferred intelligences through which they learn more effectively. These intelligences include the following:
  — logical-mathematical;

To learn effectively, children need to be engaged and interested in learning.

- verbal-linguistic;
- bodily-kinaesthetic;
- visual-spatial;
- musical;
- intrapersonal;
- interpersonal;
- naturalistic.

As a teacher you need to identify each child's preferred intelligences and use learning experiences that will include each of these ways of learning. Often teachers use their own preferred intelligence in their teaching and so many children in their class miss out on engaging effectively in learning. To find out more about the Multiple Intelligences theory and the creative arts turn to Chapter 8, 'Integration and the arts'.

- **Eye contact.** Keep children involved and engaged when you are teaching by using frequent eye contact with them. This helps give you feedback on whether or not they are understanding the lesson and also helps with behaviour management.
- **Clear explanations.** Think through your explanations before you give them. Make them simple, brief and clear and use visual aids if possible. Avoid giving multiple explanations before checking for understanding.
- **Check for understanding.** Consistently check with the children that they understand. Avoid asking them 'do you understand' as you will receive a chorus answer and not really know who understands and who does not. Clarify the explanation or instruction, ask children to repeat what they have to do or what steps need to be taken and so on, question individuals, and look for puzzled or enthusiastic faces and other signs of understanding.
- **Repeat important points.** If something is really important for the children to learn, you may need to communicate it at least three times in three different ways. Use kinaesthetic, visual and aural ways of repeating important information to assist all children to learn.
- **Learn through *doing*!** Children learn through doing much more than through listening, so it is important to engage all children in interactive learning experiences. The arts are easy to provide children with such experiences, as children can be moving, painting, drawing, playing instruments, taking photos, working on the computer, dancing and singing as they learn important concepts and knowledge.

Review for feedback

Review the lesson and reflect on its effectiveness. If you have the opportunity, videotape your lesson and review it in relation to the seven SPEAKER points:

Self-confidence: How believable are you?

Posture: What does your body language say?

Enthusiasm: Does your use of gestures and voice aid your presentation?

Aids: How effective was the use of these?

Know your subject: Was it clear that you knew your children and the content and purpose of what you were teaching?

Engage your students: How were they involved?

Review: Reflect on your teaching, gain feedback from a video, ask someone to be your mentor and/or discuss your lesson with your supervising teacher.

Based on this feedback, ask yourself, what sort of SPEAKER are you?

Behaviour management strategies

Effective communication is one aspect of creating a positive classroom. However, despite being good communicators, many teachers avoid teaching music, media, visual arts, dance and drama because these lessons are seen to present more behaviour management challenges than other lessons. This may be because children are moving around, expressing themselves and using exciting resources such as instruments, paint, music, art materials and cameras, whereas other lessons involve children sitting down in the one place, writing, reading or listening to the teacher. When involved in the arts, children are constantly engaged in learning through practical kinaesthetic, aural and visual learning experiences. Teachers sometimes think that children will become excited and may be disruptive in these types of lesson; however, when children are focused, involved and engaged in learning, they are often well behaved and cause few problems. But, as with all lessons, certain strategies need to be put into place for behaviour to be acceptable and positive throughout the teaching period.

Using the mnemonic of CREATIVE, here are some behaviour management strategies which will help you to prepare to teach arts (or any other) lessons.

Behaviour management strategies

Children

Rewards, rules and routines

Environment

Attitude

Time and resource management

Interactive activities

Variety

Enthusiasm

Children

Know your children well. Know:
- *who* to sit them next to (and who *not* to sit them next to);
- *what* their interests and prior learning experiences are;
- *where* they come from (home and cultural background);
- *why* they act as they do;
- *how* they learn (learning styles, intelligences and so on);
- *what* methods of positive reinforcement work best with them;
- *what* their preferred intelligences and learning styles are.

Based on the above information, include relevant learning experiences in your lessons so all children can learn; this may mean including a wide variety of activities in each lesson or program of work.

Rewards, rules and routines

Rewards

At the start of your lesson, clearly set out your expectations for positive classroom behaviour. Use different forms of positive reinforcement where appropriate; these could include *social* reinforcement (a smile or a gentle touch on the shoulder or head), *verbal* reinforcement ('Well done!', 'Great work!' and so on), *token* reinforcement (stickers, awards, jelly beans, and so on) or *physical* reinforcement where the child is given free time, privileges and so on. Ensure you make your praise authentic, meaningful and frequent to increase its effectiveness. Reward good behaviour instead of drawing attention to bad behaviour; for example, if a child is not on task in an art lesson, focus on a child who is working well and praise that child; if someone is being silly during a dance sequence, praise a child who is concentrating on doing the sequence. Used effectively, positive reinforcement can be an extremely powerful tool for promoting a positive classroom environment. In arts appreciation sessions, encourage every child to make positive remarks about each other's work; when they want to criticise artworks, encourage them to praise what they like about the work, and then make constructive critical comments about it.

Rules

At the beginning of the lesson, set out the rules, consequences and rewards clearly. These should initially be discussed and agreed upon by the children so that they understand and have ownership of them, rather than your dictating them. Make sure that you are consistent and follow through on the rules and consequences. Children will try you to see if they can outsmart you, so be sure that you enforce the rules from the start.

Routines

When giving instructions, make sure children are quiet *before* you talk as this will save your voice and make it more likely that they will hear you. If you talk over their noise, they will most likely just become noisier! Make your instructions clear and simple and avoid chorus answers. Phrase your questions so that children will answer individually when asked, not altogether; for example, asking 'Does everyone have a paintbrush?' results in most children calling out and waving their brushes, and doesn't give you the information you require! If you ask, 'Put your hand up if you do not have a paintbrush', you will know immediately, without fuss and noise, who does not have a brush.

Give clear explanations and make sure every child understands what is expected of them. For example, when starting a painting lesson, tell them how the paints, paintbrushes, paper and water will be distributed, have them repeat the instructions, and then recap them briefly. If you just say, 'Go and get the paints and brushes' there could be chaos, and spilled paint and water. Establish a routine and have children go through it with you verbally before they put it into practice. Ask for feedback to ensure children understand instructions. After several weeks, the routine will be established and children will know what to do with minimal instruction.

Create a signal for being quiet: blow a whistle, clap a rhythm and have them clap it back, sing a phrase and have them repeat it, hit a triangle, count to three or hold your hand in the air. Whatever signal you decide upon, practise this with the children and make it into a fun game, with them making a noise and praising the first children to obey the signal. Reinforce the signal at the start of each lesson, and gradually it will become part of the day's routine and children will need less and less reminding.

Work out how children will move from the mat to their desks, from one lesson to another, and in and out of the classroom. Develop a routine that the children will begin to do automatically and this will cut down on noise, fuss and possible behaviour problems.

Environment

Consideration of the environment of the arts classroom needs to include both the physical and the emotional setting. Physically, the classroom needs to be well organised, tidy and attractive with all resources carefully prepared beforehand. The children need to be nurtured in an emotionally safe, caring and respectful environment where their creativity is encouraged and their learning styles and preferences are considered. An emotionally healthy and attractive environment can go a long way in creating positive behaviour in the classroom.

Attitude

Attitudes are caught and not taught! In the arts, as in any other subjects, teachers need to be positive and inspiring, enthusing the children to participate in the learning experiences and be creative in their work. They need to provide their children with a powerful role model, being ready to learn new information and skills themselves, respecting differences and encouraging acceptance of everyone. These characteristics of a good teacher will influence the children's attitudes, so that they learn to value and respect both themselves and others and be ready to learn. When children learn to respect people and things, they will be less likely to cause behaviour problems.

Time and resource management

In order to promote positive behaviour, teachers need to be well organised in relation to both time and resource management. They need to set a well-paced lesson, being aware how long the activities should take and when they need to finish. The length of the different parts of the lesson needs to relate to the children's attention span. Younger children can concentrate for less time than older children, so plan accordingly. Constantly monitor your children visually for signs of boredom, misunderstanding or completed work. Always have an activity prepared for early finishers. This doesn't need to be 'more of the same', but it could be a fun activity, an extension activity, peer

Check out what resources the school has.

teaching, having time out to read quietly or spending time on the computer.

Have all required resources prepared and ready to use, know how they work and how to use them. Behaviour problems can often be caused by an unprepared teacher who needs to have the class sit still as he/she tries to find the appropriate CD, computer program, extension cord, artwork, paint or other vital resource. Plan how the materials are to be distributed and collected at the beginning and end of the activity or lesson and ensure children are clear about these routines.

Interactive activities

Focus on having less teacher talk and more child-centred activities in each lesson. Teachers generally talk too much in lessons and many children do not learn effectively by just listening; rather they learn in a variety of different ways and have preferred intelligences and learning styles through which they learn best. Aim to include interactive activities based on a variety of intelligences and learning styles. Remember and practise the old Chinese proverb:

I hear and I forget
I see and I remember
I do and I understand

Variety

Children need variety. Spend a few minutes watching a children's television show and you will see constant changes of colour, plot, characters, action, voices, movement, activities and so on. In some ways, teachers have to compete with technology as children are so used to being entertained through computer games and TV shows that sitting down, being quiet and listening to a teacher talk throughout the lesson can be a challenge. To gain and keep children's attention and so create positive behaviour in the arts classroom, use variations in your voice (make it faster or slower, higher or lower as is appropriate), vary your use of body language to create interest, and move around the classroom to stand close to different children. Encourage the children to be involved in a variety of activities, cater for their preferred intelligences and learning styles, and ensure they are engaged in authentic, real-life experiences and children will respond positively and enthusiastically.

Enthusiasm

Learn as much about the arts as you can and develop an enthusiastic interest in teaching each of the art forms in your classroom. Be enthusiastic about each child; it's easy to say negative things about some children in the staffroom or even to their face, but try to avoid this and focus on the positive abilities and character traits of each child. Be enthusiastic about lifelong learning and show the children that you are still learning. Take up watercolour painting, learn to play the guitar, go to dance or drama classes or learn more about using your computer and then share your learning experiences with your class. This will increase your skills in the arts as well as modelling to the children the importance of lifelong learning. If you model this enthusiasm for the arts, for teaching and for each of the children, they will pick this up and become enthusiastic, too. Children who are inspired and excited about learning will rarely cause significant behaviour problems in the classroom. However, be careful about hyping them up with too much overt enthusiasm as this could be counterproductive to positive classroom behaviour!

Lesson planning in the arts

When preparing your lessons, work out how you will implement these behaviour management strategies and you will find that the children will respond positively to you and to what you are teaching.

When planning creative arts lessons, sequence the lessons and activities so each lesson builds on the learning from the previous lesson. Ensure there is a smooth closure for each lesson and the transition to the next lesson is planned carefully.

Make sure the activities are content, age and stage appropriate. Be aware that some children may not be able to read confidently so use visuals to complement written words. Use visual aids to enhance your teaching, communicate effectively to visual learners, add interest and variety to the lesson, and clarify instructions and activities.

Think creatively, overcome possible challenges to teaching the arts and ensure that the children are engaged in authentic learning experiences. Avoid superficial arts activities such as colouring in or filling out a stencil; instead, use activities that involve the children exploring the elements and skills related to an art form so that they can become confident, creative artists in each of the art forms.

Be involved with the children in the learning experiences. If you expect them to sing a song, sing along with them; if they are to make a clay pinch pot, make one too; if they are to participate in dance or drama activities, join in with them; and if they are taking photos, take some too! Refer to the section 'Practical considerations', in each chapter for further details about planning and teaching lessons in each art form.

Preservice teachers are required to write lesson plans to help them work out the step-by-step procedures of teaching a lesson. As they become more confident with lesson planning and teaching they will then begin to write programs, as 'real' teachers do. Here are some pointers for planning and writing lesson plans for the creative arts. For details on programming in the arts, see Chapter 9 'Putting it all together: An introduction to programming in the arts'.

When writing lesson plans, remember that these are formal, professional documents, so an excellent standard of literacy is expected. One criticism of some teachers today is that they do not seem to be able to spell or use correct grammar! Work at using the correct grammar, punctuation, spelling and use of apostrophes to ensure clarity of expression and a professional piece of work. Children will learn from you how to spell and have correct grammar. You need to know that you are a good model for them!

Make good teaching *great*!

With a good teacher, students will learn, and they will love and respect their teacher.
With a great teacher, they will learn to love and respect themselves. (Erin Christian, 2004)

We have many good teachers in Australia — teachers who are committed and work hard to teach their children effectively. Work hard to join this group of teachers and then aim to make your good teaching even better and become a *great* teacher!

Great teachers know their children well; they know their home and cultural backgrounds, their interests, their attitudes and preferred intelligences as well as their social, cognitive, physical, emotional and creative abilities and skills. They then cater for all these in their lessons. They realise that they are setting an example to the children through their actions and attitudes and are therefore energetic, industrious, motivated, dedicated and caring. In all their interactions with their children they are firm, fair and friendly. They believe in the value of what they are doing and show their children respect and courtesy. They know why, what, where and how they are teaching their lessons. Aim to be a great teacher and remember, in each of your lessons, you should teach so as to challenge all the children some of the time, yet at the same time ensure that they each experience a reasonable chance of success. Here are some considerations for planning lessons in the arts that can help you become a great teacher!

Lesson planning in the arts

Make good teaching *great*!

Resources

Teacher's presentation

Lesson plans

Reflection and evaluation

Using learning centres

Resources

When writing a lesson plan, work out what resources you need to help the children achieve the indicators in each lesson. Include details of each of the resources in your lesson plan or program to help you gather them together before the lesson, and so another teacher could find and use these resources if they are required (or the teacher may want to teach your lesson). You may remember now that a selected track of music is on a certain CD, but next year when you want to use that track again, you may have forgotten, so write down the details of the CD in the lesson plan. If appropriate, include the Readers' Theatre script, a copy of the song, story, diagram of charts, overhead transparencies and so on for future reference. Before the lesson, learn to sing the song, do the dance, read the poem, script or story, work the computer program or camera and so on confidently so you do not waste time in the lesson.

Once you have identified all the resources required for the lesson write them down and think through how you will use the resources in each lesson, for example:

- What space do you need for the activities?
- How will you set up the classroom for each lesson?
- What children will sit where? Who works best with whom? Which children work well in groups?
- What rules and consequences will you make clear at the start of the lesson and reinforce through the lessons until they become instilled in the children's understanding?
- What positive reinforcement techniques will you use throughout the lesson?

- Where will you store the resources required for the lesson?
- Do you need an extension cord, power board or batteries for using CD/cassette players, computers or overhead projectors?
- What routines for resource distribution and collection do you need to set in place before or at the start of teaching the lesson?
- If you are using a big book or graphic score, is there an easel or blackboard ledge on which it can be placed? If not, work out how you will hold it up for everyone to see.
- Where will you store the wet or unfinished artworks?

Teacher's preparation

Before teaching a lesson, you need to work out who you are teaching, what you are teaching, why you are teaching it and what you hope to achieve from the lesson so you can use this information as you plan the lesson.

- **Contextual description.** Identify children's previous learning experiences, knowledge and skills in the particular art form presented in the lesson. Know their difference in achievement levels and stages, and be aware of their cultural, cognitive, creative, emotional and social differences and their entering attitudes, needs and interests.
- **Syllabus outcomes.** Decide what outcomes you want the children to work towards achieving and take these directly from the relevant state or territory syllabus. Be realistic about what you can achieve and avoid expecting children to achieve too many outcomes in one lesson.
- **Purpose of the lesson.** Identify how the purpose of the lesson fits in with the overall work program. Work out why you are teaching this particular lesson to this particular group of children, given their current knowledge, skills and attitudes.
- **Specific indicators.** Now you have the big picture of *who* you are teaching, what outcomes you wish to achieve and why you are teaching the lesson, narrow down the focus to what you want children to achieve in each lesson. Specific indicators in the lesson can be used to show that your lesson has been effective. These should be related to each activity in the lesson and should be observable and assessable. Achievement of a series of related specific indicators can be used to document what outcomes are being worked towards or achieved.
- **Links to other key learning areas.** If possible, show relevant links between this lesson and other key learning areas so children see their learning at school as a cohesive whole and not broken down into discrete, unrelated lessons.
- **Behaviour management strategies.** Think through which methods of positive reinforcement you will use throughout the lesson. Work out with the children what routines, rules and consequences you will use so children will know what is expected of them. Decide on appropriate signals for *quiet, finishing up, listening to the teacher* and so on.
- **Classroom organisation.** Work out where the children will be at the beginning of the lesson and if (how and where) they need to move during the lesson.

Identify procedures and routines for setting up and clearing away art materials and how you will distribute and collect instruments or other resources. Know which children should not be seated together, and which children work best with other children if you are doing group work.

- **Resources.** Schools have limited resources, and only minimal use of photocopying and other consumable resources may be available to use at the school. If you are a student teacher you may need to provide your own materials and resources; however, discuss what resources the school is able to provide and what materials are available in the classroom with your supervising teacher. Make a comprehensive list of all resources required, such as CDs, CD player, extension cord, storybook, graphic score, flashcards, scarves, computer, software program, script, art materials, digital camera and so on, and remember that you need to learn the song or dance and so on yourself as well!

Lesson plans

Introduction

Grab children's attention with a motivating start to the lesson. Use a puppet, a story, an artwork, a picture or flashcards, an object hidden in a bag, or an artefact related to the theme or a sound. It is vital to focus the children's attention on the lesson right from the start as this will give it a strong beginning and motivate the children to stay on task.

Introduce the element, theme or activity briefly, but don't overdo the teacher talk. Children can lose motivation quickly if all they hear is the teacher talking with no visual or kinaesthetic aids! Avoid extensive questioning or discussions as this may involve only a few children and the rest will become bored or not feel involved.

Body of lesson

Describe the lesson fully, referring to what the teacher will do and what the children will do. Use the third person, not 'I'; for example: 'Teacher sings song while children clap the beat' and not 'I will sing the song and ask the children to clap the beat'.

Detail each activity clearly and ensure that the learning experiences are sequenced carefully, with each building on the previous one, and are related to the stated indicators, outcomes and purpose of the lesson.

Closure activity

Close with an activity that summarises what has been taught; avoid generalised discussions that include only a few children. Closure should be activity-based and should bring together the main teaching points from the lesson giving you feedback about which children have achieved the indicators. You may also like to give children the opportunity to reflect on, and summarise, what they have learned by writing in their arts journal or sharing what they have learned or enjoyed with a friend.

Reflection and evaluation

Self-reflection

Great teachers reflect on what they have done. Remember the valuable lessons you have learned and realise that mistakes are part of learning: if you don't make mistakes, you won't learn much!

Reflect on, and write down, what worked and what didn't work and why! Use what worked in the next lesson; learn from what didn't work!

Reflect on:
- the lesson content;
- the lesson procedures;
- the children's responses;
- what worked, what didn't work and why;
- how effectively the indicators were achieved;
- what you have learned;
- suggestions for future related lessons.

Formal lesson evaluations

Self-reflections can then form the basis of your formal evaluations of the lesson and the assessment of the children. In your evaluations, include:
- How effective was the content?
- What strategies challenged children to learn?
- What were the most successful sections?
- Were there any difficulties in the lesson?
- What could have been done better?
- How many children achieved the indicators? How do I know this?
- How effective were the aids and resources?
- What might I change or modify next time?
- What will I teach to follow up this lesson?

Using learning centres

Why use learning centres?

As well as teaching whole-class lessons and using group work to teach elements, skills and knowledge in arts education, the use of learning centres can also contribute to effective learning in the classroom. Learning centres can be used by individual children, pairs or small groups of children who work by themselves, completing the tasks and then sharing them with others. They encourage independent and cooperative learning, and are activity-based and child-centred. They can include problem-solving tasks that are open-ended to allow all children to succeed and create a unique artwork, while working at their own pace. The tasks should be related to the needs and interests of the children, their previous learning experiences and the stage they are at in each art form. They can introduce, revise or extend children's understanding about the elements, skills and procedures with the arts.

Learning centres can be for individual children.

MMADD about the arts

Working together in learning centres can help develop cooperative skills.

How to set up learning centres

To use learning centres effectively children need to be self-directed and able to work by themselves or in a small group without constant supervision. It is often advisable to demonstrate or work through the learning centre tasks with the whole class so children are aware of what is required of them before they start.

Learning centres can be situated in a corner of the classroom and children work at them in 'free' or designated times. Alternatively, the whole class can work at different learning centres at the same time and rotate around them at a given signal or in their own time. To keep track of the activities they have completed, they could each have a contract card listing all the activities, which they stamp or mark when they have completed one activity then move on to the next activity.

All resources and instructions should be included in each learning centre so children can be self-directed and work independently. Workcards should be attractive visually, be simple enough for every child to understand, and have clear and detailed instructions. It may take considerable time to set up effective learning centres but this will pay off as children work in their own time and develop problem-solving and cooperative skills as well as learning about the elements, concepts, knowledge and skills related to each art form.

Examples of Learning Centre Workcards in each artform can be found as a pdf file on the accompanying CD.

Assessment in arts education

Observation

Consultation

Using outcomes and indicators

Self-assessment

Peer assessment

Other forms of assessment

Assessment in arts education

Assessment is an important part of the arts education program as teachers need to know how well children have achieved the indicators and outcomes. It needs to be appropriate to the learning experiences and the children's background, knowledge and skills so children are not being set up for failure. The assessment criteria need to be explicit and clearly communicated to children and parents. Assessment tasks should be varied and continuous over the year so the development of the children within each of the art forms can be documented and discussed with the individual children and their parents. These tasks can take many forms. They can include in-class observation, consultation with the children, the development of yearlong portfolios of children's work, self-assessment and peer assessment, and they should be based on relevant outcomes and indicators. Formal assessment in the arts can focus on knowledge and content, responses to artworks and responses related to personal performances. It should include the process of collecting, analysing and recording details about each child's progress in relation to specified indicators and syllabus outcomes. This assessment data can then be used to develop the next program of work for the children, building on and developing what they have already demonstrated they know, can do and understand.

Observation

Often assessment is done intuitively, with teachers noticing who is paying attention, who can move their bodies to the beat, who can sing the song confidently, who can use their voices expressively, who can mix paints to create secondary and tertiary colours, who needs help with certain tasks and so on. They then alter their teaching to repeat or move on from the learning experience, depending on how many children have achieved the indicators, thus responding to the needs of the teaching situation and the learners.

Teachers also find that they are consciously assessing children both throughout the lessons (formative assessment) and at the end of the program of work (summative assessment) and that assessment is an integral part of instruction. They can assess children's work in relation to how well they sing, draw, move, follow instructions or present a Readers' Theatre, and how well they demonstrate they understand each of the elements of music, drama, dance, media and visual arts. Assessing values and attitudes is a little more difficult; the better teachers know their children, the easier this is.

Consultation

Assessment can involve asking questions of children and talking with them about their work, but this is better done individually or in small groups to ensure that teachers are getting feedback from all the children and not just the bright or artistically experienced children. Ensure discussion questions are stimulating, relevant and clear, and that they stretch the children's thinking and allow them to demonstrate and discuss what they understand or value. Wait for answers; don't expect children to have the answer immediately. Vary the length and difficulty of questions to allow all children to be involved and avoid simple 'yes' or 'no' answers. Ask single questions; avoid asking several questions at once. Listen to the answers carefully and use them as a springboard for the next question, delving into the meaning and understanding behind the artwork. Consultation can consolidate assessment details already collected and can clarify anything that is unclear. It can also be undertaken with the child and their parents, to show the parents the importance of the children's varied artworks, why and how they have created them and the child's development in this area over the year.

Using outcomes and indicators

In order to develop effective assessment techniques, teachers need to be very clear about the general purpose or outcomes of the overall unit and the specific indicators for each activity until the children can demonstrate that they have achieved all the outcomes for that stage. The state and territory syllabus documents assist teachers with determining the outcomes the children are working towards within the program and some also provide sample indicators for teachers to use as guides when writing their own. Indicators should be observable and should show how the learner will demonstrate they have achieved the specified learning to be achieved. An indicator that states: 'children will be able to understand the concept of dynamics' is non-specific, cannot be observed and is difficult to assess. An indicator that states: 'children will demonstrate that they can sing and play loudly and softly in response to large and small flashcards' is specific to the activity and can be observed and assessed. Assessment techniques need to be authentic and relevant in that children will need to be able to demonstrate their knowledge, understanding, attitude or skill, not just talk about it or fill in a stencil.

Self-assessment

Children could assess themselves or be involved in peer assessment and occasionally it may be relevant to have children assessed by parents or by outside specialists. When involved in self-assessment children could be asked to give a short oral presentation and identify what they had set out to achieve, why they used the resources that they did, if they were happy with the results, what would they like to change and why, and what would they like to do next. They could be asked to assess the quality of their own performance or composition or they could write about their progress in a creative arts journal to assess their artistic growth within each of the art forms. They could record their composition and then talk about it onto the same (video or aural) tape, explaining how and why they created it and what they learned while creating and playing their composition. This could form part of an electronic portfolio of work to show their development throughout the year.

Peer assessment

Children could also assess the quality of the performance by others in their class (peer assessment) based on discussed criteria. To avoid children being negative to those they do not like, the teacher should encourage comments that are positive and constructive. Children could be asked to comment on what they liked about the artwork or performance in relation to the criteria, or make at least one positive comment and one suggestion for improvement. Another method is to ask the class to show with their fingers a number out of ten that indicates how well they thought a group performed. The teacher can then lead a discussion about the ratings.

Other forms of assessment

Assessment can also take the form of creating checklists for each child and having them, their peers or their teacher tick off when they can consistently achieve certain criteria, pointers, indicators or outcomes. Often assessment is done by observation, but there could be times when children's work can be assessed using more formalised procedures, such as written tests or exams. Interviews, audio and visual recordings, annotated work samples and reflective journals can be other forms of assessment as could a teacher's anecdotal notes in a journal or against a list of the children's names. Portfolios with dated examples of children's work throughout the year to show their developmental progress can be another effective form of assessment. Throughout all assessment procedures, it is very important that assessment is not used as a way of 'putting down' a student, but should, instead, be used to encourage, praise, acknowledge and celebrate children's achievements and development within the arts.

SPRINGBOARDS FOR DISCUSSION AND APPLICATION

1. Prepare a brochure for parents which explains clearly the reasons for including the arts in the core curriculum in primary schools.
2. Teach a simple arts-related skill to peers, using effective communication skills; have them review it using the SPEAKER mnemonic.
3. Select an art form and prepare a lesson for a hypothetical class, listing at least five behaviour management strategies that will be used in the lesson and indicating appropriate assessment strategies to be used.

FURTHER READING

Barrett, M. (1996), *Learning centres in music education* (video and book), University of Tasmania, Launceston.

Office for Standards in Education (OFSTED) (1998), *The arts inspected: Good teaching in art, dance, drama, music*, Heinemann, Oxford.

REFERENCES

Christian, E. (2004), *Motivating Moments*, <www.motivateus.com>.

Combs, M. (1991), Decline in arts education lessens student creativity, specialists say, *Boston Sunday Globe*, 10 March.

Finn, B. (1991), *Young people's participation in post-compulsory education and training*, Australian Education Council, Melbourne.

Fiske, E. (1999), *Champions of change: The impact of the arts on learning*, The Arts Education Partnership, Washington, DC.

Fowler, C. (1989), 'The arts are essential to education', *Educational Leadership*, pp. 60–63.

Jensen, E. (2001), *Arts with the brain in mind*, Association for Supervision and Curriculum Development, Alexandria, Virginia.

Mahlmann, J. (no date), *What students should know and be able to do in the arts: Summary statement,* <http://www.menc.org/tour/summary.html>.

Mayer Committee (1992), *Putting education to work: The key competencies report*, Australian Education Council/Ministerial Council of Vocational Education, Employment and Training, Melbourne.

Oddliefson, E. (1994), 'What do we want our schools to do?', *Phi Delta Kappan*, vol. 75, no. 5, pp. 446–452.

Perrin, S. (1994), 'Education in the arts is an education for life', *Phi Delta Kappan*, pp. 452–453.

Smith, R. (2002), 'Spend (slightly) less on health and more on the arts', *British Medical Journal*, 21 Dec.–28 Dec., vol. 325, iss. 7378, pp. 1432–1433.

Ultan, L. (1989), 'Crises in society: The role of the arts', *Arts in Education*, May 1989.

chapter three
Introduction to music education

Music education provides powerful learning experiences for our children and has the potential to assist them in achieving diverse and valuable educational outcomes. (The Hon. Dr Brendan Nelson, MP, 26 March 2005)

Learning outcomes
By the end of this chapter, students will be able to:
- define the main elements in music and demonstrate how they can be practically applied in the primary classroom;
- demonstrate how a suggested learning experience can be simplified or made more challenging for different ages and stages of children;
- create a music program which teaches and reinforces the elements and activity areas of music.

MMADD about the arts

Engagement in music helps children develop cooperation skills.

Introduction

Making music is fun! Most children love to clap, move to music, sing and play instruments! Music education is vital to every child's holistic development and can help them reach their fullest potential. Through an effective music education program, children can develop an aesthetic sense; enhance their self-esteem; engage in authentic, real-life learning experiences; and use music as a way of expressing themselves and communicating. Engagement in a quality music program helps children develop self-discipline and social, cooperative skills; discover an enjoyment in listening to a variety of different styles of music; learn about different cultures through their music; develop both fine and gross motor skills; challenge and develop their critical thinking and problem-solving skills; and . . . have fun!

Why teach music education?

Music is a way of knowing and learning about the world and expressing one's identity within the world. It is a means of self-expression and as such has been used in every culture throughout history. Music reflects the beliefs and identity of the composer, the performer and those who hear it as well as reflecting the social and cultural context in which it was written. Music engages us emotionally and intellectually, stimulating both the right and left sides of the brain, and uses many of the basic intelligences through which children learn.

Music needs to be experienced, not just through listening, but by making music — by playing, improvising, composing, organising sound, moving and singing. Through these varied ways of experiencing music children learn the basic elements of pitch, duration, tone colour, dynamics and structure and gain a deeper understanding and appreciation of music. They will learn to become intelligent consumers of music, and be able to talk about how music makes them feel, why they like it and what is happening in the music they hear at school, at home and in their adult life.

Through participating in sequential music programs, children can develop their self-esteem, self-discipline and confidence as they learn to perform a variety of music. They can develop their ability to cooperate in groups and become strong leaders and team members through group compositions, learning experiences and performances. Children can learn more about themselves, their peers and people from different cultures as they make, perform and appreciate a variety of music. They can become critical thinkers, reflective learners and creative problem solvers as they analyse music and its cultural context, create their own music and learn to take risks in making and appreciating different kinds of music.

As well as the personal, interpersonal and musical benefits of an effective music education, music can also be used to create authentic, engaging learning experiences in other subjects across the curriculum. For example, there are significant associations between music and achievement in mathematics and reading, as well as social, emotional and behavioural benefits for the whole child (Fiske, 1999). Through using music to learn other subjects and skills, children who may not be able to learn using other methods may achieve significant results in these subjects.

Music is a multimillion dollar economy. Listening to commercial music is a major pastime of many children and young people. Across the country parents see the value of a quality music education and are paying for their children to learn to play an instrument. Live and recorded choirs, bands, rock groups, ensembles, orchestras and musical productions are providing audiences with great enjoyment so that music is an integral part of life and of the Australian economy.

Teachers can implement quality music lessons with their class.

Music in the primary classroom

All children come to school with a wealth of musical experiences and many move and sing spontaneously to music. This needs to be nurtured and developed throughout their primary school years. However, many generalist primary classroom teachers feel that they don't have the skills, knowledge or resources to implement effective music education programs for their children. Teachers say, 'I can't sing!', 'I can't play the piano', 'I don't have any musical instruments in the classroom', 'I don't have songs or music that relate to my classroom themes, and if I did, how do I teach music instead of just having the children sing the song?'

Most good teachers who are committed to ensuring their children have a well-rounded and holistic education overcome these barriers, develop their skills and knowledge, check out the library for appropriate songs and music, and attend professional development courses to get skills, knowledge and inspiration for music lessons! However 'unmusical' teachers may think they are, if they are committed to their children, have a positive and enthusiastic attitude and are keen to learn, they can succeed in implementing music lessons in their classrooms.

Start at the very beginning

But where do we start? As Maria, in *The Sound of Music* sang, 'Let's start at the very beginning, a very good place to start!' In order to talk about music, we need to learn some basic terms. Music can be broken down into five main elements or concepts: *Pitch*, *dynamics*, *tone colour*, *structure* and *duration*. Once these terms are understood, lessons can be planned which incorporate activities focusing on each of these elements. Each concept can be introduced at a simple level, and then developed further through movement, singing, listening, and instrumental and creative activities. At each level, as children develop their confidence and understanding of the elements of music, they will develop a much deeper understanding and appreciation of the music which is part of their life. They will also expand their repertoire of music of different styles and cultures that they may not have previously encountered.

They will also begin to learn to play a variety of classroom instruments, and this may inspire them to have further music lessons within or outside school, to learn a

Start teaching duration using simple clapping activities.

particular instrument such as the piano, guitar, violin, saxophone or drums. Through the implementation of an effective music education program, children will learn to value music as a means of personal expression, for the way it is created and played and for its cultural value, as well as developing a positive attitude to learning about music.

Remember that in one class, some children may have a deeper understanding and experience of music education than others. Don't presume that just because children are in a Stage 3 class they are ready for Stage 3 music lessons. Also, some children in a Stage 1 class may actually be at Stage 2 in relation to music education. Some 10-year-olds may never have had music lessons that cover these elements of music before, while some 6-year-olds may have been immersed in such instruction from their first years both at home and at school. All children deserve an effective music education program throughout their primary school experiences, and teachers should aim to challenge and develop each child musically within their classroom by implementing regular and developmental music lessons throughout each school year.

Other approaches to music education

The music activities and suggestions included in this chapter are based on an eclectic approach to music education. However, other philosophies could also be used to achieve quality music programs, and these include the Dalcroze, Kodaly and Orff methods of teaching music. The Swiss educator Emile Jacques-Dalcroze (1865–1950) believed that rhythm is the main element in music and that the human body can be the source for all musical rhythms and as such focuses much of his philosophy of music education on movement. Zoltan Kodaly (1882–1967), a Hungarian educator, believed that singing was the best foundation for musicianship and developed an approach to music education which involved singing folk songs using hand signs to show relative pitch and through this developed children's musical literacy and understanding. The German composer Carl Orff (1895–1982) developed a music education curriculum in which children would physically experience the elements of music through movement and playing child-friendly instruments, which he created. For further information about these and other philosophies of music education, refer to the reading list at the end of this chapter.

Carl Orff created child-friendly instruments for children.

Elements of music

In this section, the five elements of music are each defined and then discussed in more depth. Specific classroom learning experiences to teach each of these elements then follow to help the generalist classroom teacher implement an effective music education program throughout the year.

Introduction to music education — Chapter 3

Duration

Duration includes the rhythm, beat, tempo, accent, length of notes and time signatures, for example:

- rhythm (long and short notes, the patterns of sounds and silences);
- beat (underlying steady pulse, like the heartbeat of the music);
- accent (first, strong, accented beat of each bar);
- tempo (speed of beat; tempos can change in a piece of music);
- rhythmic ostinato (repeated rhythmic phrase).

Pitch

The element of pitch includes high and low notes, melodies, melodic ostinato, chords, harmonies, and rising and falling pitch, for example:

- melody (a series of pitched notes, a tune);
- harmony (different notes played together);
- definite pitch (sounds which can play a tune, e.g. xylophone, piano, violin);
- indefinite pitch (sounds which cannot play a tune, e.g. triangle, tambourine);
- melodic ostinato (repeated melodic phrase).

Tone colour

Tone colour involves the quality of sound produced by different instruments and the ways these sounds are made, for example:

- sound source material (e.g. made from wood, metal, plastic, string and so on);
- sound production or how the sound is made (e.g. sounds made by hitting, shaking, blowing and scraping);
- sounds heard singly (unison);
- sounds played together (ensemble).

Dynamics

Dynamics includes loud and soft sounds, increasing and decreasing volume of sounds; contrasting dynamics can be used to create character and expressiveness in a piece of music. See 'Italian terms' in 'Some musical terms explained' on page 53 for further details of specific dynamic levels.

Structure

The element of structure identifies how the piece of music is put together: which sections or phrases are the same or different and which are repeated; is there an introduction, ending, bridge and so on; or does the song have verses and a chorus, for example:

- the design or form of the music (which can create unity or variety);
- same or different sections or phrases (i.e. repetition or contrast);
- different parts of the music, (i.e. verse, chorus, phrase, theme, section, motif, introduction, bridge, coda or ending);

47

- simple structures include:
  — binary form: A B
  — ternary form: A B A
  — rondo form: A B A C A D A
  — verse – chorus – verse – chorus
  — introduction – main section – ending (coda).

Repertoire in music

A variety of different types of music can be used to teach these elements and to develop a repertoire of music that children can appreciate, enjoy, analyse, sing and play. Children should be encouraged to use music from their own cultural traditions and those of others when singing, playing, moving and listening to music. Bring in a variety of music for the children to engage with; include music from different eras, styles, countries and cultures. Encourage children to listen, analyse and learn to appreciate the differences and cultural contexts of the music.

Repertoire in music can include the following:

Vocal music
Learn to sing age-appropriate songs covering a variety of styles.

Chants and raps
- Use the words of an appropriate song or poem as a chant.
- Have children create their own raps or chants about relevant subjects.

Children's songs and rhymes
- Simple nursery rhymes are ideal for the first introduction of the elements with young children.
- Rhymes and children's songs can also be used with older children as a springboard to more challenging activities; they are usually easy to sing and have simple words so children can concentrate on more difficult activities such as adding a simple accompaniment on a tuned instrument or creating an instrumental non-tuned accompaniment to the song.

Game songs
These are generally easy to learn and can incorporate singing and movement.

Appropriate popular songs
- Check lyrics, pitch and rhythms first to ensure these are appropriate.
- Some popular songs have sexually explicit, violent or other lyrics that would not be suitable for the primary classroom.
- Many popular songs are difficult to sing as they have a wide pitch range and difficult rhythms.
- However, the careful use of appropriate popular songs can create considerable motivation and interest in music lessons.

Introduction to music education   Chapter 3

Some musical terms explained

If teachers are to implement music lessons, it is helpful to know some basic musical terms.

1. Beat (Duration)

This can also be called the pulse of the music. Like your own pulse, it is <u>regular and steady</u>. When you clap to a piece of music, you generally clap the pulse, or *beat* of the music, for example:

2. Rhythm (Duration)

Music is usually made up of a combination of long and short notes. These create the *rhythm* of a song or melody. We can use the following notes to create simple rhythms:

♩	=	1 crotchet	=	**Taa**
♫	=	2 quavers	=	**Ta-te**
𝅗𝅥	=	1 minim	=	**Taa-aa**
𝅝	=	1 semibreve		**Taa-aa-aa-aa**

These four notes can be used in combinations to make a rhythm. Clap these rhythms to a steady beat:

3. Time signatures (Duration)

Rhythms are divided into groups of notes to make reading rhythms easier. Bar lines divide the groups. Each group, or bar, has the same value of beats in it.

The number and type of beats within each bar is indicated at the start of the rhythm or music, by the *time signature*. Note:

- The *top number* tells us how many beats are in each bar.
- The *bottom number* tells us what kind of note represents one beat.

MMADD about the arts

Top	4	=	4 beats in each bar
Bottom	4	=	Crotchet, or 1/4 note represents one beat
	2/4	=	2 crotchet, or 1/4, beats in each bar
	6/8	=	6 quaver, or 1/8, beats in each bar

Clap these rhythms, tap the beat.

4. Pitch and note names

Pitch refers to high and low sounds in music. Every note has a name and can be written on a music staff. Note names follow the first seven letters of the alphabet: A B C D E F G , and then they repeat the sequence, going higher each time, for example:

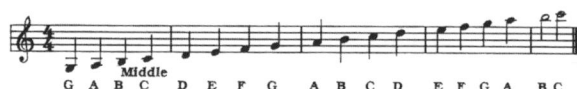

G A B C D E F G A B C D E F G A B C
     Middle

Each letter name and note responds to a note on an instrument, for example:

The piano keyboard:

| C | D | E | F | G | A | B | C | D | E | F |

Middle C (at the centre of the keyboard)

5. Note and rest values

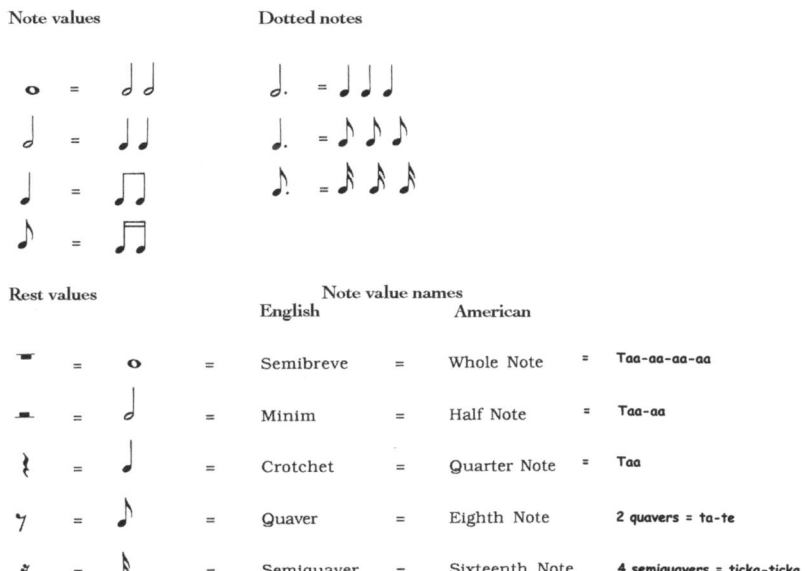

Rest		Note		English		American		
𝄻	=	𝅝	=	Semibreve	=	Whole Note	=	Taa-aa-aa-aa
𝄼	=	𝅗𝅥	=	Minim	=	Half Note	=	Taa-aa
𝄽	=	♩	=	Crotchet	=	Quarter Note	=	Taa
𝄾	=	♪	=	Quaver	=	Eighth Note	=	2 quavers = ta-te
𝄿	=	♪	=	Semiquaver	=	Sixteenth Note	=	4 semiquavers = ticka-ticka

6. Scales

A *scale* is a series of notes set out to a prescribed formula of tones and semitones. A major scale has eight notes, for example C major ascending and descending:

A scale can be played ascending or descending; that is, in the C scale, from middle C to high C, or from high C to middle C. All scales start and end on the same letter name.

7. Chords

A chord is created when two or more notes are played together. They may sound dissonant and harsh, or harmonious and pleasing to the ear. A basic three-note chord (triad) uses the first, third and fifth notes in a scale, starting on the letter name of that scale, for example:

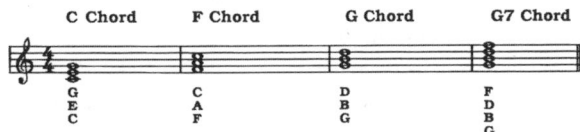

8. Bass notes

The *bass note* of a chord is the note indicated by the name of the chord; for example, in a C chord, the bass note is C; in a G7 chord, the bass note is G.

9. Pentatonic (5 note) scale

A *pentatonic scale* uses the first, second, third, fifth and sixth notes of the scale, for example:

If a song is written using only the notes of a pentatonic scale, any or all of the five notes may be used to form an ostinato to accompany the song.

10. Ostinato

An *ostinato* is a repeated rhythm or melody that can be used to accompany a pentatonic song. In a pentatonic song, any combination of the pentatonic notes played in a rhythmic pattern will harmonise with the song, for example:

11. Graphic scores

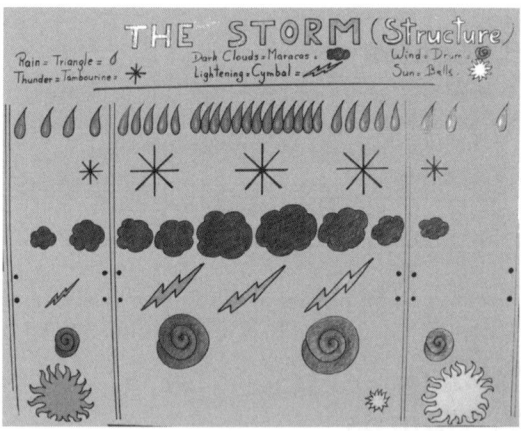

A graphic score is a symbolic representation of a story, landscape, event or description. Instruments, body percussion and/or voices are used to interpret the symbols. The conductor can move his/her pointer from left to right across the score, to indicate the tempo of the piece and when each instrument plays.

12. Italian terms

Many instructions indicating how to play a piece of music are written in Italian, for example:

Tempo	=	Speed of music, fast or slow, and so on
Ritardando	=	Slowing down
Accellerando	=	Speeding up
Staccato	=	Make the notes sound short, sharp and detached
Legato	=	Play the notes smoothly
Crescendo	=	Becoming louder
Diminuendo	=	Becoming softer
Pianissimo	= **pp** =	Very soft
Piano	= **p** =	Soft
Mezzo piano	= **mp** =	Moderately soft

Mezzo forte	=	**mf**	=	Moderately loud
Forte	=	**f**	=	Loud
Fortissimio	=	**ff**	=	Very loud

13. Phrases

A phrase is like a musical sentence. Phrases are sometimes marked above the music like this:

14. Tuned and untuned percussion instruments

Some percussion instruments can play different notes, and can be used to play a melody or add an accompaniment to a song. These are called tuned or melodic percussion instruments, for example xylophone, glockenspiel and chime bars.

Other percussion instruments cannot play melodies—they can only play rhythms. They are called untuned instruments, for example triangles, maracas, tambourines and bells.

Xylophone (Wooden bars)   Glockenspiel (Metal bars)

Tuned/Melodic Percussion Instruments
→ play diff. notes; melody, add accompaniment.

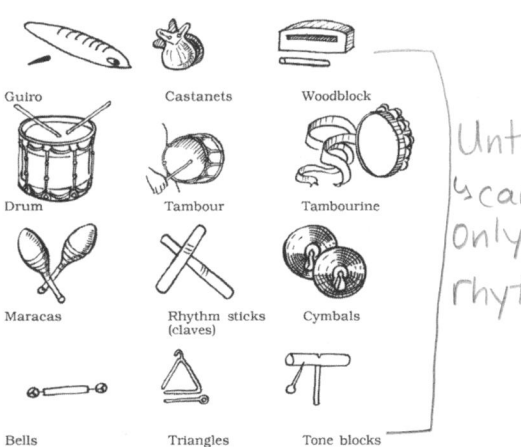

Untuned can only play rhythm.

a) Using tuned instruments.

b) Using untuned instruments.

Making, performing and appreciating

The above elements of music and musical terms should not be taught solely by rote or teacher-talk. Rather, children should be engaged in practical, interactive, meaningful learning experiences that include making, performing (singing, playing instruments and moving) and appreciating. It is more important that children experience and understand the elements of music through these activities than that they are able to recite a definition of dynamics, pitch and so on. When engaged in a developmental music program, children will learn and understand the names of these elements of music as they are covered at a more challenging level at each stage, but it is the actual meaningful involvement in the activities that are the important learning experience.

Making

When children have been engaged in a variety of structured activities, they can then build on these experiences, using a variety of sound sources to create their own pieces of music or develop interpretations of songs or music through:

- experimenting with different sounds, structures and musical elements;
- imitating ideas or styles they know and enjoy;
- improvising different sequences of sounds and music;
- arranging their ideas into a formalised structure;
- composing and creating new pieces of music to sing or play.

Performing

Singing

Through singing, children learn to sing in tune and sing with confidence. They also experience musical elements such as loud and soft, fast and slow, high and low, and different styles in music as they sing songs.

Singing activities can include:
- chants, rhymes and raps;
- choral speaking and singing;
- singing games;
- age-appropriate songs;
- two-part songs/three-part songs;
- rounds.

Playing instruments

Children need to be given the opportunity to make and play their own music using a variety of instruments. These do not need to be expensive and any teacher can gather enough instruments for the class to use regularly, such as:

- body percussion (clapping, stamping, clicking fingers and so on);
- classroom objects (ruler tapped on chair leg, pencil tapped on desk, tins tapped together and so on);

- found or junk materials (rocks, sticks, cans and so on);
- student-made instruments (empty plastic bottle filled with rice, stick with bottle tops nailed to it and so on);
- untuned percussion instruments (tambourines, triangles, rhythm sticks);
- tuned instruments (xylophone, piano, guitar, recorder);
- electronic and computer-based instruments;
- instruments from different cultures or movement, when creating a piece of music or to explore musical elements.

Using untuned instruments to keep the beat.

Moving

Children can move in response to music, to experience the musical elements and to communicate their emotions. Movement can be used as a stimulus for classroom activities, and can be accompanied with a piece of music, a sound or series of sounds, or short musical phrases.

Movement activities embrace locomotor and non-locomotor movements.

- **Locomotor movements.** These include:
  - folk dancing;
  - modern dancing;
  - singing games;
  - improvised movement sequences;
  - creative dances and so on.

- **Non-locomotor movements.** These include:
  - body percussion;
  - swaying;
  - stretching;
  - twisting;
  - bending and so on.

Appreciating

In order to appreciate music, children's listening skills need to be developed. This is important to ensure a sound basis for their general and music education. Musical listening activities can enhance and focus children's listening abilities across the curriculum as well as developing their ability to listen to, and appreciate, music of their own and that of others. Listening activities should help children to:

- be aware of different sounds heard in music;
- be able to discriminate between the different sounds heard in music;
- remember sounds they have heard;
- recognise and remember sequences of sounds in music;
- imagine sounds without hearing them.

When children listen carefully to their singing and playing, they can learn to create sensitive and expressive performances. Through listening to, and appreciating, a variety of music from different cultures and contexts children can learn about, and respond to, the music of other people, critically analyse the elements and

styles used in that work together to create music and evaluate and interpret their own and others' music.

Practical considerations

When planning music lessons, know what activities the children have done, what musical skills they have developed, which children take music lessons outside of school and what stage and outcomes the children are working towards (this could be different for different children).

Singing and . . .

Teachers and students often note the difficulty children have when asked to sing *and* do another activity simultaneously, for example playing instruments, body percussion, moving!

Ensure children have learned the song well and can sing it confidently before adding another activity.

Ground rules

Set clear ground rules at the start of the lesson. Simple rules for the music lesson could be:

- **Movement.** No touching anyone else unless instructed and no talking.
- **Playing instruments.** Stop playing on prearranged signal and keep instruments quiet ('put them to sleep') unless playing.
- **Singing.** Sit up straight with no talking, open mouths, enunciate words clearly, show expression, and so on.
- **Listening.** No talking or distracting others.

Teaching a song

Teach each song so that children will enjoy it, and also sing it with accuracy and appropriate interpretation. Through singing songs, children can develop their understanding and skills related to the basic musical elements that occur in the material.

Children actually need to be *taught* the song; don't expect them to be able to sing the song just by listening to it once. Use a variety of ways to teach the songs (see the next section in this chapter, 'Five ways of learning music', for further ideas on teaching songs). Choose songs children can actually sing, keep the songs within children's vocal range and check that the lyrics are suitable for children. Use a CD or cassette tape of the song for pitch if you are not a confident, in-tune singer.

Suggested structure of a music lesson

- Start with a motivating introduction to grab the children's attention.
- Briefly introduce the main concept or skill to be taught through an activity.
- Develop the concept, skill or activity, building on previous knowledge and experiences. Challenge those with previous music experience and support those with no background in music.

- Close with an activity that summarises and consolidates what has been taught and provides you with observable feedback on the achievement of the indicators and outcomes.

Five ways of learning music

The five ways of learning music that are covered by the activity areas of performing (singing, playing instruments, moving), making and appreciating are now discussed more fully with practical classroom implementation ideas. These activity areas can be used individually and with each other to ensure children engage in a variety of effective learning experiences which achieve the set indicators and outcomes for the lesson or program of work.

Singing

Many music lessons are centred around a song. However, often teachers feel they can't sing in tune and so they avoid singing with the children. This may communicate to the children that the teacher isn't interested in singing and so they may copy that attitude. To avoid this, teachers should sing along softly with the CD and the children, regardless of how they think they may sound. The children will appreciate their making the attempt to sing. Remember that the more you sing, while listening carefully to a CD, the better you will become. With good models, teaching and lots of practice, you can become more confident with singing with the children and be able to lead them in a song, even without a CD.

There are various ways to teach a song. Teachers should try to be creative in the different ways they introduce and teach the songs and determine the most effective method for each song. Don't forget that children need lots of repetition of the song in order to learn to sing the song confidently, so build this into the lesson when a new song is being taught. Remember to teach so that all the children are challenged at least some of the time within a lesson. But at the same time, make sure that they also all experience a reasonable chance of success.

Consider the following questions when you select a method of teaching a song and when you plan your lesson:
- What is the musical experience of the children?
- What are their musical abilities?
- How difficult is the song in relation to the above?
- What elements of music do you want to develop in the lesson?
- What skills do you want to develop?
- What attitudes and values do you want to encourage?
- How will you assess the children's progress and development?

Why sing?

There are many musical and other reasons for having singing in the classroom. Here are a few ideas; try to think up some more:
- It's fun to sing!
- Musical elements can be taught through singing.

- Singing helps children move creatively and lose some of their inhibitions.
- Children can learn to sing in harmony (two or more notes sounded together).
- Children can develop their fine and gross motor skills through singing games and action songs.
- Songs can provide effective integration into theme work across the curriculum.

Teaching a song

Teach each song so that children will enjoy it and sing it with accuracy and appropriate interpretation. Through singing songs, children can focus on the development of musical elements that appear in the material and on skills related to these elements. When appropriate, children should also learn about the cultural context of the song.

It is important to take note of the following in order to confidently and competently teach songs to a class:

- Choose songs that reflect the children's interests and likes, and/or that relate to classroom themes or elements being taught.
- Choose songs that can be sung comfortably by the children, as related to their age, range and vocal ability.
- Know the song very well.
- Practise playing and singing it.
- Sing or play the whole song through first so that everyone hears how it goes.
- Check that children understand the lyrics and cultural context of the song.
- Use eye contact for feedback and discipline.
- Ensure you give the starting note clearly and correctly.
- Check posture, diction, voice production, phrasing, breath control and vocal care throughout singing lessons.
- Set the tempo (speed) of the song, for example by counting in one bar of the song before starting singing, or by playing an introduction first. If the song is in 4/4 time, count in four beats; if it is in 3/4 time count in three beats and so on.
- Vary each repetition of the song to avoid boredom, both by the teacher and the children! Sing it softly, loudly, quickly, slowly; add instruments; clap the beat or rhythm; add simple actions or movements; and add a repeated rhythm (ostinato) to the song.
- Be enthusiastic and positive! Remember, attitudes are caught and not taught.

Different ways of teaching songs

There are many ways to teach a song. Here are a few suggestions:

1. **Learning the song as a whole, with questions.** Sing and/or play the whole song through. Introduce each repetition of the song with different focus questions or activities; for example, listen for the high notes or clap the beat.
2. **Learning the song phrase by phrase.** Some songs may be easier to teach line by line or phrase by phrase. Sing the first phrase together, and then sing the first two phrases. Repeat. Sing the third phrase, then the first three phrases. When

children can do this, sing the fourth phrase. Sing the first four phrases again. Repeat the procedure for the rest of the song.

3. **Teaching a song by following the words and music.** If there is a hard copy of the music and words of the song to be taught, use this to develop and further children's knowledge of written music. Ask children questions about the high, low, fast, slow notes, repeated phrases, chords, dynamics and so on that are on the written music.

4. **Rhythmic approach to teaching songs.** Some songs have difficult or often repeated rhythmic patterns. In this case, it may be advisable to focus on learning the rhythm first before the rest of the song is taught.

5. **Teaching songs using a recording.** Often a song will be taught using a recording on a CD or cassette. In this case, children can be encouraged to focus on listening to the performance of the song and the musical elements within the song. After listening and clapping the beat, they can then learn to sing (for example) the chorus. On the next listening they can begin to sing the first verse and so on.

How can teachers assess if the children have learned the song?

- **Accuracy.** Can the children sing the song accurately in pitch, melody and rhythm without help?
- **Interpretation.** Can the children show their sensitive interpretation of the style and mood of the song, using appropriate dynamics and tempo?
- **Elements of music.** Are the children showing a development in their understanding of elements of music such as melody, rhythm, dynamics, pitch, harmony, tone colour and structure? This can be observed through their responses in related performing, making and appreciating activities.
- **Skills.** Are the children developing their listening, singing, moving, playing and creative skills?
- **Cultural context.** Can the children briefly discuss key points about the cultural context of the song?

Listening and appreciating

1. Developing children's listening ability

As teachers, it is difficult to develop children's musical ability unless they can really listen. When listening, they need to learn to concentrate, they must be able to understand what they are listening to, and they should learn to remember what they have heard. As they develop these listening skills, children also need to develop their ability to analyse, reflect on and respond to music, both to their own and to music by other people and from other cultures, and make personal and informed judgements about the music to which they listen.

Teachers can help children develop effective listening skills through a variety of games and activities which can be experienced every day to improve their listening skills. For example, encourage children to listen to the sounds around them, in the classroom, in the playground, on the street and at home. Discuss the sounds, and categorise them into loud and soft sounds, high and low sounds, fast and slow

sounds, and near and far sounds. Try to imitate them with voice, body percussion or instruments. Draw and write about them.

2. Checklist for a music appreciation lesson

Children should be given the opportunity to appreciate music from a wide variety of different types, styles and cultures. An excellent resource to start with as you introduce children to the world of classical music is the ABC's *The classic kids album* or *ABC classic kids*. Resources such as *World sound matters* (Stock, 1996) will give you ideas to help you introduce multicultural music into the classroom. Encourage children to share music from their culture as well as their favourite popular music and have them tell the class about the music they are sharing.

When taking a music appreciation segment of a music lesson, check the following points before starting the lesson:

- Start with very short excerpts of music, and gradually build them up in length as children gain experience.
- Ensure the music is relevant to the outcomes and indicators or pointers of the lesson.
- If possible, use a high-quality recording of the music and ensure you have a good reproduction of the music.
- Try to ensure the room is free from outside noise and distractions.
- Check everything is working before the lesson. If using cassettes, make sure they are cued to the correct track.
- Check if you need a double adaptor or extension cord in order to plug in the CD/cassette player (or does it use batteries?). Check that the power is switched on.
- As you play the music, give it your undivided attention if you expect your pupils to do the same.
- Become very familiar with the piece of music before you share it with the class. Include other musical experiences related to the music, such as a song, movement, a creative activity and listening quiz.
- Have the children respond in some way to the music; for example, draw, move, write a story or poem, create a similar piece of music or answer questions afterwards.

3. Make listening sessions relevant

Children will respond more to music that is seen to be of relevance to them or their studies. Relate the music to:

- their experiences;
- other curriculum areas;
- a holiday, event or season;
- a poem, story or legend the class has been reading;
- some artwork they have been examining;
- a song the children may have learned or are learning;

- music heard on TV or the radio;
- to the work being covered in English, social studies, science and so on.

4. Ensure children know *why* they are listening to the music

Avoid putting on music and telling children to listen to it without motivating them and giving them a reason to listen carefully to the music. Encourage them to develop focused listening skills by participating in some of these activities:

- Listen to teach about musical elements — such as pitch, dynamics, structure, beat, rhythm, tempo and tone colour.
- Listen to learn about the history, changing styles of music or cultural contexts of music.
- Listen to interpret music in movement.
- Listen to music that describes a scene, a story or an event. In response, write a story or poem, compose a piece of music or paint about it.
- Listen to music as a springboard for creative, dramatic movement or composition.
- Listen to music for pleasure.
- Listen to music to identify the instruments heard.
- Listen to respond with art, and create a graphic score that can then be played by the children.
- At times, provide children with the opportunity for free, unfocused listening.

5. Encourage children to analyse and respond to music

- Expose children to a wide variety of music, not just the top 40!
- Have them bring in their favourite music, music from their own culture, and music their parents and their grandparents like, as well as bringing in CDs from your own collection. Find out and discuss the cultural context of the music.
- Give them the tools to analyse the music; that is, as they experience and learn about the five elements of music they can use this knowledge to be able to analyse and appreciate the variety of music they hear every day.
- Encourage children to express their personal responses to a variety of music, through movement, drawing, written work, singing, composing, improvising, discussion and so on.
- Have them listen to a variety of music, make an initial judgement about whether or not they like it, and then explore it further through, for example, movement, composition, visual arts, drama, dance, understanding its cultural context, and analysing its content. Then listen a final time and ask them for their personal judgements on the music. Discuss if these changed from the initial judgements and why.

6. Placing music within its cultural context

When music is written, sung or played it is generally within a given context and performed for a reason. It is important that children realise the cultural context of the music they sing, listen to and play and be able to discuss the context of their own

compositions. Music can give a person or cultural group an identity, reinforce values, create meaning, be a form of communication, and embody values and opinions. However, be aware of different cultural attitudes to music and check with your children to see if this influences their responses to music.

Music has been created and performed since the start of history and each period of history developed its own unique way of creating and performing music. For hundreds of years music of one generation has been criticised and not understood by the previous generation. When children sing a Negro spiritual, a lullaby, a 1960s protest song, an aria or a madrigal, they need to know why the song was written and the social and cultural context of the song in order to understand the song in a more holistic way. This may need some research by the teacher or the children, but the work is worth the effort. For new pieces of music or songs, see if you and the children can find out:

- where it was written or created;
- when it was originally sung or played;
- why it was created;
- what instruments or voices originally sang or played it;
- who created it or first sang or played it.

Moving

Movement can be divided into six main elements:

- action (what we move);
- dynamics (how we move);
- time (when we move);
- space (where we move);
- relationships (with whom we move);
- structure (form in movement sequences).

(For further details about these six main elements of movement, see Chapter 6, 'Introduction to dance education'.)

Although it is important to work on these six elements separately in order for children to identify and experience them, the elements should not be allowed to stay in isolation for any length of time. Children should develop an awareness of them within the overall context of movement as well as studying these elements individually. Children should be given the opportunity to develop both fine and gross motor skills through movement, though younger children should initially begin with gross motor movements as they find these easier.

1. Listening can be a good stimulus for movement

Musical elements such as beat, rhythm, tempo, dynamics and pitch can be experienced in a very meaningful way as children are encouraged to explore these elements by moving to relevant music. Encourage children to develop control and coordination throughout their movements. Provide them with opportunities to move freely to music as well as to structured directions.

2. Using instruments to stimulate and develop movement

- Have children move in a certain way when they hear a drum being played, and then move in a different way when a triangle is played.
- Act out stories with instrumental accompaniment to aid characterisation and sound effects, for example *The Three Bears*, *The Three Little Pigs*, *The Three Billy Goats Gruff* and so on.
- Improvise on a tuned instrument, using the notes C, D, E, G and A initially, and have children respond in movement to the high, medium and low sounds being played.
- Improvise on a non-tuned instrument as children respond to the loud and soft sounds, and fast and slow sounds being played.
- Have children step out a repeated rhythmic pattern that is played on the drum.
- Have children invent animals to be identified with different percussion instruments. When these instruments are played, the children move as the relevant animal.

3. Sing songs as an aid to movement

Many songs can be adapted for movement purposes to ensure children experience the songs in a variety of ways. Many songs already have set actions and movements to them; however, creative children and teachers can easily invent relevant movements to songs without set actions. Movement can be used to describe the content of each verse, to describe characters or animals, to evoke the mood of the song or to explore the theme of the song. Young children may be very familiar with songs by the Wiggles and Hi-5 which provide excellent examples of putting movement to songs. Other songs could include:

- movement songs (e.g. 'Pizza Hut');
- finger action songs, (e.g. 'Incy Wincy Spider');
- counting songs, (e.g. 'Five Little Monkeys, There Were Ten in the Bed');
- whole body movement songs, (e.g. 'Skip to the Right', 'Hokey Pokey');
- movement to describe content, (e.g. 'How Did You Travel to School?' 'Old MacDonald');
- games and dances, (e.g. 'Looby Loo', 'The Farmer in the Dell').

4. Creating with movement

Given a theme, most teachers and children could create movement sequences to explore the theme further, for example:

- Tell a familiar story, legend or folk tale in movement.
- Create original dances to favourite pieces of music.
- Make up a dance to a familiar song.
- Create a movement sequence to a piece of music you enjoy.
- Create a movement picture which shows the content of the theme being explored, for example games we play, discovering gold, or the lifecycle of a butterfly.

- Paint a movement picture, for example a factory, the Olympics, getting up in the morning, or at the beach.

Playing instruments

Use this checklist before using instruments in the classroom.

- Have a variety of durable and attractive instruments readily available for music lessons. Have children make their own instruments from found and junk materials if the school does not have sufficient for each class or grade level.
- Make sure all instruments are easily accessible, before the lesson.
- Choose instruments that are suited to the children's physical abilities and coordination.
- Explain and demonstrate correct care and handling of each instrument as it is introduced in a lesson.
- Explain the correct technique for playing each instrument and check that children are playing the instruments correctly, but also give them the opportunity to explore different ways of playing the instruments.
- Establish a signal to which children respond by keeping their instruments quiet or 'putting them to sleep'. This might be a hand raised in the air, a whistle being blown, clapping hands and so on. Practise this with the children until they are all responding quickly.
- Distribute instruments singly, let small groups of children choose their instruments together or have monitors distribute different instruments to different groups.
- Let children experiment with their instruments to find out how many sounds they can make with them, within reason!
- Let playing an instrument be a privilege; that is, if children abuse the privilege, they are warned, and then if they continue abusing the privilege, the instrument is taken from them for a short while.
- While speaking and giving instructions, make sure all instruments and voices are kept quiet so everyone can listen to what is being said.
- When children are reading a rhythm from a score, practise each part separately with the class before playing it together as a whole.
- Give children the opportunity to improvise and perform solos, duets, in small group ensembles and as a class.

Let children experiment with making sounds on their instruments.

Instruments can be used for a variety of reasons in a music lesson

Musical instruments can be used to integrate into other areas of singing, listening, movement and making music. They can also be used to play a musical score, either a commercial one or one which the children have written. Here are some other ideas for using instruments in the classroom:

- to accompany songs, for example playing the bass line (following the guitar chords of a song to a steady beat, have different children play the corresponding notes on chime bars or xylophones to accompany the song);
- to describe content of a song, for example in 'Old MacDonald' use instruments to identify each animal as its verse is sung;
- to read a score, whether an original or commercial score, a graphic score or a standard notation score;
- to teach about musical elements, for example high and low sounds can be explored on tuned instruments; loud and soft sounds, fast and slow sounds, beat, accent and rhythm can be explored on non-tuned instruments;
- to stimulate movement;
- to aid creativity, by making up pieces of instrumental music;
- to create a focus for listening to music, for example play the triangle whenever you hear a flute playing; or play the drum when you hear loud music and play finger cymbals when you hear soft music.

Using instruments to read scores.

Making music

Creativity is the ability to put together old ideas in new combinations. The more meaningful musical experiences with which children have been provided, the better equipped they are to create satisfying creations of their own. An encouraging, positive atmosphere needs to be fostered, to ensure success in any creative activity and original thinking.

Making music can be integrated readily with each of the other music activities of singing, listening, moving and playing instruments. Making music can include:

- composing: creating new melodies;
- improvising: playing creatively with sound, sometimes as a performance;
- arranging: creating arrangements to pieces of music or songs, adding appropriate dynamics, adding extra parts, adding an introduction and ending and so on.

Other ways of making music in the classroom include:

- adding new words to a familiar tune;
- making up a new tune to a favourite poem;
- adding instruments to describe the lyrics of a song;

Experiment with a pentatonic scale to create a simple tune.

- telling a familiar story, legend, folk tale: add movement, add descriptive instruments, create a graphic score about it, and then put this all together;
- experimenting with different body percussion sounds to create an interesting piece of music, and then write it down as a graphic score;
- creating and playing ostinati rhythms to favourite songs;
- writing an original orchestration to a favourite song, by adding several rhythmic ostinati and a bass line;
- experimenting with (for example) the C pentatonic scale (notes are C, D, E, G, A) to create a simple tune, and then adding words to the tune.

Children should be encouraged to explore a variety of vocal, instrumental, environmental and body percussion sounds as they improvise and create music and be given the choice at times of working individually, in pairs or in groups to create a piece of music or movement sequence.

Activities to introduce and teach the musical elements

The following activities will provide the musically hesitant teacher with some ideas and learning experiences that will help to build the teacher's confidence and knowledge as well as providing children with practical and valuable opportunities to engage in music education. To give an introduction and overview of teaching the five elements of music, the first set of activities uses one song to introduce each element briefly.

Each element is then covered separately with both simple and more challenging activities included to suit children at all stages. However, the learning experiences are not set at specific stages as each one can be made easier or more challenging, depending on the children's prior knowledge, abilities and background experiences. If older children have not had much structured music education before, the simple activities can still be used but adapted for their interest level; for example, a more age-relevant song could be used with the same activities as suggested here.

The songs included are suggestions only, and are used because most of them appear on the included CD. Teachers should use songs with which they are confident and which are age-appropriate to the children. Note that some songs may initially seem to be for younger children, but with a positive attitude and challenging related activities they could also be used with older children to teach a specific element or skill.

Introducing the five musical elements using 'Pizza Hut'

Introduction

Ask children what is their favourite food.

Listen to the song 'The Fast Food Song' by the Fast Food Rockers (*Hits for Kids 5*) and clap the beat. Discuss what fast food outlets were mentioned in the song.

Teach the song 'Pizza Hut' line by line, with actions:
- Pizza: show a large-sized family round pizza with arms.

- Hut: make pointed hut shape with hands above head.
- Kentucky Fried Chicken: put fingers in armpits and flap elbows like a chicken.
- McDonald's: draw a large 'M' in the air.

Duration (beat/rhythm)
- Walk around in a circle while clapping the rhythm and stepping the beat.
- Split the circle and have half the children clap the rhythm and half clap the beat.
- Change from rhythm to beat or beat to rhythm when an imaginary line drawn across the circle is crossed.

Duration (tempo)
- Sing half the song fast and the other half slowly.
- Change around, singing the first half slowly and the second half fast.
- Reflect on which sounds better.

Pitch (melodic contour)
- Show the melodic contour with hands (i.e. show when the tune goes high and when it goes low).
- Prepare pitch cards which show the pitch contour/shape of each phrase of the song. Have children put the pitch cards into the correct order.

Structure (same and different phrases):
Identify the structure of the song from the ordered pitch cards (i.e. A B A B C D C D).

A Pizza Hut, a Pizza Hut	A
Kentucky Fried Chicken and a Pizza Hut	B
A Pizza Hut, a Pizza Hut	A
Kentucky Fried Chicken and a Pizza Hut	B
McDonald's, McDonald's	C
Kentucky Fried Chicken and a Pizza Hut	D
McDonald's, McDonald's	C
Kentucky Fried Chicken and a Pizza Hut	D

Dynamics (loud, soft and medium sounds)
Use flashcards of a large, a medium and a small pizza, the different fast food logos, or dynamic markings and so on to indicate loud, soft and medium sound levels of singing.

Duration (rhythm)
Introduce each ostinato (repeated rhythms which continue throughout the song) to the whole class with body percussion, and then have a small group of children perform each ostinato as the rest of the class sings the song, for example:

Ostinato 1	Food!				Food!			
Ostinato 2	Fast		Food!		Fast		Food!	
Ostinato 3	Yum	Yum!	Yum!	Yum!	Yum	Yum!	Yum!	Yum!
Sing	Piz-	za	Hut	a	Pi-	za	Hut	Ken-

Tone colour
Add instruments to play the ostinati rhythms in small groups.

Pitch/Structure
When the children can sing the song confidently, have them sing it as a round, in two parts. If they can do that confidently and in tune, try it in four parts. Avoid the children shouting, but ensure each group of children sing their part clearly and confidently.

Note: Songs that can be sung as a round usually say this at the top of the song. *Do not* try to sing other songs as rounds — most songs do not work harmonically when sung as a round!

Putting it all together
Have three small groups perform the three ostinati, with instruments and voices, with two larger groups singing the song as a round, for example:

Introduction: Ostinato 1: Food, food (4×)
Add in Ostinato 2: Fast food, Fast food (4×)
Add in Ostinato 3: Yum, yum, yum, yum (4×)
Body: Sing the song together (in unison) and then sing it as a round, accompanied by the three ostinati.
Coda: (Ending) Ostinati 1, 2 and 3: Yum, yum / Fast food / Food (4×)
Ostinati 1 and 2: Fast food / Food, food (4×)
Ostinati 1: Food (4×)

Extension
Sing the song 'Healthy Foods' to the same tune from the CD and repeat the above activities.

Create a new song to this tune, using healthy food, good breakfast foods, multicultural food and so on as the words for the new song.

In the remainder of the chapter, activities are suggested relating to each of the five elements (duration, dynamics, pitch, tone colour and structure) separately.

Duration

Beat
Have each child lead the rest of the class in non-locomotor and locomotor movements to the beat of a piece of music, for example sway, hop, jump, run, twist, hit, punch, spin or kick.

Beat and rhythm improvisation
As a known song is sung or a piece of music with a strong beat is played, pass an instrument around a circle to the beat of the music. When the music stops, or at the end of a verse, the child with the instrument plays a rhythm pattern until the music starts again.

Extension: Pass two instruments around the circle. When the music stops, each child holding an instrument plays their own original improvised rhythm in turn. Add to the number of instruments as children become confident in this activity.

Silent singing to the beat
Suggested song: 'If You're Happy'
Omit key words when singing; for example, omit 'happy' and 'clap your hands' but keep in the movements. Brainstorm different emotions and have children act out a selected emotion. Add appropriate movements and new verses to the song in response to different emotions, for example:

> If you're angry and you know it, stamp your feet!
> If you're sad and you know it, give a sigh!

Omit key words when singing, but keep in the movements.

Beanbag beat
Play a piece of music that has a strong beat. Have children pass a beanbag around the circle to the beat of the music, as the children clap the beat. As children become more competent in doing this, add two and then three beanbags to be passed around the circle to the beat. As a child is passed the beanbag, he/she touches it on the floor to the beat, and then passes it on to the next child on the next beat.
Extension: Choose a simple song with four lines or phrases in it. On the first phrase clap the beat to the song, on the second phrase tap shoulders to the beat, and then on the third and fourth phrases pass the beanbags around the circle to the beat.

Pass the beat
Add body percussion and repeated movements to the beat of a piece of popular music. Pass two beat patterns around the circle; that is, one child does a two-beat body percussion pattern (for example, click right, click left) and the rest of the class copy the child; and then the next child does a different two-beat pattern (e.g. stamp feet, tap shoulders) and the rest of the class follows. Continue around the circle.

Pokare kare ana
Have children sit cross-legged in circle. Each child has a pair of rhythm sticks. Demonstrate and then ask them to create simple rhythm and movement sequences to the song with the sticks, for example:
- Tap floor, tap sticks together, tap floor, tap sticks together.

  Experiment with sequences in pairs, for example:
- Tap floor, tap sticks together with partner, tap floor, cross arms and tap sticks together with partner.
- Tap floor, tap right sticks together with partner, tap floor, tap left sticks together with partner.

Rhythmic names
Give each student a musical instrument. Have each student say the name twice, tapping out the rhythm of the name each time with his/her instrument.

Beat and rhythm
As children sing a known song, one child plays either the beat or the rhythm. The class identifies which was played. Take this activity in turns, so all children have a turn at choosing to clap the beat or rhythm of a known song.

MMADD about the arts

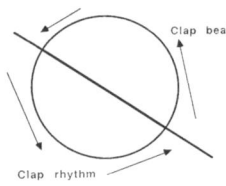

Circle to the beat, circle to the rhythm

Form a circle and draw an imaginary (or real) line through it to cut it in half. The children on one side of the line will clap the beat as they sing a favourite song and the children on the other side will clap the rhythm. Both groups of children will step the beat. Have them walk around the circle in an anticlockwise direction, either clapping the beat or the rhythm. As they cross the line, they change from clapping the beat to clapping the rhythm, or vice versa.

Beat, accent, rhythm

Suggested song: 'Waltzing Matilda'

Divide the class into three groups, each with a different set of instruments (e.g. triangles, drums and woodblocks). As the song is sung, one group plays the steady beat (triangle), one plays the accent — that is, the first strong beat in each bar (drum), and the third group plays the rhythm — that is, the fast and slow notes (woodblock).

Tempo

Suggested song: 'Pizza Hut'

Create a four-beat body percussion ostinato or movement sequence to show the beat of 'Pizza Hut' or other selected music; for example, slap thighs/clap/left click/right click for four beats. Use both locomotor and non-locomotor movements. Change the tempo and sing the song either faster or slower. Reflect on which is easier, more difficult, more effective and so on, and why.

Suggested music: 'Minoeskja', from *Off the Wall* by Gary and Carol Crees

Form a circle and indicate the changing speed of the music using bodies, scarves or ribbon sticks. Play 'Follow the Leader' with movements, changing leaders each time the fast music is heard.

Music can be fast or slow

Suggested song: 'Moving'

Listen through the whole song. Respond to each verse with pastels, crayons, felt pens or pencils on paper, showing the different types of movement heard in the song using lines, colours, shapes and so on. Listen to the song again, this time adding different body movements as each verse is sung. Sing the song through, adding different instruments for each verse.

Rhythm

Suggested song: 'Who Let the Dogs Out?' (Baha Men: *Hits for Kids 3*)

Learn to clap the rhythms 'Who Let the Dogs Out?' and 'Woof, woof, woof, woof, woof'. Divide the children into two groups, one for the 'Who Let the Dogs Out?' rhythm, and one for the 'Woof' rhythm; all clap the beat to other sections of the song.

BINGO

Suggested song: 'BINGO'

- Sing the song through and clap the rhythm.
- Use the rhythm of the words B-I-N-G-O as a repeated ostinato throughout the song.
- Select five children to play five different percussion instruments, with a different

Introduction to music education   Chapter 3

one to be played on each note of the B-I-N-G-O rhythm, and have them play as the song is sung.

Echo clapping

- Echo clap a variety of simple rhythms; for example, teacher claps the rhythm and class repeats it.
- Echo clap the rhythm of 'Who Let the Dogs Out?'
- Have the class suggest different symbols to indicate long and short beats in the rhythm pattern.

Writing rhythms

- Echo clap one rhythm several times until the class can repeat it confidently, for example:

  long – short – short – short – short – long – long – long – short – short – long.

Clapping rhythms.

- Decide on symbols to denote the short and long notes in the rhythm, for example:

- Later, when children have all had an opportunity to read and write rhythms using graphic symbols, introduce them to the idea of formal, or standard notation, by changing the symbols to musical notation, for example:

Rhythm grids

Play a rhythm grid, starting with simple symbols, and then develop the activity by introducing standard musical notation. Experiment by moving the pointer forwards, backwards, up, down and diagonally to a steady beat. As the pointer touches a square in the grid, the class claps or plays a long note, two short notes or a rest, depending on what is indicated in the square, for example:

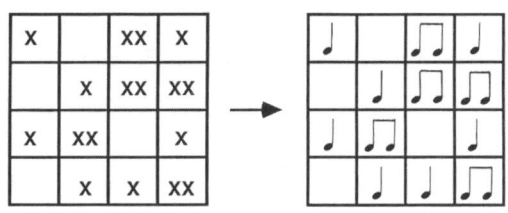

Creating and playing rhythms.

71

MMADD about the arts

Beat and rhythm wheel
Prepare a Beat Wheel (see diagram) on the blackboard or whiteboard, on a sheet of cardboard, or as an overhead transparency. Let the children know that the circled numbers are to be clapped at a steady beat (long notes) and the non-circled numbers are to be played as two short notes. Clap, make other body percussion sounds or play instruments to the rhythm indicated clockwise around the wheel to a piece of music with a strong beat.

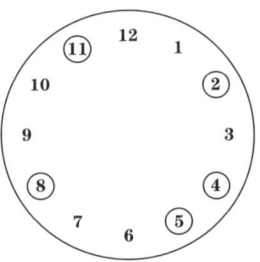

Reading rhythms
Prepare a series of flashcards, each showing a different rhythm. The teacher claps the rhythm of one card, and the children identify which card it is.

Rhythmic cards
Prepare a class set of flashcards with multiple copies of the different note values and rests covered in class, for example:

Give each of the children a card to place in front of them as they sit in a circle. Clap the rhythm shown, around the circle. Add instruments to play the rhythm. Rearrange the order of the cards and play the new rhythm. Have a child step the rhythm as the other children clap it.

Extension: Arrange the cards in groups of (for example) four beats. Place a ruler between each set of four beats to show the bar lines. Note that some cards may have to be changed or added in order to have exactly the number of beats required in each bar, for example:

Play, clap and step the rhythm, accenting the first beat in each bar. Rearrange the cards into groups of 2s, then 3s and play each new rhythm created. Use these rhythms to accompany known songs in 2/4, 3/4 or 4/4 time.

Rhythm grid
Decide on three different rhythms and label them A, B and C. Construct a rhythm grid with nine squares. Write the letters A, B or C and combinations of pairs or triplets of these letters in each of the squares. Point to one square at a time and have children play the

A	B	C
AB	BC	AC
ABC	AA	BB

Key: A = ♩ ♩ ♫
      B = ♫ ♫ ♫
      C = ♩ ♩ ♩

corresponding rhythms to a steady beat. Repeat this activity to music with a strong beat.

Body percussion rhythms
In groups, have children make up their own rhythms and play them back using body percussion. Add music with a strong beat as background to the music.

Creating rhythms
Have children make up their own rhythms with note value flashcards, for example:

Have them clap their rhythm and then play it on an instrument. Ask them to step out their rhythm and add body movements to show the rhythm. Working in pairs, put the two rhythms together. Have one child play an ostinato as a simple rhythmic accompaniment while the other child claps or plays the two rhythms, one after the other. Have them arrange the rhythms and ostinato into a structured piece of music. Use the ostinato by itself as an introduction, then add the rhythm played loudly and repeated softly, and then repeated a third time, loudly. Finish with the ostinato played several times by itself as a coda or ending.

Music moves in groups of 2s, 3s and 4s
Work out different movements to respond to music moving in 2s, 3s and 4s, for example using body percussion:
- 2/4 can be shown by clap/click.
- 3/4 can be shown by clap/click/click.
- 4/4 can be shown by tap knees/clap/click/tap shoulders.

Alternatively, use movements from everyday activities to move to the music and show the different time signatures, for example in the playground:
- 2/4 Up and down on a seesaw
- 3/4 Pushing a swing (1 beat)
  Standing back waiting for the next push (2 beats)
- 4/4 Hopscotch: Jump feet together (1 beat)
  Hop (3 beats)

Conducting time signatures
Another way to explore the different time signatures, or the way music moves in 2s, 3s, 4s, 6s and so on is to draw different shapes on paper or in the air, in time to the music, for example:

Geometric shapes
- 2/4 Straight line, up and down
- 3/4 Triangle
- 4/4 Square

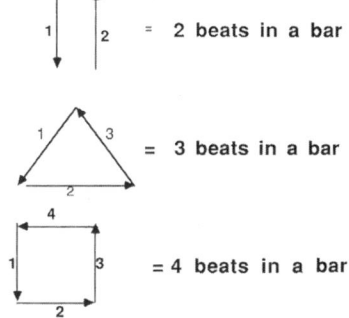

Exploring time signatures

Listen to a selection of songs and respond with appropriate movements showing the different time signatures of selected songs, for example:

- 'Click Go the Shears'   Groups of 4
- 'Waltzing Matilda'   Groups of 4
- 'Two Times' (Ann Lee)   Groups of 4
- 'Think Pink' (Beyond Pink)   Groups of 4
- 'Botany Bay'   Groups of 3
- 'One Hand, One Heart' (Dene Warwick)   Groups of 3
- 'Hero' (Chad Kroeger: *Spiderman* movie track)   Groups of 3
- 'Wild Colonial Boy'   Groups of 2
- 'Doodah' (Cartoons)   Groups of 2

Extension: In groups, using rhythm cards, write one simple rhythm in 2/4, one in 3/4 and one in 4/4, and clap the appropriate one as an ostinato to the music heard.

Environmental sounds

Go out into a selected environment (e.g. playground, roadside or library) and listen for 30 seconds. Note down all the sounds that have been heard in that 30 seconds. Categorise them into:

Long	Short
Fast	Slow
Regular	Irregular sounds

Try to reproduce these sounds using environmental instruments (sticks, stones, leaves and so on), body percussion or conventional instruments. Create a graphic score to represent the environment and the sounds heard. Play it using different types of instruments.

Rhythm dramas

Have children use instruments and rhythms to describe a rhythm drama, devised by the teacher or suggested by the children. Add movement to depict the scene visually. Each scene should involve a contrast of long and short sounds; that is, have two characters, one that can be recognised by long sounds and one that can be recognised by short sounds. Put in several silences in appropriate places.

Some examples of rhythm dramas could include:

- Describe a stormy sea followed by a calm sea.
- Describe an old man swimming slowly, while a young board rider surfs quickly past him.
- Describe a lady sunbaking, while her children splash and play in the water.
- Describe a small fish swimming through the water, when suddenly it is attacked by a shark.

Tempo dramas

Encourage children to make up a story about two characters, one fast and one slow. As the children retell their story, have them represent the slow character with an instrument played slowly, and the fast character with an instrument played quickly.

Suggestions for stories:
- the hare and the tortoise;
- a steam train and an electric train going up a hill and coming down the other side;
- a mouse and an elephant;
- an aeroplane and a hot-air balloon;
- a whale and a little fish;
- running late for school on a weekday and getting up slowly on a Sunday.

Extension: Choose one of the stories and make up a class graphic score about it, showing the two characters (fast and slow) and other relevant events or sound effects. Divide the children into groups and have each group make up their own graphics score for their own story.

Dynamics

Ribbon sticks or scarves
Using ribbon sticks or scarves, have students say their names loudly or softly while they make large or small movements to match the dynamic level.

Using a puppet to show dynamic levels
Suggested song: 'Pizza Hut'
Sing the song loudly when the puppet faces the class, and softly when the puppet hides its face. Let students work the puppet to create loud and soft singing by the class.

Using scarves or ribbon sticks to show dynamic levels
Suggested music: Excerpt from *Carmina Burana* by Carl Orff (Track: 'Fortuna plango vulnera': Spring)
Work out big and small movements to make in response to the soft, medium and loud sounds. Use scarves or ribbon sticks if children are initially inhibited about using their bodies.

Using the radio/CD player to show dynamic levels
Switch on a CD or the radio. Use the volume control to alter the dynamic levels of the music. Have children show the dynamic changes with their bodies. For example, for loud music children walk tall with arms above their heads and stamp the ground; and for soft music children crouch low, fold their arms to their chests and tiptoe.

Using flashcards to show dynamic levels
Suggested song: 'John Brown's Holden'
Have a leader indicate when to sing loudly or softly by holding up large, medium and small flashcards of a car to indicate loud, medium and soft dynamic levels.

Using arm movements to show dynamics
Suggested song: 'If You're Happy and You Know It'
Have a leader indicate that the class is to use a different dynamic level for each line, by holding arms wide apart (loud singing), closer together (medium singing) or very

close together (soft singing). Accompany singing with varied body percussion to accentuate the different dynamic levels.

Using Italian musical terms to show dynamics
Suggested song: 'Rock My Soul'
Prepare a set of dynamic symbol flashcards. Discuss meanings of the Italian words: *pianissimo, piano, mezzo piano, mezzo forte, forte, fortissimo, crescendo* and *diminuendo* as written on flashcards. Add movements to show the difference in meaning. (See 'Italian terms' on page 53 for the definitions of these dynamic levels.)

Sing 'Rock My Soul' and point to flashcards indicating the different dynamic levels throughout the song. Have a child indicate the different dynamic levels when singing the song through again.

Guess the dynamics
Select three of the dynamic flashcards. Choose two children to sit back to back, each with some instruments in front of them. Child 1 arranges the cards in a chosen order and plays an instrument to show the order chosen. Child 2 guesses the order and plays it back to the first child. The class say whether it was correct or not. Develop the activity by adding to the number of flashcards used to create a sequence of dynamic levels.

Crescendo and *diminuendo*
Suggested song: 'Trains'
Learn to sing the song, noting that the melody is built on the C major scale. Say the beginning and ending sections, and sing the middle section. Identify the dynamic markings in the music and start singing the song softly and ending loudly (without shouting!).

Passing parade
Sing a known song, adding instruments to play the beat and an ostinato. Imitate a passing parade which is singing and playing the chosen song, by starting softly as the parade is in the distance, becoming louder and louder as it comes closer, and then becoming softer as it goes off into the distance.

'Bydlo' by Moussorgsky
Listen to the piece of music 'Bydlo' from Moussorgsky's *Pictures at an Exhibition* (from *ABC Classic Kids*). Discuss the dynamic changes heard and what the children imagined was being described, for example a passing procession. Have the children, either in groups or as a whole class, create a piece of music to describe a similar event. Draw and play a graphic score about it.

Add dynamics to popular recorded music
Select a recorded piece of music; listen with the children to identify which sections are loud, soft or medium; and add different dynamic markings to the different sections. Accompany the music with percussion instruments or body percussion, according to the different dynamic markings. Suggested songs with clear dynamic differences: 'It's All Coming Back to Me', Celine Dion or 'Nothing's Changing My Life' by the Hoodoo Gurus (Mach Schau)

Using instruments to show dynamics

Allow all children to select an instrument and experiment with it, playing it loudly and softly. These could be chopsticks, pencils on the desk, or conventional non-tuned instruments, depending on the classroom resources. In a circle, each student tells the name of their instrument and demonstrates how it can be played loudly and softly.

Classroom dynamics

Have each child select a sound source from within the classroom, for example a ruler, pen, chair or fingers. Have them try to find three different dynamic levels of sound (i.e. loud, medium and soft) from their chosen sound source/instrument. Share these with the rest of the class.

Extension: Each child chooses one of their sounds and makes up a rhythm with it. To help them remember their rhythm, suggest to the children that they use words, for example:
- Mary Brown eats noodles and rice, or
- Pawpaw, pears, passionfruit and apples.

Play this rhythm at three different dynamic levels, using their selected sound instrument, to the rest of the class.

Make up a class piece of music, by tapping a steady beat and playing the rhythms around the circle. Each child plays his/her rhythm once at one selected dynamic level and then the next child plays his/her rhythm immediately after at a different dynamic level, and so on around the circle.

Which dynamics?

Choose a known song to sing. Divide the class in half. Each half decides on a way of singing the song showing different dynamic variations in each line, section or phrase. As one half of the class sings their dynamic arrangement of the song, the other half identifies the order of the dynamic changes. Repeat with the other half of the class presenting their dynamic arrangement of the song.

Hide and seek

One student leaves the room while a puppet or other object is hidden. The student returns and has to find the puppet or object guided by the loudness or softness of the playing of the instruments by other students.

Parking the car

Blindfold a child who pretends he/she is driving a car and looking for a parking space in a busy shopping centre car park. The other children decide on a parking spot, and have to lead the driver in the car to it, by playing their instruments softly when the car is far away from the parking spot and loudly when the car is approaching it.

Can you play this loudly?

Have children invent ways of indicating when the class is to make loud sounds and when they are to make soft sounds. Let different children experiment with conducting the class with these movements, for example raise arms for loud sounds, and

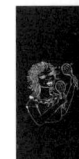

MMADD about the arts

lower arms for soft sounds. The class can play instruments, make sounds with voices or experiment with found objects to make loud and soft sounds.

Extension: Have two conductors, one for each half of the class. Have them both conduct their half of the class at the same time. Experiment with the different effects of (for example) loud against soft, both loud, both soft, one half silent and so on.

Dynamic grid

Divide the class into four groups, each group having a different set of instruments, for example triangles, drums, maracas and rhythm sticks. Have each group experiment with making loud, medium and soft sounds (for younger children, start only with loud and soft sounds). Create a dynamics grid which indicates when to play what instruments and how loudly each instrument is to be played, for example:

pp	*mf*	*ff*
T	**T**	**T**
D	**D**	**D**
RS	**RS**	**RS**
M	**M**	**M**

Key:
T = Triangle
D = Drum
RS = Rhythm sticks
M = Maracas

Dynamic graphic scores

With the class, create a simple graphic score. Select (for example) five instruments for the score and create a simple icon to represent each instrument. List these in the key or legend of the score. Draw the icons across the page, having the instruments played together at times and at other times played by themselves. Add dynamic markings to create interest and contrast to the graphic score. Play the score by moving a pointer from left to right across the score. When the pointer touches an icon, that instrument is played, and when it is past the icon, playing on that instrument stops. Use the selected instruments with the appropriate dynamic levels, for example:

Vocal dynamics

Using vocal sounds (e.g. *ooo*, *eee*, *zzz*, *ahhh*, *brrrrm*) develop a soundscape using varied dynamic levels. Divide the children into five groups, each having a different sound and a different dynamic level. Practise the parts individually and then put them together, for example:

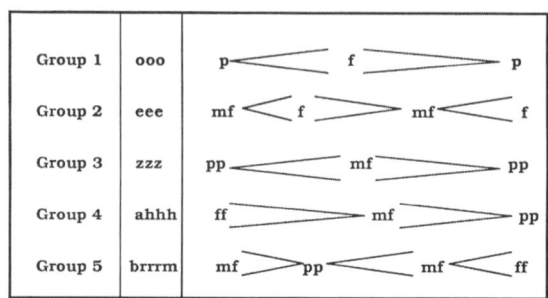

Thematic scores

Create a graphic score about the literacy, science or social science theme the class is currently studying. Use symbols to create the score and have different instruments represent each symbol. Draw some symbols large and some small to indicate how loudly or softly the instruments should be played at that particular time.

Big books/Graphic scores

Suggested text: *The Farm Concert*

Read through *The Farm Concert* saying the first section loudly and the second section softly. Add appropriate instruments to represent the different characters, playing the instruments loudly in the first section and softly in the second section. Create a graphic score that tells the story in big and small pictures instead of words.

Graphic Score: *The Farm Concert*.

Suggested text: *The Three Billy Goats Gruff*

Read through the story and decide on instruments to represent each of the goats, the troll, the bridge, the 'trip trap' across the bridge and the green grass on the other side. Discuss how the concept of dynamics could be used with this story (loud sounds for Big Billy Goat, medium sounds for Middle Billy Goat and soft sounds for Little Billy Goat and so on). Read through the story again and have children play their instruments loudly, medium or softly at the appropriate times throughout the story. Create and play a graphic score based on *The Three Billy Goats Gruff* so that the story is told only by instruments, with no words.

MMADD about the arts

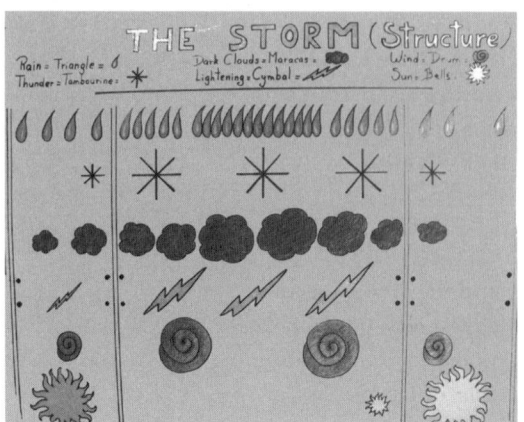

Create a storm with body percussion

Discuss what sounds are heard and sights seen in a storm, for example rain pitter-pattering down, rain pouring down, wind whistling, thunder roaring, lightning flashing and trees swaying. Decide on different body percussion to represent each of these sights and sounds. Build the storm by starting with the rain pitter-pattering down; add the rain pouring down, the wind whistling and the trees swaying; and then add the thunder roaring and the lightning flashing as the climax to the storm. Gradually soften and take away each of the sights and sounds in reverse order so the last sound heard is the soft pitter-patter of raindrops.

Create a graphic score depicting the story that has been created using body percussion. Use the score to repeat the sound of the storm, either with body percussion, or classroom instruments to create the sounds instead. Reflect on how effective was the creation of the sights and sounds of the storm.

Create a story to show dynamics

In groups or as a whole class, have children decide on three characters that could be represented by instruments played loudly, medium and softly. Work out a beginning, middle, climax and ending and tell the story using words and instruments. Create a graphic score that tells the story visually. Play it using only instruments and no words.

Pitch

High and low names

Give each of the children a scarf and have them say their name one by one at either a high or low pitch making movements with their scarves to show the same relative pitch.

How high is that?

Sing a known song in a high key, then in a low key and then in the normal key. Discuss which is easier or better to sing and why. Sing it again at the pitch that sounds the best.

Follow the conductor

Have children explore how many high and low sounds they can make with their voices. Encourage them to 'follow' the sounds with arm movements to show the relative pitch of the sounds.

Extension: Choose one child as a conductor. Every time the child raises an arm the class makes high sounds; every time the arm is lowered the class makes low sounds. Experiment to make a sequence of varied pitches that can be repeated. Work in two groups, one following the conductor's right arm and the other following the conductor's left arm.

Introduction to music education — Chapter 3

Movement to accompany changing pitch

Show flashcards, pictures or fluffy toys of several animals and birds (e.g. wombat, snake, kookaburra and kangaroo). Ask the children to make high sounds and high movements for the kookaburra card, medium sounds and movements for the kangaroo card, and low sounds and low movements for the wombat and snake card.

Suggested song: 'Australian Animals'

Add a simple xylophone accompaniment to the beat to match the changing pitch of each line to represent animals, for example:

- Wombat: Middle C down to low G, repeat
- Snake: Middle C up to E, repeat
- Kookaburra: G up to top C, repeat
- Kangaroo: E down to Middle C, repeat

Add movement to represent each of the animals and their respective pitch.

Extension: Create harmony by singing the song as a round in four parts.

Limbo

The teacher or a selected student improvises on a tuned percussion instrument. Try using the C pentatonic scale (C, D, E, G, A), so that any notes played after each other, or together, are not discordant. Two children hold a broom; children step under the broomstick when low sounds are played and over it when high sounds are played on a xylophone.

Chime bars back to back

Select two children to sit back to back, each with three chime bars, handbells or three notes of a xylophone. Have Child A play a series of notes on the chime bars, and then Child B repeats the series on his/her instrument. The class shows pitch with arm movements and sings the notes that have been played, for example high — low — medium.

Extension: Seat two children back to back, each with a similar xylophone. Child A plays a pattern that illustrates one of the following:

- going up;
- going down;
- on the same note.

Child B identifies the pattern and then imitates the sound on the xylophone.

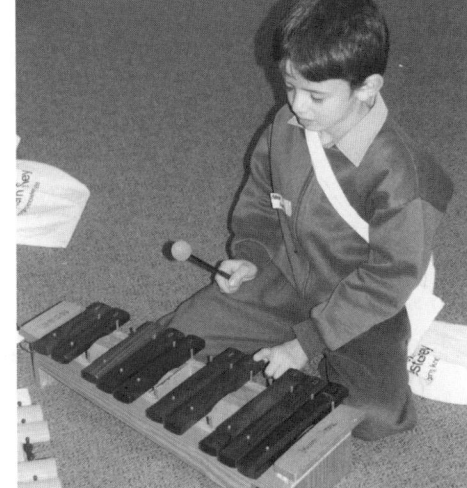

Adding a simple xylophone accompaniment to a song.

Sing the pitch

Form a circle and pass three different chime bars around the circle to the beat of a drum or to a piece of music with a strong beat. When the drum or music stops, three children are left holding the chime bars. Each of the children hits their chime bar and sings the note that they have just played. The rest of the class identify which note is the highest, which is the lowest and which is the medium-sounding chime bar. Mix up the chime bars and repeat the activity.

81

My name is . . .

Pass three or four chime bars around the circle to a given beat or a piece of music, or as a song is sung. When the beat or music stops, the children holding the chime bars play their note, and then sing a sentence on that note, such as, 'My name is Julia', or 'I am feeling happy', or 'Today is Wednesday'. The teacher can vary the order in which the chime bars are played around the circle.

Chime bars in order

Eight students are each given one of the eight chime bars or handbells from the C major scale (C, D, E, F, G, A, B, C) and stand at the front of the class. The rest of the children identify the lowest and the highest notes, and then order the chime bars from low to high in sound just by listening to their sound. (For younger children, start with only two notes and have them identify which is higher and which is lower. Then add another note and so on until the full eight notes are used.)

When the eight-note scale has been ordered, have the children who are holding the chime bars or handbells visually show the pitch of their note — that is, by the first child kneeling low down to the ground and the last child standing on a chair or table (check this is safe and stable first!) and the other six children showing ascending heights with their bodies.

Extension: Have a conductor point to the children with the chime bars or handbells one at a time, in a varied order, to create a new melody.

Suggested song: 'Pigs' or 'Lamb Stew'

Have the chime bar students play the melody, which is based on the C major scale. Have children use small flashcards of pigs or lambs, or use scarves to show the relative pitch of the song with their bodies.

Trains

Suggested song: 'Trains'

Learn to sing the song 'Trains', noting that the melody is built on the C major scale. Use chime bars, handbells or xylophones to play the melody line. Speak the beginning and ending sections to the set rhythm, and then sing the song, showing the rising pitch with arm movements. Start singing the song softly and end loudly, as indicated by the dynamics.

Bass lines

The bass note of a guitar chord is the note indicated by the name of the chord written in capital letters above the music. To play the bass line of a song, follow the guitar chords written above the music. Using a xylophone or other tuned instrument, play the letter names of the guitar chords to the beat and change them when the letter names change.

Suggested song: 'Kookaburra'

The two guitar chords used are D and G. The notes of the D chord are D, F#, A and the notes of the G chord are G, B, D. The bass notes are the first note in each chord, for example, D and G respectively.

To play the bass line to the song, start on the note D and play it to the beat until the word 'sits' when it changes to G. The bass note changes back to D on the word 'old'. The bass line for 'Kookaburra' would look like this:

D, D, G, G, D, D, D, D
D, D, G, G, D, D, D, D
D, D, G, G, D, D, D, D
D, D, G, G, D, D, D, D

Harmony
Suggested song: 'My Paddle's Keen and Bright'
Add a simple accompaniment to the song by playing the chord to the beat on tuned percussion or keyboard. The guitar chord in this song is D minor and this chord does not change throughout the song. Play the notes of the D minor chord (D, F, A) together to the beat throughout the song. Add a melodic ostinato throughout the song by using the notes of the last line ('Dip, dip and swing') played on a tuned instrument, for example DD – C – D.

Use the ostinato and accompaniment as an introduction and ending to the song. When children can do this confidently, sing the song as a round.

Life cycles
Suggested song: 'Just a little seed'
Sing a song which describes a plant's life cycle, for example a plant growing from a seed to a tall flower — 'Just a Little Seed'.

Add class movements to show the growth of the plant as the song is sung. Have three children hold three flashcards of parts of the plant, for example petals (high), stem (medium) and roots (low). Point to them in random order and have the rest of the children move in response to them, making high, medium or low sounds with their voices.

Suggested song: 'Caterpillar'
Similar activities can be done with this song while it is sung, showing a caterpillar changing into a butterfly.

Whose phone is that?
Have children experiment with tuned percussion instruments to play the tunes used on mobile phones, computers and video games. Have the children try to match the pitch of the first notes of their mobile phone tune, a TV advertisement or their door bell at home, with a tuned instrument. Experiment to find other things at home and school that make a definite pitched sound.

Playing cards
Prepare a series of graphic notation pitch flashcards, for example:

Have individual children or small groups interpret each card using tuned percussion instruments or voices. Have a child select one card that he/she doesn't show to anyone else and then play the card. The rest of the class identifies which card was 'played'. Arrange the cards in an order and have the whole class 'play' them through. Rearrange the cards for a different piece.

MMADD about the arts

Extension: Have children draw their own pitch flashcards and interpret them on tuned percussion instruments or using their voices. In pairs, one child plays from a selected pitch flashcard, and the other child, without seeing the flashcard, either repeats what has been played, or draws the pitches heard symbolically on a piece of paper.

Playing more cards

Prepare a set of pitch flashcards, for example:

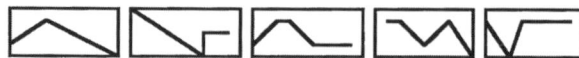

Divide the class into five groups, giving each group a flashcard. Have half of each group describe their card symbol with movement, while the other half describes it with tuned percussion or voices. The teacher conducts the five groups to compose a piece of music; that is, the teacher points to groups in a random or predetermined order, using contrasts and repetition to build up a musical composition.

Extension: Add dynamic variations to repetition of played flashcards. Add short periods of silence.

Suggestion: Use lengths of wool or string instead of flashcards and have each group create their own melodic picture showing when they will sing high and when they will sing low and so on. Each group then performs it, with appropriate movements to the rest of the class.

Back-to-back flashcards

Seat two children back to back, each having an identical set of pitch flashcards. Child A plays or sings his series of flashcards in a particular order. Child B has to put her flashcards in the order she has just heard, and then sing or play them. Child A says if this is accurate; if not, child A repeats playing or singing his series of flashcards until Child B can repeat it accurately.

Extension: Start with two flashcards, and then gradually add more as children increase their confidence with the activity. Have the rest of the class sing and show with their hands the pitch of what Child A has played or sung.

Pitch contours

Suggested song: 'L.O.V.E' (Hi-5)

Show the rise and fall of the song (this mainly happens in 'L-O-V-E') with scarves in the air. For the verse, show the relative pitch with scarves. Later, children will be able to show the actual pitch contours of the whole song with scarves or whole body movements.

Show the pitch to recorded music

Using suitable recorded music, have children show the high or low pitch of the music using their hands, scarves or ribbon sticks, or drawing on paper with felt pens or pastels.

Suggested song: 'My Paddle's Keen and Bright'

Show the pitch contour or each phrase with hands in the air. Have children identify which is the highest note in the song, which is the lowest note and which notes are the same pitch. Show contour cards for each phrase of the above song and have the class order them.

Extension: Listen to a favourite song on a CD and try to record the pitch contour of the chorus, and then of each verse and other sections of the song.

Play the bottles

Have children fill several glass bottles with different quantities of water. One at a time, tap them (gently) in turn with a spoon or beater, to obtain a different pitched sound from each of them. Have the children order the bottles from high sounds to low sounds. Discuss with the children how the amount of water in the bottle relates to the pitch of the sound produced.

Extension: Select a chime bar or note on a recorder, piano or xylophone and have the children fill one of the bottles with water until it produces a note similar in pitch to that of the chime bar. Repeat until a pentatonic scale of C (C, D, E, G, A) has been created using the bottles. Create a piece of music using the bottles as a tuned instrument. This activity might work best in small groups after the teacher has demonstrated what is required of the children.

Telephone call

Have ten children stand in a circle. Give each child a number, in order, from zero to nine. Give out ten sequenced chime bars, or notes on a xylophone or recorder (e.g. C, D, E, F, G, A, B, C, D, E) so that each child has a different note. Choose one child's telephone number, (e.g. 9758 3841) and as each part of the number is called out, the child in the circle with the appropriate number plays his/her note.

Extensions
- Children can sing the melody created by the telephone number after hearing it played.
- Play four telephone numbers, one after the other, to create a four-phrase melody.
- Using (for example) three telephone numbers, sequence them with some repeats, to make up a longer, unified piece of music.
- Add an introduction and an ending to create a finished composition.

Pitch in literature

Use stories that involve big, medium and small characters, for example *Three Little Pigs*, *Goldilocks and the Three Bears* and *The Three Billy Goats Gruff*, and play a note each on a low, medium and high tuned instrument to represent the different characters. Decide which pitched note can be played for which character, for example in *Goldilocks and the Three Bears*, baby bear could be represented by a high note, mother bear by a medium note, father bear

by a low note and Goldilocks by bells. Each time the character appears in the story, play its respective note or instrument. Add sound effects with non-tuned percussion instruments to make the story more interesting; that is, use rhythm sticks for the chairs and tambourines for the porridge and so on.

Extension: Improvise a pentatonic melody (e.g. uses the note C, D, E, G, A in the C pentatonic scale, or use the notes G, A, B, D, E for the G pentatonic scale) for each of the bears, using a high melody for baby bear, a medium melody for mother bear and a low melody for father bear. Play these short melodies whenever the bears are heard in the story. Create a graphic score based on the story showing the pitch levels clearly.

Creating melodies to poems

Find some simple poems or have children make them up. Say a poem through several times to find the beat and rhythm of the poem. Experiment using three to five notes (e.g. C, D and E; or use the pentatonic scale (see below) with the notes C, D, E, G, A) to create a simple melody to the poem. Start and finish on C, and use any note *except* C on the last note of the second line. Write the pitches above the words. Practise singing and playing the song, for example:

Create a melody to a poem.

See the leaves are blowing round
In the sky and on the ground.
Windy days are here to stay,
Let us all go out and play!

OR

Kick the football in the sky
See it flying through the sky,
Score a goal, the team has won,
Now it's time to say goodbye!

OR

All around the flowers he goes,
Busy little bee.
Buzzing here and buzzing there,
Please don't buzz near me!

Pitch grids

Use a 5 × 5 grid to create melodic patterns. Write the names of the notes from a pentatonic scale down the left side of the grid (e.g. a G pentatonic scale uses the notes G, A, B, D, E). Start by using symbols for note values and then develop this by using standard notation, for example:

Play the score across from left to right, from right to left, line by line, all five lines together, randomly and so on to create different sequences of sounds.

G	X		XX	X
A		X	X	
B	XX	XX		X
D	X	X		XX
E	XX		XX	

G	♩	𝄽	♫	♩
A	𝄽	♩	♩	𝄽
B	♫	♫	𝄽	♩
D	♩	♩	𝄽	♫
E	♫	𝄽	♫	𝄽

Pentatonic music

Using the C pentatonic scale (i.e. use the notes C, D, E, G, A on a tuned percussion instrument), have children create a simple pentatonic melody of eight bars (4 beats in each bar) using the following steps:

1. **The pentatonic scale is made up of 5 notes, the first, second, third, fifth and sixth notes in the scale.** For example:
   (a) In the scale of C major, the pentatonic scale is C, D, E, G, A.
   (b) In the scale of G major, the pentatonic scale is G, A, B, D, E.
   (c) In the scale of F major, the pentatonic scale is F, G, A, C, D.
2. **Select a pentatonic scale with which to work.** Take out the notes you don't need from a tuned percussion instrument.
3. **Make up a simple eight bar rhythm.** Practise clapping it until you are sure of the rhythm.
4. **Write down notes from the pentatonic scale underneath the rhythm notes and experiment with how they sound by playing them on the tuned instrument.** As a suggestion:
   (a) Start and end on the first note of the scale; that is, start and end on C in the C major pentatonic scale.
   (b) Finish the fourth bar with any note except the first note of the scale.
   (c) Use lots of repeated notes to make the melody easier to play!
5. **Write this melody and rhythm on music manuscript paper.**
6. **Work out a melodic ostinato.** For example, use a simple two-note melody which is repeated throughout the song, choosing notes from the selected pentatonic scale (e.g. 'E' and 'A' in the C pentatonic scale).
7. **Use these as two beat notes (minims) to accompany the melody.** Write them on the second staff (set of five lines), underneath the melody.

Rhythm Score Title_____

Introduction:

Pentatonic Melody

1
2   4
3
4   4
5

Ending:_____

Key to instruments: 1 =
                     2 =
                     3 =
                     4 =
                     5 =

Structure:

MMADD about the arts

Tone colour

Different sound sources
Each student selects an instrument and demonstrates different ways of making sounds with it. Using hoops placed on the floor, categorise instruments into what they are made from (wood, skin, plastic, metal and so on). Take back the instruments and categorise them into the hoops to indicate how they are played (scraped, hit, shaken and so on). Take back the instruments again, but have children remember from which hoop they took their instrument. Have one child step from hoop to hoop. As the child steps (for example) in the 'hitting' hoop all children with instruments that produce a sound by being hit play their instrument. Continue from hoop to hoop to create an improvised piece of music.

Tone colour wheel
Use a Beat Wheel to indicate when to play instruments that are scraped, hit or shaken to make a sound. Number the Beat Wheel from one to 12. Then circle the numbers that are to be played by scraped instruments, draw a square around those numbers that are to be played by hit instruments and leave blank the ones that are to be played by shaken instruments, for example:

Point to each number in turn, to a steady beat, and have children play the appropriate instruments when the different numbers are pointed to.

Metal	xxx	xxxxxxxx	xxxx		x
Wood	v vvv	vvvv	vv		vvvvvvvvv
Plastic	ooo	oo o o	o	oo	
Skin	| |	||||||||| |||||	||| ||	|||||	|

What is it made from?
Divide the class into groups. Have each group select a variety of instruments and experiment with their sounds. Categorise the instruments into groups (e.g. what they are made from). Create and perform a graphic score using one of the selected categories.

Match the sound
Have children bring in various containers (matchboxes, film capsules, plastic bottles and so on) and a variety of seeds (lentils, rice and so on). Have them make a variety of instruments using these materials. Make sure the lids are secured firmly! Play each instrument and match them according to the sound made. Discover how size, shape, material and the way the sound is produced affect the actual sound of the instrument.

Move to the sound
Encourage the children, in pairs, to explore the different sounds one instrument can make. Ask them to create movements in response to these different sounds with one child playing the instrument and the other child moving to the sound. Develop a

sound-and-movement sequence and write this up as a graphic score. Share both the movement sequence and graphic score with the rest of the class.

Metal soundscape
Divide the class into three groups. Have one group choose only wooden instruments. Another group is to choose only metal instruments. The third group chooses only plastic instruments. Note that some instruments have both wood, metal and/or plastic on them; the children will have to decide whether the sound is made mainly from the wood, metal or plastic parts.

Each group should then make up their own piece of music which describes an event, a person, a story or a landscape. Have them share these pieces with each other and discuss the different categories of instruments used, and how these affected the sounds produced.

Extension: Repeat the activity, but this time divide instruments into how they are played (scraped, hit, shaken and so on).

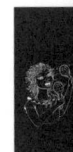

Different instruments make different sounds
Listen to 'Treaty' by Yothu Yindi or another piece of music with a variety of instruments. Identify different instruments and then categorise them into what they are made of and how they are played.

Extension: Select a piece of music that has only a few instruments playing. Have children listen to the piece and identify which instruments are playing. Choose different percussion instruments to represent the instruments heard on the recording. Play these instruments as their counterparts are played on the recording.

Name the voice
Children sit in a circle around a blindfolded child. A ball is passed around the circle to the beat as a known song is sung. On the teacher's signal the ball stops, and the person holding the ball sings the next line of the song alone. The centre child identifies the singer. If the child is correct, the singer changes places with the centre child; if incorrect, the centre child has another turn.

Animal sounds
Select the names of six animals. Have the class stand in a large circle. Whisper to each child the name of one of the animals. On the word 'go', the children close their eyes, make the sound of their own particular animal and, by listening, try to find others making the same sound. When like animals find each other, they sit down together, continuing to make their sound until every person is in a group.

Extension: Give the children pictures or names of animals, birds and so forth on cards and do the same activity. This is a fun way of having children form groups or teams for another game or activity as well as developing their listening skills.

Noah's Ark
Suggested song: 'Noah's Ark'
While singing this song, add instruments to represent Noah and the animals in each verse, that is:
- Verse 1:   Noah

MMADD about the arts

Using instruments to represent animals in a song.

- Verse 2: Elephants
- Verse 3: Rhinoceros and kangaroo
- Verse 4: Bear, bug and bumble bee
- Verse 5: Hippopotamus
- Verse 6: Noah
- Verse 7: Monkeys
- Verse 8: Ant and elephant
- Verse 9: Noah
- Verse 10: All animals and Noah

Extension: Add the instruments cumulatively to match the number mentioned in the verse. Other instruments can play to the beat through the chorus.

Body sounds or instrument grid

Draw a grid on the blackboard or whiteboard, or on a piece of cardboard, with four body or instrument sounds along the top, and four voice sounds down the side, for example:

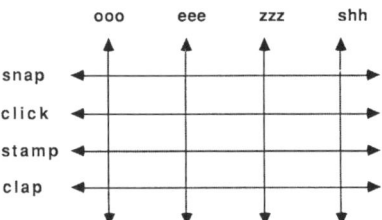

Divide the class into eight groups, each group taking a different sound and its corresponding line on the grid. Move a pointer slowly across the grid in random directions. Each time a line is crossed, the group makes its noise as indicated. Vary the speed and the direction of the pointer.

Tone colour rhymes

Select or create a speech rhyme or song. Accompany it in different ways, for example with:
- one instrument;
- two instruments;
- no instruments;
- vocal sounds.

Use flashcards to assist with this activity (i.e. each card has one way of accompanying the song written on it). Split the class into two (and later four) groups. Each group selects several ways of accompanying the rhyme or song, with a different accompaniment on each line. Each group presents its version of the rhyme or song and other groups identify which accompaniments were used on which lines.

Using instruments in a tone colour grid.

Giving directions
Divide the class into two teams; each team has one member blindfolded. One team directs its member to catch the other team's member, using only instruments to communicate directions, for example:

Team One	**Direction**	**Team Two**
Tambourine	Backwards	Cymbal
Triangle	Forwards	Slide whistle
Guiro	Turn right	Maracas
Woodblock	Turn left	Castanets

Back-to-back teams
Have children form two teams, lining up back to back down the room. Give each team an identical set of instruments, one to each child. The teacher points to one of the children on the first team, and that child plays his/her instrument. The child from the second team who has the same instrument plays it. If they are correct, a child from the second team plays his/her instrument and the child from the first team responds by playing the same instrument.
Extension 1: Have two children from the same team play their instruments together, and then the two children on the other team have to play their corresponding instruments together.
Extension 2: Increase the number of instruments that are to play together, as children become more confident with this activity.
Extension 3: Have all the children but one on the team play their instruments. The children on the other team have to guess which instrument was not playing. They then all play their instruments, except for the child with that instrument.
Extension 4: Repeat Extension 3, but omit two instruments instead of one.

Tone colour walk
Take the class for a walk around the schoolyard. Have them touch as many differently textured surfaces as possible, and note down how they feel. Do texture rubbings of the different surfaces. Back in the classroom, discuss the different textures of each of the objects touched. Experiment with a variety of instruments to see if the felt textures can be shown aurally with instrument sounds. Discuss the results and share the different sounds and related textures the children have discovered.

Instruments to represent characters and events
Add appropriate instruments and movement to represent different characters in each song.
Suggested song: 'Our Family'
Motivation: In groups make up movements and instrument sounds to represent family members. Make up a simple sentence about what grandfather, grandmother, father, mother and children could be doing (grandfather is walking to the shop; mother is CEO of the bank and so on).

Listen to the song and keep the beat by clapping softly. Learn the song phrase by phrase. Add in the made up-lines to create new verses, for example:

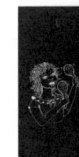

MMADD about the arts

Let's move like grandfather moves, walking to the shop,
Let's move like grandfather moves, walking like this.

Let's move like mother moves, working hard, at the bank,
Let's move like mother moves, working like this.

In five groups, add appropriate instruments and movements to represent the different verses.

Suggested song: 'When You Grow Up'
Show pictures or flashcards presenting different occupations. Ask children to identify the different occupations. Listen to the song, and add body percussion to the beat while learning it. Create appropriate movements to the third line of each verse. In six groups, each group takes a verse and adds appropriate instruments for each verse.

Extension: Make up other verses with instruments and movement to show other occupations.

Adding instruments to books

Add appropriate instruments and movements to represent different characters in a simple children's book; explain why each instrument was chosen to represent the characters or events, for example:

Text: *I thought I heard* ... by Alan Baker, 1996, Alan Books, or similar text with different sounds in the story.

Read through the story. Identify what sounds were heard in the story. Give out instruments to represent each of the sounds. Add these instruments in when reading the story. Have the children use their instrument to very carefully depict the actual sound; bring in dynamics, pitch, duration and so on if appropriate.

Instrumental pictures

Select a variety of paintings or art prints that show different styles, media, subjects, emotions and so on. Divide the class into several groups and have each group select one picture and describe it with percussion instruments, or create a musical picture using the artwork as a stimulus. Have each group share its musical pictures with the rest of the class. The other groups guess which picture is being described. Discuss the musical pictures created in relation to how well they described the artworks, and how the sounds created related to the mood, style, media, and so on of each picture.

Listening to music

Select a short piece of descriptive music. (If you are not sure where to start, listen to an excerpt from the *Carnival of the Animals* by Saint-Saëns or *Pictures at an Exhibition* by Moussorgsky, on the ABC CDs: *The Classic Kids Album* and *ABC Classic Kids*.) As the children listen to it, have them draw their impressions of it in an abstract way. Emphasise that they are listening for the different sounds of the instruments, the mood of the piece, and the high and low, loud and soft, sharp and smooth sounds and so on. Different colours, lines or shapes could be used to identify the above sounds. Discuss the different drawings, leading children into thinking about how music can be portrayed in a visual way.

Divide the children into groups. Each group chooses one of its member's drawings and uses it as a graphic score, interpreting each line, colour, shape and so on with a different instrument. Share these creative pieces with the rest of the class.
Extension: Have each group use all its members' drawings and order them in such a way as to make a complete piece of music.

Sounds may be sung or spoken
Suggested song: 'Going on a Bear Hunt' (page 34, *'Bananas in Pyjamas Songbook'*, ABC). Listen to the whole song, and then learn to sing it. Note the parts that are *sung*, that is:

> We're going on a bear hunt, we're going on a bear hunt,
> We're going to catch a big one, we're going to catch a big one,

and

> We can't go over it, we can't go over it,
> We can't go under it, we can't go under it,

and the remaining parts which are *spoken*.

Ensure the difference is heard when singing through the song. Add different instruments to represent the different part of the story (i.e. the mud, the grass and so on).

Speak and sing in a circle
Have the class stand in a circle. Draw a real or imaginary line through the centre of the circle. Children on the left-hand side of the circle walk around the circle to the beat, singing a known song. When they cross the line they speak the words of the song to the rhythm. When they cross the other end of the line, they return to singing the song. Children on the right-hand side of the circle do the opposite; that is, they start singing the song, cross the line and speak the song, and then sing the song when they cross the line again.

Spoken ostinato to a song
Suggested song: 'She'll Be Coming Round the Mountain'
Have a small group add a spoken ostinato to the song; that is, select a short phrase (e.g. *Round the mountain*) and speak it rhythmically while the song is being sung. Divide the class into four groups. Have each group create a different ostinato for each verse. Sing the song through with each group repeating its spoken ostinato in its verse.

Adding tone colour to songs
In four groups, add different instruments and ostinato to one of four selected songs, for example:
- 'Click Go the Shears';
- 'John Brown's Holden';
- 'Old MacDonald';
- 'He's Got the Whole World'.

Extension: Select a popular song, and write up the words to it so all children can see them. Attach cards representing the different instruments to different phrases or sections of the song. Have children sing the song and play their instrument when it is indicated by the instrument cards on the word chart.

Colour poems

Encourage children to make up a poem or pieces of prose, each one being thoughts about, or associations with, a different colour, for example:

> Red is danger, anger, fright,
> Red is blood spilled in a fight,
> Red is splashed on the evening sky,
> Red is a scream of pain, and a cry.
>
> White is ice, pure without heart,
> White is a wedding, and paper for art,
> White is the snow on evergreen trees,
> White is gardenias attracting bees.

Accompany the reading of these with different instruments, used to sensitively portray the feelings and descriptions represented in each poem.

Sound poems

Make up a class sound poem. Use words which evoke feelings and sounds, or describe events or things happening around us, for example:

> **The Storm**
> Drip!
> Drip, drop!
> Drip, drop, drip, drop!
> Pitter, patter, pitter, patter!
> Splish, splosh, splish, splash!
> Pouring rain, down it comes!
> Pouring rain, down it comes!
> Dark clouds looming, thunder crashes!
> Blackness then the lightning flashes!
> Dark clouds, thunder, blackness, lightning!
> Blackness, then the lightning flashes!
> Dark clouds clearing, thunder crashes!
> Rain is easing, gently falling!
> Rain is easing, gently falling!
> Splish, splosh, splish, splash!
> Pitter, patter, pitter, patter!
> Drip, drop, drip, drop!
> Drip, drop!
> Drip!

Have children read the poem through, and then add suitable instruments or body percussion to describe or represent different parts of the poem.

Extension: Play the instruments to accompany the poem, but don't speak the poem aloud, so that only instruments describing the approaching and then disappearing storm are heard.

Graphic scores
In the jungle: Using a picture of a jungle, select instruments to represent each of the animals. Play them as the pointer moves across the picture and indicates the different animals.

On the farm: Make multiple pictures of farm animals and the farmer. Glue them randomly around a piece of cardboard. Select instruments or vocal sounds to represent each animal. When the pointer indicates each animal, play the corresponding instrument.

Structure
Same and different phrases
The teacher plays a series of walking notes (taa notes or crotchets) on the drum, interspersed with some running notes (ta-te notes or quavers). Alternate the sequence of walking notes with the running notes, firstly at even, regular intervals and then randomly. Children walk when the walking notes are played and run when the running notes are played.

Answering phrases
Suggested song: 'Jabbin, Jabbin'
Listen to the whole song while clapping the beat. Identify the same and different phrases; that is 'Jabbin jabbin, kirrooka' = A and 'Kirroo, kirroo, kirrooka' = B. In pairs, work out body percussion sequences to show the same and different phrases, with the movements to the A phrases being quite different from those in the B phrases.

If possible, have the children watch videos of traditional Aboriginal dancing and try to create their own similar movements to represent birds waking up in the morning. Sing the song with some children playing the beat on rhythm sticks. As phrase A is sung, the A movement sequence is performed and then freezes in position as the B phrase is sung and the B movement sequence is performed.

Same and different rhythms
Use two sets of four rhythm flashcards, for example:

One child puts one set of flashcards in a selected order and plays it to the rest of the class. Without seeing these flashcards, the rest of the children identify the sequence played by arranging the second set in the same order as was played by the first child.

Extension: Have two children sit back-to-back, each having an identical set of four rhythm flashcards. Child A orders the cards and claps the rhythm. Child B listens and then rearranges the cards to form the order of the rhythm clapped by Child A.

Note: For younger, or less experienced children, start with two flashcards each, and then build up as children become more confident at the game.

Verse and chorus

Sing a known song with a verse and chorus, for example:
- 'Waltzing Matilda';
- 'Click Go the Shears';
- 'Botany Bay';
- 'John Brown's Holden';
- 'I Am Me!'.

Use one sequence of movements to accompany the verses and a different sequence for the chorus. Accompany the verse with different instruments from those used in the chorus.

Same and different sections in a song

Suggested song: 'Old MacDonald'
Sing the whole song and show the different phrases by playing different instruments or doing different movements for each phrase.
Suggested song: 'When You Grow Up'
Listen to the whole song first on the CD; identify the same and different phrases. Sing the song through and use body percussion to show the different phrases; for example:
- Line 1: Clap hands.
- Line 2: Click fingers.
- Line 3: Clap hands (same as Line 1).
- Line 4: Tap shoulders.

Select a popular piece of music and show the same and different phrases by accompanying them with different instruments.

Rondo

Improvise a rondo — a series of different short pieces of music interspersed with a repeated melody or rhythm (i.e. A B A C A D A) where the rhythm or melody (A) is repeated, but is interspersed with a variety of other rhythms or melodies (B, C, D and so on). Individual children could improvise a rhythm or melody for parts B, C, D and so on.

My name is . . .

(A) Class claps a selected rhythm (e.g. taa taa ta-te taa, ta-te ta-te ta-te taa).

(B) Individual student says and claps: 'My name is XXX'.

(A) Class claps first rhythm (e.g. taa taa ta-te taa, ta-te ta-te ta-te taa).

Repeat around the circle, with A being the same repeated rhythm alternating with B, which is a different rhythm for each student.

Storm is coming (rondo form)

Have the class sit in a circle. Each student says a different phrase about a storm and does an appropriate movement, alternating with the whole class saying 'Storm is coming'. Sound starts off softly and increases around the circle, and then dies down.

At the zoo

Divide the class into five groups (B, C, D, E and F) and have each group select instruments to represent a different animal from picture cards or photographs. One student (A) is the zoo keeper and selects an instrument to describe her job. The class listens to each group and identifies each animal from the sounds they created to describe that animal. Order the way the groups play their instruments to create a story about the zoo keeper visiting the animals at the zoo, for example:

A B A C A D A E A F A B A D A

Write the created piece of music down using graphic notation.

Ostinati (melodic and spoken) to accompany songs

Suggested song: 'Christmas Round'
Listen to the song and learn to sing it; identify the same and different phrases (i.e. they are all different: A B C D). Play a melodic ostinato to the beat: D G A D (i.e. the melodic ostinato can be the bass line which follows guitar chords).

Suggested song: 'Bound for South Australia'
Sing through the song once; identify the same or different phrases (A B C D E B F D). Select one phrase as a spoken ostinato (e.g. 'Heave away, haul away') and speak this throughout the song; or create a dance to show the same and different phrases of the song.

Writing a graphic score

Create a musical picture with instruments describing an event; write it down in symbols and play it back. Try to include other elements apart from tone colour and

Graphic score for the text *Who's in the Shed?*

structure (e.g. dynamics). Give the graphic score to another group and have the group interpret the score. Comment on how easy/difficult it was to write down how the score should be played and to play a score someone else had written.

Talking xylophones

Seat children in pairs, each with a pentatonic scale on chime bars or xylophones (e.g. use the notes C, D, E, G, A or G, A, B, D, E). Child A improvises a simple melody using these five notes. Child B plays back an answering melody (i.e. not an echo or a repeat of the melody, but a different melody).

Note: For young children, start with only two of the five notes, and build up to using the five notes as they gain confidence in the activity.

Extension: Have four children seated, each with a pentatonic scale on a xylophone in front of them. Child A plays a melody, Child B answers with a complementary melody. Child C plays a melody and Child D plays an answering melody. Continue, with two children playing together sometimes and at other times individual children playing and another child 'answering' them on their instrument as they have a musical conversation.

Conversations with xylophones.

Cooperative composing

Divide the class into four groups. Name the groups A, B, C and D. Each group creates a rhythm on untuned instruments or a melody on tuned instruments. Develop a form or structure for the total composition, for example:

A B A C A D A
or
A B C B D B A
or
A B B A C C A D D A
or
Introduction A B C D A Ending

Play the composition through according to the specified structure. Record it on a video or cassette player and reflect on how the piece sounded and what changes could be made. Experiment with changing the order of the groups to create a satisfying and finished composition.

Pentatonic melodies

Divide the class into three groups (A, B, C). Have children experiment with notes from a pentatonic scale, for example:
- C pentatonic scale = C, D, E, G, A
- G pentatonic scale = G, A, B, D, E
- F pentatonic scale = F, G, A, C, D

Each group creates a short melody that it can repeat several times, if necessary. Organise the order of the whole piece using letter names for each group, with bracketed letter names indicating these groups play together to create harmonies, for example:

A (AB) (BC) (AC) A
or
A (AB) B (BC) C (AC) A
or
A (AB) loudly (AB) softly (AC) loudly (AC) softly A (BC) loudly (BC) softly A

Play the piece through; record it and reflect on any changes that need to be made. Change the order and combinations of groups to create different compositions. Add dynamic variations to contrast repetitions of each melody.
Extension: Have a small group of children play an ostinato through the piece of music.
Note: For young children, this activity can be simplified either by using just two notes from a pentatonic scale or by using only non-tuned percussion instruments.

'I Know an Old Lady'
Read through a poem or a story or sing a song that has repeated phrases in the structure or content of the lyrics or text.
Poem/Song: 'I Know an Old Lady Who Swallowed a Fly'
Select a different instrument for each of the animals or characters mentioned. Read the poem or sing the song through, using the instruments to describe the animals.
Extension: Draw a symbol on a card to represent each animal. Organise the cards into a selected order to form a score, and then play the score. Add movement to accompany the instrumental sounds. Rearrange the order of cards to create a new movement sequence and soundscape. Create a graphic score to record these experiments.

Using instruments to represent different characters in a poem.

Writing a graphic score
In groups create musical pictures, using found, made and/or commercial percussion instruments to represent, for example:
- storm and calm at sea;
- at the beach;
- train starting up and travelling into the distance;
- fireworks at night;
- jungle adventure;

- at a football match;
- the Melbourne Cup;
- a traffic accident;
- a cricket match.

Write down the music symbolically to create a graphic score using the following steps:
- Decide what happens at the start, middle and finish of the event.
- Decide on instruments that could be used to describe the sounds associated with this event.
- Create a piece of music describing this event.
- Using symbolic notation, write down the score that has just been played.
- If applicable, try to show differences in dynamics (loud and soft), pitch (high and low) and tempo (fast and slow) in the piece of music.
- Practise the composition, and then share it with the rest of the class.

Re-create sounds in the environment

In small groups, take a piece of paper and pencil outside. Listen for (for example) one minute and list all the sounds heard. Where applicable, categorise them into:
- loud and soft sounds;
- sounds which get louder or softer;
- fast and slow sounds;
- regular and irregular sounds;
- high and low sounds;
- faraway and close-at-hand sounds.

Experiment with instruments found in the environment to re-create the sounds heard in the first one minute of listening. Write down these sounds on a graphic score, showing differences in dynamics (loud and soft), pitch (high and low) and tempo (fast and slow) in the piece of music. Practise the composition, and then share it with the rest of the class.

Tell a new story

Think of some characters who could be part of a story. Brainstorm ideas about what could be included in the story. Work out the introduction, the problem, the climax and the conclusion to the story. Experiment with instruments to help tell the story without using any words. Write down the musical story as a graphic score, using symbolic notation, showing differences in dynamics (loud and soft), pitch (high and low) and tempo (fast and slow) in the piece of music. Practise the composition, and then share it with the rest of the class.

Experiment with sound and/or body sounds

Explore all the different sounds that can be made with the materials around the classroom (pencils, backpacks, drink containers, cupboards, bins, chairs and so on). Form these sounds into a continuous piece of music using a variety of different ways to play these sounds (fast, slow, loud, soft, high, low and so on). Write down these sounds on a graphic score, showing differences in dynamics (loud and soft), pitch (high and low) and tempo (fast and slow) in the piece of music. Practise the composition, and then share it with the rest of the class.

Retell a favourite story

Select a simple story and read it through. Work out who are the characters and what are the events in the story. Select appropriate instruments that can be used to represent the characters and events in the story. Read through the story adding the instruments. Write down the sounds that were played in the story on a graphic score, showing differences, where applicable, in dynamics (loud and soft), pitch (high and low) and tempo (fast and slow) in the piece of music. Practise the composition using only instruments to tell the story (no words), and then share it with the rest of the class.

Suggested children's stories that can be made into graphic scores:
- *Three Billy Goats Gruff*
- *Going on a Bear Hunt*
- *To Town*
- *Who's in the Shed?*
- *The Three Little Pigs*
- *Goldilocks and the Three Bears*
- *The Farm Concert*

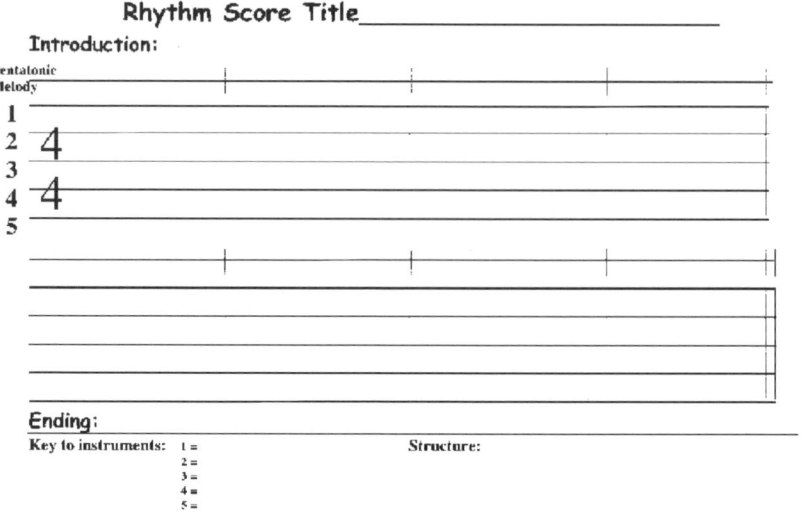

Read through the story; decide on events and characters depicted in the story; decide on the musical concept to be reinforced in the story; and add instruments to represent events and characters. Present the story read and accompanied by instruments to a younger grade. Notate the instrument playing symbolically to create a graphic score; play the score to the rest of the class, using only instruments — that is, with no words being read (similar to a story map).

Writing music using standard notation

- **Duration: Make up a rhythm.** Individually, using cards (include taa beats = crotchets; ta-te beats = quavers; taa taa beats = minims; and taa-taa-taa-taa beats = semibreves) have children make up an eight-bar rhythm, and then practise it using an instrument of choice. Write down the rhythm on one line of scored paper.
- **Tone colour.** Join with four other students, each having a different instrument. Create a five-part rhythm, and write down each rhythm on a different line of music. Practise this as a group.
- **Dynamics.** Repeat the five-part, eight-bar rhythm, at a different dynamic level.
- **Structure.** Add an introduction and an ending, and present the finished piece to the rest of the class, for example: Introduction/1 × loudly/1 × softly/Ending.
- **Pitch.** Add in pentatonic notes to create a melody to go above the rhythms. Write the rhythm on the score and the note names above the rhythm. Have children who can write music using the treble clef write out their pentatonic melody on a five-line staff.

SPRINGBOARDS FOR DISCUSSION AND APPLICATION

1. Select a song and decide how you can teach each of the five elements (duration, dynamics, pitch, tone colour and structure) of music using the song as a starting point. Identify what children would need to know and be able to do prior to engaging in these activities. Identify what indicators or pointers could be used to assess children's learning in each of the five elements of music. Write your ideas in lesson-plan formats.

2. Select one of the above activities from each of the five musical elements and identify how each activity can be made more simple for children with very little experience in music, and can be made more challenging for children with a strong background in music. Identify what indicators could be used to assess children's learning in each of the activities.

3. Select a children's picture book or simple storybook and identify how you could teach and develop one or more of the elements of music using the book as a stimulus or starting point. Identify what indicators and outcomes could be used to assess children's learning in relation to the elements of music covered. Write your ideas in a programmed format, indicating which activity areas (singing, listening, playing instruments, moving and making music) and what elements (duration, dynamics, pitch tone colour and structure) are being taught and developed. Indicate what syllabus outcomes the children are working towards by engaging in these activities.

FURTHER READING

Abeles, H., Hoffer, C. & Klotman, R. (1984), *Foundations of music education*, Schirmer, New York.

Anderson, W. & Lawrence, J. (2001), *Integrating music into the elementary classroom*, 5th edn, Wadsworth, California.

Askew, G. (1993), *Music education in the primary school*, Longman and Cheshire, Melbourne.

Barrs, K. (1994), *Music works: Music education in the classroom with children from five to nine years*, Belair Publications, London.

Choksy, L., Abramson, R., Gillespie, A., Woods, D. & York, F. (2001), *Teaching music in the twenty-first century*, Prentice Hall, Upper Saddle River, New Jersey.

Hackett, P. & Lindeman, C. (2004), *The musical classroom*, 6th edn, Pearson Prentice Hall, Upper Saddle River, New Jersey.

Leask, J. (1984), *Upbeat: Music education in the classroom*, Levels 1–6, Scholastic, Sydney.

Mark, M. (1986), *Contemporary music education*, 2nd edn, Schirmer, New York.

Miché, M. *Weaving music into young minds*, Thomson Learning, New York.

Mills, J. (1993), *Music in the primary school*, rev. edn, Cambridge University Press, Cambridge.

NSW Department of Education (1985), *Music and dance* Booklets 1 and 2, Sydney.

NSW Department of School Education (1997), *Sync or swim*, Author, Sydney.

Nye, R. & Nye, V. (1992), *Music in the elementary school*, Simon & Schuster, Parsippany, New Jersey.

Russell-Bowie, D. (1989), *Music is everywhere*, Educational Supplies, Sydney.

Russell-Bowie, D. (1989), *Music is alive*, Educational Supplies, Sydney.

REFERENCES

Fiske, E. (1999), *Champions of change: The impact of the arts on learning*. The Arts Education Partnership: Washington, DC.

Nelson, Hon. Dr Brendan (2005), 'Music takes centre stage', media release, 26 March.

Stock, J. (1996), *World sound matters*, Schott, London.

chapter four
Introduction to media education

Media literacy seeks to empower citizens and to transform their passive relationship to media into an active, critical engagement.
(Wally Bowen)

Learning outcomes
By the end of this chapter, students will be able to:
- create suitable thematic learning experiences for children exploring at least four different forms of media;
- integrate media learning experiences across the arts and across the other key learning areas;
- present a clear argument for the importance of media education within the primary curriculum;
- write a unit of work that shows their understanding of how children can design, make and analyse media in the primary classroom.

MMADD about the arts

Introduction

Imagine a world without media, without technology! There would be no television (TV), radio or telephones; no computers, CDs or video games; and no books, magazines, comics or advertising. Although media is all around us and has been for many years, media education has developed only relatively recently in schools.

The term *media* can include any form of communication — books, magazines, comics, newspapers, films, videos, DVDs, compact discs-read only memory (CD ROMs), overhead transparencies, computers, cameras, telephones, email, Short Message Service (SMS) texting, TV and radio. For thousands of years, communication was generally undertaken face to face. However, now we have such powerful technology and means of communication that people thousands of kilometres apart can have immediate, live conversations through SMS texting, phone calls, internet chatting and video conferencing. Information can flash around the world in milliseconds as we celebrate the latest sporting victory or see a royal wedding as it happens, or are stunned by the news and video clips of a tsunami, the tragic death of a famous person, a terrorist attack or the atrocities of war.

Media changes and is updated constantly; what was new and 'cool' last week, last month or last year is regarded as old-fashioned and cumbersome today. In the 1980s the desktop computer revolutionised our work and leisure times, and a computer with 512 kilobytes of memory complete with a floppy disk drive was considered powerful and efficient, until it was outdated by the state-of-the-art 1-megabyte computer. Today's children would find it difficult to understand how one worked on such a computer, as they work with programs, documents, graphics and songs using more memory than could ever have been imagined 20 years ago. Even in the past five years, the development of mobile phones, digital audio and video cameras, DVD players and TVs has accelerated so quickly and prices have dropped so dramatically that most families own and use a range of new technological equipment that their parents would never have thought could exist.

Media and the child

From birth, most children are touched by media, in their homes, the shopping centre and the cinemas, and as they play and work with their computers during their leisure hours and while doing homework. Media influences each child's conception of reality and of their understanding about the world. Within their personal lives, most Australian children are knowledgeable and enthusiastic consumers of films, videos, DVDs, mobile phones, computers and software, digital cameras, printers, CDs, MP3 players, books, magazines, comics and newspapers. Media education acknowledges this total immersion in media and aims to use it to develop children's critical appreciation, knowledge, creativity, understanding and skills in relation to what they watch and how they interact daily with the media. This prepares them for lifelong learning and critical appreciation of the ever-changing world of the media.

However, teachers should also be aware that there is an ever-widening chasm between the media-rich and the media-poor children. The stereotype of today's child is that of the *cyber kid*, who is playing on the computer for hours on end; they are communicating on their mobile phones, surfing the web, chatting on the Internet

Children need to learn and practise relevant skills.

and gaining confidence and skills in using the tools that will help make them successful in the workplace. This stereotype ignores the technology poverty that entraps so many children, especially those in the low socioeconomic areas.

This may be attributed to lack of financial or cultural access to computers, software programs, printers, scanners, the Internet and mobile phones; however, there could be other reasons which need to be identified by each teacher in relation to their class of children. It would be an important fact-finding mission for the teacher to establish how many children have easy and ready access to this technology and how many children are technology-poor. Perhaps there is a computer in the home, but older siblings or parents work on it all the time and do not allow the younger children access. The children may not see the relevance of using the technology in their day-to-day life, or their non-use of available technology may even be as simple and powerful as someone having told them they are stupid (or they are girls!) and therefore could not possibly understand how to use a computer or camera. The more teachers know about the children, their culture and their background, the more effective their teaching in the area of media education will be in meeting the needs of the children and developing their knowledge, skills and attitudes further in this area.

Within the school setting, children need to develop their ability to critically analyse the media and to use it in creative processes. As with each of the art forms, children need to explore and learn the skills, concepts and knowledge required to understand the many facets of media, and then use these practical, creative and analytically critical skills across the arts curriculum and into other key learning areas. Teachers should aim to give children systematic and developmental practical activities to gain the knowledge, concepts and skills related to media education and to learn about the media that shapes and reflects their culture, through structured, creative and reflective processes.

Why teach media education?

In the first half of the 20th century, media education was introduced to protect children against the mass media which promulgated popular culture, as this was seen to be an infectious disease which contaminated traditional, accepted culture, manipulated and exploited audiences, corrupted children's language and was underpinned by greed and consumerism. Popular culture, whether it was portrayed in music, film, dance, drama or visual arts, was seen as not being suitable for children to study in school, as it was more important that they should concentrate on the superior 'high' art subjects and literature. By the 1960s media education was used, not to protect children against the media, but rather to help them see the difference between good and bad media, realising that some of the popular media could be of similar quality and standing as 'good' literature and art. However, the main emphasis was on discriminating between good and bad films, and other aspects of media were not generally considered as important.

Towards the end of the century, ideas moved away from judgements about good and bad media, and focused on children learning to study and critically analyse the conventions, codes, signs and symbols used in media. Media education taught children to question the power, techniques and ideologies behind the representations of reality within media and to delve into current political and social issues as portrayed and embedded in the media.

More recently, trends in media education are encouraging children to realise that the main function of the media is to market and sell products to certain audiences. Marketers and governments are increasingly in control of the media and it is becoming more difficult to find information that is not influenced by certain biases and agendas. Children need to become media-literate and be able to analyse media in relation to the four areas of *producer — message — medium — audience*. They need to realise that information (the *message*) can either be sold as just another commodity or it may be freely given for its intrinsic social value. Within media education, children need to learn how media texts work and how they are used to represent and create meaning. They also need to be aware of who produces media (the *producer*) and how these institutions and industries are organised. They need to question what lies behind the media productions they see every day, what are the motives, who funds it, why it was funded, what values are shown and who owns the media used. They also need to have some knowledge about the actual media technologies of film, TV, photography, radio, print and electronic media (the *medium*) that are used to convey the messages from the producers to the audiences. As *audiences* to a wealth of media in their everyday lives, children need to be able to make sense of these media products and the different forms of technologies they use inside and outside their homes.

Much research has focused on the negative effects of violence being depicted in the media and how children become aggressive and violent themselves after a steady diet of TV, video games, music, films and videos that portray violent acts and events. However, it has also been found that the more children are able to analyse and talk about these programs, films and games, and understand how they have been made and how they influence values, beliefs and actions, the less affected they are by what they see. Thus media literacy and media education are both vital to developing children, to empower them to understand and resist the subconscious messages conveyed in what they see, hear and read and to be more thoughtful about what they consume.

This chapter examines media education in relation to designing, making and analysing media, and suggests classroom activities which may be undertaken to enhance children's knowledge of these facets of media education.

Forms of media

Television
Genres include:
- family shows
- quiz shows
- reality shows
- documentaries
- romance
- science fiction
- drama
- sports shows
- news
- fashion
- cartoons
- educational programs
- advertising and so on

Film
Genres include:
- documentaries
- romance
- non-fiction
- science fiction
- fiction
- drama
- cartoons
- educational films and so on

Photography
Genres include:
- still photography (shooting and printing)
  — 35mm single lens reflex (SLR)
  — instant-focus cameras
  — polaroid cameras
  — digital cameras
  — black-and-white or colour photography
- video photography and so on

Print
Genres include:
- posters
- books
- magazines
- comics
- journals
- newspapers
- overhead transparencies and so on

Radio
Genres include:
- variety
- talkback
- news
- drama
- sport
- music
- interviews
- advertising and so on

Computer and electronic media
Genres include:
- CD-ROMs
- computer software
- scanners and printers
- shareware and freeware
- web pages
- email
- Internet
- mobile phones and so on

Designing, making and appreciating media

Children need to learn about media, about how it is made and produced, and how it shapes and represents reality, but they also need the practical hands-on experiences of designing and creating the ideas and then actually producing media themselves. Another important facet of their learning about media is to develop their ability to analyse and appreciate the media they engage in and produce themselves. Even young children can start the analytical process to broaden their awareness of who is sending the message, and how and to whom it is being sent. Real-life activities should be included in your term's program so children can understand how media is used inside and outside the classroom.

Skills and processes to design and make media artworks

To learn about the art form of media children need to learn the skills, processes and techniques unique to each of the forms of media so that they can become competent in producing media artworks. Such skills, understandings and processes can include the following:

- **Framing.** This is putting a border or frame around a picture or section of a picture to draw attention to it, to put it in context and to exclude dead space in the image. It includes extreme close-up, close-up, mid-shot, long shot and wide angle.

- **Lighting.** Lighting is used to emphasise or highlight a subject. Lighting can be from behind, above, below or to the side, depending on the desired effect.
- **Positioning.** This involves placing an object or subject in a certain place in relation to others for a specific reason.
- **Focal point.** The focal point of a picture, poster or photograph is the main subject. When composing an image, know what the focal point is and plan the photo or picture accordingly.
- **Cropping.** Material in a picture that is not required can be cut out so that the subject is highlighted more clearly. This can be done on a computer program for digital images or using mats, scissors or frames for print photos.
- **Displaying.** This includes using mats, borders, frames, captions and so on to display the media artworks to portray their message clearly.
- **Designing.** This involves planning or sketching ideas for an artwork, detailing layout techniques, formatting and processes to be used to prepare the artwork.
- **Layout.** This is the arranging of pictures, headlines, text and so on to create a clear message using a readable, attractive design.
- **Formatting.** Fonts, tabbing, styles and so on are used to present text and graphics clearly to convey a specified message.
- **Interviewing.** A series of questions, comments, anecdotes and so on are scripted to elicit information from one or more subjects; this skill can be used in TV, film or radio.
- **Sequencing.** This involves ordering a storyboard or series of images to tell a story or present a message clearly.
- **Scripting.** This is writing the text for a film, video or radio show.
- **Writing.** This is creating text for print media.
- **Storyboarding.** A series of scenes or pictures are created to show the planned sequence of a film or video.
- **Shooting.** This involves taking images using video or still cameras.
- **Special effects.** Sounds or visuals are created to produce a certain effect within a film, video, TV or radio show.
- **Recording.** This is the process of putting audio and visual sounds and images into digital or analogue format to be viewed or listened to at a later date.
- **Editing.** This involves preparing and/or modifying information, data, graphics and text prior to production.
- **Adapting.** This includes adjusting, modifying and clarifying visual and/or audio text prior to production.
- **Distributing.** The hard copy of the completed production is dispersed to selected audiences.
- **Publishing.** This is printing the completed text in a professional format and presentation.
- **Transmitting.** The completed electronic, digital or audio production is dispersed to selected audiences.

Analysing and appreciating media

Analysis of content

Children also need to be able to do quantitative analysis of content in various forms of media as part of evaluating the medium. For example, they may visually analyse how much of a magazine is devoted to pictures and how much to text and so on. What does this imply about the audience? Compare this with an academic journal and a comic book. Alternatively, children may compare the number of advertisements with the number of articles. They may categorise the types of article and count the number in each category. When watching a short documentary, they may count the number of angles taken of a subject and discuss why these have been included and what different messages are being portrayed by the different viewpoints.

Analysis of text

Meaning can be explored through an analysis of the media text, which includes identifying and understanding the codes, symbols and conventions used in paintings, sound, graphics, comics, magazines and so on. Children can learn to become literate in sound and visuals as well as with written text. For example, children can watch an advertisement or short excerpt from a movie without the sound and discuss what message is being conveyed. How did they know this? Did they all receive the same message? How were lighting, close-up/medium/distance shots, movement and colour used to give a message? Then listen only to the sound to see if this message opposes or consolidates what was seen in the visuals. How were the music and the vocal expression used to contribute to the message? Put both sound and visuals together and see if this is a more powerful way of communicating the message. This discussion can then develop into a practical experience of creating their own short movie to promote a message using the techniques they have discussed previously. This may be a more in-depth learning experience than just asking them to create a movie themselves without any lead-in, input, discussion or reflection. When children know how and why media text is constructed they will be able to create more powerful media artworks as well as know how to critically analyse what they see and hear in the media in their daily lives.

Meaning can be explored through an analysis of the media text.

Thematic approach

Another aspect of media education can be to take a thematic approach where one topic is observed and discussed through a variety of forms of media. There may be an advertisement or a news story which appears on the TV, in magazines, in the newspaper and on the radio. Each form of media can be analysed and discussed in relation to what message is being conveyed and how effective each form is in presenting the message. Are there any clear differences or biases in the information portrayed and why is this so? What techniques have been used? This helps children understand the range of issues to be considered in choosing the appropriate media to convey a message and how meaning can be altered depending on the media used and the bias of the producer. Children could then decide on a theme or message to be conveyed and select appropriate media to present this message in a variety of ways.

Producer – message – media – audience

Another way of analysing media is to look at the 'big picture' and ask questions about the sender, the message, the media used and the audience to whom the message is being sent. When children can analyse media using this framework they should be encouraged to put this analysis into practice in their home use of media as well as when they are in the classroom.

Producer (Who? Why?)

- **Who?** Who has created the media, do they own it, what biases or influences might they have, and what is the political, social, economic and/or cultural context in which the media work has been made?
- **Why?** Why is the message being sent? What obvious and underlying reasons does the producer have in creating this message using this particular type of media?

Message (What? How?)

- **Obvious and underlying messages.** What is the obvious message being sent? Are there any other messages that can be heard through the use of language, codes and conventions of the particular form of media, the representations of people and objects, and the genre being used?
- **Language.** What is the language used and how does it affect the communication of the message? How is the language of the different media forms used, such as clothing, settings, gestures, symbols, composition, movement, graphics, sound effects, narration and voice-overs, written word, headlines and captions, and how effective is this? Is there an obvious and a hidden meaning in the text?
- **Codes.** What are the technical codes used to convey the desired message? How are the processes such as editing, framing, composition, lighting, angles, flashbacks, volume of music, sentence construction, fade in/out of sound and picture and so on used and to what purpose? What are the symbolic codes used in sending the message? How are the use of movements, body language, symbolic objects, sound effects, dialogue, set design, lighting, words and so on used and to what purpose? Are these codes dependent on a certain cultural context or are they relevant in any culture or context?
- **Conventions.** What conventions are being used within the chosen media to convey the message? How effectively are conventions related to the representation, composition, programming, content, genre, advertisements and so on used?
- **Representations.** What people, objects, animals, places, events, gender, occupations and so on are shown and how are they represented? Are these true to life or are they stereotyped?
- **Genre.** What genre is being used and how effective is it? For example, is the TV program a family show, a quiz, news, a documentary, a sports show, cartoons, a drama, a romance, a reality show and so on?

Media (What? How?)

What media is being used and how is it being used?

- **Film.** Is the film an animation, drama, documentary and so on?
- **Television.** Discuss the programming (time of show, serials, movies, ratings and one-off shows), who funds the program, live TV (news, events, sports and reality TV), genre and so on.
- **Photography.** Discuss presentation (black-and-white or colour photographs, digital or photo print, slides), composition and framing techniques, uses of photography (newspapers, magazines, fashion, sport, advertisements and news) and so on.
- **Radio.** Discuss programming (music, talkback, drama, sport and so on), sound effects used, advertising and content.

Discuss the design, message and format of illustrations in a children's book.

- **Print media.** Discuss how design, formats and layout are being used to convey a message — that is: newspapers (headlines, photos, sections, format and advertisements), posters and brochures (size, colours, font, space, visuals, words and symbols), comic books and cartoons (speech bubbles, simplification of content and action, detail and presentation, story), children's books (illustrations, and use of fonts, colour, space, words and symbols) and magazines (targeted audience, content, layout photographs, text and advertisements).
- **Computer and electronic media.** Discuss hardware, software, shareware, freeware, use of equipment, CD-ROMs, mobile phones, email, Internet, and so on.
- **In general.** What form of media is being used and how is it used? How effective is it in portraying the message? Why did the producer choose this form of media to convey the message? Would another form of media have produced the same message as effectively? What costs might have been involved?

Audience (To whom?)

- **Cultural context.** To whom is the message being sent — that is: to one person, to a general group or to people in a certain time and place, culture, age, gender, income group and so on? How do you know? Is the message different when it is received by someone in the targeted group from when it is received by someone outside the targeted group? How does the producer ensure the specified audience receives the message?
- **Feedback.** Is there any form of feedback from the audience to the producer to assess the effectiveness of the message and the media used?

Practical considerations

Preparation

Media lessons often involve technical equipment, so get to know how each piece of equipment works yourself so you can use it confidently before the lesson. You will need to work out where the equipment is stored and how it can be borrowed, and always ensure that you return it as soon as you are finished with it. Establish clear instructions and routines on using the equipment, identify and address equity issues, and demonstrate how each piece of equipment is used. Indicate any safety procedures required when using it and emphasis that children need to be careful of the equipment when they are handling it. Know what media activities the children have been involved in prior to the lesson and find out how familiar they are with each piece of technology being used.

Resources

When using media technologies, children need to know:
- what resources are required;
- where to find the appropriate equipment;
- how to borrow, use and return it;
- whether or not they need an adult to assist or supervise them as they use a piece of equipment;
- care of the equipment;
- what level of noise and movement is acceptable both inside and outside the classroom;
- what the rules are for leaving the classroom (e.g. go with a friend, be no longer than five minutes and take a note);
- how to talk about and appreciate their own and others' artworks;
- how to be positive and reflective in their comments and give constructive, helpful criticism and so on.

Ensure children have time to practise using the equipment.

Skill development

When teaching children how to use equipment, teachers need to know how to use it themselves and work out how all children will learn to use it. If for example, there is only one video camera, teachers need to work out logistically how this will be structured; they could demonstrate how to use it, and then have the children suggest the key points which are written down on the blackboard or whiteboard and later onto a work card which is attached to the camera. When individual children have the opportunity to use the video camera, a child who has already learned the skills could act as a peer tutor with the child learning the skill, using the work card for reference and reminder as needed.

Develop this idea into creating a media learning centre (see Chapter 2, 'The creative arts classroom') with a series of work cards detailing various learning experiences children can complete with different media. These may be used by children in their free time, for fast finishers, for the whole class during a set period of time or on a rotation basis, or as other children complete learning-centre work in different art forms.

Teachers may find it helpful to develop a roster system so that every child has the opportunity to use each piece of media equipment at least once each term. This will allow even the most hesitant child to have some practical hands-on experience to learn how to use the equipment. Monitor access to the equipment during the week to ensure everyone has equal access; for example, if computers are only used when children have finished their work, some children may never have the opportunity to use them.

Computers can be used for different purposes both in the home and at school.

Using computers

Ensure that the software for computers is of interest to both boys and girls, that it is suitable for the age group and that all children know how to use it. It may be useful to have several children who are competent users of a piece of software teach other children how to use it. Encourage children to use computers for a variety of reasons, for example playing, writing stories, drawing pictures, playing games, reading stories, learning about and writing music, and learning spelling.

Talk with parents about the use of computers and other technology in the home and encourage them to give their children regular access to using this equipment, if this is possible. Show them the different ways computers can be used so they don't think computers are just for playing games. If you expect a piece of homework to be completed on a computer, work out how children without a home computer can finish the work.

Child-centred activities

Know your children and be aware of those who learn best when working by themselves and those who prefer to learn in a group. Plan learning experiences using different media so that children can learn individually or with other children, depending on their preferred intelligence. Ensure that the learning experiences are child-centred and children are allowed to experiment and explore the technology, learning to use the relevant tools and language to design, create and analyse their own media artworks. Try to include a variety of forms of media in your term's program so that children are exposed to learning experiences that involve TV, film, photography, print and radio as well as computers and electronic media.

Real-life activities

Part of a media program should involve children participating in simulations of, or actual, real-life situations, such as being a TV director and programming an afternoon and evening's TV viewing, creating a newspaper for a designated audience, designing an advertisement for an upcoming school event or setting up an art exhibition on a given theme.

Children need to be able to identify each step that is required in the organisation of the chosen task: who will be responsible for each part of it; what equipment and resources are required; where they can be obtained; the timeframe of the project; and what needs to be done each hour/day/week and so on. As the children work on their particular part of the project they can develop team working, cooperation and other social skills, self-esteem, creativity and leadership abilities as well as engaging in in-depth learning about the techniques, practicalities and processes of media making.

Real-life media activities can be readily integrated within the arts as children can video a dance or drama production and use the video to reflect on the performance, photograph an artwork and write about how it was produced, or audio tape one of their creative musical pieces and use this as the stimulus for dance or for reflective feedback. In these activities, the different media are being used as tools to achieve the outcomes and indicators of the other art forms. As with any art form there needs to be a balance between using dance, drama, music, media or visual arts to learn about one specific art form, or to use this art form to achieve an outcome or indicator from another subject or key learning area — that is, learning *about* the art form or learning *through* the art form.

Suggested structure of a media lesson

- **Introduction.** Start with a motivating, relevant introduction to gain children's attention. Introduce or revise and familiarise children with the skills and equipment for the lesson.
- **Skill building.** Work out clear steps to cover content and how children will learn and practise relevant skills.
- **Designing and making.** Ensure sufficient time and resources are available for children to complete the relevant production tasks.
- **Closure.** Using reflection, appreciation and analysis, share the completed artworks and discuss the techniques, procedures and equipment used.

Activities to introduce and teach forms of media

Based on a spiral curriculum, these classroom activities can be introduced simply with young children and then repeated each term or year using age-appropriate examples and deepening the level of learning expected from the children. Preservice and in-service teachers should use their particular state or territory syllabus as a framework for teaching media education and adapt these suggestions to suit the requirements of the syllabus and their children's needs, interests, previous experiences and skills, and the resources available in the school and classroom.

Television

The influence of TV on children's lives is clearly documented, and in one week children often spend more hours in front of the TV than they do at school. It is important, therefore, that they learn to engage analytically with the medium so that any harmful effects are lessened through knowledge, understanding and discussion about the programs they watch. Media education can make children aware of the influences, messages and biases behind the programs and they can also learn, through engaging in practical activities, about processes involved in the production of TV programs, including storyboarding, scripting, sequencing, shooting, special effects, editing, publishing and producing.

Elements of narrative

Discuss a favourite TV program and identify the key narrative elements in them (i.e. setting, characters, costumes, introduction, middle, climax and ending). Watch a news program or a games show and identify if these key elements are evident. Create a news program about events in the school. Determine the setting and the news reader, what news events will be presented, what will be the key point or climax in the show and how it will end.

Watch the ads!

Prepare a spreadsheet with hourly timeslots during the day from 6 am to 9 pm down the left-hand side and columns across the page headed with the different TV stations of your state or territory. During the week or during the holidays/weekend and so on have children write down what is being advertised at what time on what channel. On a designated day, have them bring in their completed sheets and pool the data they have collected. What can they discover or deduce about the times of day that certain products are advertised? Why would producers advertise (say) fast foods around 6 pm, children's toys between 4 pm and 6 pm or home products between 11 am and 12 noon? Help the children to understand that they are being specifically targeted when they watch TV at certain times.

When will we advertise it?

Following on from the above activity, have groups of children select a product and decide when it would be best to advertise this product on TV and why they made this decision. Discuss the different categories that advertisers use to appeal to different audiences; for example, it looks good, it will make you happy/sexy/beautiful/younger, or be like the famous stars or everyone is buying it, and so on. Identify which one applies to advertising the selected product. Have the children storyboard an advertisement for their product and present this to the rest of the class.

What do you watch when?

Have each child prepare seven spreadsheets with hourly timeslots during the day from 6 am to 9 pm down the side and columns across the page headed with the names of different family members. Write a different day of the week across the top of each worksheet. Over one week, have them write down what programs and channels each member of the family watched. Encourage children to have the rest of the family join in to help them with this activity! Ask them to bring the completed activity sheets in to class and collate and graph all the data. Discuss the findings with them in relation to what age groups watch what sorts of programs and channels at what times during the day and evenings. Do these change at the weekend? Does it make a difference if there is only one TV in the house, compared with those families who have several TVs? How would this information help producers in designing TV programs throughout the day and evening, and advertisers booking timeslots to advertise their products?

Producer for a day!

Based on the above information, divide children into groups with each group representing a different TV channel. Have them pretend that they are a producer for that channel and they have to design the program for a full day's TV viewing. What sort of programs would they put in the early morning and why? What would they program for the middle of the day and why? What programs would they put on after school, around 6 pm and in the evening? Why did they make these decisions? List the types of product that could be advertised at different times of the day.

Scripts and storyboards

View a short excerpt of a suitable soap opera or children's show. Analyse it with the children in relation to what sort of instructions the writer would need to put into the film script to let the actors know where and when to move and how to act out their

Experiment with different framing of subjects: wide shot, mid-shot and close-up.

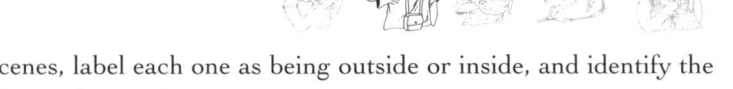

part. Number the scenes, label each one as being outside or inside, and identify the time or day in relation to the previous scene.

Write up a shooting script for the scenes, numbering the different shots, describing the action in each shot, and indicating what sort of framing the camera needs to take (i.e. extreme close up, close-up, mid-shot, long shot or wide shot).

Using the shooting script they have prepared, have children draw up a storyboard which will show what each shot would look like as a still picture.

What product is that?

Record the soundtrack or jingle behind several TV advertisements and play them back with just the sound and no visuals. Have the children identify what products are being advertised. Discuss which aspects of the music helped portray the message the producers wanted to send to the audience in each advertisement. Who is the targeted audience and was the music suitable for them? Why/why not?

Create your own jingle

In groups, select a product to be advertised, and create a jingle to be sung and/or played alongside the visuals. Think about what sort of product it is, what is the targeted audience, what sort of message you want to portray and so on. Use computer software, vocals, and tune and/or non-tuned percussion instruments to create the music.

Create a television advertisement jingle on tuned instruments.

Be a TV star!

Discuss with the children their favourite TV programs and their favourite characters in these programs. Using felt pens, crayons or a computer-drawing program, have them create themselves as their favourite character.

Extension: Have children take a photo of their face, print it out and paste it onto a piece of paper, and then draw themselves as their favourite TV character using their own face as the face of the character. Alternatively, have the children cut out a picture of their favourite TV star and paste a photo of their own face on top of the star's face. Write short paragraph about 'My life as a star!'.

Comic TV

Show an excerpt of a film that has a comic-strip parallel (e.g. superman or the phantom). Have children talk about a TV program they have seen recently, or a short excerpt shown in class, and then create the series of events in the program in comic-strip format. Share these with the rest of the class, and compare and contrast the film and the comic-strip versions.

Australia through the TV

Find excerpts of Australian films and advertisements featuring 'typical' Australia. Discuss what impression these would give overseas viewers about what sort of country Australia is, and what the people are like. Ask children if the excerpts are typical of the life they know in Australia. Prepare and video your own class advertisement which shows important features of the local community. If possible send this to a buddy school in a different part of Australia and have them do the same; discuss the similarities and differences between the lives and communities of the children in each of the schools.

Weather report

Have children observe the weather reports from different channels on TV. Discuss how they are similar or different. Identify the different symbols used in the weather report and have children find out what they mean. Identify the structure of the weather reports and compare each one, checking if they use the same or different structures. In groups, have children research, prepare, present and video a weather report, using different towns across Australia and different times of the year for each group. Present these to the rest of the class for feedback, reflection and comment.

Film

Children are very familiar with the concept of films, but many know little about the conventions, codes, signs and symbols used to convey emotions, messages, ideas and actions. As they view excerpts of suitable films, children can be challenged to look at the big picture and analyse how certain emotions are evoked in films, how characters are portrayed, and how they know what is going to happen by noting the lighting, framing, positioning of characters, camera angle, music and so on. This level of analysis can then be used in their own creations using a video camera and dramatised situations, which are then analysed to see how effective their use of these conventions was in conveying what they had set out to portray.

Censorship classifications

Have children examine posters or advertisements about current films and identify their classification. Find out about different classification categories from the Office of Film and Literature Classification website (www.oflc.gov.au). Discuss why they think the different classifications have been designated for these particular films. List the classifications that children are allowed to watch and those that are not allowed to be watched by children. Discuss what kind of action and events should not be included in children's films and why.

What film shall we see?

Ask children how they decide what films they will see. Where can they find out about the films? List the sources of information they could look up to find the content, reviews, classification and main actors in the films. Using a variety of media, see how much information children can find out about a newly released children's film.

Check out the poster!

View different film posters. Discuss what genre of film they are presenting. How do children know, just from the poster, that a film could be an adventure, a romance, a science fiction or a documentary? Identify the key elements in a film poster (title, actors, picture from the film, rating, and short sentence or hook to grab attention and make you want to see the movie) and have children design their own poster for a movie they have seen recently.

Which genre?
Collect posters or brochures about films from a variety of genres (romance, horror, documentary, drama, children's, science fiction and so on) or print off small posters from the relevant websites. Have children identify and classify the different genres and list reasons for coming up with these classifications. Divide the class into groups and have each group create a brief outline for a film using one of the genres and illustrate it with an imagined scene from the film.

More about genre
List four different genres and have children discuss in groups what setting, characters, story, costumes, music, props and title would be considered typical of a film in this genre. Present their lists to the rest of the class using expression and dramatisation.

Match the genre
Identify five different genres of film with which the children are familiar. Divide the class into five groups, one for each genre, and have each group decide on two different titles for films within their genre. Write these all up on the blackboard or whiteboard and have the groups work out which title would fit best into which genre.

Have children identify the setting of different films.

In the beginning
Show excerpts from the beginning of several films and have children identify how much they can find out about the setting, era, characters, story, special effects, genre, music and so on of the film just from viewing the first few minutes of it. Have them each select one of the films and draw a picture or poster which shows as many of these aspects as possible, and then create some music on percussion instruments to be played as the picture is viewed.

Opening shots
Ask the children to choose a story they have written recently and create a picture or poster showing the title and key scene for the story, as though they were preparing to advertise it as a film. Have them think carefully about the setting, characters, framing and action portrayed in the picture so that key aspects of the story are represented in the title picture.

Film plots
Some film plots tend to be fairly similar within genres; for example, romance: man meets woman; they fight; they fall in love; they endure a crisis which challenges their love; and they make up and live happily ever after! Identify several genres with which the children are familiar and divide the class into groups, one per genre. Have each group prepare on a word processor a brief synopsis of a hypothetical film on four separate cards:
1. Introduction of characters and setting

2. Problem
3. Working through the problem
4. Climax
5. Resolution

Put all the cards from the different groups together and try to sort out the different stories and genres.

Wide angle and close-ups
View excerpts from suitable films which show the big picture with a wide-angle shot and then focuses in on a close-up of a subject. Compare the information and message conveyed in the wide-angle shot with what is conveyed using the close-up view. Draw both scenes and write about the different information given and why the producer has used these two approaches to the subject.

Big and small
Have children select a character from their favourite film and draw it as though taken from different frames, for example:
1. wide-angle shot
2. mid-shot
3. close-up
4. extreme close-up

Write a sentence under each picture describing why the producer used this particular framing technique.

High and low
View excerpts of films that show different camera angles of the same subject — that is, viewing them from above, from below and at eye level. Discuss what messages are being portrayed using the different angles; for example, in the movie *Stuart Little*, at times the parents are viewed from below, the cat is viewed from eye level and Stuart is viewed from above to show the contrast in size. Have children select a favourite character from a film and draw it as though filmed from above, from below and at eye level, and write a sentence about why the subject is viewed from a different angle in each picture.

Audio and visual
View a few excerpts of films where the music is an important aspect of communicating what is happening in the story. Play an excerpt without any sound, just the visuals. Discuss what is happening. Play just the sound with no visuals from another excerpt, and discuss what the children think is happening. Identify how the music can be an important factor in telling a story, setting a scene, portraying an emotion, foretelling what will be happening and so on. Show the first excerpt, and have children create their own music using classroom percussion instruments, as a backing track to the film, to describe the emotion or what is happening in the music. Draw a picture to show what could be happening in the film, as they listen to the second excerpt without the visuals. Watch and listen to the two excerpts and discuss

the children's music and drawings in relation to what they saw and heard in the films.

One-liners
Collect a series of newspaper or Internet advertisements for films, which have a one-liner telling briefly about the film. Write up the one-liners onto separate pieces of paper and then blank these out on the advertisements. Have the children match the one-liners with the advertisements. Discuss how the visual information in the advertisement helped them be able to do this. Have them create their own one-liners for their favourite movies. Share these with the rest of the class and ask the children to guess which movie is represented by the one-liner.

What's the plot?
Discuss the plot of a movie that the children have all seen recently. Identify the characters and the setting, and then write down how it started, what the problem was, how this was worked through, the climax to the movie and the resolution to the problem. Discuss these actors in relation to a movie of a different genre and see if each genre follows the same format.

Plotting ideas
Have each child cut out an object or person from a magazine or newspaper. In groups share the pictures and create an oral story that includes action involving all the pictures. Using the visual clues from the pictures, children will need to identify the characters of the people, the setting, the motivation for the action, how it will start, the problem to be solved, steps towards solving the problem, the climax and the resolution of the problem. Present the story orally to the rest of the class.

What do you see?
Show a film excerpt, without the sound, of two people talking (e.g. two girls talking and pointing to a group of boys). Ask the children to write down what they think the girls were talking about, and then share their answers. Note that although they all saw the one set of images, interpretations of the images differ. Show the excerpt again, with the before-and-after sections of the film and with sound, to put it into context and discuss how the 'correct' interpretation was presented on film when the images were seen in context.

Light and dark
View several excerpts of film showing light and dark being used to represent certain characteristics; for example, dark can portray fear, sadness and evil, and bright lighting can portray happiness, love, trust, joy and goodness. Identify with the children what messages are being conveyed in the excerpts through the use of lighting, even without any music or words.

Colours and characters
Brainstorm with the children the role that colours have in conveying the character of a person in a film, for example, black can convey the feeling of evil, white can represent goodness, and red can portray danger. Identify characters in films who are dressed in a specific colour which represents their character. Note that in more

recent times there has been a change from black being evil (e.g. in the use of the white witch in the *The Lion, the Witch and the Wardrobe* as an evil being). Discuss why these colours are used and what emotions and characters can be portrayed by the use of different colours.

'Clothes do not make the man'

Show the children short excerpts from films of different genres and eras. Have them identify as much information as possible about the characters of the people shown just by observing their costumes and props. If possible, show the same character in several costumes in the same film. Discuss if the change in costume confirms or negates the character and information identified from the first costume they wore. In groups, have children write a character description of a selected person (past, present or fictional) and dress up one child in their group to represent this person. Reflect on how important the role of costume is in portraying character in film.

Create a video

A class video may take a whole term to complete. It could be a documentary about an excursion or other school event, or about a topical issue the children are researching, or it may be based on a story written by an individual, a group or the whole class. This project will need to be planned carefully in advance, and each of the children should have a particular task for which they are responsible. A planned audience for the completed production is also important.

Creating a class video.

Include the following processes in the preparation and implementation of the video:

- Watch a variety of different genres of film excerpts and discuss the particular styles, conventions, codes and representations used.
- Brainstorm ideas or issues that could be included in the video.
- Spend time in groups or individually working these ideas into a format which is then briefly presented to the whole class.
- Vote to determine some of the most popular ideas or stories.
- Decide to go with one particular story, or divide the class into groups and have each group follow through with one of the stories, ideas or issues.
- Organise the different jobs and roles to be undertaken in the project, for example producer, director, camera person, publicity officer, sound person, actors, costume designer and assistants.
- Ensure camera and sound people know how to use the equipment; provide them with short activities to practise skills such as composition, framing, lighting, angles, sound recording and sound effects.
- Experiment with and practise interviewing, dramatising, recording and videoing ideas, and encourage the children to be creative in their use of the camera, sound, lighting and action. Play the recorded excerpts back to the group for feedback and to allow further ideas to develop.

- Develop a storyboard of the main action to occur in the video; this could include the basic sequence of shots drawn in comic-strip style, paintings or as a series of photos.
- Share ideas and storyboard, and brainstorm for any further ideas; ensure there is an attention-grabbing opening, a clear development of story, a climax and a well-rounded closing section.
- Create more detail in the storyboard to include these further ideas; finalise the storyboard.
- Work out where the scenes are to be shot, walk around the area and finalise angles, lighting, composition and framing.
- Create a shooting script which could include three columns: 1. Shot number; 2. Action to be shot; and 3. Audio to be heard. In the 2nd column include angles (close-up/medium/wide-angle shots to be used), framing, lighting, composition of shots and so on as well as actions to be shot. In the 3rd column include the sound effects and music to be heard.
- If there is to be dramatisation or narrative, create a film script which show who says what, when, how and where.
- Work out sets, costumes and props to be used where relevant.
- Design and print an attractive sleeve jacket for the video case.
- Prepare an equipment checklist of all equipment required for the shoot and who is responsible for getting it ready and using it.
- Determine if there are video-editing equipment and/or skills available, or if the first shoot will be the final shoot. On Macintosh computers, iMovie is a very easy video editing program which comes with Operating System 10 (OSX) and which most children could learn to use.
- Check that everything and everyone is ready for the shoot.
- Set aside a significant amount of time for the shoot; always allow much more time than initially planned!
- Shoot the video.
- Edit it!
- Advertise it!
- Launch it! This is really important as it affirms all the creative hard work the students (and teachers) have put into producing the video and lets others share in their creativity.

Photography

This area of media is perhaps one of the most familiar in which children can be involved. It is important to move them away from the 'happy snappy' shots and think about the framing, lighting, positioning and cropping of the subject to convey certain messages. As well as involving children in classroom photography activities, take them to a photographic exhibition and have them see and learn about the works of photographers and analyse these in relation to what they have learned about photography.

What sign is that?

Have children photograph different signs and symbols around the school and community, print them out and share them with the rest of the class. Have children identify what each sign means and whether the symbol could change its meaning if the context changed.

Big picture, close-up

Have children identify a subject and take a photo of it, firstly within the larger context as a wide-angle picture, and then frame it close-up to convey particular information or a message about the subject. Print and display the two photos and write a paragraph about why the different frames were selected, and what different information is given about the subject in each photo and why some information was deleted in the close-up.

Angles

Have children select a subject (i.e. flower, pet, friend, family member and so on) and then take photos from different angles (e.g. eye level, from above looking down on them, and from below looking up). Print these out and write a short paragraph about what message each angle could portray about the subject.

Framed landscapes

Collect a series of photographs of landscapes. Prepare three mats of different sizes (to serve as frames) which can be put over the landscape:

1. Use a narrow mat to frame the full landscape.
2. Use a medium mat to frame a mid-sized object within the landscape.
3. Use a wide mat to frame and focus attention onto a small object in the landscape.

Experiment with the different mats on each of the landscape photos and have children discuss what they see in each landscape with the different mats. Discuss the fact that what we see in a picture is often influenced by the framing of the subject.

Cropping

Discuss what was learned in the previous activity, and then have children take a photo of an object in a setting. Ask them to download the photo onto the computer, print out the original, crop about half the landscape around the object and print the photo; and then crop the photo until just the object with a little of its setting is seen and print this off. Display the three photos and write about what each photo shows about the object and its setting.

What's outside?

Select a photograph of an action shot or landscape. Cut a piece of paper the same size as the photo and cut out a square to create a frame to show one section of the photo. Put this over the photo and ask children what they see, and then what they think might be on the rest of the photo that they cannot see. Discuss how photographers and film makers sometimes show a close-up and let the audience imagine what is outside the frame. Have children cut out a picture from a magazine, paste it onto a piece of blank paper and draw what is outside the picture.

Cropping helps to highlight the subject.

Light and dark
Have children photograph an object or a person in bright sunlight, and then again in shadows and dim light (without using flash). Encourage them to reflect on any differences they can see visually and whether the lighting of the object or person changes the character, feeling, mood or message of the photo. Ask them to write down their responses to the two photos and print these out, displaying them under the photos.

Describing my day
Use photographs to show what happens in each part of a typical school day. Print these out, put them in order and write a caption for each photograph.

I am me!
Have each child learn how to take a still photo, scan or download it onto the computer, and transfer it into a word-processing program. Ask them to write a short paragraph describing their lives, interests, homes, hobbies and family under the photos. Display these around the room.
Extension: Print off the picture separate from the text for each child. Mix up the photos and the text and have the children match the text to the correct photo.

Rule of thirds
Let children experiment with the traditional rule of thumb for composition (i.e. the rule of thirds). Have them look through the viewfinder of a camera and imagine two vertical lines and two horizontal lines spaced evenly across the picture they see (like a noughts-and-crosses grid). Ask them to move the camera so that the main element on which they are focusing, such as the eyes of a person in a portrait or the horizon

Horizontal line two thirds down picture.

Horizontal line half way down picture.

in a landscape picture, is on or near where the lines intersect. When the subject or other important parts of the composition are placed in any of these four points, the picture will end up having a satisfying feeling to it, with the viewer's eye going straight to the focal point. Ensure the horizon runs along one of the horizontal (rule of thirds) lines and is not directly in the middle of the photo. Take pictures using this rule, and then take others of the same subject, placing it directly in the centre of the picture. Compare the two versions of the same subject, and discuss which works best and why.

Check your viewpoint

Have children experiment with taking a subject from different viewpoints. Ask them to select an object and take it from eye level. Then have them take more shots of it from different viewpoints: above, below, from the side, closer, further away and so on. Print out the photos and discuss how the different viewpoints can change the overall message in the picture and give a different interpretation of the subject.

Fill the frame

As children are photographing a subject, have them experiment with taking photos of it from different distances and/or using a zoom lens to fill the frame with the subject. Print these out and discuss the differences in audience focus in the different photos and which distances worked well and which didn't. Alternatively, using a digital camera, take a wide-angle view of a subject, download it into the computer and experiment with cropping the subject, firstly so that there is a large amount of extra picture around the subject, and then repeatedly cutting away a little more from the subject until finally the subject fills the frame completely. Compare the different photos and decide which one gives the best message about the subject. Print this out and write a few sentences about the techniques used to produce the picture.

Lines, repetitions and patterns

When composing an image, have children look for lines that draw the viewer's eye through the photo. These can be lines on a playing field, rows of trees or houses, power lines, tall buildings and so on. Look also for patterns and repeated images in landscapes and other pictures and include these in the photo to add depth and interest. Encourage children to explore the use of symmetry and asymmetry when composing a photo. When they have taken several photos using these guidelines, ask them to print them out and write about the techniques they used to create the photos.

Foreground, middle ground and background

Display a variety of landscape photos or pictures, some with foregrounds and some without. Talk about the concept of foreground, middle ground and background. Discuss which photos work best and why having some foreground in the front of the picture can add to the depth and effective composition of the image. Ask children to take a photo of a landscape including an interesting foreground and one without a foreground. Print them out and write a few sentences about their thoughts on the procedure and product.

Surprise!

Encourage children to take photos from extraordinary viewpoints or angles; for example, take a landscape through a side-view mirror of a car, or take a portrait of someone through a mirror or lying on the floor facing up to the camera.

Up or down?

Ask the children to select several subjects around the playground or inside the classroom. Have them take each subject, first holding the camera horizontally (landscape) and then vertically (portrait). Print out the photos or download them to the computer and have them decide which orientation worked best for which subject.

As a group, discuss if there is a general rule of thumb for when to take horizontal photos and when to take them vertically. Prepare a poster that explains visually and through words what they have learned about the orientation of photos.

Experiment with using landscape and portrait formats.

Light and shade
A photo can be enhanced by the use of effective lighting. Have children experiment with taking photos of a subject outside at different times of the day. Assist them to discover that on a clear day, the early morning and late afternoon light often has a yellow–orange glow and angles of shadows are generally longer, which can add depth and interest to the subject. In the middle of the day, if the sun is bright, the shadows become shorter, the light becomes brighter and harsher, contrasts are strong and colours tend to become more natural. If the sky is overcast, shadows will be much lighter and there is usually less contrast. Print, document and display their findings about the effect of light and shade during the day on a subject.

Angle of light
The angle that light strikes an object will change the mood and message of the photo. Have children experiment with placing a strong light to the back, at the front, at the top and at the sides of different subjects and take photos of each subject using four different lighting angles. Print the photos or download them onto a computer, compare them and discuss which light worked best for different subjects. Write a few sentences about what they learned and publish this information with illustrations.

Shoot a drama
When children have practised a dramatisation of a favourite story, have them take photos of a sequence of actions throughout the story. Ask the children to place these in the correct order and write a caption for each photo on a separate piece of paper. **Extension:** Mix up the photos and the captions and have the children put them in the correct order, matching the photos with the captions. (The dramatisation can also be videoed for feedback and reflection.)

Comparing cultures
Collect a selection of photos showing different cultures and countries. Ask the children to comment on what they can find out about the culture or country by looking at the photos. Compare these with similar photos of Australia; for example, if there is a photo of a Vietnamese family, find a photo of a multi-generational Australian family to compare the cultures and countries.

Print
Design and production of print media needs to be carefully undertaken to ensure clarity and legibility, with diagrams being bold and simple, lettering and fonts clear and large enough to read by the selected audience, the format uncluttered and conveying the message effectively, colours carefully used and the text suitable to the audience. For example, if it is a poster advertising an upcoming school event in a multicultural school, consider using several languages. Analysis of concepts such as design, layout, use of fonts and space, content of text, publishing and displaying techniques need to be learned through instruction, demonstration and practical activities.

Signs and symbols

Signs and symbols are a shorthand way of conveying a message. Select a sign or symbol, for example the letter *X*, and identify different contexts, cultures and meanings given to this letter. Some examples might include:

- a kiss at the end of a letter;
- a wrong answer in a test;
- 'X' to mark the spot where treasure is buried on a map.

A cross in different settings and contexts may represent a church, death or a crossroads. Make a list of signs and indicate if they can convey different messages in different contexts.

Character signs

Look at crests, logos, coats of arms and so on and discuss how symbols are used to portray the character of a person or company. Brainstorm positive words to describe each child in the class. Have each of the children create their own coat of arms, logo or crest to portray their character strengths. Display these around the classroom along with a photo of the child.

Print advertisements

Collect a variety of child-appropriate magazines and have each group look through one, identifying for what age group and sex the magazine is targeted. Have them explain how they know this. Ask them to identify and write down comments about each advertisement in relation to:

- what product it is advertising;
- if there is a photo or image of the product in the advertisement;
- how it is advertised;
- whether or not the product matches the sex and age group for which they think the magazine is targeted;
- any other general comments about the advertisement, the product and the appropriateness or otherwise for the targeted consumers.

Display the answers to these questions, along with the advertisement, in the classroom.

Who? What? Where? When?

In small groups, discuss a recent event that has been on the news. Write an opening paragraph for a news story, covering the main points (Who? What? Where? When? Why?) succinctly. Read an actual account of the news story and compare their paragraph with that written by the journalist. What differences or similarities were there?

Colours and the message

Find or create some black-and-white drawings of people. Make duplicate copies of each drawing. Have children colour in one drawing using bright colours and the other drawing using dark colours, and then write a description about the character portrayed in each drawing. Discuss how the use of different colours may influence the representation of characters in pictures.

What did she say?
Examine a comic strip with the class and discuss the use of speech bubbles to let the reader know what each person in the cartoon is saying. Collect a number of photos, cartoons or pictures about a variety of people in different situations. Photocopy them and distribute them to the children. Ask them to think about what each person in the picture is saying and to write what they are saying in a speech bubble above their heads. (**Note:** This can be an effective introduction to the use of speech quotation marks in a literacy lesson.)

Caption it!
Collect a series of pictures (from magazines, drawings, artworks or photographs) and share one or two with the class, asking them to suggest a suitable succinct caption for the picture(s). Photocopy and distribute a variety of these pictures to the children and have them write a caption for their picture. Alternatively, have them photograph an event or interaction in the playground or classroom, print it out and type a caption under it to explain what is happening. The captions may be humorous or purely descriptive.

Caption the family
Ask children to take a photo of their family and bring it to class. Have them paste it onto a piece of paper and create a caption for the photo, and then write a sentence about each person in the photo.

Having a great time!
Share a variety of postcards from different countries with the children. Discuss what are the similar aspects of the postcards (e.g. clear photos of significant icons, scenes or buildings of that country or city). Have the children create their own postcard using their own holiday photos or drawings, or by making a collage of suitable magazine pictures. On the back, have them write to a penpal, telling that person about themselves and where they live, referring to the picture on the front of the postcard.

Having a wonderful time — wish you were here.

Wrap it up!
Bring in a variety of boxes, packaging and wrappers for toys, food or other objects. Discuss with the children the key aspects of packaging, for example information about the product, picture or clear wrapping so the customer can see what the product looks like, large print for important information and colours used effectively. Have children design their own packaging for a selected toy, food or object and share with the class why they included certain aspects in their packaging.

Come to our show!
Using computer-generated or hand drawings, have children create invitations, brochures and posters to advertise a coming event such as the school assembly

performance, a sports carnival, a spell-a-thon, a school art exhibition or a concert. Design a logo and decide on what information should be included. Determine what is the most important information (this should be written large and towards the top of the page) and what information is not so important (this could be written smaller and towards the bottom of the page). Share the draft versions of the posters, brochures and invitations and encourage children to make comments about their effectiveness and what could be improved. Either decide on one poster, brochure and invitation, finalise it and make copies of it for distribution, or have each of the children finalise their own advertisement.

Create a cover
After children have written and published a story, have them design a cover for the story and publish it either by hand or using the computer.

Signs rule!
At the start of the year, decide cooperatively on classroom rules and have children create symbols to show each rule visually. Draw these or print them off on the computer and display them around the room, accompanied by written text to remind children what the symbols mean.

Flip the picture
Collect and share with the children several flip books which show an image in slightly different positions on each page; when the pages are flipped quickly, it appears as though the image is moving. Have the children create their own flip books, and then make up some music using percussion instruments or voices to accompany the sequence.

Sounds and a story
Read through a simple picture book and have children determine the characters and events. Let them experiment with a variety of classroom instruments to create suitable sounds to represent each of the characters and what is happening in the story. Encourage them to determine if they need to use loud or soft sounds, fast or slow sounds, regular or irregular sounds and/or high or low sounds to make the story accompaniment more effective. Record the reading of the story with the sounds and play it back. Discuss how effective the sounds were in representing the story.

See a story
After children have written a story, encourage them to create pictures to depict what happened in the story, so that it is told through pictures. (**Note:** Have children who are visual-spatial learners create the series of drawings and then write the story. You may be surprised at the quality of written work they produce if they have done the drawings first!) Have them use the pictures to tell the story orally to the rest of the class or to a younger grade.
Extension: Give each child one of the pictures and have each child tell what happened in the story before and after the picture.

How tall are you?
Take full-length photos of each child in the class and create a display of these photos, Write captions under each picture detailing the name, height, weight (if this won't

embarrass children) and favourite pastime of the child. Order them from tallest to smallest, or from lightest to heaviest or by grouping together those with similar favourite pastimes.

Focal point

Have children create a poster about themselves, their pet, a member of their family or their favourite TV character. Ask them to position a picture of the subject so that it is the focal point of the poster, and then place information and other pictures telling about the subject around the main picture, ensuring that they do not detract from the picture.

Calendar

Create a class calendar for the next year, by collecting photos of the class taken over the current year showing them involved in a variety of different activities. Ensure that a caption is included for each photo. Publish the calendar and, if possible, make copies so that each child can have one.

Media stereotypes

Ask children to bring in pictures from a variety of printed forms (e.g. newspapers, magazines, comics, brochures, and recent and old children's picture books). Have them identify the people in each of the pictures and talk about who they are, where they are from and what they are doing. Discuss whether or not children think that this is a true representation of these types of people, why the production manager has created these images of people and why they are represented this way.

Children can analyse pictures and text from a variety of printed forms.

Heroes and villains

Have children collect representations of heroes and villains from storybooks, newspaper articles, films and comic books. List the visual characteristics of them and discuss if there are any clear stereotypes in any of the representations; for example, is the villain a dark-skinned male with a scar on his face? Is the hero blonde, handsome/beautiful, rich? Encourage the children to write and illustrate a story reversing the common stereotypes of heroes and villains.

Create a brochure

Have children create a brochure which clearly conveys a message; for example: the importance of involvement in the arts in a child's life; the importance of eating healthy food rather than junk food; why road safety rules are important; or what your child needs to know when he/she comes to kindergarten. Give them the alternative of creating their brochure on the computer or by hand. Share the completed brochures with each other for reflection and comment. Make copies and distribute them to the targeted audience for comment and feedback.

Front page news

Bring two different newspapers with the same cover story to class and share these with the children. Have them identify how each paper has told the story, in relation

MMADD about the arts

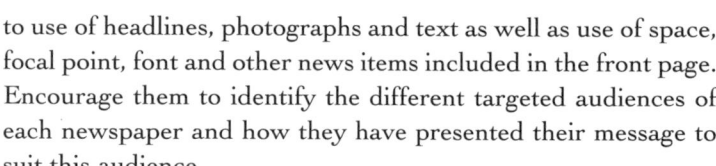

This is a poster designed during a social studies program on rainforests.

to use of headlines, photographs and text as well as use of space, focal point, font and other news items included in the front page. Encourage them to identify the different targeted audiences of each newspaper and how they have presented their message to suit this audience.

My favourite things!

Collect a variety of magazines and other print media texts (suitable for the age group in your class) and have them select and cut out pictures that show their favourite food, hobbies, clothes, people, and so on. Ask them to create a collage of these pictures and write a few sentences below their collage explaining the process and product.

Extension: Have them select pictures that are in a certain category (e.g. fast-food advertisements, animals and famous people) and create a collage on a theme; and then write about the process and product.

Showing what we learned

Have children design and make posters to show what they have learned in other key learning areas.

Radio

In past decades, most classrooms had access to the radio and a speaker was attached above the blackboard so everyone could listen to the ABC music programs or science lessons and so on. Nowadays, the radios are more likely to be part of a small, compact CD/radio/cassette player and rarely used as a teaching resource. However, radio is an important aspect of media education.

If playing a radio program to the whole class you will need to check that the sound is loud enough for every child to hear — perhaps a plug-in speaker could assist with this. Radio is a very important part of many homes with music, news, traffic reports, documentaries, sport and other programs being broadcast constantly throughout the day. Children need to become aware of the different genres of radio and the conventions and codes used to convey messages using this medium as well as the techniques used in interviewing, scripting, special effects, playing music and advertising on radio.

Sound effects

Have the children find objects around the room which make a clearly identifiable sound or create a sound with their voices or body percussion. Have each of the children record their sounds onto an audio tape and then have the class identify each sound and how it was made, and write or draw how the sound was made.

Title song

Many radio programs have clearly identifiable signature tunes that are played at the start of the program. Record several of these and have the children identify them. Have the class create their own chant or short song as the signature tune for different parts of their day (e.g. recess, maths lesson, sport and quiet reading time). Record these and play them at the appropriate times during the day.

Whose voice is that?

Have a group of children record their voices saying a few sentences. Play them back and ask the rest of the class to identify whose voice it is and discuss how they knew this. Listen to audio excerpts from TV and radio shows and try to identify who is speaking.

Radio interview

Decide on one or more people in the school or local community whom children would like to interview. Have them prepare the topic, decide whom they will interview, prepare the questions and set up the interview. They need to decide why they are doing the interview — that is, to provide new information, to entertain, to let others know about this person or to educate their audience about a certain topic. They may also interview people to ascertain responses to a decision or event, to bring out an emotional aspect of a news item or topic, or to make their audience think about something they may never have considered before.

Recording vocal sounds onto an audio disk.

When the children are ready to do the interview, have them create and complete a checklist to ensure everything has been covered, for example:

- Have I done my background research to get the most from the interview?
- What are the three main points I wish to make from the interview?
- Have I practised doing the interview with parents or friends so I can gain confidence?
- Where will the interview be held and how long will it be?
- Has the person/people been contacted and are they ready for the interview?
- Has all the relevant equipment been organised using the correct procedures?
- Who is doing the recording and do they know how to work the equipment?
- Have I decided on a great opening question and a question to round up the interview and close it off?
- Are my questions short, clear and to the point?
- Have I worked out how I will present myself before and during the interview? That is, start with a smile, put the interviewee at ease by chatting and letting him/her ask any questions before the recording session, project my voice and speak clearly when asking the questions, show attentive listening through affirming body language when the interviewee is talking, and avoid rustling papers if using notes.
- Have I decided on one or more strategies to use if the interviewee talks too much, won't talk much or goes off on a tangent?
- How do I feel about doing the interview? This will often come across in the interview, so, generally, the more enthusiastic, practised and relaxed I am about doing it, the better the outcomes!

Interviewing peers on a given topic.

When the recording is completed play it back to the rest of the class for feedback and comments.

Traffic report

Listen to excerpts of traffic reports from different radio stations. Compare and contrast the detail, presentation, areas covered, use of expression, live versus scripted presentation and so on. Have children stand near the road in the school playground before the start or after the end of school (check they are safely away from any cars, and have permission forms completed to let parents know children may be late or need to come to school early). Have them observe any traffic problems on the road outside the school. Ask some children to write down notes and then present a scripted report about the situation. Ask others to present a live report about what is happening and have it recorded. Compare the two types of presentation and discuss what strategies the different children used to make the report sound interesting and informative.

What sound is that?

Record or obtain a series of audio clips (Microsoft PowerPoint has some of these) which are of recognisable sounds, for example a fire engine, glass breaking, applause, a rooster crowing, a scream or laughing. Play them to the children and have them identify what the sounds could represent. Let the children select several sounds and write a story that incorporates these sounds. Develop the text into a radio story and use these and other sound effects to bring the story to life as it is read. Record it on audio tape and have children reflect and comment on its effectiveness.

Take a mike for a walk

Select a suitable recording device (portable cassette player, laptop, iPod with recording accessory and so on) and have a small group of children take it with them on a walk around the playground. Ask them to record sounds during their walk, and then play them back in the classroom. Have children identify the sounds recorded, and then create a story for radio using the sounds as part of the story. Record the whole story and sounds, and play it back for reflection and feedback.

Computer and electronic media

Every school has computers that can be used by the children. How these are allocated across classrooms and the library varies from school to school. Some schools have a computer room where every child can work on a computer at the one time. Others allocate a certain number to each classroom so that pairs or small groups of children can work together on the one computer. This set-up allows children to use the computers in spare or planned classroom time, as a reward or as part of a learning centre.

A key factor in the use of computers in the classroom is the professional development of the teacher. Try to use the computer as much as possible in your own preparation and teaching, to model its effective use to children, and participate in professional development courses to upgrade your skills in areas in which you feel challenged.

There is a growing chasm between the children who have had access to computers since they were very young, are confident with a variety of software and can surf the Internet for hours, chatting, emailing and finding information, and those who do not have a computer in the home, may not be familiar with any program and have never worked on the Internet. Be aware of such inequities in your classroom and try to encourage those with few skills in this area to have equal if not more time on the computers, compared with those who are very confident in using them. Maybe you could set up a peer-tutoring system and have those who know about using them work with those who are not so confident, but ensure that the skilled children do not do all the work instead!

Creating signs

Have the children create their own signs on the computer for different instructions around the classroom or school; for example: Do not place books here, Quiet while reading, or Switch computer off when not in use. Share these with the class and discuss how clearly they convey the desired message.

My word!

Introduce the children to using Microsoft Word or another word-processing package. Once they have mastered one specific technique or tool, have them learn another one. These activities should be applied to real-life experiences, so children can see their application to publishing stories, posters and other literacy genres. Skills for children to master could include:
- put a story they have written on a word processor;
- check the spelling; change misspelled words if necessary;
- edit and save the document;
- use the 'save as' feature and understand why it is different from 'save';
- change the font of some or all of the text;
- change the format of the font and/or paragraphs;
- add tabs;
- add graphics;
- wrap text around graphics;
- add word art to a document;
- use 'find and replace';
- set margins;
- change document to landscape;
- add headers and/or footers;
- create a table;

- sort the information in a table;
- use different preset styles in a document;
- for longer stories, learn how to build an index and a table of contents;
- create columns for the text;
- create a newspaper or magazine article in columns with graphics;
- create a story and then give it to a friend who makes changes using the 'tracking changes' and 'adding comments' tools;
- create a 'merge' document and print customised letters to all the children in the class.

PowerPoint

Have the children create a PowerPoint presentation about a topic they have researched. As they become more confident in using this software, have them include another tool or use a more challenging technique each time they prepare a PowerPoint presentation, for example:

- use text boxes to write in text about the topic;
- create a master page which can be used for each page of the presentation; add a footer and page numbers to the slides;
- change the original set-up, for example add or delete a slide, move a slide, and change the layout;
- add graphics to the slide, either from clip art or from photos they have taken;
- print out the presentation in greyscale or colour, one slide a page or with several slides per page;
- create a new design template;
- use a colour scheme;
- add transitions to the presentation;

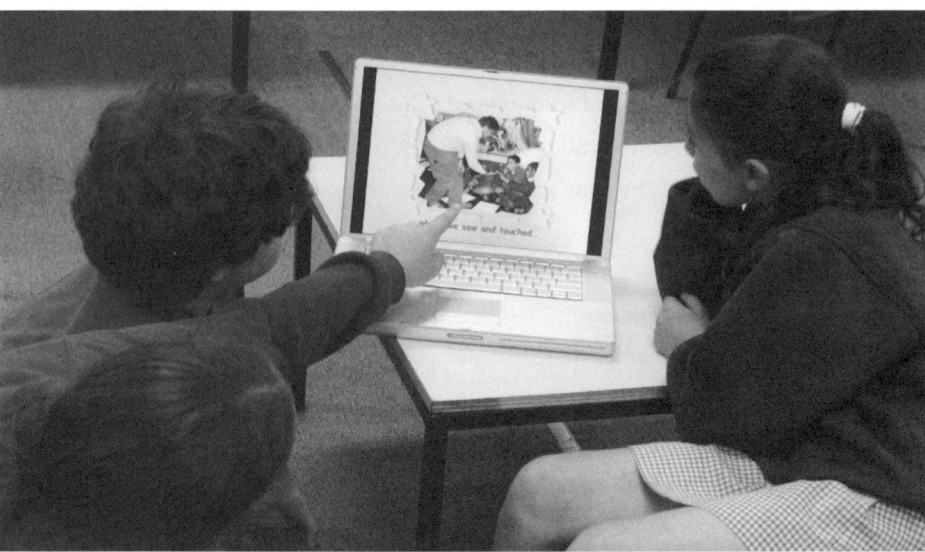

Have children create a PowerPoint presentation about a topic they have researched.

- add animations to each slide;
- add a hyperlink to a slide;
- set the timings manually;
- set the timings to show the slides automatically;
- add a sound clip to one slide;
- add a sound track to the whole presentation;
- set up a self-running show;
- add in tables and/or charts;
- turn the PowerPoint presentation into a QuickTime movie.

Ideas for PowerPoint presentations:
- sharing special moments from a sports carnival;
- advertising a school concert;
- documenting an integrated arts project;
- publishing a story with graphics;
- demonstrating how to do long division;
- introducing the children in the class to each other;
- explaining the steps in a dance;
- sharing people's view on a topic;
- presenting a research project.

Spell this!
Type correctly spelled words on the computer that are used often but sometimes misspelled. Use a large font, add appropriate graphics, print these off and display them around the room.

Our logo!
Examine different logos from well-known brands. Discuss the shapes, fonts, words and colours used, and the simplicity or otherwise of the design. In groups brainstorm each child's personalities, interests and skills and then decide on a logo which represents the commonalities of the group. Design a simple logo on the computer, print it out and display it on each of the children's desks.

Happy birthday!
Give each child another child's birth date. On that day, have the child send the birthday child an appropriate e-card.

Congratulations!
When one or more children have achieved success in a task (e.g. sport, music or academic work) select a few children to send them appropriate e-cards or emails with graphics attached to congratulate them. Make sure that over a set time period, for example a month, every child has both sent and received at least one electronic card.

Music media
Have the children explore the variety of shareware and freeware music software available for download on the Internet and encourage them to learn how to use the software and to create and play their own music. If the school has the resources, use commercial software to learn more about music using the computer.

Art media
There is an amazing amount of commercial, freeware and shareware art software available for children to use to explore a variety of art concepts and skills. Give them the opportunity to create their own artworks using the computer, and then share the process and products with the rest of the class.

General media activities
These activities may be applied to, or integrated across, a variety of media forms.

What do you like?
Interview each of the children to find out what form of media they like best and why, and if there are any forms of media they do not like and why. Have the children collate their answers in a graph and make a list of the reasons for and against each form of media. Ask them to repeat this activity with older and younger children and compare the lists and graphs from the different age ranges. Are there any differences or similarities? Ask the children why they think this is so.

Where is it set?
Select a variety of media texts (film excerpt, picture book, TV excerpt, photograph and so on) and ask the children to identify the particular time, place and/or culture in which the text is set. Have them write a few sentences describing how they know it was set in this particular context.

How did it feel?
Using a variety of media texts, or just focus on one, have the children describe verbally, graphically or in written words what emotions were evoked, and what techniques were used by the producers to make them feel that way.

Create a feeling
Have the children select a form of media with which they feel comfortable and create the presentation of a feeling or emotion using this media. They will need to have learned about different techniques used to portray emotions in the different media, and practised using the media before attempting this activity.

Create an ad
Ask children to select a product or object and then create an advertisement for it using print, still photography, computer software or video, or a combination of these. Remind them of the different languages, codes, conventions and so on related to each of the media so that they can create a clear and relevant message in their advertisement, and target it to a particular audience.

Present a story

Encourage children to write a story that could be adapted for presentation using video, radio, still photography, comic strips or the computer. Work through the production steps of adapting the story to a script or storyboard, shooting, editing, reviewing and producing the final presentation. Share these with each other and have children comment on the content and structure of the presentation and how effectively they have used the techniques and conventions of the selected media to portray the story.

Surfing for the media

Have children use the Internet to find out as much as they can about the codes, conventions and language used in a selected form of media. Ask them to present the information they have found to the rest of the class, using that form of media.

How things have changed!

Collect a series of examples of different media from a variety of eras (e.g. posters, photos, advertisements, photos, film excerpts and radio clips). Select one form of media and show the different examples to the children, asking them to identify the cultural context of each example. Discuss how they were able to identify the differences and what techniques, conventions, costumes, voices, content, structure and so on were different from those used today.

Extension: Ask children to create a similar text but for today's audience. Discuss what sort of changes they need to make to do this.

Audiovisual procedures

After working through a set of procedures such as a recipe, doing a craft, borrowing a book from the library, playing a game or learning how to work a piece of equipment, have children create visual and/or auditory sequences explaining the procedures. This may be undertaken using the video camera with voice-overs, a series of still photos and written captions, drawings (computer-generated or freehand) and captions, or a PowerPoint presentation.

Using the Internet as a research tool.

Document the changes

Encourage children to use a variety or one selected form of media to document observed change in (say) a science experiment, a growing plant or chicks hatching. Have children present this with a verbal description accompanying the visual. This could be completed using drawings and a story to create a poster, a series of still photos and captions, a video movie with voice-overs, a radio report or interview with sound effects, or a PowerPoint presentation.

A day or hour in the life of . . .

As a class determine a set timeframe and have children identify what they do/did in a particular amount of time; for example 7 am–9 am: getting out of bed and going to school; 2 pm–4 pm: working at a science project in class, packing up, waiting for the bus and going home; 10 am–1 pm, Saturday: playing with friends and then going shopping. Have the children decide on the key actions and create a storyboard illustrating these aspects within the given timeframe.

Extension 1: Develop the storyboard into a video, sequence of photos or computer-generated drawings to tell the story of what happened in the designated timeframe.

Extension 2: Resequence the storyboard to create a different order of events and write a story based on this new sequence.

Walking in our suburb

Organise a walking excursion for the children around the local suburb. Have them take photos and video what they see as well as sketching aspects of their community. Back in the classroom, publish these photos, writing captions and stories about each picture. Ask them then to search the web for text and images representing that community, visiting local government, tourist and council websites. Compare the two sets of representations of the one community. Identify if they are the same or different, and if they are different why do they think this is so.

My favourite media text

Ask the children to decide on their favourite media text, for example comic, computer game, TV show, photograph or magazine; have them bring a sample of it to class and share with the rest of the children why they chose this particular piece of media.

Extension: Have children describe orally and/or in a written format how media affects their lives; what media they use for education, information, leisure and entertainment; and why they use and enjoy it. Encourage them to use the language of media in their explanations, and to discuss the use of images, music, sound and content.

Journalist for a day

Set aside a day, an afternoon or some non-school time for children to pretend they are journalists. They will need to decide what their article is to be about, select one or more relevant people to interview, take a photo of them, write up the story and publish it using a computer program.

Things to consider when writing for the media:

- Ensure the story includes all the information expressed clearly (i.e. include Who? What? Where? When? Why? and How?).

- Appeal to the readers' emotions (e.g. pride, joy, excitement, wonder and sadness).

- Make the writing clear, succinct, newsworthy and relevant to the target audience.

- Think about how it will be formatted in the final publication. Use a clear, large, succinct headline, write it in the present tense and include action verbs. Keep the text short and include the main message of the story in the opening paragraph, which should be no longer than 25 words. Make sure the most important information is presented in the first paragraphs and the least important information is included at the end. Use colourful, descriptive, specific words, put in an interesting quote, and avoid generalisations.

- Give the completed article to a friend to read for comment. Make any necessary changes.

- Add the appropriate photos with a suitable caption.
- Publish the story and photo; the class may decide to make this project into a class newspaper. If many copies are to be made, it would be cheaper to make them in black and white on a photocopier. However, if only a few copies are to be made, print them on a colour printer for maximum impact.
- This could also be made into a video or PowerPoint presentation using other forms of media.

SPRINGBOARDS FOR DISCUSSION AND APPLICATION

1. Select a theme and decide how you can teach the skills and content related to the theme using at least three different forms of media. Identify what children would need to know and be able to do prior to engaging in these activities. Describe the indicators and outcomes that could be used to assess children's learning in each of the forms of media. Write your ideas in lesson-plan formats.

2. Plan a series of media-related learning experiences to work towards achieving outcomes from another key learning area as well as from media, using at least one form of media and at least one other art form.

3. Design and create a poster, brochure, video or a PowerPoint presentation, suitable to be shown at a parents' meeting, arguing the importance of media education within the primary curriculum.

4. Write a unit of work on a selected theme that shows a clear understanding of how children can design, make and analyse media in the primary classroom.

FURTHER READING

ACT Department of Education and Training and Children's Youth and Family Services Bureau (1996), *Gateways: Information technology and the learning process — A collection of teacher practices from Australian schools*, Commonwealth of Australia, Canberra.

Bowen, W. (1996), *Citizens for media literacy*, Asheville, North Carolina, reported in Media Awareness Network, 2004.

Evans, R. (2002), *On air: A practical resource for today's viewing*, Australian Teaching Aids Publishing, Osborne Park, Western Australia.

Fatouros, C., Downes, T. & Blackwell, S. (1994), *In control: Young children learning with computers*, Social Science Press, Sydney.

Ferres, S. & Ferres, G. (1998), *Mouse art: Creating art on the computer*, McGraw-Hill, Sydney.

Mathieson, K. (1993), *Children's art and the computer*, Hodder & Stoughton, London.

NSW Department of School Education Curriculum Directorate (1997), *Computer-based technologies in the creative arts KLA*, Author, Sydney.

chapter five
Introduction to visual arts education

Every child is an artist. The problem is how to remain an artist once he grows up.
(Picasso)

Learning outcomes
By the end of this chapter, students will be able to:
- create a portfolio of work to show their understanding of the main elements and forms in visual arts;
- design a lesson plan to demonstrate how to teach a particular visual arts skill;
- develop a visual arts education program using art appreciation as a starting point for implementation in a selected primary classroom.

Introduction

Archaeologists can gather a significant amount of information about a civilisation just from its artworks! From the beginning of time, people have created artworks to tell stories; depict events, rituals, celebrations and achievements; and decorate their clothes, walls, floors, ceilings, and their cooking and eating utensils. From the first cave painting to the most recent graffiti, from ancient Chinese pottery to computer-generated art, from patterned rabbit-skin cloaks to the latest Armani suit, from a child's finger painting to the megamillion-dollar artwork in the local gallery, art has been used to communicate and to bring aesthetic pleasure into the lives of ordinary and important people.

Artworks reflect the ideas, attitudes, aspirations, perceptions, values and practices of the artists who create them and also the society, culture and context in which they live. Children need to engage in authentic art experiences that will allow them to learn about themselves and the world around them. As well as being an important factor of a child's aesthetic development, the visual arts are a vital vehicle for self-expression, learning and observation that children need to develop through their primary school years.

Designing, making and appreciating

When involved in a visual arts program, children should be given the opportunity to interpret and respond to their observations and experiences of the world around them, both real and fantasy, through designing, making and appreciating art. A quality, developmental visual arts program should allow children to develop their skills from making simple marks and symbols on paper, to designing and making sophisticated and creative representations of their world using well-practised skills.

Children should be given the opportunity to view and appreciate a range of artworks from different cultures and contexts, and learn about the development of visual arts through history, and history through visual arts. They should be exposed to a wide variety of types and styles of art and learn about other world cultures as well as their own through appreciating artworks from these cultures. Children will need to develop and use research skills to find out specific information about art and artists through the library and the Internet and be able to use the language of visual arts to discuss, analyse, interpret and respond to artworks.

Through these experiences they should learn to value the visual arts for aesthetic reasons as well as their being a medium to learn about the world around them and respond to artworks in an individual and unique way. They can also use the visual arts to express what they have learned in other key learning areas. In a quality visual arts program, children should be given the opportunity to experiment creatively with a wide range of materials to discover different ways of making artworks, and then select, design and arrange materials, graphics and techniques to enable them to express their ideas, observations and emotions.

As they learn to appreciate the artworks of both unknown and famous artists children can learn to discover meaning, form opinions and give reasons for their responses to the artworks. Such a visual arts program would provide children with

Introduction to visual arts education   Chapter 5

Collaged rainforest: Children can use the visual arts to express what they have learned in other key learning areas.

a sound foundation of knowledge, skills and understandings as they make and appreciate art.

Designing and making

The process of designing and making art is a valuable and rewarding activity and can be a rich learning experience. Children should be given the opportunity to explore a wide variety of materials, media and techniques to design and create their own unique artworks. Artworks can be designed and created to represent people, emotions, other living things, objects, places, spaces and events, and can be responses to stimuli such as music, pictures, sounds, stories, artworks, imagination and movement. Through designing and making art children can learn the language of visual arts and explore and discuss the effective use of tone, texture, line, space, shape and form in their artworks. They should be exposed to both two- and three-dimensional art-making activities, learning to paint and draw, design and make prints and photographs, as well as working with clay, collages, sculptures, ceramics, textiles and digital forms of art.

Appreciating

Children can appreciate artworks at different levels to help them make sense of what they see. Personal, reflective and spontaneous responses to artworks are valuable and help children understand their own and other people's art. They can respond about their personal likes and dislikes about the artwork, as well as analysing an artwork in terms of the use of colour, space, form, line, tone and patterns, or in terms of the style or era in which it was painted. They can explore the possible intentions of the artist though discussion or they can use visual arts, music, dance, drama or other expressive medium to respond non-verbally to the artwork.

Knowledge about relevant contextual art history and the language of visual arts can enrich and deepen children's

The process of designing and making art is a valuable and rewarding activity.

Let children visit the local or state art gallery to see the professional artworks exhibited.

appreciation of artworks. Children should be given the opportunity to appreciate the artworks of their peers as well as those of commercial and well-known artists. They can explore the Internet for user-friendly sites of artworks which can be shown and discussed. An important aspect of appreciating art is to have children visit the local or state art gallery to see professional artworks exhibited. Contact your local art gallery or museum to find out the procedures and costs involved for bringing children to see their artworks.

When appreciating artworks, whether a child's freshly completed painting, an illustration in a children's book, an abstract sculpture in the local community or a famous artwork in a gallery, discuss with them some of the following questions, as relevant:

- What is it?
- Who created it?
- What is it called?
- Why was it created?
- Was it created for a specific audience? If so, how do you know?
- What media and techniques were used to create it?
- In what historical, cultural and geographical context was it created?
- How do you know?
- What message and/or emotions does it convey?
- What might have happened before/after what is portrayed in the artwork?
- What elements of visual arts were used to convey this message?
- How does it compare with other artworks you have explored?
- What utilitarian use does it have, if any?
- What is your personal response to the artwork?

Subject matter in visual arts

When making and appreciating art, children can explore a variety of subject matter and forms in visual arts.

Subject matter

Quality visual arts programs encourage children to use a variety of subject matter in their artworks, which should be derived from their direct experiences of life and interests as well as from their imagination. Subject matter can include people, emotions, other living things, objects, places, landscapes and events and can be created from direct observation, from pictures or from unknown places, pretend and fantasy worlds. Children can begin with depicting the subjects realistically, and then extend their learning experience by examining different styles of artworks through history. They can consolidate this learning by depicting the same subject using a contrasting style (cubism, impressionism, geometric and so on).

(a) This pastel artwork shows members of family in the style of Picasso.

(b) This self-portrait is decorated with 'my favourite things'.

People

Children can learn to create artworks based on real and imagined people who are known or unknown to them and who come from different cultures and contexts. They can learn to draw portraits of themselves and others, by careful observation of each other, photographs and pictures. Show the children different artists' styles of portrait painting and compare and contrast the techniques and media used, and then have the children create their own portraits using a selected styles and medium. Portraits can be used to tell the viewer much about the subjects, including their personality, character, emotions, age and stage in life, culture and context.

Emotions

Children can use art to express their emotions and use their emotions as a stimulus for art. As they explore the different mediums, techniques and elements of art they can learn to find a way to communicate how they are feeling using visual expression. Some children will find it easier to draw what they are feeling and thinking than write or talk about it.

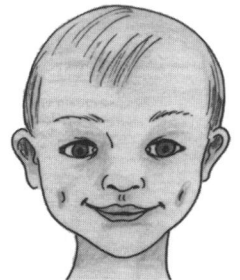

Other living things

As well as people, children can create artworks based on animals, birds, fish, reptiles, plants and so on. Encourage children to talk about their own pets, the different parts of animals, their texture, colour and shape and how these can be depicted using a selected medium. If possible allow the children to observe and touch the live subject and to create their artworks from observation; alternatively, provide a wide variety of pictures of living things as stimulus.

Title: *Unknown joy*; 'Unknown joy is a mystery but we keep trying to find it in the world around us' Jamie B.

MMADD about the arts

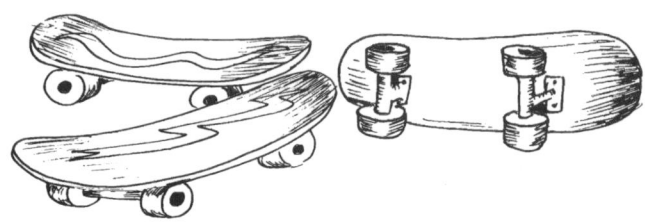

Title: *I am the independent falcon*. 'I am like the independent falcon who lives by itself and doesn't need anyone to follow. I am strong and I never give up.' Taha D.

Objects

Still-life artworks can be created using objects such as fruit, flowers, vegetables, rocks, toys, fabricated constructions and cultural objects as the stimulus. Create representations of these standing alone or place them in a selected context within the artwork.

Places and spaces

Have children examine artworks of landscapes and cityscapes in Australia and other countries and use these to stimulate creative artworks about known and unknown places; local, regional, national and international places; real and fantasy places, outer space and so on from a variety of other contexts and cultures.

Sketch of Sydney Harbour Bridge.

Events

Celebrations, events and festivals can be an exciting stimulus for visual arts lessons. Learn about them through direct experience, videos, Internet research, photos and pictures, and then create artworks depicting celebration rituals, sporting events, cultural events, historical and religious events, and so on from a variety of cultures and contexts.

Title: *The Country*: 'Australia is a very dry country, so I chose yellow and orange to show this. I hope that one day I can see a windmill in the country.' Jennifer L.

Wax resistant artwork depicting New Years Eve on Sydney Harbour.

Title: *My life rules*. 'This artwork represents my life because everything in it means something to me. The big heart stands for kindness. The four-coloured ball represents fun. The fish represents love and hate. The road signifies my love of cars.' Khader H.

Visual arts elements

When creating artworks, children should be encouraged to think about how they are using each of the elements that form the building blocks of art. These are discussed briefly below so teachers and children can use the language of art as they make and appreciate artworks.

Line

Lines give an artwork shape and are combined or used separately to create drawings, plans and sketches. They can be used to bring focus to an object or to emphasise it, define it or separate it from other objects.

Introductory learning experiences: Experiment drawing contours, life drawings, still life, buildings, squiggle pictures and so on.

Tone

The use of light and shade is often described as tone. Light can be bright and intense, focusing on, and emphasising, one side of an object, resulting in the other side being darker. The tonal quality of an artwork can be affected by the artist's use of light and dark colours.

Introductory learning experiences: Use a spotlight or lamp on an object to show how light on one side can cause darkness on the other side. Draw or paint the effect of light and dark on the subject.

Colour

Colours can be described as primary, secondary or tertiary.

- **Primary colours.** These are red, blue and yellow and from these (plus white and black) all other colours can be made.
- **Secondary colours.** These are made by mixing two primary colours together; yellow and blue = green, yellow and red = orange, and red and blue = purple.

Picasso self-portrait uses tone to express the artist's emotions.

MMADD about the arts

The colour wheel

The colour wheel shows warm and cool colours.

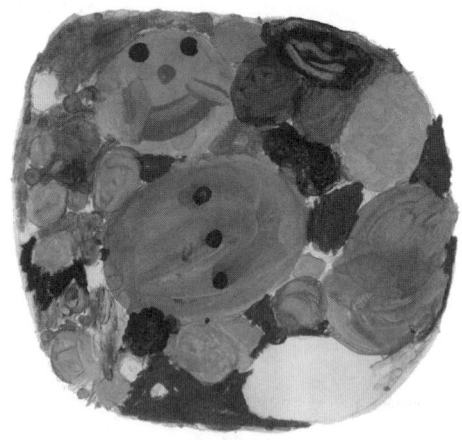

Title: *Me and the Universe*. 'I am the centre of the circle. The largest circle represents the world around me and the small circles represent the people that I know.' Fatoum El C

- **Tertiary colours.** These are brown and grey, and are created by mixing all three primary colours together.

  Differences in *hues* can be created by using different proportions of colour.
- **Complementary colours.** These colours are opposite on the colour wheel, for example yellow and purple, green and red, and blue and orange.
- **Analogous colours.** These colours are near each other on the colour wheel.
- **Cool colours.** These suggest coolness — they are blue, purple and green.
- **Warm colours.** These suggest warmth — they are red, yellow and orange.
- **Monochromatic colours.** These use only one colour plus white or black. A *tint* is created when white is added to a colour and a *shade* is created when black is added to a colour. (Tip: to remember the difference between a tint and a shade, *white* and *tint* have both the letter 'i' in them; *black* and *shade* have both the letter 'a' in them.)

Introductory learning experiences: Create secondary and tertiary colours, tints and shades. Create artworks exploring the use of each of these different categories of colour; for example, paint a winter scene using only cool colours and a beach scene using only warm colours.

Texture

All surfaces have a texture: some can be smooth and others can be rough, silky, sharp, prickly or bumpy. The impression of texture can be created in a two-dimensional artwork, and actual textures that can be felt can be achieved in a three-dimensional work of art. An impression of a three-dimensional texture can be taken by placing a thin piece of paper over the texture and rubbing a soft lead pencil over it.

Introductory learning experiences: Create rubbings and photos of actual textures (e.g. bark, cement, fabric and leaves); experiment with creating simulated textures using pencil, pen, printing, clay, wood and computer designs; and create collages with materials of different textures.

Shape

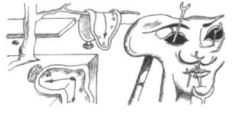

A shape is a flat, two-dimensional area defined by a boundary. Shapes can be regular or geometric such as circles, squares and triangles, or irregular such as the outline of a person or a tree. Shapes use lines to form boundaries and, as such, are two dimensional although they are often used to represent three-dimensional objects. They can be realistic, stylised or symbolic.

Introductory learning experiences: Draw or paint three-dimensional objects on a piece of paper concentrating on the outline and shape, and the positive (object) and negative (area around object) space.

Form

Form is a three-dimensional shape — the space that an object takes up in its environment. If viewed from different angles, the form of the object will appear to change.

Introductory learning experiences: Construct sculptures, carvings and papier mâché artworks. Draw them from different angles.

Space

The area between shapes and forms is called *space*. A challenge for artists is to draw or paint the space between three-dimensional objects or forms in a two-dimensional artwork. The use of perspective drawing can give a feeling of depth and reality to a two-dimensional painting or drawing. Space can be crowded or empty, and it can be positive or negative, depending on the intent of the artist.

Introductory learning experiences: Draw landscapes with a background, middle ground and foreground; create three-dimensional paper tole designs with three layers; examine paintings (e.g. from the Renaissance period) showing clear perspective (the further away an object is from you, the smaller it looks) and create similar artworks; and explore the use of negative and positive space in your own and others' artworks.

Pattern

Patterns are all around us in nature and can be used with great effect in artworks. Patterns can be symmetrical or asymmetrical, organised and geometrical or more free-flowing and irregular.

Introductory learning experiences: Create both geometrical and irregular patterns, using different printing techniques and on the computer; and explore the works of Escher and create similar artworks.

This black-and-white photo of power pylons was taken from below.

Composition and design in visual arts

Many of the design and compositional concepts discussed in Chapter 4, 'Introduction to media education' are relevant to creating effective compositions in visual arts. Composition uses the elements of art (line, tone, colour, texture, shape, form and space) in conjunction with the principles of contrast, emphasis, focus, balance, movement, harmony, perspective, repetition and variety to create artworks which are satisfying to view. Key principles in design are coherence, movement, proportion, balance and central focus. Through exploring these concepts and principles children can create satisfying and unique artworks using both two- and three-dimensional forms.

In visual arts activities, students should be given the opportunity to experiment with, and explore, each medium, and then develop their expertise in using this medium separately and in combination with other forms to create meaningful artworks that can be shared with others. Different forms of art are discussed here with examples of some specific techniques and skills for lessons. Explore the wealth of art learning experiences on the Internet and in local libraries to extend this introduction to visual arts activities.

Two-dimensional forms

Drawing

Drawing can be boring busy work or it can be an exciting and fun activity. Children can be challenged to observe the subjects carefully, explore the use of artistic conventions such as design, perspective and composition, become personally and aesthetically involved with the subject matter and use a variety of media to create satisfying, meaningful representations of the world around them. To explore the form of drawing children can use pencils, ink, felt pens, charcoal, crayons or oil pastels. Subjects can be drawn from direct observation of objects, people or animals, or from remembered or imagined images. Through drawing children can learn about the outline (the line drawn around an object), hatching (shading using a set of parallel lines), cross-hatching (creating shading and the impression of depth by drawing series of parallel lines intersecting across other sets of similar lines) and stippling (a section shaded with dots). Children can also use drawing to tell stories, document an experiment or excursion, show their feelings, recall an event, share their thoughts and experiences, and solve problems.

Drawing birds using pastels.

Painting

Through painting, children can learn to mix colours and to explore their visual qualities of light, dark, warm, cool, colour, tone and texture using acrylic paints, dyes, inks, oil paints and so on. They can explore the works of famous artists and identify how they used colour and paint; for example, they can compare the works of the impressionists, the expressionists and the cubists in their use of colour and then create their own works in one of these styles. They can study paintings from different cultures and learn about different countries and customs in relation to what they can observe in the artworks, and then create paintings depicting their own culture and life in a selected style. Children should be given the opportunity to experiment with different media such as acrylic and oil paints, finger paints, watercolours, glass, wax resist, fabric and silk painting, and discover the unique qualities of each medium. Through painting children can explore and create representations of still life, portraits,

Painting display.

Self-portrait.

landscapes, nature, emotions, real and imagined experiences, stories, songs and poems, science experiments, famous artworks, and art from other cultures and contexts.

Glass painting

Everyday Kolor is a child-friendly glass paint that comes in a variety of brightly coloured opaque paints and may be applied to most surfaces. It can be painted onto plastic and placed on mirrors, windows, glasses and so on then can be peeled off if desired at a later stage and leave no mark. A similar product can be created by mixing polyvinyl acetate (PVA) glue with vegetable dyes, acrylic paints or food colours. Other commercial glass paints tend to be more expensive and require more developed skills and so could be used by older children.

- **Glass painting — peel a picture.** Have children select a picture or create their own outline, put it behind a clear sheet of plastic and then paint it with glass paint. When their painting is complete and dry, peel it off slowly and use it to make fridge or window decorations.
- **Collages.** Make colourful collages on paper or cardboard and add on sand, fabric, sticks, leaves, cotton, flowers and so on to give it a three-dimensional effect.
- **Paint on paper.** Everyday Kolor can also be used on paper, wood and cardboard using fingers, brushes or applicators and, because it is thick, interesting textures can be created.

Using glass paints on plastic before removing dried picture to attach to a window.

MMADD about the arts

Printmaking

Printmaking

When paper was invented in China about two thousand years ago, the Chinese were the first people to use woodcuts to create prints. The technique of printmaking allowed artists to create multiple copies of their works using the processes of relief printmaking (where the design area stands out as with stamps, rubbings and woodcuts), surface printmaking (where the artwork is applied directly to the surface such as with lithography), stencil printmaking (where a stencil is attached to a screen and ink passes around the stencil to create the image on the paper) and intaglio printmaking (such as etching, where the image is scratched into the surface). Modern techniques using photocopiers and printers widen children's printmaking opportunities to produce repeated images, which may be abstract, real life, expressive or symbolic.

- **Printing with objects.** Almost any object may be used for printing: bottles, string, fruits, vegetables, lino, clay, junk, environmental materials, cloth, sponges, polystyrene, nuts and bolts, paint, newspaper, cardboard, leaves, ferns, and so on. Put a small amount of paint in a saucer or other flat container. Dip the object with which you will print in the paint, and then print it on paper to create the desired planned effect.
- **Rubbings.** Using lightweight paper, have children use crayons, pastels or soft pencils to rub over the paper which is placed on an interesting texture, such as a piece of tree bark, a coin, the pavement or a piece of fabric.
- **Monoprinting.** Spread paint over a sheet of glass (cover the edges with masking tape to avoid cutting fingers) or use a piece of lino or masonite. Have children create their design or image in the paint using their finger or other implement and then place a piece of paper carefully over the paint, press it down gently and peel it off to create the print.
- **Newspaper and cardboard printing.** Scrunch up a ball of newspaper, dab it in paint and print. Cut out shapes of thick cardboard and, using the edges that have been dipped in paint, print different patterns.
- **Nature printing.** Collect gum nuts, leaves, ferns, stones and so on. Dip them in paint and use them for printing interesting patterns.
- **Fruit and vegetable printing.** Cut the fruit or vegetable (a potato works well) in half. Use a blunt knife to make a simple raised up surface design on the cut side. Dip it in paint and print patterns. Experiment with different fruits and vegetables for different textures and prints.
- **Junk printing.** Collect odds and ends from around the kitchen, garage, playground and so on. Use these, dipped in paint, to create a variety of prints.
- **Paint blob printing.** Select a piece of paper and fold it in half. Place blobs of paint on one-half of the paper and then fold the other half on top of it. Open it up carefully to reveal a brightly

Natural objects are being used for printing.

158

coloured symmetrical pattern. Create a picture from this pattern by drawing over it with a dark felt pen, or leave it as an abstract painting.

- **Toothbrush printing.** Make paint into a watery consistency. Make a frame by stapling flyscreen wire onto an old picture frame (see 'Paper making' on page 164). Cut out simple designs from paper and place these on the paper to be painted. Put the screen on top and then flick paint with a toothbrush through the screen. Remove the paper cut-outs to reveal the design on a speckled background.
- **Polystyrene printing.** Using a blunt instrument, press a design into a piece of polystyrene. Roll on ink over the polystyrene design and then use this to print patterns. Alternatively, place the paper onto the inked polystyrene design and roll it carefully, and then remove the paper to reveal the design. Extend this technique and create prints using linocuts and woodcuts.
- **Screen printing.** Cut out a simple design from paper and place it on another piece of paper. Carefully place the screen over the cut-out design. Put the paint or ink along one edge of the screen. Pull the ink towards you with a squeegee once or twice. Carefully lift the screen off the paper at an angle. The design should be stuck to the screen and the paper should reveal the print, which has just been made. This process can be repeated with other clean sheets of paper to make multiple copies of the same design.

Marbling

Originally the ancient art of marbling was used to decorate the endpapers of fine books and was used for centuries in Asia and Europe and more recently in Western countries. Nowadays marbling is used on virtually anything made of paper or fabric. In the past, throughout the world, marbling required very specialised knowledge, tools and techniques. However, new types of non-toxic, child-friendly marbling inks are available which allow virtually all ordinary materials which can soak up water (e.g. paper, cloth, hide and wood) to be marbled. Sakura Innovative Marbling Dyes are recommended for this activity and are manufactured by Boku-Undo Company in Japan and available through your local school supply store.

- **Marbling.** Half-fill a large shallow container with water. Submerge the 'float paper' (small circle of cardboard) with a brush. When it rises to the top gently place one drop of ink from the tube directly on the paper so that the ink will spread to the water surface. Continue to apply desired colours to the float paper. To create designs, gently stir the ink on the surface with a brush or wooden skewer. Pick up the material or object to be marbled and, starting with one end, gently lay the material on the surface of the water where the coloured pattern is. Do not allow air pockets to form between the water and the material. When the entire material or object is soaked with water, gently lift it by one edge, peel it back from the water surface and place it face up on a sheet of newspaper.

Creating prints using marbling.

Blot with a paper towel to remove the excess water. While there is a design on the water surface, successive prints can be made. Clean the water with newspaper and add new colour for brighter patterns. To make secondary colours, mix inks in a small dish and apply them to the float paper with a brush or eye dropper. To darken colours, simply use more ink.

- **Sponge marbling.** Ensure the background is clean and dry. Moisten a sea sponge or ceramic sponge. Dab the sponge in the desired colour of acrylic paint and then dab on the background in every direction. Dry the piece in between colours (a hairdryer may be used for this). Add another colour and dry; and then add another colour and dry. Repeat this process until the desired effect is achieved. It is generally best to start off with the darkest colour and finish with the lightest colour.

Photography

Another significant development in the creation of artworks was the 19th-century invention of the camera. Partly because of the camera's ability to represent subjects exactly, some artists moved away from realism into impressionism, expressionism, cubism, surrealism and fauvism. Later, artists began to use the camera to create unusual artworks by distorting images, changing colours and creating multiple images on the one page. Children should become familiar with using a variety of cameras such as single lens reflex (SLR), instant-focus, polaroid, and digital still or movie to explore ways of artistically capturing events or creating abstract artworks. They can create portraits and landscapes; illustrate their stories; document an excursion or sports carnival; gain feedback about a dance they have created by filming it and reflecting on their performance; capture a drama activity on film, print it off and display it; design and print posters and brochures advertising a school event; and create artworks based on nature, people, events, excursions and so on using photographic media techniques to distort and change the original photo. For further suggestions on the use of photography in the classroom, see Chapter 4, 'Introduction to media education'.

Photographing the community.

Three-dimensional forms

Sculpture

Sculpture has been a significant part of cultures for thousands of years and is still a highly respected form of art. Sculpture may include free-standing artworks which may be viewed from all sides, or relief sculptures which are generally viewed from the front and attached to a wall or other surface. Provide children with the opportunity to observe a variety of different types of sculpture and discuss how and why they were made.

Children can learn to model, carve and construct three-dimensional sculptures in response to a story, poem, piece of music or a picture, or they can be inspired by their own imagination to create a fantastic spaceship or alien, plant or vehicle. Children can

The simplest forms of sculpture can be made from boxes and masking tape.

experiment with wood, paper, cardboard, plastic, wire, metal, plaster, clay and textiles to create objects such as sculptures, textured collages, puppets, masks and models. They can learn about the unique characteristics of each medium and how it can be used by itself or in combination with other media, to create an effective and aesthetically pleasing artwork. The simplest forms of sculpture can be made from boxes, masking tape, glue and paint. Then children can develop their skills in creating free-standing sculptures from paper, cardboard, textiles, wire, rolled-up newspapers and other assorted materials. Children can also create sculptures such as masks and puppets to be used in drama lessons. They should be encouraged to plan and design their proposed sculpture prior to creating it so that they have determined its relative size, nature, character, shape and construction materials.

Mask making

Masks can be used as a creative artwork for self-expression and aesthetic purposes as well as in conjunction with a drama activity. There are a variety of different ways of making masks, which depend on the time and resources available, and the age and experience of the children. For further information see:

- www.cln.org/themes/masks.html
- www.noteaccess.com/MATERIALS/MatMaskMaking.htm
- home.att.net/~tisone/masks.htm

Here are some ways of making masks:

- **Paper-plate masks.** Use paper plates or cardboard and have children design a mask, adding materials such as wool, leather, egg cartons, pipe-cleaners and textiles to give it a three-dimensional effect. Tie elastic or wool to the sides so it can be attached to the child's head.
- **Papier-mâché masks.** Blow up a balloon and tie it. Cover the balloon with vaseline and then paste several layers of small torn squares of paper that have been soaked in paste or water on it to make papier-mâché. When the papier-mâché is completely dry, extract the balloon from inside it, and cut out the required shape of the mask. Decorate it as desired using a variety of media, or just paint.
- **Gypsona masks.** Gypsona is a plaster of Paris bandage, available from a chemist or educational art suppliers. When wet, it is very flexible; then it dries hard, taking on the shape into which it has been formed. It is a very quick and effective method of creating custom-made masks to fit a child's face. Cover the child's hair with plastic wrap and spread vaseline over the face. Have the child close his/her eyes and relax while small squares of gypsona are dipped in water, gently squeezed to get rid of excess water and then applied evenly

This bear mask is made from cardboard.

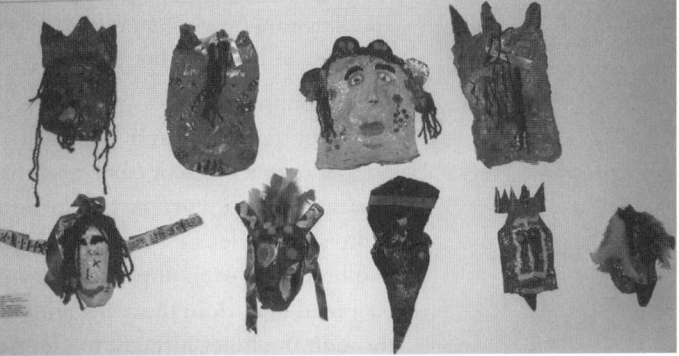

These masks are made from papier-mâché.

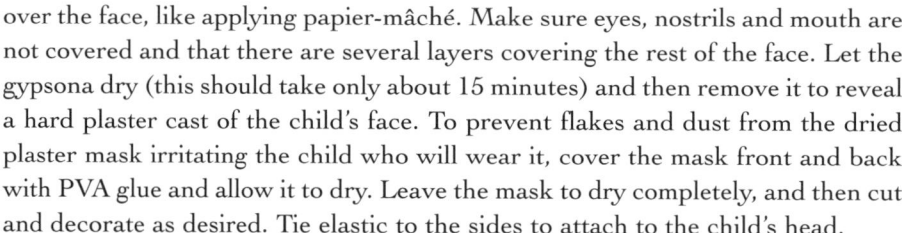

MMADD about the arts

over the face, like applying papier-mâché. Make sure eyes, nostrils and mouth are not covered and that there are several layers covering the rest of the face. Let the gypsona dry (this should take only about 15 minutes) and then remove it to reveal a hard plaster cast of the child's face. To prevent flakes and dust from the dried plaster mask irritating the child who will wear it, cover the mask front and back with PVA glue and allow it to dry. Leave the mask to dry completely, and then cut and decorate as desired. Tie elastic to the sides to attach to the child's head.

Puppets

Puppets have been popular with a wide variety of people for many hundreds of years. They have been used to entertain and to teach, and they can be moved around and made to act and talk just like people. Puppets can be made as artworks in themselves or developed for and used in conjunction with a drama activity. For further information about puppets, see:
www.noteaccess.com/MATERIALS/MatPuppets.htm

Here are some suggested methods of making puppets, which can then be used in many creative ways:

- **Finger puppets.** Fingers can be painted with non-toxic paint or felt pens and used as finger puppets. Alternatively, use decorated scraps of felt or paper tubes to slip over the children's fingers. Lay the child's finger on a piece of felt and draw around it. Cut out two pieces of felt to this pattern and sew or glue them together. Decorate each puppet to represent a different character using felt pens, wool, extra felt and scraps of material.
- **Cardboard puppets.** Design these puppets on thin card, decorate them, and then cut out holes through which the children can put their fingers to create the character's legs, the elephant's trunk and so on.
- **Glove puppets.** These puppets fit onto the child's hand and when they move their fingers, the puppet's arms and head move. If children make two glove puppets, one for each hand, they can make them 'talk' to each other. Lay the child's hand on a piece of felt and spread out his/her thumb and little finger. Draw a line around the hand leaving 4 centimetres between the hand and the line. Cut out two pieces of felt to this pattern. Pin the sides together and then sew around the outside, leaving the bottom open (for the child's hand). Turn the puppet inside out and decorate by gluing on felt shapes, adding wool, and drawing in features using felt pens or fabric paint. Similar glove puppets can be made using (clean!) socks.
- **Jiggle puppets.** These puppets are made from card and have movable joints so that they jiggle around when their strings are pulled. Draw the body of the puppet onto a piece of card, and then draw the upper and lower legs and arms all separate, but in correct proportions, onto the card as well. Cut these out and make small holes at the top of each arm and each bottom leg joint and at the top and bottom of each upper leg, as well as on the body where the arms and legs will be joined to it. Join the arms and legs to the body using 'butterfly' paper fasteners through the holes already made. Sew and knot a large stitch between the top of both arms as well as between the top of both upper legs. Attach a piece of string

to the top of the head. Attach another piece of string to the large knotted stitch between the arms, and then tie it to the large knotted stitch between the upper legs and thread a bead onto the bottom. Hold the puppets by the head string and pull the bead to make it jiggle.

- **Shadow puppets.** These are used extensively in Asia to tell stories from one generation to another. The puppets are moved behind a back-lit see-through screen so that only their shadows can be seen. They can also be used in front of a wall with a light shining behind them, so that their shadows show up on the wall. Draw the simple shape of the character onto a piece of black card. Cut it out and then cut out smaller shapes within the main shape to create the character's features. Glue coloured tissue paper or cellophane paper to the back of the cardboard cut-out, making sure the coloured paper doesn't show outside the main puppet shape. Attach (say) a chopstick or ruler to the back of the puppet so it can be held from below.

These are shadow puppets.

- **Papier-mâché puppets.** Cut off the top of a 1-litre plastic soft-drink bottle and place some stones in it. Attach a large ball of plasticine (about 10 centimetres in diameter) into the top of the bottle. Work the plasticine to make a head, neck and shoulders above the bottle and then model a face overemphasising the features so they can be seen from a distance. Tear up newspaper into small squares, cover the head with paste, smooth on the newspaper squares, cover with paste, smooth on more newspaper squares and so on until the whole head is covered with two layers of newspaper. Leave to dry, and then repeat this process three more times so that there are eight layers of newspaper over the plasticine head. When the last layers are dry, gently ease the head off the bottle. Scoop out as much plasticine as possible and then glue a tube of cardboard inside the neck of the puppet. Paint and decorate the puppet's head as desired; for example, cut out a circle of material and glue it around the puppet's neck to give it a costume. Add props and/or decorations unique to that particular character as desired. Make the puppet 'come alive' by placing two fingers up the cardboard tube into the neck, and moving the puppet around.

  Alternative papier-mâché recipe: Tear newspapers into small pieces and soak overnight in water. Place in a cotton cloth and wring out excess water. Add glue or paste to bind it (experiment beforehand with the amounts required) stir until it has a clay-like consistency. Papier-maché made like this can then be modelled like clay and used instead of the plasticene.

Collage

Collage is the process of attaching a variety of materials onto paper or cardboard to create a textured effect. Find some books by Jeannie Baker (e.g. *One hungry spider*, *Millicent*, *Where the forest meets the sea* and *Window*) and identify the collage techniques and media she has used and why they are effective.

Photo and coloured pencil collage.

Collage

Select a theme, subject or topic and have children find or make objects and materials to assemble a collage of this theme or topic. To create a collage, children could attach photos, magazine pictures, different types and textures of papers, or found, made or natural objects to a piece of cardboard to produce a textured artwork. Extension collage activities can include paper making and creating different types of cards.

Paper making

Paper can be made from almost any paper product; this reinforces the principle of recycling as it can use 'rubbish' to create something useful. Paper-making screens can be bought through educational art suppliers or made using a cheap picture frame (without the glass) with flyscreen wire attached across it.

Recycled paper used to create textured paper and pictures.

- **Paper making:** Tear paper into small pieces and soak in water overnight. Put about a litre of water in a blender and add several handfuls of the soaked pulp. Blend it until it is smooth and then tip it into a container. Repeat until all the paper is blended thoroughly. Cover a pile of newspapers with dampened Chux wipes to form a 'couch'. Put about 10 centimetres of water into a large flat tub. Wet the screen. Pour in several handfuls of pulp and mix it around in the water. Put the screen down the inside wall of the tub and across the bottom, and then lift it straight up. It should now be full of the watery pulp. Drain off excess water and tip the screen upside down onto the newspaper/Chux couch, rock it, and then roll off the blended pulp. Write the child's name on a piece of paper and put it on this newly made paper. Cover with another Chux, and another child can repeat the process. When all the children have had a turn, stack newspapers on top of the pile to soak up all the water. Cover it with a board and weight for about one hour. Peel semidried paper off and hang it up to dry.

Extension: Flowers, leaves, tissue paper, onions, food colouring and other materials may be added to create colour and textures in the paper.

Cards for different reasons and different seasons

Throw out the stencils for Mother's Day cards! Homemade cards are a very personal and welcome way of passing on good wishes and so on, and can be a unique form of self-expression. Encourage children to experiment with a variety of types of card throughout the year, making special cards for Father's Day, Mother's Day, Easter, Christmas, the Islamic festival of Eid or the Jewish celebration of Hanukkah.

- **Cards using rubber stamps.** Make cards by adding pictures and greetings using rubber stamps and embossing powder.
- **Paper tole cards.** Select wrapping paper that has repeated designs on it. Cut out three identical designs. Paste the first design onto the front of the card as the background. Using the second design, cut out some more of the design and discard. Attach what is left to the appropriate place on the first design using small strips of double-sided adhesive foam tape. Using the third design, cut out the parts of the design that appear closest to the front. Attach these to the appropriate place on the second design using small strips of double-sided adhesive foam tape to form the foreground of the picture.
- **Marbled cards.** Use marbling to cover blank cards and then add cut-out pictures, or decorate with paper tole pictures or rubber stamps.
- **Cut-out cards.** Cut out a simple shape from the front of the blank card. Glue a piece of marbled paper, a picture, a piece of silk painting or an embossed design so that it can be seen through the cut-out shape.

Ceramics

Clay is a wonderful tactile medium for children to play and create with, whatever their age. Clay can be bought from educational art suppliers, or in some areas it can be dug up from the ground but then all lumps and foreign objects need to be removed. Clay may be fired or just air-dried; often it is the process of creating which is the most important objective, not necessarily the quality of the finished product. Children can use clay to create three-dimensional artworks by modelling sculptures, making coil or thumb pots with their hands, or using a wheel and throwing pots.

For further information about using clay in the classroom see:
- www.noteaccess.com/MATERIALS/MatMatCEClay.htm
- www.claystation.com/guides/teachers.html
- www.nsead.org/search/results.asp

MMADD about the arts

1. Select wrapping paper with distinct repeated patterns or designs.

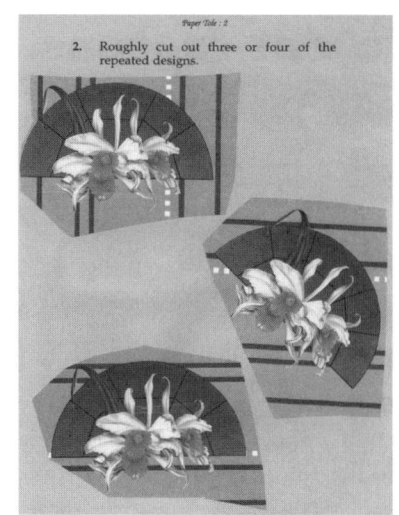

2. Roughly cut out three or four of the repeated designs.

3. Cut one of these designs out carefully and glue to the front of the card.

4. Take the second design and cut out the middle- and fore-ground of the design.

   Using double-sided adhesive foam tape (or glue and polystyrene pieces, cardboard, etc) fix the second design over the first, background design.

5. Take the third design, and only cut out the foreground.

   Using double-sided adhesive foam tape (or glue and polystyrene pieces, cardboard, etc) fix the third (foreground) design over the second, middle-ground design.

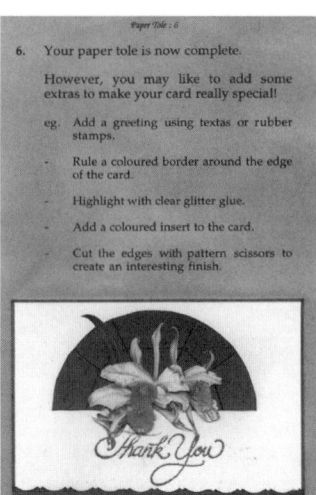

6. Your paper tole is now complete.

   However, you may like to add some extras to make your card really special!

   eg. Add a greeting using textas or rubber stamps.

   - Rule a coloured border around the edge of the card.
   - Highlight with clear glitter glue.
   - Add a coloured insert to the card.
   - Cut the edges with pattern scissors to create an interesting finish.

Tole cards.

Experiment with using glazes on clay artworks.

Different textures can be created in clay by using a range of utensils.

Ceramics

Ensure all the children are wearing aprons or garbage bags to protect their clothing. Give them each a lump of clay on a board and allow them to play with it in order to learn about how it feels and what can be done with it. Have them experiment with punching it, rolling it, twisting it, kneading it, beating it, smoothing it and so on to ensure all air bubbles are out of the clay. Have children join two pieces together by roughing up each edge to be joined with a wet toothbrush and then pushing the two parts together. Have them try to create different textures on the clay by rolling it on material or any other textured surface and then try cutting it with fishing line, decorating the edges with paddle-pop sticks, and using a comb or cookie cutter to create different textures and shapes, all the time keeping it moist with water from a spray bottle. Encourage the children to create their own unique object or sculpture such as pinch pots, clay creatures or sculptures, puppet heads and jewellery. Leave to air-dry or dry in a kiln. If the resources are available, experiment with using glazes on the clay artworks.

Textiles

Working with a variety of textiles and fabrics children can explore ways of changing their colour and creating patterns, through batik, wax resist, tie-dyeing and screen printing, and painting with fabric paints. They can also develop hand-sewing and machine-sewing skills to design artworks using techniques such as quilting, embroidery, felting, tapestry, cross-stitch, embroidery, weaving, appliqué and beading. There may be some parents who are able to assist in teaching the children these skills if you are not confident with them.

Create a class quilt with every child creating a design on a square.

167

Silk painting

Silk painting is an ancient technique that originally came from China, the homeland of silk. In the early 1900s it was rediscovered and developed in France where it quickly became a popular craft. Today silk painting has developed into a successful retail business around the world. Within the classroom it can be used to create individual and unique works of art.

For further details about silk painting see:
www.nsead.org and search for 'Silk painting' and 'Lesson plans'.

There are various types of silk dye that can be used:
- cold-fix dyes (fix the colour using special fixer, e.g. SilkFix and cold water);
- heat-fix dyes (fix with an iron to set the colour);
- steam-fix dyes (steam the dyed material to set the colour).

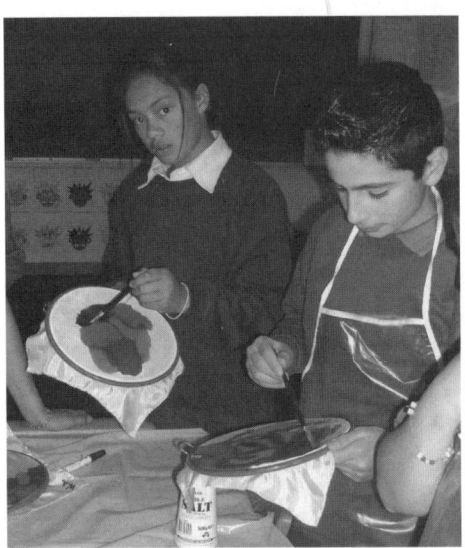

Children are painting silk stretched over embroidery hoops.

- **Silk painting.** Depending on the type of dye used, you will need to follow the directions on the dye container for fixing the colour. Stretch the silk over an embroidery hoop or other frame until it is taut. Put a small amount of several different colours of dye into a plastic ice-cube tray or similar compartmented container. Using a soft brush, apply dyes to the fabric, allowing the colours to blend into each other. When the dyes are still wet, sprinkle salt over the dyed material and watch each salt crystal draw the dye to itself and create unique and beautiful patterns. Allow it to dry, and then set the colours according to the dye manufacturer's instructions. Rinse in cold water with a little vinegar, blot the excess water and iron with a cool iron on the back of the fabric.

Extension: Using the resist method, prepare the silk as above and then draw a pattern or picture lightly on the taut fabric with a water-soluble pencil. Using a resist medium which keeps the dye from spreading, (i.e. gutta) draw over the pattern or picture, ensuring the nib of the gutta bottle or tube is touching and pressing down slightly on the silk as the resist is applied. Do not press too hard as the silk should not touch any hard surface underneath. All lines must join up and there should be no gaps in the gutta lines. Allow the resist to dry, and then apply silk dye to the different sections of the pattern or picture. The dye will spread until it touches the resist and then it should stop spreading further. Set the dye according to the manufacturer's instructions.

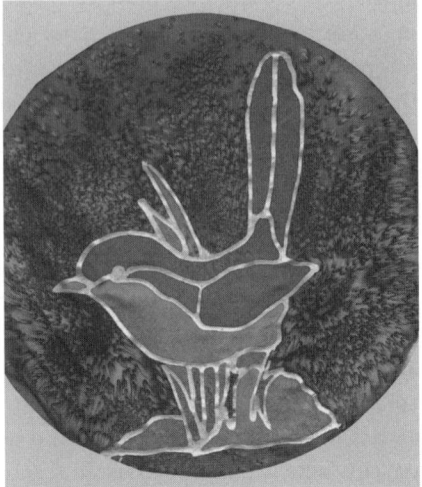

Silk painting of wren.

Tie-dyeing

Tie-dyeing is based on the principle of tying up part of the material to be dyed so tightly that the dye will not penetrate that section. When dry and untied, an interesting pattern will be produced. Wear an old shirt or an apron to protect clothes and use rubber gloves when working with the dye. For further details about tie-dyeing see: www.nsead.org and search for 'Tie-dyeing lesson plans'.

- **Tie-dyeing.** Wash new material to remove the dressing so that the dye will work more effectively. Fold or scrunch up the cloth and tie parts of it very tightly with string, rubber bands and so on so no dye can penetrate to the material. Suggested ties with which to experiment are:
    — lift material from the centre and tie at regular intervals;
    — knot the folded material;
    — concertina the material and tie at regular intervals;
    — scrunch material into a ball and tie string all around it.
  Make up dye according manufacturer's instructions. Immerse tied material in a bucket of dye for at least one hour, realising that the longer it is left, the darker the colour will be. Remember that the colour will appear much lighter when it is dried. Remove tied and dyed material and rinse it well in water; drain on a pile of newspapers. Some or all of the ties may then be undone, depending on the final design required. If another colour dye is available and/or required, retie material in different places and dye in the second colour. Rinse well in water, and leave it to drain on newspapers. When fairly dry, untie the material and iron.

Tie-dyeing can create interesting designs.

Batik

Batik uses the principle that water and wax will not mix, so when a line of wax is drawn on the cotton material, the surface is protected. The material may then be dipped in dye and only the unwaxed material will take the colour, leaving the waxed drawing the colour of the original fabric. For further details about batik see www.nsead.org and search for 'Batik lesson plans'.

- **Batik.** Select a piece of white fabric with a smooth surface (e.g. cotton or rayon). Wash it thoroughly in boiling water and washing soda to remove all traces of dressing, and then dry and iron it. Melt the wax in a frying pan or double boiler. Sketch the design lightly onto the material with a pencil. Place the piece of material on several newspapers near the melted wax. Apply wax with an Indonesian *Tjanting* or brush to the part of the design that is to remain white. When waxing

Batik bear.

is complete, have children name their material and then drop it into a bucket of dye and leave it for an hour or so. Rinse it in cold water until the water runs clear and hang the cloth up to dry. When dry, remove the wax by placing the material between newspapers and ironing it.

Digital forms

Children can use the forms of photography, film and video to integrate visual arts and media as well as creating digital works using computers and other forms of technology. Computer hardware and software should be used as tools to create individual and unique artworks and not as an end in themselves. Through using software programs such as Microsoft Word, AppleWorks, Kids Pix, Kids Pix Studio, Microsoft Fine Artist and Paintbrush children can explore further their understanding about line, shape, colour, tone, space, texture, pattern and form, and develop their skills in composition and framing. Print out the children's artworks and display them. Note that colour printing can be expensive but is very exciting for children to use. With the cost of colour cartridges coming down it may become more accessible for using regularly in visual arts and other lessons.

As well as being used as a tool to assist with the creativity process, technology can be used to document and store children's artworks in an electronic portfolio, using still or movie cameras or scanning the artworks into the computer or to create a virtual class or school art gallery. Using the Internet, children can share their artworks with other children within their class or across the world and receive their comments and reflections on their artworks, as well as research the history and context of artists and designers throughout the centuries and view artworks from galleries and museums in other countries.

Practical considerations

Some teachers mistakenly think that an effective classroom environment is always quiet and tidy! If this were true the only 'art' children might do would be colouring in. But quality art experiences can happen within a well-ordered and organised classroom through careful planning and preparation of resources, and the setting up and modelling of routines, rules and clear expectations.

Preparation for visual arts lessons

Well before a visual arts lesson, think carefully about how the materials and children will be managed. Plan thoroughly how you will set up and clear away the visual arts materials. Have all the resources ready before the lesson and set up before school, at recess or at lunchtime, as appropriate. You may like to establish a routine where the children assist with setting up and clearing away — this will save you a lot of time. For example, appoint class monitors to distribute and collect the paint, brushes, paper and so on; or have the

Identify where the school art resources are stored.

children working in pairs with one collecting and returning the paint and brushes, and the other collecting and returning the paper.

Know what art activities children have done previously, what skills they have developed and what stage they are working towards (this could be different for different children). Always have children name their artwork at the start; this will alleviate much confusion later. Work out where you will store the completed artworks or the artworks in process so they do not get destroyed or put (say) paint on classroom furniture or other materials. Demonstrate techniques, such as how to put paint on a brush, how to mix paints, how to knead clay and so on before children are expected to do this. Teach and model to the children how to respect other people's property and artworks. Work out how you will clean up. Will you do it or will you appoint monitors? Will everyone do a part of cleaning up or will they clean up their own materials and mess in pairs?

Resources

- Start collecting resources now! At the start of the year check out newsagents and bookstores for cheap calendars of art prints, animals, birds, landscapes, buildings, different cultures and contexts, and so on, so you can use these as stimulus pictures in your art lessons. Label and store them neatly so you have ready access to them.
- Surf the Internet looking for relevant sites of artworks and clip art; note down the web address or download prints you might use in your lessons.
- Check out the multitude of art lesson plans on the web — read them through carefully to ensure they will provide the children with quality learning experiences as some of them can be rather gimmicky and superficial.
- Check out the school art room or resource cupboard; you may be surprised to find some unused visual arts materials hidden away.
- Visit the school, university and local libraries to find books of art activities; read these and adapt them to suit your class, resources available and outcomes to be achieved.

Brief overview of art history

For further information on these styles and artists, check out your local library or the Internet.

Style	Dates	Key art and artists
Prehistoric	40 000–5000 BC	Aboriginal art, European Stone Age art
Ancient	4500–30 BC	Egyptian, Sumerian, Assyrian, Persian, Islamic, Asian, Minoan, Indian, Chinese, Japanese, Pre-Columbian, Native American/ Canadian Indian, African
Classical	500 BC	Greek, Roman (79 AD: Pompeii destroyed by Vesuvius)
Medieval	300–1300 AD	Art based in the church (*Book of Kells* and so on) Flat images, Gothic art, stained glass
Renaissance	1300–1600 AD	Italy: 'rediscovery' of classic Greek art Use of perspective and chiaroscuro (use of light and shadow in painting) Artists: Donatello, Botticelli High Renaissance artists: da Vinci, Michelangelo, Pieter Brueghel the Elder, van Eyck, Hans Holbein

Style	Dates	Key art and artists
Baroque art	1600–1750 AD	Based in Rome, used swirling figures, romantic, religious and mystic subjects Artists: El Greco, Rubens, Caravaggio, Velázquez Dutch baroque: painted portraits, landscapes and interior scenes Artists: Rembrandt, Vermeer
Rococo art	1700–89 AD	Refined, elegant and highly decorated artworks Artists: Watteau, Fragonard, Reynolds, Gainsborough
Neoclassicism	18th century	Pompeii in Italy was rediscovered and reawakened artists' interest in classical art Artists: Ingres, Reynolds, Jacques Louis David
Romanticism	Mid-19th century	French Revolution, Industrial Revolution, America freed from British rule — all these changes were reflected in a change in art; paintings reflected common life and passions Artists: Goya, Constable, Turner

- Find out what the visual arts budget is and how to order in specific art resources, such as clay, textiles, and silk and glass paints. Plan this well before you need to do the activity so that the materials arrive in time and you have the opportunity to practise using them.
- Keep your classroom visual arts materials clean, tidy and clearly labelled, and develop routines for ensuring they are kept this way.
- Collect piles of newspapers and magazines throughout the year, and use them for covering desk tops and for collage work.
- Visit Reverse Garbage (if you have this valuable resource in your state or territory) and keep a large bin full of 'junk' that can be added to throughout the year for children to use when creating collages, sculptures and other three-dimensional artworks.
- Have all children bring in an art smock at the start of the year, label them clearly with the child's name and store them neatly. Expect children to wear them for messy art lessons.
- Familiarise yourself with the art programs on the computers in the school and make sure you know how to work the computers, software programs, scanners, printers, cameras and other technology available in your classroom and in the school.

Safety

As well as the safety considerations listed in Chapter 2, 'The creative arts classroom', teachers of visual arts lessons need to be vigilant in ensuring a safe classroom for their children. Check all materials are non-toxic and know what to do if a child swallows paint, glue and so on or gets it in their eyes. When using sharp utensils, hot-glue guns, hammers, screwdrivers, an iron or hot plate, ensure that an adult is supervising the activity. Model the use of a potentially dangerous resource; that is, when finished with an hot-glue gun, turn it off, unplug it and put it away from children on a surface which will not melt. Teach children to clean up everything they have used in the art lesson to avoid accidental spills and mess later in the day.

Expectations in the classroom

Set and model clear expectations such as wearing a painting smock, covering tables with newspaper, not walking around with wet artworks, storing clean paintbrushes with bristles up, being responsible for the tidiness and cleanliness of a child's individual work space, valuing other people and their artworks, and cleaning up on completion of the activity. Discuss and create routines, rules, rewards and consequences for the visual arts lesson so children have ownership of these and see their relevance. For further details about behaviour management strategies, see the section in Chapter 2, 'The creative arts classroom'.

Displaying work

Displaying children's work attractively indicates that you value and respect their creative artworks. Consider why and where the artwork will be displayed, how it will be mounted, if and how you will use borders, as well as the composition and presentation of the display area. Sometimes all the children's artwork will be able to be displayed, and at other times there may be room for only a few pieces. If this is the case, ensure that over a period of time all children have their artworks displayed, not just the gifted children. Mount each piece of art on backing paper and frame special artworks. Have the children caption their artworks to explain the title, medium used and any interesting information the viewer may need to know about the work.

Lesson planning for a visual arts lesson

Introduction

Start the lesson in a motivating way, using a picture, music, artwork, story, poem and so on as a stimulus for the designing, creating and/or art appreciation lesson. You may like to show an example of the sort of artwork children will be making in the lesson but encourage children not to copy yours, but rather to create their own individual artwork.

Style	Dates	Key art and artists
Impressionism	1870	Explored the effect of light on nature Artists: Manet, Monet, Renoir
Post-impressionism	1880	Developed ideas of impressionists to make subjects look more durable and solid Artists: Cézanne, Van Gogh, Gaugain, Seurat
Cubism	1890	Beginning of abstract art, used geometric elements, simple lines and angular shapes Artists: Picasso, Braque, Delaunay
Expressionism	Early 20th century	Aimed to express internal emotions and experiences rather than represent the external world Artist: Kandinsky
Surrealism	20th century	Painted dreamlike, fantasy pictures with people and objects merging together Artists: Dali, Paul Klee, Miró, Magritte
Abstract expressionism	1950–1960	First major American art movement Abstract art conveying energy and mood Artists: Pollock, Krasner, Rothko

Style	Dates	Key art and artists
Pop art	1960s	Concentrated on everyday objects. Artists: Warhol, Lichtenstein, Hockney, Johns
Optical art	Late 20th century	Used patterns, lines and colours to create optical illusions. Artists: Vasarely, Riley, M.C. Escher
Art of the present		Goldsworthy, Kemp, Whiteley, Whiteread, Hanson, Hirst, Gordon, Patterson and so on Check out your local artists' work at a gallery near you for contemporary Australian artworks

Demonstration

If the lesson involves the development of skills or learning a new craft activity, demonstrate how to do the activity, making explanations and instructions clear and simple. Repeat instructions for the activity and question for understanding.

Development of skills, techniques and creative artworks

Allow children time to develop their skills, techniques and creativity as they work on designing and making their artworks. Be available to comment, praise, encourage, extend and keep children on task throughout the lesson. Be prepared for early finishers and decide beforehand what they will do when they have completed their artworks. If the activity is planned to continue in another lesson decide where the works in progress will be stored safely.

Reflection and sharing

When most or all children have completed their artworks, or when it is time to finish the lesson, talk with the children about what they have created, teaching and reinforcing the language of art, reflect on what they have learned and check on the achievement of the indicators for the lesson. Maybe have them write about their experiences in their creative arts journal. Ensure all children are involved in cleaning up their work space and putting their artworks away safely.

Activities to introduce the different forms of visual arts

The following art examples using different visual art forms have been based on quality children's literary texts. See the list of references at the end of the chapter for the publishing details of each text. In these examples art can be seen as being an integral part of the curriculum with meaning and context. However, these form-based activities can be used and adapted to other content and contexts depending on the needs, interests, abilities and prior art experiences of your children and themes with which you are working in the classroom program.

Two Summers by John Heffernan

Art appreciation: Australian landscape artists

Examine works by Australian artists depicting dry, outback landscapes, for example:
- *Dry Weather* by Blamire Young;
- *The Rabbiters* by Russell Drysdale;

- *Emus in a Landscape* by Russell Drysdale;
- *Wimmera Landscape* by Arthur Boyd;
- *Upway Landscape* by Fred Williams;
- *My Camp* by Henri Bastin;
- *The Overlanders* by S.T. Gill;
- *Murchison Sand Plain* by Robert Juniper.

Discuss the different styles, techniques and media used by the different artists. How have they used space, line, colour, texture and so on to create the impression of the outback? How effective is this?

2D drawing: Landscapes

Have children view two-dimensional (2D) photos of different arid landscapes (e.g. from calendars or books, or from the Internet) and then create their own artwork using one of the techniques, media and/or styles as discussed in the initial art appreciation activity.

As the children work, play music by Peter Sculthorpe or another Australian composer, which depicts the dry Australian outback, for example *Sun Music I, II, III* and *IV, Red Landscape, Rain, A Burke and Wills Suite* or *Tailitnama Song* by Peter Sculthorpe.

On another piece of paper have children draw the same landscape as represented in the activity above, but as though it has had lots of rain and is lush and green. Use the same style and materials to create the second landscape. Display the two landscapes and write a sentence about each of them.

Cat and Fish by Joan Grant

2D artwork: Lines and space

The illustrator, Neil Curtis, has made decisions about how space is going to be used positively or negatively. Compare the dramatic use of white space when Cat and Fish are on the mountain or when Fish carries Cat under the sea, with the use of large areas of black for the cover and the back endpapers. Have the children experiment using positive and negative space with a variety of mediums such as paint and pen, using Cat or Fish or both or another simple shape or animal.

2D line drawings

Discuss with the children the detailed line drawings that illustrate the story, how they were drawn and how effective they are. Ask them questions about the illustrations, for example:
- How are the lines used?
- How effective are they?
- Why did the artist not use colour?
- How do the lines show depth in the pictures?

Have the children draw an outline of an animal on a piece of paper, and then fill it in with black-and-white lines, showing contours and different parts of the animal in

the same way as the illustrator did in the text. Display their work along with a sentence explaining how they created their artwork.

2D drawing: Visual sentences

Read through the story and identify pages where the content of the text is portrayed visually, for example:

- He showed Fish how to climb (words go up the page).
- Fish was lonely for the water (words are wavy, like water).
- Float (letters are floating).
- Where the land and sea meet (circular text — the end meets the beginning).

Have children make up their own sentence about any subject they like and then ask them to write the sentence in a way that describes visually the content of the words. Share these with the rest of the class and have each child explain what he/she has done and how it was done. Display their artworks with explanatory sentences.

Grandpa and Thomas by Pamela Allen

Art appreciation: Comparing styles

Examine a selection of photos, artworks and pictures about the sea. Use calendars, children's storybooks, photographs, posters or prints of famous artworks, postcards and so on. Have the children discuss questions such as:

- How do they know it is a picture of the sea?
- Describe what is happening in the picture.
- What colours have been used?
- How did the artist show if the sea is calm or stormy?
- What materials (media) have been used to create the picture?
- What other animals or objects are in the picture which tell us more about what is happening in the picture?
- How do they know where the land is and where the sea is?
- How much of the page does the picture fill? How effective is this?

2D painting: Watercolours

Based on the above discussion, have the children paint a beach scene by first wetting the paper in three sections. Wet the top third first and then apply small amounts of paint to create the sky. Wet the next third and apply small amounts of paint to create the water and then the sand. Allow the paints to 'bleed' into each other for effect. When the painting is dry, draw in Grandpa and Thomas, the seagulls, the beach umbrella, the sandcastle and any other relevant details. Have the children add a caption and display their paintings.

Little Humpty by Margaret Wild

2D painting: Warm and cool colours

Little Humpty lived in the hot, hot desert. Look at the colours on the first double-page spread. Ask the following questions:

- What colours can you see?
- How do they make you feel?
- How are these warm colours created? (red, yellow, red + yellow and so on)

Ann James, the illustrator, uses yellow in the centre of the first double-page spread and then adds red to create orange as she moves away from the centre. Ask the children to paint a desert scene using only warm colours — reds, oranges and yellows. Show the children how to make colour variations by adding more yellow or red. When the painting is dry, have the children draw Little Humpty on one side of the paper. On the other side have them write words to describe how each of the warm colours makes them feel. Look at pictures or photos created using mainly blue, green and purples. Ask them the same questions as above, for example:

- What colours can you see?
- How do they make you feel?
- How are these cool colours created? (blue, blue + red, blue + yellow and so on)

Encourage the children to paint a contrasting scene (e.g. a rainforest) using only these colours to give an impression of coolness.

2D drawing: Observations from real life and photos

Find a selection of real-life drawings and photographs of camels, elephants, hippos and crocodiles. As each photo or picture is shown to the children ask them to describe each animal (the shape of its eyes, its mouth, its nose, its feet, the length of its legs, its body, its tail and so on). When they have examined the pictures carefully, have each child select an animal and draw it, using the photo as an example of what their real-life drawing should look like. Display the finished artworks and include a sentence about how children drew the animals and what they noticed particularly about the animal they drew.

3D artworks: Ceramic model

As an extension to the above activity, have children then model their animal from clay (or plasticine, if you do not have access to clay), ensuring they include all the details discussed and illustrated in their drawings.

Read through the story and identify all the different objects and animals mentioned in the story (e.g. sand, Little Humpty, Big Humpty, palm trees, sand dunes, twisty rocks, scraggly bushes, small pebbles, hippos, elephants, crocodiles, elephants, camels and the waterhole).

As a class create a 3D model of the desert using clay or plasticine. Include all of the identified plants and other objects from the story. Add the clay sculptures of the animals to the completed model. Write a summary of the story and attach this to the artwork.

Jethro Byrde, Fairy Child by Bob Graham

3D artworks: Textiles

Using pegs, small dolls or pipe-cleaners, have children create their own fantasy friend. Bring along a range of cloth scraps, needles, thread, scissors, glue, tinsel, cellophane, buttons, glitter paint, wool and so on, so that children can dress and decorate their fantasy friend. Alternatively, the teacher may prefer children to create fairies like the ones in the story. Display these created friends and have children write a paragraph about them.

2D painting: Colours and shapes

Have the children look at the pictures of the fairy cakes that Annabelle's mum made for afternoon tea. Discuss how she decorated each one differently. Look at the colours, shapes and positioning of the decorations. On a paper plate, have each child draw five or six fairy cakes as viewed from above, and paint their tops with a variety of decorations. Encourage the children to make the icing on each cake a different colour and to use a variety of shapes in the decorations. You may like to have children use only primary colours, use only secondary colours or focus on mixing colours for the icing, if children need practice in these skills.

Diary of a wombat by Jackie French

2D drawing: Animal sketching

Examine photos and pictures of a variety of Australian animals. Divide the children into two groups. One group creates a picture of an Australian animal, either from memory or from observing a picture, with no background, just white space. The other group draws the same animal but fills in the background, such as trees, grass and sky to cover the page. Each group writes a few sentences about their drawings and their use of white space or background.

Compare the drawings with those illustrating the text of this book:

- Is the style of text different depending on how the illustration is drawn?
- Why does the illustrator leave so much white space on each page?
- Does this match the way the text has been written?
- Do the illustrations need more background?

Illustrator Bruce Whatley uses a minimalist approach by providing only the essential elements in his illustrations. This is regarded as using space positively. Ask:

- Do you think the author and the illustrator have a sense of humour?
- How do you know? Find written and illustrated examples of this.

Look at the illustrations of the wombat throughout the book. Have the children describe the line, colour and shape used to portray the wombat in her different positions. Ask them to copy in pencil one of the illustrations, trying to make it an exact replica. Then ask them to think of another four-legged animal (e.g. a cat, dog or a possum) and try to draw it in the same position as they drew the wombat, taking note of line, colour and shape. Share their artwork with the rest of the class.

3D sculpture
Using clay, playdough or plasticine, have children create their own wombat in one of the positions seen in the book.

The Potato People by Pamela Allen

3D sculptures and textiles

Look at Pamela Allen's illustration of the Potato People and discuss how to make model Potato People:
- What will we need to make our own Potato People?
- What else can we use?

Record the children's responses. Have the children bring in two potatoes — one large and one small and whatever else they need to create their own potato character. Provide them with some scraps of cloth and other fabrics as well as scissors, needles and thread. Look at the pictures of the Potato People in the book and discuss how these were made. Ask children to create their own Potato People using the collected resources.

Digital forms: Digital images
Have children write a biography on the computer about the Potato People they have created. Illustrate the text with digital images taken of their Potato People artworks.
- What is his/her name?
- Where does he/she live?
- Are there others in the family?
- Do they go to school or to work?
- What games do they like to play? and so on.

2D drawing: Cross-hatching
In *The Potato People* Pamela Allen uses cross-hatching (where parallel lines cross and intersect) as a background in many of her illustrations; for example, when grandma is sitting at the table, her own cross-hatching creates the background. Have the children create their own picture and experiment with cross-hatching as a part of the background using pencil, pen or felt-tipped pen, or a combination of all three.

A year on our farm by Penny Matthews

2D drawings: Mixed media

Andrew McLean used charcoal pencil, watercolour and pastels to illustrate *A year on our farm*. Create a class mural of the farm showing the seasons and using the same types of mixed media. Include parts of the story as captions.

MMADD about the arts

3D collage: Seasons on the farm

As a class, list the different jobs that are done in each season on the farm, for example:

- *Summer*   Picking fruit
  Spreading hay
  Checking water troughs
- *Autumn*   Planting vegetables
  Milking cows
  Looking after lambs
- *Winter*   Mending fences
  Planting trees
  Crutching sheep
- *Spring*   Shearing sheep
  Baling hay
  Watering trees

Look at the illustrations for each of these tasks and discuss what is happening in each picture. In pairs have children make a picture collage of one of these jobs, using a variety of found and school resource materials. Label them clearly and display them in sequence.

2D drawing: From memory and from observation

Examine the trees on the bottom left-hand side of each double page. Discuss with the children the following questions:

- How do these trees change?
- What is happening to them as the book progresses?
- Why is this happening?

Take a walk around the schoolyard and examine a tree, or set this task for homework and have the children look in their neighbourhood for a tree. Have them draw the tree from observation. See if they can remember how it looked during another season (obviously deciduous trees would be best for this activity, but even native trees register some changes throughout the year, for example they grow flowers, flowers die, gumnuts grow and new shoots appear). Children may have to ask their parents or neighbours to help them remember how the tree looked several months ago. Have the children draw another version of the same tree, showing it in another season. Have them write about how it changes during the year.

The slightly true story of Cedar B. Hartley (who planned to live an unusual life) by Martine Murray

Digital forms: Posters

Using the computer and clip art, create a flyer or poster to advertise 'Circus Berzerkus'. Alternatively, create a 'Lost Pet' poster (see page 18 of the book). Photograph or scan an image of a pet and include this in the poster, as well as details of rewards and contacts.

2D drawing: From written description and observation

Read the descriptions of the gardens on page 7 of the book and from these draw the row of gardens side by side as described in the text: The Bartons', Cedar B's, Mrs Trinka's and the Motts' gardens. Then have children draw their own neighbourhood and the gardens alongside their house or apartment.

2D drawing from observation/art appreciation

If possible, bring a live cat into the classroom (check the relevant 'Animals in schools' policy first!). Alternately some museums lend out stuffed animals to schools, so find out if you can arrange this. Another possibility would be for children to photograph their cat in various positions and bring these photos to school. Observe the cat (or the photos) closely from different angles; discuss its features, colouring, movements and so on; have children touch it; and then draw their impressions of the cat on paper. Show other artists' impressions of cats, both realistic and abstract; encourage children to use one of these techniques in drawing another representation of the cat. Compare the differences and similarities.

The Barrumbi kids by Leonie Norrington

3D artwork: Didgeridoos and clap sticks

Research different sorts of Aboriginal artwork within the context of their spirituality and legends as well as the techniques and media used. If possible, have someone from the local Aboriginal community talk to the children about this and demonstrate different kinds of artwork.

If this is not possible, the teacher should talk with local Aboriginal people about what learning experiences would be appropriate and culturally sensitive within that particular community. If appropriate, after relevant research and/or demonstration, boys could design, make and decorate their own didgeridoos, and the girls could decorate cut pieces of 2.5-centimetre dowel with paint to use as clap sticks to accompany their singing. As stimulus and examples, use the pictures from references books, art prints and information from the Internet. Find out which Aboriginal groups use the didgeridoos and clap sticks in their corroborees and when and why they used them. Use the painted didgeridoos and clap sticks when engaged in appropriate music and dance activities.

3D collage

List all the Aboriginal words from the Mayali language and their meanings as found in the book. These are found at the back of the book (pages 195–196) but are also sprinkled throughout the story. Give one word to a small group of children and have them create a collage illustrating the word, and then have them write the Mayali language word clearly underneath the picture. Display these around the room.

The singing hat by Tohby Riddle

Art appreciation and 2D artworks: Mixed media

Examine the illustrations in the story and discuss what mixed media have been used in each picture. Ask the children why they think this variety of media have been used, and how effective their use has been.

Identify and list the different media and techniques used, for example:
- simple black-and-white line drawings;
- collage using photos, material or magazine pictures;
- watercolours;
- silhouettes: plain paper cut-outs or filled-in blocks of colour.

Have each child select an illustration from the book and copy it, using a similar variety of media. Share their artworks and discuss the difficulties and effectiveness (or otherwise) of using these media all together in one picture.

Extension: Using similar mixed media, create Colin Jenkins and his singing hat in a different situation, for example:
- in a boat at sea;
- on a farm;
- teaching a class;
- visiting his Aunt Mary.

In the artwork, show the responses from those around him to his unusual hat.

Digital forms: Word-processed sound cards

Have children examine how the following words have been written in the text. Note the use of size, colour, font and so on, and discuss how effective this is in making the word look just as it sounds.
- Tweet! Tweet! Twitter, Twit!
- Cwark!
- Squark!
- Tweet
- Clunk

Have children choose their own words, and then create them on the computer using colours, textures, fonts, shapes, size and so on to make them to look just as they sound. Print them out on separate cards and display them around the room.

A is for aunty by Elaine Russell

3D collage

Alphabet books have traditionally been used to help young children identify familiar objects as well as letters and sounds. Alphabet books were among the first books published for children. Have the children look at a number of alphabet books such as *Alice and Aldo* by Alison Lester, *A Apple pie* by Kate Greenaway and reprinted, *ABC* by Jan Pienkowski, *Animal capers* by Kerry Argent and *Animalia* by Graeme Base.

- What are the characteristics of alphabet books?
- List these on the blackboard or whiteboard.

Have each child select a different letter of the alphabet and draw it clearly in the centre of a blank sheet of paper. On another piece of paper, and with the help of a dictionary (or *Animalia*), have them list a variety of words beginning with that letter. Using magazines pictures, illustrate the first sheet of paper with pictures of objects that start with that letter. (Alternatively, allow children to photograph objects around the school starting with their selected letter.) Add a sentence describing their artwork. Collect the illustrations and make them into an Alphabetical Big Book of the class's artwork or scan/digitally photograph the pictures and make them into a PowerPoint presentation.

Art appreciation: Naïve art

The style used in the illustrations in *A is for aunty* is called naïve art, where the figures are simplified and often take on a symbolic rather than a real appearance. Ask the children the following questions:

- How does the illustrator use this technique?
- Why do you think the illustrator has chosen not to use a traditional Aboriginal painting style?
- How does the illustrator use colour?
- How does the illustrator use brushstrokes?

The dust jacket on *A is for aunty* folds out to become a large map. In groups, have children create a large map of their school, using the same style of painting as the illustrator. The children can then individually use the same style of illustration to create a picture of their own house and yard.

The lost thing by Shaun Tan

Art appreciation: Illustrations

Show the children the book and allow time for them to look carefully at the illustrations, using a magnifying glass to reveal the details in each page. Ask them what they discovered about the Lost Thing:

- Is it lovable?
- Would you find it a home?
- Why has Shaun Tan drawn the Lost Thing the way he has?
- What media has the illustrator used to construct his pictures (e.g. collage)?
- How does the illustrator use colour, line and texture to convey meaning?
- How do the illustrations make you feel through the use of colour, light, shade, line, shape and character expressions?
- What symbols does the illustrator use (e.g. the arrow)?
- What do the symbols mean?
- How does the illustrator use perspective; what is happening in the foreground and in the background?

- How does the page layout influence where you look on the page?
- What is happening at the top, middle and bottom of the page?
- Does the layout divide the page into top, middle and bottom?
- If yes, what techniques does the illustrator use to divide the page (e.g. text placement)?
- What story are the illustrations telling? Is there a message in *The lost thing*?
- Do the illustrations 'fill in the gaps' by extending the information from the text?

Art appreciation: Surrealism

Examine the works of Salvador Dali and other surrealist painters such as René Magritte and Joan Miro. Discuss the similarities and differences between the illustrations of *The lost thing* and these artworks. Discuss the techniques used by surrealist artists, the content of their paintings and what they are expressing. In response to learning about surrealism, investigating surrealist artworks and examining the illustrations from *The lost thing*, have the children select a familiar object and draw it from observation. Ask them to draw it a second time and distort it using some of the techniques discussed above, as used by surrealist artists. Share the artworks with the rest of the class and explain what has been done to distort the object.

Extension: Children could scan their original picture into a relevant software program (e.g. Photoshop or Photoshop Elements) and use distortion techniques to create a surrealist image from their picture.

3D sculpture: Design a 'lost thing'

Create a 3D sculpture of an imaginary 'lost thing'. Write a few sentences about what it eats, how it moves, how it communicates, what it looks like, how big it is and so on, and display this next to the completed sculpture.

2D printmaking: Patterns

Turn to the right-hand side of the second last page of the book. Look at the four pictures, which show the same scene from a sequence of distances: close-up of a tram's windows, three whole trams, twenty or more trams and fifty plus trams. These now create a pattern where the individual tram is not the important focus; rather, the pattern that multiple trams create is the overriding effect.

Have children divide a piece of paper into four equal quarters.

- First quarter: Draw one object close up and filling the quarter.
- Second quarter: Draw three identical objects filling the space.
- Third quarter: Draw seven rows of the three identical objects, filling the space.
- Fourth quarter: Cover the space with fifty or more identical pictures of the chosen object.

Extension: This activity could be completed on the computer as children create one drawing, and then use the *copy-and-paste* facility to make the repeated patterns of multiple copies of the initial drawing as suggested above. Alternatively, they could use a printing technique such as lino, potato or screen printing and adapt the above activity to suit the chosen medium.

An ordinary day by Libby Gleeson

2D drawing: Evolution of an object

Look at the pages in the story that show the dull-coloured cars and buses jammed together. Discover how, throughout the story, they gradually become brightly coloured whales swimming in the sea, and then turn back again into buses and cars. Examine the work of M.C. Escher and discuss any similarities or differences. Have children take a common object and draw it in several repetitions, with each repeated drawing changed slightly until it has turned into another object. Display these in sequence with a title describing the series of pictures.

Papunya School Book of Country and History by Papunya School Publishing Committee

Art appreciation: Aboriginal art

Examine the Aboriginal paintings throughout the book. Find out what the symbols, colours, shapes and lines mean. Read the explanation on page 40 of the book about the picture on page 41: the teachers' vision for education at Papunya. Explore the different symbols and meanings in the picture in the light of the explanation.

Compare the painting style of Albert Namatjira to the traditional style of the Arrente people. How are they different? Create paintings of local landscapes which imitate both styles. Which style do you prefer? Why? (See pages 18–19 of the book.)

Check out these websites:

- www.abc.net.au/btn/australians/namat.htm
- www.aboriginalpottery.com/namatjira.html

The Anangu artists painted their stories onto canvas in the Papunya style. Discuss and develop your original class or group style of painting and paint your story onto paper. (See pages 32–33 of the book.)

Check out these websites:

- www.aboriginal-art.de/art_eng/maleriei.htm
- www.aboriginal-art.de/art_eng/aborigine.htm
- www.aboriginalpainting.com/papunya.html
- www.lib.latrobe.edu.au/AHR/archive/Issue-December-2000/bonyhady2.html

2D drawing: Comparing cultures

Read the section 'Going on a bush trip'. Discuss a recent excursion the class has been involved in. List the differences between the class's excursion and the children from the Papunya School's bush trip. Have children fold a piece of paper in half and list several aspects of an excursion down the middle (e.g. transport, venue, food and activities). On one half of the paper have the children illustrate the Papunya excursion, and on the other half illustrate the class's excursion, focusing on showing clear details in their artwork. Have them write a caption explaining which one they would prefer to be involved in and display this with their artwork.

Baby Bilby, Where do you sleep? by Narelle Oliver

Art appreciation: Realistic representations of animals

Have the children look carefully at each of the pictures in the book and describe the different footprints, habitats and other characteristics they can find out about each of the animals before reading the text. List these on the blackboard or whiteboard. Examine the prickly spinifex grass, the mulga branches and the gibber stones. List how many tiny animals they can find camouflaged in these pictures. Discuss what artistic techniques the artist used to camouflage them in these pictures.

2D drawing: From observation

Take children for a walk around the playground. Have them draw from observation a part of nature (e.g. a tree, a patch of grassy ground, a stony path or a flower-filled garden). Ask them then to draw tiny animals and insects into their picture, camouflaging them and using the same techniques that Narelle Oliver used in her illustrations.

2D printmaking: Marbling

Have children add marbling to a piece of A4 paper. When it is dry, cut it in half. On one half, draw several small animals or insects and cut them out. Paste these onto the other half of the marbled paper. See how the animals and insects are camouflaged against the marbled paper!

SPRINGBOARDS FOR DISCUSSION AND APPLICATION

1. Create a portfolio of works demonstrating each of the elements and forms of visual arts. Annotate each artwork with dot points detailing key teaching strategies and processes.

2. Select one form of visual arts and develop it into a lesson plan showing clearly the preparation prior to the lesson, the purpose of the lesson, the indicators and how learning will be assessed, resources required for the lesson, as well as step-by-step details of the lesson procedure.

3. Select a children's picture book or other relevant artwork and identify how you could use this in an art appreciation lesson which extends into a 'making art' lesson. Identify what indicators could be used to assess children's learning in relation to the elements of visual arts covered. Write up your ideas in a programmed format, indicating which subject matter and forms of visual art are being taught and developed. Indicate what syllabus outcomes the children are working towards by engaging in these activities.

FURTHER READING

Chamberlin, L. (2003), *Art smart*, rev. edn, McGraw-Hill, Sydney.
Chambers, J. & Watson, S. (2000), *Art in the sun*, Educational Supplies, Sydney.
Dineen, J. & Barber, N. (1997), *The world of art*, Evans Brothers, London.
Gaitskell, C., Hurwitz, A. & Day, M. (1991), *Children and their art*, Harcourt Brace Jovanovich, New York.
Holroyd, V. (2003), *Beyond faces: Creative activities for early years children using art galleries and visual arts for starting points and inspiration*, Artists in Warwickshire Education, Warwickshire.
Hurwitz, A. & Day, M. (2001), *Children and their art: Methods for the elementary school*, 7th edn, Harcourt College Publishers, Orlando, Florida.
Mathieson, K. (1993), *Children's art and the computer*, Hodder & Stoughton, London.
Meltor, S. & Lavers, L. (2000), *Creating Art*, Holding Educational Aids, Sydney.
Ministry of Education, Victoria (1988), *Art maps: Art explorations for children*, Author, Melbourne.
NSW Department of School Education Curriculum Directorate (1990), *Aboriginal vision*, Author, Sydney.
NSW Department of School Education Curriculum Directorate (2000), *Beyond the frame*, Author, Sydney.
NSW Department of School Education Curriculum Directorate (2000), *Enter art*, Author, Sydney.
Stockley, M. (1991), *Art detective*, Reed International Books, Melbourne.
Stoikovich, V. (1993), *Visual Arts for teachers*, Holding Educational Aids, Sydney.
Wachowiak, R. & Clements, D. (2001), *Emphasis art: A qualitative art program for elementary and middle schools,* 7th edn, Longmans, Sydney.

USEFUL WEBSITES
National Society for Education in Arts and Design (UK)
www.nsead.org/search
National Art Education Association (USA)
www.naea-reston.org
National Art Education Association: Electronic Media Interest Group (USA)
www.cedarnet.org/emig/nb.html

The J. Paul Getty Trust (USA)
www.getty.edu/artsednet
Virtual teachers centre (UK)
www.vtc.ngfl.gov.uk/docserver.php?temid=57
Grove's dictionary of art terms
www.groveart.com
National Association for Gallery Education, London
www.engage.org
Art Gallery of New South Wales
www.artgallery.nsw.gov.au/collection
Virtual Art Galleries
www.theartgallery.com.au
www.art.com
http://gallery.euroweb.hu
Art Education
www.questia.com/Index.jsp?CRID=art_education&OFFID=se1&KEY=art_education_quotes
Art education ideas and posters
www.art-rageous.net
Kids Pix Integration Ideas
http://www.forsyth.k12.ga.us/sbeck/kid_pix_integration_ideas.htm

REFERENCES

Allen, P. (2004), *Grandpa and Thomas*, Penguin Books, Camberwell, Vic.
Allen, P. (2003), *The Potato People*, Penguin Books, Camberwell, Vic.
Baker, J. (1980), *Millicent*, Scholastic, Sydney.
Baker, J. (1989), *Where the forest meets the sea*, Scholastic, Sydney.
Baker, J. (1995), *The story of Rosy Dock*, Random House, Sydney.
Baker, J. (2004), *The hidden forest*, Scholastic, Sydney.
Baker, J. (2005), *Belonging*, Scholastic, Sydney.
French, J. (2003), *Diary of a wombat*, HarperCollins, Pymble, NSW.
Gleeson, L. (2002), *An ordinary day*, Scholastic Press, Gosford, NSW.
Graham, R. (2003), *Jethro Byrde, Fairy Child*, Walker Books, Newtown, NSW.
Grant, J. (2004), *Cat and fish*, Lothian Books, Melbourne, Vic.
Heffernan, J. (2004), *Two summers*, Scholastic Press, Gosford, NSW.
Matthews, P. (2003), *A year on our farm*, Omnibus Books, Gosford, NSW.
Murray, M. (2003), *The slightly true story of Cedar B. Hartley (who planned to live an unusual life)*, Allen & Unwin, Melbourne, Vic.
Norrington, L. (2003), *The Barrumbi kids*, Omnibus Books, Gosford, NSW.
Oliver, N. (2002), *Bilby Bilby, where do you sleep?*, Lothian Books, Melbourne, Vic.
Papunya School Publishing Committee (2003), *Papunya School Book of Country and History*, Allen & Unwin, Melbourne, Vic.
Riddle, T. (2001), *The singing hat*, Penguin Books, Camberwell, Vic.
Russell, E. (2001), *A is for aunty*, ABC Books, Sydney, NSW.
Tan, S. (2001), *The lost thing*, Lothian Books, Melbourne, Vic.
Wild, M. (2004), *Little Humpty*, Little Hare, Surry Hills, NSW.

chapter six
Introduction to dance education

Dance is a poem of which each movement is a word.
(Mata Hari)

Learning outcomes
By the end of this chapter, students will be able to:
- identify skills, knowledge and attitudes that children can learn both *through* and *in* dance;
- list the main elements in dance and demonstrate how they can be practically applied in the primary classroom;
- develop a dance education program showing how the three areas of making, performing and appreciating can be developed and implemented in a selected primary classroom.

Introduction

Children love to move! Babies learn about their world through movement and young children spontaneously respond to the music in their environment by moving their bodies. In many cultures, for thousands of years, movement, music, singing and dancing are an integral part of each person's life and being, with dance used as an expression of who they are within their community — an act of being, rather than a performance. Within this context, dance is a means of passing knowledge, skills and attitudes from one person to another, and from one generation to the next; it is a celebration of life, a ritual and a way of expressing grief, happiness, surprise, sorrow, joy and achievement.

Dance is a powerful vehicle for non-verbal communication, self-expression, creativity, and ways of knowing and learning and, as such, should be encouraged at all levels of schooling. Through active involvement in dance children develop physical, social, interpersonal, problem-solving, communication, creative and aesthetic skills. Every primary schoolteacher needs to understand, appreciate and utilise the power of dance within the classroom. Dance engages the physical, mental, creative and emotional self and through this unique medium children can learn about themselves and their world. Dance can be a work of art, it can be a ritual within a given context of culture, it can be a means of self-expression and it can give children the opportunity to create and communicate meaning about themselves and the world around them.

Learning *through* dance

Many children come to school with strong, well-developed musical and kinaesthetic intelligences and will learn much more easily if they are allowed to utilise these intelligences as they learn. But often they are told to sit still and stop wiggling, and are expected to learn using their weaker intelligences (e.g. verbal–linguistic or mathematical–logical); and so, in some cases, they are being set up for failure. Perhaps if they were allowed to learn the subject matter through movement and be able to express what they know through dance, they may learn more quickly and achieve success in the classroom.

Children can develop their physical fitness skills through dance.

Ways of learning *through* dance

There are at least six ways in which learning about other knowledge, skills and attitudes can be achieved through dance; these include the following:

Physical fitness

Dance can be part of a physical fitness program to develop children's physical skills of coordination, stamina and rhythm. These types of activity often occur in a physical education program when children learn dances from other cultures and contexts, such as the barn dance, the hokey pokey, the macarena

Space (where we move)

Space in dance includes:
- personal space and common space;
- patterns (straight, zigzag, curved);
- body shapes in space (straight, curled, stretched);
- size in space (big, small);
- extension (near, far);
- levels (high, medium, low);
- directions (up, down, sideways, forwards, backwards).

Relationships (with whom we move)

In dance we sometimes move by ourselves but often we move in relation to others. Relationships in dance explores:
- **Partner relationships.** These include:
  — meeting and greeting a partner;
  — being with a partner or parting from a partner;
  — leading a friend and being led by a friend.
- **Trio and small groups.** These include:
  — moving in line and circle formations;
  — moving simultaneously or separately;
  — moving together or away;
  — repeated movements in unison or individually;
  — individual movements relating to others in the group.
- **Large group movements.** These include:
  — structured or improvised movements as a whole group;
  — moving as a group individually or in unison.

Structure (how dance is organised)

Structure gives a dance form and unity. It includes:
- form of a dance — the same and different sections;
- unity and cohesiveness of a dance;
- repetition and contrasting movements;
- variety of movements including the same and different ones, movements and stillness, and contrasts in dynamics, time, space, relationships and action;
- transitions between individual movements and movement sequences.

Making, performing and appreciating dances

The key areas of learning in dance are making dances, performing dances and appreciating dances.

Making dances

As children become familiar with exploring and learning different movement techniques, skills and elements, they can begin to create their own dances, shaping them carefully using a variety of dance elements. Teachers should avoid the temptation of putting on a piece of music and expecting children to 'dance to it' if they have not had any previous instruction or experience in dance movements. Children should be introduced to making dances through simple, structured problem-solving activities so that they begin to learn about the process and language of creative dance. As they develop a more expansive movement vocabulary and gain more experience in creating dances, they will be able to work in a less structured environment.

Using varied stimuli, children can develop a simple sequence of dance movements. They can then develop, extend and adapt the original sequence to extend or enrich it. For example, the sequence of movements could be:

- repeated;
- performed backwards;
- performed facing a different direction;
- danced twice as quickly or twice as slowly;
- changed in relation to quality (i.e. smooth movements could be repeated in a jerky manner, or light movements could become heavy);
- performed at a different level (i.e. at a low level instead of at a high level);
- performed with another movement added in.

Once a series of movements has been decided upon, encourage children to use different structures in their dances. They may like to create a dance in A B, or binary, form, with one series of movements (A) followed by a different series of movements (B). Or they may like to extend this to ternary form, A B A, where A is danced, followed by B and then A is repeated. A rondo form of dance (A B A C A D A) has one series of movements (A) repeated and followed each time by a different series of movements (B C D and so on). Alternatively, the dance may follow the life cycle of a butterfly or a plant, it may tell a story or create an impression or emotion, or it may be a collage of different movement sequences put together to create a cohesive whole.

Steps in creating a dance

Creating a dance can include the following steps:

- **Problem.** The children are presented with a movement problem to be solved, for example: create a dance in response to an artwork, a story or a piece of music; create a dance using specified movements or focusing on one element; or dramatise a beach scene and then develop a series of movements from this dramatisation to create a dance.
- **Parameters.** Certain parameters or limitations are set for the creation of the dance, for example: use a designated amount of space within the classroom; the dance must use only four main movements; the dance must be in ternary form (e.g. A B A); and the dance must focus on using a variety of levels.

- **Problem solving.** Within the given parameters, the children then explore, improvise and experiment with ways to solve the problem using a variety of elements of dance. Children may start with a basic idea and then create a simple sequence of dance movements which they discuss, repeat, change and improvise further as the dance evolves. This can take some time as children with different abilities and skills work together to create a cohesive and aesthetic dance that portrays their solution to the given problem.

Children performing a rap they have created.

- **Practice.** Once the basic dance has been created and agreed upon, the children then practise this several times, making changes, adapting, refining further and rehearsing it until they are ready to share it with their peers.
- **Performance.** This should not be the main aim of the activity, as the learning achieved through the process is more important. However, performing a dance to an audience, however small, can build children's self-esteem and confidence and also provide them with constructive feedback so that they can improve and develop their dance further.
- **Ponder.** After creating and sharing their dance, children need to take the time to reflect and ponder on the creative process and appreciate their finalised dance in relation to what they have learned and experienced, and how effective their dance was in solving the given problem. This can be done individually, in pairs, in groups or as a class. Using a video of the performance can enhance and focus this reflection process.

Performing dances

Children need the opportunity to perform dances whether they are their own created dances, those directed by the teacher or traditional folk and cultural dances. Performance of dances can involve accurately performing phrases, sequences of movement or full dances with expression and musical rhythm. Performance can be as simple as one child demonstrating a single action he has developed to another child, a small group performing a short dance composition to their peers or the whole class presenting their rehearsed and polished dance to the rest of the school. Dance performances should include a variety of dance elements to create interest, should be structured with a clear beginning, middle and ending, and should start and end in stillness.

Structured dances

Learning to perform set dances can be developed through three stages:
1. **Cognitive and verbal stage.** In this beginning stage, the movements are verbalised as they are demonstrated, using cues and instructions. They are broken down

Encourage children to create their own dances.

into small segments that are rehearsed with feedback to identify difficulties and what is working well.

2. **Physical motor stage.** During this next stage, there is less input by the teacher, specific problems and difficulties are focused upon and rectified, and the children begin to take responsibility for the quality of their performance.

3. **Automatic stage.** This final stage occurs when children can complete the dance by themselves with few cues, instructions or directions from the teacher.

Different types of dance

As well as teaching structured dances for performance, ensure that a variety of different types of dance are included in a year's dance education program. These could include:

- teacher-directed dances;
- student compositions;
- cultural, traditional and historical dances.

Appreciating dances

Appreciation of dances involves observing and viewing dances; perceiving what the dance is about and what it is communicating; describing, analysing and interpreting what they see; and evaluating this using the language of dance. Dances can be viewed in the classroom as peers perform, or they can be viewed on video or at a live concert. As children develop in their learning about the process of dance making they will learn the language of dance and be able to use this as they discuss and reflect on their own dances and those of their peers. With experience, they will also develop skills to be actively involved in a discussion about their interpretations and reactions to dances they see in the classroom, on stage and on a video, using the language of dance.

Through their discussions, children should be able to show their understanding about how dance is different from normal human movement, how the language of dance can be used to describe what they see, and how different cultures and contexts produce different kinds of dance. Children should be encouraged to use metaphors and analogy to interpret the ideas seen in dances, show their understanding of the roles that music, lighting, costuming, props and sets play in the dances, if appropriate, and discuss intelligently the cultural and contextual differences seen in a variety of dances.

Practical considerations

Teaching dance lessons brings different challenges and rewards from teaching many other subjects. Many teachers do not feel comfortable in dancing themselves, let alone teaching dance, and there are significant safety issues to be considered as well as working out where to hold the class, how to manage the behaviour of the children, what to include in a dance lesson, and how to use music and other resources effectively. These are covered in the following section.

I'm not a dancer!

Some teachers have had the wonderful experience of learning a wide variety of dances for many years through private dance lessons, and many of these teachers have taught dance to small and large groups inside and outside of the school situation. They are well equipped with the knowledge, skills and abilities to teach and perform dances. However, the majority of generalist primary school teachers have had very little background in dance or dance education and may feel hesitant to implement dance lessons in their classroom. But teaching creative dance lessons can be exciting and rewarding for all teachers if they are willing to approach the experience with enthusiasm, creativity, a desire to learn and a positive attitude! Be prepared to try something new, to have fun and to be creative with the children.

Preparation

- When you set up the classroom or hall for dance ensure you have a safe, clear space free from obstacles.
- Decide beforehand if you want children to take off their shoes and socks, in view of the type of activities you are going to do with them, the smell (especially on a hot summer day), the time this may take out of your lesson, whether or not the children can find and put on their shoes themselves at the end of the lesson, and whether their shoes are suitable for the dance activity.
- Establish physical boundaries and let the children know what areas of the hall, classroom or playground are out of bounds.
- Establish clear signals for simple instructions instead of shouting them out; for example clapping hands or blowing a whistle could indicate they have one more minute to complete their activity, or that everyone should freeze still. Practise these until they become routine and children follow them immediately.
- Know what activities children have done, what skills they have developed and what stage and outcomes they are working towards (this could be different for different children). Teach the elements, techniques and structures for dance before expecting children to create their own dances.

Safety

As children are moving freely and expressively around the room or hall, it is imperative that safety considerations are thought through beforehand and implemented carefully.

Warm-ups

Always do a warm-up activity when children start a dance class. Warm-ups increase the blood supply and circulation of blood to the muscles; they allow the muscles to contract and relax more quickly; and they loosen the muscles, tendons and ligaments to help prevent injuries. As well as their physical benefits, warm-ups also assist students in focusing on the present learning experience and develop a unity of purpose.

Neck rolls

Avoid asking children to do full neck rolls (i.e. a complete rotation of the head) as this could cause injury. Rather, have them gently and slowly roll their heads from the left shoulder, down to their chest and then up to the right shoulder and back. They can also move their head to their right shoulder and then to their left shoulder and repeat. If any child has had a neck problem, advise that child not to do this exercise.

Room to move

Ensure that there is sufficient space for the number of children to move comfortably without them invading the personal space of other children. If this is impossible in the classroom, consider moving to the school hall or outside in the playground. Do not allow children to climb on stacked chairs, desks or the stage and so on, or to play with equipment around the hall. Ensure that there are no obstacles in the space in which children are moving. Be aware and act to prevent possible collisions with stacked chairs when you tell children to run to the sides of a hall or classroom. If children are to lie down or do floor work ensure the floor is clean.

Know your children

Children need to be taught and encouraged to identify and take notice of what their body is telling them in relation to pain or fatigue. Avoid making children do exercises or activities which their body type or fitness levels do not allow them to do safely (e.g. running and jumping, tumbling, or doing cartwheels or head stands). Be aware of cultural and gender issues that might be relevant in your classroom, such as asking children of the opposite sex to hold hands, certain beliefs about dance held by some cultures, walking over bodies or sitting with the soles of the feet facing another person. Be aware also of those children who will need to be encouraged to join in because they are shy or scared of being embarrassed.

If a child is injured

If an injury such as a strained muscle does occur, use the **RICED** method:

R: *Rest* the injured limb or body part.

I: Apply *ice* to the injured area; this can be a bag of frozen peas, a cold pack or ice cubes (wrapped in a towel to prevent ice burns). Apply the ice for 10–20 minutes at frequent intervals. Avoid putting ice on an open wound in case of infection.

C: Apply a *compression* or moderately firm bandage to reduce the swelling. Bandage the area above, below and on the injured area. Do not bandage too tightly or this might constrict circulation.

E: *Elevate* and support the limb or injured area above the level of the heart as this will encourage the blood to flow back to the heart.

D: Take the child to a doctor as soon as possible for an accurate *diagnosis*.

Classroom organisation

In an ideal world, a large hall with a mirrored wall and specially designed dance floor would be perfect for dance lessons! But few primary schools have access to such a luxury. The minimum requirements for a dance lesson would be for the children to use a classroom with all the desks and chairs pushed back, leaving sufficient room for children to move in the centre of the room. As long as the floor is carpeted or wooden, has no splinters and is not slippery, it should suffice. Know where the power points are and how to work the relevant equipment and have music ready to play so time is not wasted cueing the cassette or finding the CD. If working outside, set physical parameters in the environment outside of which children are not allowed.

What to wear

Both the teacher and the children should wear loose, comfortable clothing that does not inhibit movement. Sports uniform would be preferred but this may not be possible as there may not be a place to change or children may not have brought it to wear. Shoes should be soft and flexible or children could have bare feet as this is not as slippery as wearing socks. Be aware that expecting young children to find and put on their own shoes after a dance lesson may take some time!

Discipline in the dance class

Because children are moving around and interacting with each other in a large open space, this could increase the possibility of disruption of the class by some children. Teachers need to establish their own balance of freedom and control within a dance class; however, authoritarian discipline ruled by fear is an inappropriate environment for encouraging creative activities such as dance. Read through and implement the behaviour management suggestions in Chapter 2, 'The creative arts classroom' but also consider the following suggestions.

Rules, routines and rewards

In any class setting, good discipline occurs when children use their self-control to comply and meet the set rules and expectations of the teacher. In order for this to happen, children need to be taught how to be self-controlled and the teacher, in discussion with the children, needs to set clear rules, routines and expectations for how the children should behave. Rules, routines, rewards and consequences need to be outlined clearly at the start of the lesson and the teacher should ensure that all children understand these.

Catch children being good and following instructions and praise them for it! Focus on the appropriate actions that children are doing and avoid reinforcing negative actions. Expect the children to listen carefully and follow instructions and avoid repeating these more than once or twice so children learn that they must listen carefully. Be consistent in your responses: if you ignore or reprimand one child for doing something, do the same for all children doing the same action.

As children naturally like to move, it is really important that in a dance lesson they have this opportunity. Avoid spending a lot of time talking about dance; rather, let the children experiment, explore, practise and create dance movements throughout the lesson. Be punctual, show effective time management, keep the lesson moving and give the children the respect you would like to receive. If a child is not doing the right action, and praising others doing the correct actions does not change the child's behaviour, talk to the child alone, addressing the behaviour and avoid attacking the child verbally.

Refusal to join in

Sometimes a child will refuse to join in a dance activity. In this situation, it is really important that the teacher takes the time to find out why the child is behaving this way. This should be done away from the rest of the class so the child is not embarrassed and the situation does not become a battle of wills (or won'ts!) in front of an audience. Make time to establish dialogue with any such children to find out why they do not want to join in. It may be because they have the wrong clothes or shoes, they are scared of making a fool of themselves, dance is not seen as culturally acceptable in a mixed classroom, they are upset over something that happened at home or at school, or they don't like the activity. With discussion, a compromise should be worked out; ask the student for suggestions as to how to overcome the problem and assure them that you really need and want them to join in, if this is possible. A shy child may sit out and watch the first lesson and then be encouraged to become involved a little more in each ensuing lesson.

Time-out

If a situation arises where a child needs time-out, make provision for this in the classroom. This should not have negative connotations; rather, it should be seen as giving the child the opportunity to sit apart from the rest of the class and have time to remember and practise the self-control that the child has shown in previous lessons. Make time-out sessions short and allow the children to rejoin when they think they have regained their self-control. Ensure they do not distract the rest of the class during their time-out — you may decide to have them watch the class quietly or face the wall. If time-out and talking with the child does not achieve the desired self-control and changed behaviour, you may need to separate the child from the class and follow the school's discipline policy for disruptive behaviour.

Using music and other resources

Music is a key component of the dance lesson. Choose the music carefully so that it is appropriate to the children and the dance activity. The choice of music needs to reflect the type of dance lesson (e.g. whether children are learning a social dance, doing aerobics or creating their own dance on a theme), and the teacher needs to have easy access to the CD player for stopping and starting the music. It may be easier to put all the music for one lesson onto one cassette or CD instead of taking time to cue or change the cassettes or CDs for each activity.

Locomotor movements to music.

Using songs

Check that any lyrics of songs used are appropriate to the age group; that is, avoid using songs that are of an explicitly sexual or violent nature or that show disrespect to certain groups in the community. Use a variety of styles of music and include music from different eras, cultures and contexts so children are exposed to music other than what they hear every day. Vary the music used in each lesson so children do not become bored with listening to the same piece over and over again! This will also stimulate and aid motivation within the lesson.

Beat and tempo

Generally, use music with a strong, discernible beat so, if appropriate, children can count the beats as they dance. However, some creative dance may not be performed to a beat so this may not be a consideration for all dance activities. Check that the tempo (speed) of the music that children are using for their dances is appropriate (not too fast or too slow). You may start clapping to the music in cut time, so children use two beats for each movement instead of one movement per beat, as they are learning or experimenting with the movements. Increase this to one movement per beat when children become more confident in their dance.

Percussion instruments

Using commercial music is generally a key ingredient in dance classes, but often a simple tambour or other percussion instrument can also be used as a stimulus for dance. For example, children can move in time to the beat of the tambour; they can move lightly when they hear the triangle and heavily when they hear the tambourine, or quickly when the rhythm sticks are played and slowly when the maracas are heard; and they can step the rhythms played on a drum or freeze when they hear the bells. They can create their own music with percussion instruments, record it and then develop a dance to their composed music.

Other resources

Using props such as scarves, ribbon sticks, balls and balloons help children lose their inhibitions and give them a focus for their movements. They also add colour, enjoyment and motivation to the dance lesson. The use of flashcards can also enhance a dance lesson as many children are visual learners, and young children and those from a non-English speaking background need pictures to remind them of actions or words. For example, instead of having groups of children make up a dance based on different movements which you have introduced, you could have multiple flashcards with pictures and words of several different movements and allow each group to select four flashcards, put them in the order of the dance they are creating, and use them as cues to help them in the development of their dance sequences.

Most children enjoy participating in movement lessons.

Pictures, artworks, toys, stories and action songs can also be used effectively as stimuli for creative dance and to explain about the different elements in dance. Encourage children to discuss how they could create a dance based on one of these stimuli and then ask them to move into groups and, given certain parameters, develop a dance sequence to share with the rest of the class.

Teaching social dances

When teaching social dances begin by forming the children into lines as generally teaching these dances in a circle is more difficult. After warm-ups, start by introducing some of the steps or movements from the dance. Practise these in different ways so children become accustomed to doing them as discrete movements. Make sure you face the children and mirror the movements of the dance to avoid confusion; that is, if the movement is to lift the right arm, the teacher should lift the left arm.

When teaching the dance, talk and walk through the instructions as children do the movements, before putting on the music. When children are beginning to show they understand and can do most of the movements, add the music to the dance along with giving the verbal cues. Then have the children practise the movements as a couple or in small groups.

When they are confident of the movements, have the children practise in the correct formation for the dance. As the dance progresses give verbal cues throughout to keep everyone together and to help the children remember the movements. Repeat several times, watching for sections of the dance that are causing difficulties or are going well. Praise and refine movement each time the dance is repeated. Finish with a 'cooling-down' or relaxation activity.

Developing a creative dance lesson

Dance lessons need to be well organised, thoroughly prepared and carefully paced. Establish the rules, rewards and routines at the start and keep these consistently throughout the lesson. Remind children of rules such as 'no talking, no touching' as they move, unless appropriate. Encourage them to move around the room being aware of their own personal space and that of others, and to freeze at the sound of the drum. Make sure all children listen to, and understand, the instructions and ensure that these are short and simple. Use verbal and physical cues with which children are familiar for activities such as forming two lines, freezing, facing in one direction, sitting down and standing straight. At times you will need to demonstrate the activities or movements and you may also have children demonstrate what they have practised.

Start each lesson with *warm-ups* to centre and focus the students and to prevent injury. These can be related to the theme of the lesson or to reinforce a previously learned skill. Follow this with the *introduction* of a new skill, dance element or technique and then spend time exploring and *practising* this skill, element or technique. Move around the room, watching the children as they develop and practise this technique, correcting them and praising them as appropriate. Allow the children to apply what they have learned by *creating their own dance* to reinforce and show that they have understood these skills, elements or techniques, and then share it with their peers for *reflection* and feedback. Finish the lesson with a time of *relaxation* to centre and settle the children before they leave the lesson. This could include doing simple, slow movements; sitting or lying

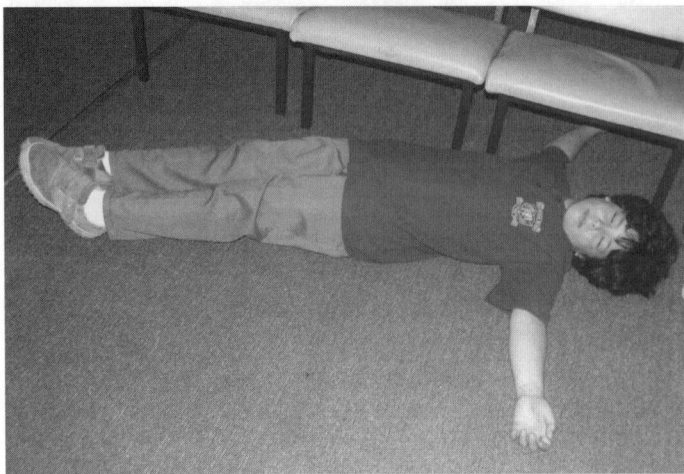
End a lesson with time to relax and cool down.

still; deep, slow breathing; resting and consciously relaxing individual parts of the body; or talking through a relaxing visualisation activity. When children (and you) are ready, have them bring movement back into their bodies slowly, turn on their sides if lying on the ground, push themselves to a sitting position, *stretch* and then stand up and stretch again. Try to finish the lesson on a bright, encouraging and positive note.

Activities to introduce the elements of dance

Here are some general warm-up activities, followed by sample learning experiences to introduce the different elements of dance and ideas for student compositions. For each element, warm-up and introductory activities are suggested, which are followed by creative dances that apply the element. A cooling-down session closes the set of activities. Start with these, adapt them for your particular class and then, using these ideas as a springboard, develop your own activities.

Warm-ups

Warm-ups can be used to develop routines, help the children focus on the theme to be covered in the lesson and learn certain rules (e.g. everyone freezes when the drum is played), release energy, develop trust and respect among their classmates, and warm up the body to prevent injury. Here are some suggestions of warm-up activities.

Keep it up!

Have the class stand fairly closely together. Throw a ball straight up in the air. The class must keep it in the air for as long as possible, counting each hit. No student should hit the ball more than once consecutively. Once the ball touches the ground, restart the game and the counting.

Extension: To change the speed of the game, use a balloon instead of a ball.

Warm-ups can help prevent injury.

Can't catch my tail!

Have every child choose a partner. All the children are given a scarf or square of material to attach to the back of their belt, skirt, collar or trousers. On the word 'go' students try to steal their partner's tail (scarf) while protecting their own. Each time a tail is stolen, the player gains a point. Points can be compared just within the pairs to find out who 'won' or as a whole-class ranking. If the teacher prefers this warm-up game to be non-competitive, every time a scarf is stolen it is given back and the game starts again, but no scores are kept.

Extension: To make this more difficult, turn it into a whole-class game, where everyone is trying to 'steal' as many tails as they can, while still protecting their own 'tail'.

Name game

Have each child clap the syllables of his/her own name, within four beats (e.g. Mary Lee). Add a different movement for each syllable, for example:

- Ma- = Clap hand above head.
- ry = Click fingers in both hands at same time.
- Lee = Turn around on the spot.

Have all children say their names and do appropriate actions around the circle, trying to vary the levels of each movement.

Extension: Have children say the names of the previous three children as well as their own, with the relevant actions, keeping to a steady beat.

Isolation of body parts

Begin at the *top of the head* and work down to the feet, isolating and moving each body part one by one (e.g. head, shoulders, arms, hands, fingers, fists, torso, bottom, knees, ankles, feet and toes). Avoid full neck rolls (see section on safety, above).

- **Spinal column.** Bend knees, touch ground with fingers, straighten one knee, relax, and straighten the other knee.
- **Legs.** Wiggle toes, rotate ankles one way and then the other, bend knees, rotate pelvis, lift knees, walk lifting knees high, run on the spot, make small jumps, make small star jumps and hop on alternate legs.
- **Arms.** Flick fingers, shake wrists, jab elbows, rotate elbows in circles backwards and then forwards, rotate shoulders backwards and then forwards, rotate arms together backwards and then forwards, and then individually.
- **General.** Walk around, shaking hands, feet, torso, head and whole body.

Dead cockroaches

The teacher calls out words at random and students respond, for example:

- **Dead cockroaches.** Lie with back on floor with feet and hands waving in the air.
- **Fish.** Lie on tummy, arms opening and closing on floor in front of head, and mouth opening and closing like a fish!
- **Dynamite.** Bend knees (say '5–4–3–2–1'), jump up and say, 'Boom!'
- **Sprinter.** Say the words and do the actions: 'Ready' (crouch); 'Steady' (raise up); 'Go' (run on the spot).

Loves me, loves me not!

Children (A and B) pair up and each child lines up at opposite walls, facing their partner. At the given word, children run to the centre, meet their partner, perform the action and then run back to the wall.

- **Phone call: Yes!** Pairs run together, pick up a pretend phone and talk to each other, gesticulating and talking excitedly in a made-up language.
- **It's love: Aaah!** Pairs run towards each other, arms outstretched, join their hands, look into each other's eyes, sigh, turn a full circle and go back to their places.
- **Proposal: Wow!** Pairs run to the centre; one person kneels and the other person stands; they hold hands and look adoringly into each other's eyes.

- **Marriage: I do!** A catches B in his/her arms; A spins B around; A puts B down and runs back to wall (or create an adaptation of this, depending on the size of the partner!).
- **Divorce: Oh dear!** Stand still in the centre, back to back without touching or talking, and arms crossed.

Action (what we move)

Warm-ups: Awareness of different parts of the body

Have the children experiment with moving single parts of the body at a time. Find out what each part can do, for example:

- Move your finger, then your hand, then your forearm and then your shoulder. Now move your whole arm.
- Move your toes, then your foot and then your knee. Now move your whole leg.
- Move your eyes, then your nose and then your tongue. Now move your whole head.
- Move your left arm, then your right arm and then your head. Now move your body from the waist up.
- Sit down and move your right leg; move your left leg; move your left arm; move your right arm; and move your head.
- Stand up and move your whole body in as many ways as possible.

Isolate different parts of the body and have the children act out the situations.

- **Fingers and toes**
  — Move these in all directions and at different speeds, pretending that they are live animals.
- **Feet and legs**
  — You are walking through quicksand. Pull each leg out in turn, as the sand tries to suck you under.
- **Hands and arms**
  — Your feet are glued to the ground.
  — Hang out a basket of washing.
  — Pick some roses.
  — Chase away flies from all around you.
  — Type a letter.
  — Be a windmill.
- **Heads and shoulders**
  — You know someone is creeping up behind you. Turn your head this way and that, trying to see who it is, while keeping your feet glued to the ground.
  — You are behind a crowd of tall people and you try to see over them, between their legs and around them. What do you see?
- **Trunk**
  — Try to open a sliding door, while holding a pile of heavy parcels.
  — Play with a ball, trying to keep it in the air without using arms, legs or head.

Isolate and move different parts of the body.

Consequences: Non-locomotor movements

Brainstorm movement words for different parts of the body. Brainstorm adverbs to describe how these actions will be done. Write the name of a body part on the top of your paper, fold it down to cover the word, and pass it to the next person. Write down an action under the doubled-over piece of paper, fold the paper to cover the word and pass the paper on to the next person. Write an adverb to describe an action at the bottom of the paper, fold it over and pass it on. Unfold the paper, read what has been written, and then do the action with the specified body part in the specified way.

Locomotor movements

Walk around the room doing a series of locomotor actions to a steady beat, for example:

- walk
- run
- leap
- hop
- jump
- skip
- gallop
- slide

Form a circle, and put these movements together in a sequence of four beats per movement, moving around the circle, to music; repeat in a different direction; repeat while facing towards the centre of the circle; and repeat moving backwards.

Divide the class into small groups and have each group select four of these movements and then create a movement sequence from them, using symmetry, contrasts and repetition. Start and end in stillness.

Move and touch

Have the children form two rows facing each other. The first person (A) takes a series of four of the locomotor movements (see above activity) and uses these to move across to the other row. A touches the first person in the other row, using a part of the body other than the hands, and sits down. The touched person (B) uses a series of four locomotor movements, different from A's or in a different order, to move across the room. B touches the next person in the first row, not using the hands and then sits down. This is repeated until everyone has had a turn.

Symmetrical body jive

Divide the class into small groups. Each group is given a different part of the body (shoulders, hands, head, arms and legs). Using some of the brainstormed movement words or other words, create an eight-beat non-locomotor sequence of activities for their body part on the right side of the body. Repetitions and contrast may be used. Repeat using the body part on the left side. This is Part A of the dance.

Repeat as a locomotor sequence, making changes where necessary. Repeat. This is Part B of the dance.

Put the two sequences together in ternary form (A B A) to create a 48-beat dance sequence to music.

Cool down

Sit or lie down in a comfortable position. Close your eyes gently. Go through each body part individually, tightening the relevant muscles and then relaxing them. Be conscious of each body part relaxing and remaining relaxed as you move onto tightening and relaxing another body part. Breathe slowly and deeply using diaphragmatic breaths. When you are ready, slowly open your eyes, stretch, roll onto your side, stretch, stand up and stretch.

Time (when we move)

Warm-ups

- Move arms fast and then slowly.
- Move legs fast and then slowly.
- Move head slowly from side to side, and then slightly more quickly (children should avoid this if they have known neck problems).
- Move shoulders slowly in a circle backwards, then becoming faster.
- Move shoulders fast forwards in a circle and then slow down.
- Walk on the spot, get faster and then slower.
- Walk to a steady beat played by a drum, around the room, swinging arms; change the speed of beat to faster or slower and make movements faster or slower in response.

Awareness of tempo (fast and slow)

- You are a large whale, slowly moving through the water. Suddenly you become a tiny fish, darting in and out of the seaweed.
- You are creeping up slowly behind a dangerous enemy. The enemy turns around and you scurry back to safety.
- You are slowly climbing a steep, rocky hill. Now you are running quickly down the other side.
- You are a fly buzzing all around the room. Someone showers you with fly spray and you gradually slow down and die on the ground.
- You are running a race that has been filmed. Play it back at twice the speed; play it back in slow motion.

Extension: Act out any everyday action using different tempos (speeds).

Fast and slow names

Have all the children work out body movements to the syllables of their name. Practise doing it fast and then slowly (e.g. Maaaaaa — ryyyyyyyy, Ma-ry). Share movements with the rest of the class who then copy it.

Ribbon sticks/scarves: *Minoeska* (Russian dance)

(Music alternates between fast and slow tempos and is from the CD *Off the wall dances* by Gary and Carol Crees.)

Practise making the ribbon sticks or scarves move fast and slowly. Experiment with different movements, making the ribbons or scarves go in, out, up and down, on different levels and in different directions. Form a circle and follow the leader, showing the fast and slow parts of the music to create a circle dance. Change the leader each time the slow section is heard. Roll up ribbons or scarves and put them away.

Hare and tortoise
Read or tell a story about characters who move quickly or slowly. Have the children move in response to the tempo of each of these characters as the story is read or told.

Moving to different time signatures
Find music in different time signatures and have children move to show the different grouping of beats. Most popular music is in either 2/4 or 4/4; music in 3/4 is more difficult to find — try waltzes, classical music or some folk songs. For example:
- 2/4   Seesaw up and down.
- 3/4   Push a swing for three beats up, pull back for three beats.
- 4/4   Throw a ball to two beats, catch it to two beats.

Chaotic factory
Have the children form groups of four. Each group is to create a machine, with each person being part of it, and each person being on a different level from each other but fitting into each other.

Follow the beat of the drum as it dictates the speed of the factory full of machines:
- slow
- getting faster
- fast
- very fast
- getting slower
- slow
- stop and freeze.

Cool down
Keep in the position held at the end of the final activity. As the xylophone plays a descending scale, slowly melt down into a liquid molten mass on the floor and find a comfortable position to lie in. Close your eyes, relax your muscles, feel yourself becoming really heavy and sink down into the earth, being fully relaxed.

When you are ready, slowly open your eyes; move your fingers, toes, arms and legs; roll on your side; sit up; stretch; stand up; and stretch again.

Create a group of machines within a factory.

Dynamics (how you move)

Warm-ups

- Tiptoe on the spot.
- Stamp your feet heavily on the spot.
- Walk around the room as though there is someone sleeping that you don't want to disturb.
- Walk as though the floor is a drum and your feet are playing it loudly.
- Move without letting your feet leave the ground.
- Pretend the floor is on fire and walk across it.
- Stride confidently in one direction in a straight line.
- Come back in a circuitous route.
- Travel as though tied in a straightjacket with feet hobbled.
- Come back light and free as a bird or butterfly.

Moving emotions
Sing: 'If You're Happy and You Know It!' and change the words to reflect different emotions and related movements, for example:

> **If You're Happy and You Know It!**
> Verse 1 If you're angry and you know it, Stamp your feet!
> Verse 2 If you're scared and you know it, Tiptoe round!
> Verse 3 If you're proud and you know it, Stride along!
> Verse 4 If you're tired and you know it, Meander slowly!
> Verse 5 If you're angry and you know it, Walk so stiff!
> Verse 6 If you're carefree and you know it, Float away!

Make the appropriate whole body movements as each verse is sung.

Heavy and light movements
- Fill a box up with solid gold bars, and try to carry the box across the room. Take all the gold out and skip back with the empty box.
- You are making a rock garden and have to move a pile of large rocks into different places. Suddenly the rocks turn into feathers and you fill a pillow with them.
- You are pulling a box of books up a steep hill. Every time you stop, it slips back. Five strong people appear and push the box up the hill, as you pull. Show the difference in your movement.
- You are carrying a large sheet of cardboard and a strong wind is blowing against you. You battle forward — every step is an effort. You turn round to go home and now the wind is behind you. Feel and show the difference in your movements.
- Play catch with a friend and an imaginary ball. Each time the ball comes back to you it has become heavier. Start with pretending to throw a ping-pong ball, and stop when you can no longer lift the large, heavy ball.

MMADD about the arts

Dynamic contrasts

Listen to the percussion instruments as you move in different, teacher-directed ways:

- skating lightly, smoothly (bells);
- stamping heavily (drum);
- marching in a straight line (xylophone: play ascending the scale);
- meandering through the forest (xylophone: moving beater quickly over the keys);
- robot (tambourine hit to beat);
- rag doll (bells).

Coloured movements

Brainstorm words associated with different colours, for example:

- red: angry, embarrassed, danger, fire;
- yellow: bright, happy, sunshine, sparkle;
- blue: sea, dreams, dolphins, sky.

Divide the class into small groups, and have each group take a colour and decide on four contrasting words that relate to their colour. Create simple, whole body movements to represent each word, putting the colour before each word, and repeat it, for example:

Red anger, red anger!
Red embarrassed, red embarrassed!
Red danger, red danger!
Red fire, red fire!

Blue sea, blue sea,
Blue dreams, blue dreams,
Blue dolphin, blue dolphin,
Blue sky, blue sky.

Coloured scarves may be used as props. Ensure that some movements are heavy and some are light, that movements are focused and clear, and that children use the whole body. Blend movements from one to the next to create a smooth movement sequence. Change direction and repeat the movement sequence.

Moving emotions

Look at pictures or masks portraying different emotions and identify these emotions. Have children demonstrate how to show each emotion with their whole body, with either heavy or light movements. Have each pair of children take four different emotions and use their whole body to portray each emotion, using contrasting movements of flow and tension (e.g. sad, surprised, happy, angry). Move through one emotion to the next, blending the four emotions together, one after the other to create a smooth sequence of movements showing contrasts in

These children are showing anger with the whole body.

heavy and light movements. Pair A shares their sequences with another pair (B) who respond with comments. Pair B shares their sequence of movements and Pair A responds with comments. Join the two sequences (A and B) together. Work out a structure for the dance:

- A B A B A
- A A B B or
- A B B A

Share the movement sequence.

Extension: Have Pair A create a sequence using heavy movements and Pair B create a sequence using light movements.

Cool down

Stand in a space by yourself. At each drum beat, you are 'zapped' with a high voltage electricity current and your whole body reacts strongly and sharply, followed by a relaxation of the tension. Repeat this a couple of times, and then the third time the electricity is so powerful that all your muscles melt and you relax smoothly and gently to the ground or to a chair. Concentrate on your breathing and feel the heaviness of each muscle as it has melted and melded with your limbs.

When you are ready, wiggle your fingers and toes, open your eyes, take a deep breath, stand up slowly and stretch.

Space (where we move)

Warm-ups: Exploring different aspects of space

Develop *spatial awareness* by having the children act out some of the following situations.

- **Common Space**
  — Pretend you are carrying a crystal bowl full of water through a large crowd. You must be very careful not to touch anyone else, or you may spill the water or drop the bowl.
    Extension: You are carrying eggs or a large sheet of glass through the crowd.
  — You are a lion, stalking a gazelle. As you hear the drum tapped, you hide and freeze, and then continue stalking.
  — Gas is leaking out all over the room. Grab it in handfuls and push and punch it into a large balloon. Collect it from all around the room: up high, down low, round behind you and in all the corners.
  — Suddenly you become the gas-filled balloon and you float anywhere in the room, being careful not to touch anyone else, or you will both burst.
  — The balloon lands on a beach, which is full of starfish. It bursts, and you have to find your way to the sea, being careful not to tread on any of the starfish.
  — You plunge into the sea, and have to find your way through its dark depths, avoiding all the fish, seaweeds, sharp coral and other dangerous sea life.

- **Personal space**
  — You are inside a large plastic bag. Try to punch a hole through it, so you can get some air to breathe. Punch it all around you, trying to find the weakest spot.

- Suddenly the bag turns into a wooden box. Your feet are stuck to the floor and you try to paste wallpaper to cover the total inside of the box.
- You decide to paint a message in bright colours over the wallpaper. Try to cover the whole surface with your message.
- The inside of the box becomes pitch black and you have to find out if there is a tiny crack or opening in it. Feel all around the box, from the ceiling to the floor, in front of you and behind you, in all directions.
- You find a crack and manage to squeeze yourself through it, only to find you have turned into a bird and you are locked in a cage. Flutter all around the small cage trying to escape.
- You are being attacked by a swarm of flies. As each one lands on you, try to hit it. They are all over you, sitting on every part of your body; try to chase away as many as you can.

- **Direction**
    - You are a bullet from a gun, shooting across the sky. See how many different directions you can go in.
      Extension: You are a shooting star, a cannon ball or a softball.
    - Your hand has taken charge of your body — everywhere your hand leads you, you follow.
      Extension: Use your elbow, foot or head, as separate leaders for your body.
    - It is autumn and you are picking apples. The best ones are at the top of the tree. Reach up for them and place them gently in a basket on the ground.
    - You are taking your two pet dogs for a walk. They both pull on the lead, and are off — each one pulling you in different directions. Follow one and then the other.
    - Your friend has fallen into the river. Reach out over the edge and pull her back to safety.

- **Patterns**
    - Your whole body is a paintbrush. You are being used to paint beautiful designs on a large wall.
    - You are a flame in a fire, leaping, twisting and sparking in the fireplace.
    - Then you rise as smoke through the chimney, and a gust of wind blows you around, making you into a constantly changing shape.
    - You are the colours in a kaleidoscope, changing your pattern at every move.

- **Body shapes in space**
    - You are at a disco, and a strobe light is flashing. Every time it lights the room you are a different shape.
    - You are a lump of hot, molten glass.

Exploring body shapes in space.

The glassblower breathes gently through his pipe, and you are constantly changing shape.
— You are a clay sculpture at an exhibition. Every time you hear the drum, change your shape.
— You are a marionette; show through your body shape emotions such as joy, fear, happiness, guilt, sadness, courage, hate and dejection.
— You are a carton of fireworks. Suddenly a match ignites the whole box and you explode into many beautiful shapes and patterns.

- **Levels (low, medium, high)**
  — You are in a desert, and have used your last food and water many days ago. You crawl along the ground, following every mirage until it disappears. Soon exhaustion overtakes you. You dream you are wading waist deep through cool water. Gently push your way through the lilies that grow on top of the water. You reach the other side, climb out and stretch up to gather an armful of the most delicious fruit you have ever tasted. The tree is tall and you have to stretch up high to pick the fruit.

Create a sculpture at a low level.

  — You are escaping from a prison, through a low, narrow, dark tunnel. Keep easing yourself forward as you look toward the pinpoint of light in the distance. The tunnel opens out into a field of corn. Run quickly through it, keeping low so no one can see you. You jump the fence, and you are free! Shout for joy and jump up high, stretching your body out to its extremities as you celebrate your freedom.
  — You are a tiny red ember, smouldering among some paper and wood. Gradually you ignite the paper and your flames crackle gently. The wood catches fire and you turn into a blazing bonfire, leaping and flaming in all directions.
  — You are dusting a very high shelf full of precious china. An expensive vase falls and breaks into a thousand pieces. Search in every nook and cranny on the floor for all the tiny pieces. Sit at a table and try to glue them back together to form the vase again.
  — Form small groups and, being conscious of different levels used, create a movement picture on a theme (e.g. a factory, a race or on the beach).

Sculptures

Create yourself into a sculpture at a high, medium or low level — make sure you are different (in level and shape) from your two neighbours. As your name is called, move to a different level and a different shape and hold it until the next person's name is called.

Groups of three

Form groups of three and call each person a different letter name: A, B or C.
- A creates a shape with her body and holds it.
- C has his back to A.

MMADD about the arts

Freeze and hold the moment.

- B describes the shape A has created and C tries to put his own body into this shape.

Repeat, changing positions.

Exploring movements in personal and common space

- **Jumping.** Jump on the spot, jump while running, make small jumps, make large jumps, jump fast and then slow, and jump on one foot and then on two feet.
- **Turning.** Turn on the spot, using a large space and then a small space; turn quickly and then slowly; turn at a high and then a low level; follow your elbow; follow your nose; and follow your ankle.
- **Moving up and down.** Move slowly, quickly, straight, sharply, down into the centre of your body, up and out into the world, kneel down on the ground and stretch out, stand up and curl into the centre of your body.
  Extension: Scatter seed in a paddock; stretch out hands and fingers. Pull a heavy fishing net full of fish into a boat.
- **Emotions.** Use the whole body to show the following emotions: sadness, happiness, surprise, anger, puzzlement and so on.
- **Stillness.** Freeze and hold the movement in the above activity, relax and stand still, make another movement and then freeze into stillness, before creating another full body movement. Repeat.

Exploring space

At a signal, move in one of the ways explored in the above activity and then freeze until the next signal. Use these movements to form a movement sequence within a given structure, for example:

- 4 beats   Jump
- 4 beats   Turn
- 4 beats   Jump
- 4 beats   Extension
- 4 beats   Move up
- 4 beats   Move down
- 4 beats   Show an emotion
- 4 beats   Stillness

Make smooth transitions from one movement to the next one.

Going to school

Improvise different floor patterns which show the way you may walk when going to school; that is, across the hall to the bathroom, back to your bedroom, down the stairs to have breakfast, up the stairs to get ready for school, down the stairs, out the door, down the path, to the bus, off the bus, to your classroom and sit down in class. Use these floor patterns to create a dance about going to school.

Initial pattern

Using the first initial of your name, move around the room, drawing it with your feet as you dance. When you can do this comfortably, write your whole name across the floor of the classroom to create a simple dance.

Move to the beat

Find a space and identify it as your own place in space. To eight drum beats, walk across the room in a straight line, returning to your place at the eighth beat.
- Repeat, walking in a zigzag pattern.
- Repeat, but with 16 beats, and use a curved pattern on the floor.
- Repeat, and at every multiple of four, reach out to a different level (e.g. 4 = high; 8 = low; 12 = medium; 16 = high).
- Repeat, but on every fourth beat, show a different size with your body in space (e.g. 4 = big; 8 = small; 12 = wide; 16 = skinny).
- Repeat, but on every fourth beat, change to move in a different direction (e.g. 4 = forwards; 8 = sideways to the right; 12 = backwards; 16 = diagonally).
- Move into groups of four; each pair becomes either A or B; pair A does four movements, each movement to four beats, showing different levels and floor patterns, for example:
    — A1 = Low and zigzag   4 beats
    — A2 = Medium and straight   4 beats
    — A3 = High and curved   4 beats
    — A4 = Medium and meandering   4 beats

Pair B does four movements to a steady beat, showing different body shapes and directions, for example:
    — B1 = Stretching up   4 beats
    — B2 = Curling down   4 beats
    — B3 = Extending sideways to the right   4 beats
    — B4 = Curling down   4 beats

Put this together to perform in unison, or alternately (A1 B1 A2 B2 A3 B3 A4 B4).
- Turn 90 degrees and repeat.
- Turn 90 degrees and repeat.
- Turn 90 degrees and repeat.

Cool down

Stretch up, curl down; and extend to the right, extend to the left. Curl down to your body centre, and continue curling right down to the floor. Relax in a comfortable position, and concentrate on slow, deep breathing. Stretch out and breathe in, and then relax in and breathe out; repeat. Relax and rest.

When you are ready, open your eyes, wiggle your toes and then your fingers, stretch, get up and stretch again.

MMADD about the arts

Relationships (with whom we move)

Warm-ups

- **Working with partners**
  - You are exploring the moon. Every time you meet another explorer, use your whole body to show surprise in different ways.
  - In pairs, one person does simple actions on a single plane while the other mirrors them.
  - In pairs, one person is a witch, casting spells on her enemy who is glued to the ground. The enemy has to react with her body to each spell that is cast.
  - You and your partner are on a seesaw.
  - You are with a friend, driving through the countryside, on a bumpy, twisting road. Sway and jolt along the journey in the same way as your partner.
  - You are with a friend in a playground. You sit on the swing and your friend pushes you.
- **Meet and greet.** Travel around the room. At a given signal, meet and greet the person nearest to you using a different part of your body each time (e.g. touching elbows, feet, heads or shoulders). Repeat several times.
- **Secret handshake.** In pairs, devise a series of at least four movements to create a 'secret handshake'; that is, Child A does the handshake and says her own name (e.g. 'Hi, my name is Mary Smith'). Then Child B repeats the handshake, and says his name. Alternatively, go around the room with all the children in turn saying their names and giving their own handshake.

Elastic angles

Have the children form pairs. Using a piece of elastic joined to form a circle, have each partner hold the elastic with both hands and both feet at different places. One partner (A) makes a movement with her body and the elastic and then holds it (4 beats). The second partner, (B) makes a related or contrasting movement and holds it (4 beats). Partner A then makes another movement which relates or contrasts with B's movements (4 beats). Continue interacting this way to music with a steady beat to create an improvised dance.

Pokare Kare Ana

Seat pairs of children in a circle, with each pair facing each other. Each person has a pair of rhythm sticks. Working with a partner have each child practise some simple movements to the Maori song from New Zealand, using the rhythm sticks, for example:

- Tap on floor, tap together, repeat.
- Tap twice on floor, tap twice together, repeat.
- Tap twice on floor, tap partner's stick diagonally twice, repeat with opposite diagonal.
- Tap twice on floor, tap own sticks twice, tap partner's stick diagonally twice, tap partner's other stick diagonally twice.

Working in groups

- Each person is a different part of a machine. Devise individual movements and put them all together.
- Move around the room as the drum plays; gradually move into a human sculpture, using different levels, shapes and patterns.
- In groups, make up a movement picture on suggested themes, with each child being a different part of the whole picture, for example:
  — **At the beach.** Have each child choose part of the beach scene to illustrate through movement and maybe sound (e.g. seagulls, waves, sun sparkling, wind in grass, crabs scuttling and children playing).
  Suggestion: The song 'The Sea' could be used as stimulus for this activity.

At the beach.

  — **Flowers.** Each child chooses to be a different flower in a garden. Show through movement the progressive growth of the flowers; that is: the seed or bulb is planted; the shoot struggles through the earth; it breaks out into the air; and it starts to grow upwards. One leaf unfolds, another one unfolds, and the bud appears and then begins to open up, fully grown. The flower sways in the breeze, the petals begin to droop and then they drop off, and the seeds dry out and fall to the ground to start the cycle over again.
  Suggestion: Use the song 'Just a Little Seed' as stimulus for this activity.
  — **Family.** Show the different people in a family and create different movements for them as they interact with each other: grandfather, grandmother, mother, father, elder daughter, elder son, younger daughter, younger son and baby.
  Suggestion: Use the song 'Our Family' as stimulus for this activity.
  — **Storm.** Show with your bodies how the lightning flashes, the thunder crashes and the rain falls — softly at first and then pouring down; the wind blows; trees bend and sway in the breeze; people run for shelter; the river grows larger and breaks its banks; and water floods everywhere. The rain eases off, the wind dies down, and the sun comes out, causing the raindrops to glisten and sparkle on the trees. Have different children become different aspects of the storm and create a group-movement sequence based on a storm. Use a graphic score of a storm, or the tone poem from Chapter 3, 'Introduction to music education', as stimulus for this activity.
  — **Transport.** Create a dance sequence by having a group of children form a train with each person being a different part (e.g. rails, wheels, people, carriages, guard and whistle).
  Suggestion: Use the song 'How Did You Travel to School?' or 'The Wheels on the Bus' as stimulus for this activity.

Four-letter words

Have the children form groups of four. Brainstorm four-letter words (not swear words!). Each group selects one four-letter word and then uses their bodies to spell out the word. For example: all start in the same still position, and the other children

in the group freeze as each person moves into the shape of his/her letter for four beats. Examples:
- L I O N
- B O A T
- S K I P

Then, as a group, show the meaning of the word with their bodies; that is: form it during four beats and then travel in the formed shape for four beats; change direction, level or floor pattern and travel for four beats; and change level, direction or floor pattern and travel for four beats. Then return to spelling out the word with their bodies. Blend and stylise these movements smoothly together to form a movement sequence. Perform to music with a steady beat.

Dance that song!

Choose familiar songs with actions and dance the songs as they are sung, for example 'Skip to the Right', 'Hokey-pokey', 'Twinkle, Twinkle Little Star', 'Here We Go Looby Loo'.

Spin the dice

Have all students travel around the room, ensuring they do not touch anyone. Then roll a dice and call the number (e.g. 4). Students form into groups of that number and perform a given action to a steady beat, for example:

1. Bounce ball.
2. See saw.
3. Hold hands and skip in a circle.
4. Form a square, and clap hands together either side.
5. Form a square with the fifth person in the centre, join hands with the centre person and skip around 360°.
6. Form pairs in a row (like a reel). The top pair holds hands and skips down between the other pairs to the end; the next top pair repeats; and the third top pair repeats.

If children are left out of a formed group, have them form their own group and do the movements that correspond to the number in their group.

The noisy factory.

The noisy factory

Have the children, individually, create a moving part of a machine (e.g. levers, pistons, wheels, clamps and whistles) and make a noise to accompany the movement.

One person moves to the centre of the room and demonstrates her machine part and sound (suggested music: *The Steel Foundry* by Mossalov). As each person is touched, that person goes to the centre of the room and adds his/her machine movement and sound to the growing machine. The machine continues to grow until all students are part of the machine. If possible, video the machine and play it back to let the children see what it looks like.

Cool down
At the beat of the drum, gradually slow down movements and melt down to the ground, concentrating on slow, deep breathing. Take a deep breath and exhale it slowly. Relax and sink deep into the floor. Take another deep breath and, as you exhale, wiggle your whole body gently. Breathe in again and as you exhale, stretch slowly. When you are ready, open your eyes, stretch again, roll over and stand up.

Structure (gives form and unity to a dance)

Warm-up
Decide on four different movements (e.g. skipping, crouching, clapping and hopping). Call out each word and have children do these movements until another word is called out. Devise a structure for the movements (e.g. 4 skips, 4 crouches, 4 skips, 4 claps, 4 skips, 4 hops, 4 skips).

'Skip to the Right'
Learn to sing and dance to this song. Discuss the element of structure in relation to 'Skip to the Right', for example where can you see the following:
- repetition
- contrast
- variety
- transitions

Heroes and villains
Have each child or group choose a story in which there are two different types of character (e.g. a hero and a villain), such as the prince and the evil stepmother in *Cinderella*. Have them create a dance in two parts; use 16 beats to describe the stepmother in dance, and then use another 16 beats to describe the prince in dance. Encourage the children to use action, space, dynamics and time to show the different characters in their dance. Have the children tell the rest of the class about how they created their dance in two sections and then have them perform the dance.
Extension: Tell the whole story in dance, using different movements to show the different characters.

Chance dance
Demonstrate this activity with the whole class, and then divide the class into groups, giving each group a die, felt pens and a large piece of paper. Each group assigns a different movement to a number from 1 to 6, and writes this down on their paper, for example:

 1 = Turn
 2 = Bend
 3 = Stretch
 4 = Jump
 5 = Skip
 6 = Freeze

219

Each group rolls the die eight times to set up a sequence of eight movements (4 beats each movement). Practise the dance to music, blending each movement smoothly into the next one (32 beats). Share the completed dance with the rest of the class.

Extension 1: Repeat it three more times using the same movements but in a contrasting direction/ level/ extension/ tempo/ floor pattern/relationship and so on each time (4 × 32 beats = 128 beats).

Extension 2: Roll the die again in each group, to determine how many repetitions are required of each movement (e.g. if 3 is rolled, then the first movement will be repeated three times).

Word dance

Brainstorm dance movement words under the categories of travel, jump, turn, gesture and stop, and write them on the blackboard or whiteboard, or as an overhead transparency, for example:

Travel	**Jump**	**Turn**	**Gesture**	**Stop**
Crawl	Bounce	Roll	Stretch	Freeze
Dart	Hop	Swirl	Contract	Pause
Gallop	Launch	Spiral	Extend	Reflect
Skip	Soar	Whirl	Curl	Sit
Tiptoe	Spring	Rotate	Push	Lie down
Slide	Leap	Twist	Pull	Collapse

Have each child take one category and create an 8-beat sequence based on this movement. Each child then joins with a partner and they share their 8-beat sequence with each other and learn the other person's 8-beat sequence. Learn to perform this 16-beat sequence confidently together. Each pair (A) joins with another pair (B) to create a foursome. They put their two 16-movement sequences together to form an extended dance, and decide on the structure of their new dance, for example:

- A B A
- A A B B
- A B A B A
- A B B A

Use repetition and contrasts to create variety, and create a dance using music with a strong beat. Practise this dance, and then share it with the rest of the class.

Cool down

Walk quietly around the room and as a word is called, move into that position briefly and then move on:

- Hover
- Settle
- Pause
- Hesitate
- Halt
- Reflect

Hold this position, and then slide gently to the ground. Close your eyes, and concentrate on your breathing: in, out, in, out. Relax your body, your neck, your head, your shoulders, your arms, your torso, your thighs, your legs and your feet. Make your breathing deeper; take a deep breath, and exhale slowly and gently. Repeat several times.

Repeat again and, as you inhale, breathe in energy; and as you exhale, wiggle your fingers and toes. Open your eyes slowly. Roll over onto your side and sit up. Stretch. Roll over to your side and push yourself up. Stretch, yawn and wriggle your whole body.

Student compositions

Warm-up: Circus performers (to circus music)

Have the children move around the room as the different circus performers as you call out their names:

- player in a marching band (choose your instrument);
- juggler, throwing balls high and low;
- acrobats balancing and swinging in the air;
- lion prowling and leaping through a hoop;
- lion tamer doing tricks with the lion;
- pairs (lion and lion tamer);
- dancing girls on the backs of prancing horses;
- elephants plodding around the ring;
- clowns running, falling, making people laugh;
- circus master orchestrating the show;
- audience clapping.

Using graphic scores as stimulus for dance

- **Class exploration of circus theme.** Divide the class into small groups. Use a circus graphic score to create a class dance, performing individually and all together. Each group develops an 8-beat dance sequence to perform in the score based on one of the circus performers.

  Extension: Use individual flashcards to indicate when each group is to move; others freeze in position until their card is pointed to.

- **Group work: graphic scores.** Use the graphic scores created by the teacher, or those from a previous music lesson, as a stimulus for creating a dance. Match movements with symbols on the graphic scores, including contrasting levels, speeds, directions, shapes in space, movements and so on.

  Extension: Instead of just using the symbols, use the concepts, story and/or ideas portrayed in the graphic score as a starting point/stimulus for a dance sequence.

Circus graphic score.

Alphabet dance

Resource: *Animalia* by Graeme Base or a similar alphabet book

Give each group of children a page from *Animalia* or a similar alphabet book and have them work out a 32-beat chant based on eight words (4 beats each) from the page, starting with the same letter, for example:

> Admiral, Athlete, Alien, Artist,
> Alligator, Arches, Apple and Ant.

Each group then needs to create a series of movements to represent these words. Practise them until the eight movements flow easily together, using a variety of levels, extensions, directions, body shapes, patterns and relationships.

Have the two groups join together. The first group shows their eight movements, and then the second pair shows their eight movements. Create a dance that includes all the movements by the two groups, for example:

- Introduction; Group 1 (4 movements); Group 2 (4 movements); Group 1 (next 4 movements); Group 2 (next 4 movements).

  OR

- Introduction; Alternate doing one movement from Group A and then one movement from Group B and so on; Ending.

  OR any other structure using movements from both groups.

Add variety by using different directions, floor patterns, levels, extensions and so on.

Admiral

Artist

Movements may be stylised, developed and extended from the initial actions so that they make use of different levels, extensions, body shapes and so on. Think through carefully the transitions from one movement to the next. Share these with the rest of the group.

Number beats

The teacher calls out a number and the children create a movement to last for that number of beats, for example:

- 0 = Freeze for 4 beats.
- 1 = Jump with two feet together (1 beat).
- 2 = Stand and shrug shoulders up and then down (2 beats).
- 3 = Crouch and tap floor, tap knees and tap shoulders (3 beats).
- 4 = Clap hands in the air as you turn 180°.
- 5 = Crouch low and then stretch up high to 5 beats.
- 6 = Hop forwards diagonally 3 steps left, 3 steps right.
- 7 = Walk backwards 7 steps, swinging arms forwards and backwards.
- 8 = Sway side to side, with arms raised for 4 beats; swing arms up and down for 4 beats.
- 9 = Turn 360° with arms outstretched, spiralling downwards to ground.

Telephone numbers dance

Write down an eight-digit telephone number. Use the relevant movements from the list in the above activity for each of the numbers. Create a dance based on these numbers to a piece of music with a strong beat. Work at smooth transitions between

numbers and contrasting movements and levels.

To simplify this dance: Have children make each movement last only four beats each and make the telephone number four digits long.

Extension: Children make up their own movements to the ten numbers (0–9) and create a dance based on an eight-digit (or longer) phone number.

Creating a dance starting with music

When children have had a significant amount of dance experience, know the language and elements of dance, and have a wide vocabulary of movements, they are ready to create their own dance to a piece of music from scratch with few given structures or parameters. Guidelines for creating a dance could include the following:

- Choose a piece of music.
- Listen to the lyrics (if the piece of music is a song) or identify the structure of the music; then work out a dance that represents the lyrics and/or structure in the actions.
- Share ideas of possible movements and structure.
- Experiment with different movements and structure.
- Refine ideas.
- Put movements to music, practise and share with peers.
- Receive comments and feedback.
- Refine ideas.
- Practise.
- Improve.
- Practise again.
- Remember.
- Perform.
- Reflect on processes and product.

Cool down

Stretch out as far as you can, and then curl into the centre of your body. Reach down to your feet, reach up to the ceiling and reach out to each side. Curl back down to your body centre, and curl down to your knees and then down onto the floor. Relax in a comfortable position, and concentrate on slow, deep breathing. Breathe in relaxation and peace, and breathe out any tension and stress. Relax your neck muscles, shoulder muscles, jaw muscles and cheek muscles. Your head feels heavy and then your shoulders feel heavy, sinking into the floor. Feel the relaxation flowing into your arms, hands and fingers. Feel your torso sink into the floor. Relax your tummy muscles and your back muscles. Feel the heaviness creep down your legs, your knees, your ankles, your feet and your toes. Your whole body feels heavy and relaxed, sinking into the floor. Relax.

Focus back on your breathing: breathe in, then out; feel the energy returning to your body as you inhale, and breath out all the stress and tension; repeat. Turn on your side, sit up, stretch, stand up and stretch.

SPRINGBOARDS FOR DISCUSSION AND APPLICATION

1. List skills, knowledge and attitudes from different subject areas that children can learn *through* dance and then list skills, knowledge and attitudes from the dance art form that children learn when involved in dance.

2. Create a lesson plan for a selected primary class, based on each of the elements of dance; include warm-ups, introducing and practising the element, applying their understanding by creating a dance based on the element, sharing this dance and a cool-down activity.

3. In groups, plan a five-week dance program on a theme for a selected primary classroom which shows the development of skills, knowledge and attitudes in the areas of making, performing and appreciating.

FURTHER READING

Allen, A. & Coley, J. (1995), *Dance for all*, David Fulton Publishers, London.
Australian Teacher Network (1993), *Creating moves*, Author, Sydney.
Australian Teacher Network (1994), *Body talk: Dance video kit*, Author, Sydney.
Education Resources Group (1995), *Making dance: A dance resource kit*, Radical Wombat Collective, Melbourne.
Kassing, G. & Jay, D.M. (2003), *Dance teaching methods and curriculum design: Comprehensive K–12 dance education*, Human Kinetics, Champaign, Illinois.
National Dance Teachers' Association (1998), *Teaching dance in the primary school* (video and booklet), Author, Burntwood, Staffordshire.
NSW Department of Education and Training Curriculum Support Directorate (1998), *Making dance work*, Author, Sydney.
NSW Department of School Education Curriculum Directorate (1997), *Qantum leaps*, Author, Sydney.
Payne, H. (2003), *Creative movement and dance in groupwork*, Speechmark Publishing, Oxford.
Shreeves, R. (1998), *Imaginary dances: More themes for children dancing*, Ward Lock Education, East Grinstead, West Sussex.
Shreeves, R. (2000), *Children dancing*, Ward Lock Educational, East Grinstead, West Sussex.
Smith-Autard, J.M. (2002), *The art of dance in education*, A & C Black, London.
Spurgeon, D. (1991), *Dance moves: From improvisation to dance*, Harcourt Brace Jovanovich, Sydney.
Thraves, B. & Williamson, D. (1994), *Now for a dance: Integrating dance and movement in primary and early childhood learning*, Phoenix Education, Melbourne.
Van Papendorp, J. & Friedman, S. (1997), *Teaching creative dance: A handbook*, Kwela Books, Cape Town.
Walker, M. (1992), *Opening the door to dance*, Ausdance National Council, Canberra.

chapter seven
Introduction to drama education

Drama is using the body in time and space to explore issues, questions, perspectives or ideas. **(Ewing & Simons, 2004)**

Learning outcomes
By the end of this chapter, students will be able to:
- list the main types of drama and demonstrate how at least three of these can be practically applied in the primary classroom by creating a series of learning experiences that develop children's ability to use these drama conventions in the process of making drama;
- identify skills and knowledge that children can learn in other key learning areas through using drama;
- show their understanding of how the three areas of making, performing and appreciating can be developed and implemented in the primary classroom by creating a drama program covering these three areas, based on a literature text.

Introduction

The three-year-old instructs her friend, 'I'll be the king and you can be the queen'; the preschooler lines up his teddies and teaches them as he looks forward to going to 'real' school; and the kindergarten children play 'Spiderman' or 'cops and robbers' in the playground. Sociodramatic play is an integral part of children's lives, weaving together physical, emotional and cognitive development as they learn about their world through this rich and unique medium. Therefore, it is vital that they use drama as a valuable and effective tool and process of learning throughout their primary school years.

For thousands of years, drama has been used as a way of communicating ideas and feelings. Every culture has a tradition of using this ancient art form to entertain, educate, communicate, celebrate and record its achievements, customs, culture, events and survival knowledge.

Drama is a way of making meaning of the world around us and allows children to live in another person's world and to explore that person's way of thinking, feeling, acting, expressing and being. Through the understanding of another's world as they engage in role-playing and other drama learning experiences, children learn tolerance and acceptance of differences and that other people's viewpoints and actions, though different from theirs, can be valid.

Some teachers may feel they have few skills or knowledge to be able to implement an effective drama program as they believe they should be giving all the input. But maybe they underestimate the amount of drama children have experienced. Teachers can be surprised at how much children have to offer, especially if they are given the opportunity to begin making drama based on their own interests and experiences and they realise that what they know and enjoy is important and their ideas will be considered.

Teachers need to learn the basics of teaching drama, acknowledge and draw on children's experiences and knowledge, and enthusiastically plan and implement drama lessons. Then they can work with, and challenge, the children to further develop their skills, knowledge and understandings in this creative and satisfying partnership for authentic engagement in learning.

Drama in the classroom

Effective drama is an integration of thought, action and emotion. Drama making can involve living life as a different person in a made-up world. Engaging in drama offers children the opportunity to explore ways of knowing and being in the world and in their interaction with others. It allows them to explore society and social behaviour, to construct their understanding of their own identity and to view the world in different ways. Participating in drama-making experiences allows children to explore an imaginary world they create by interacting with others, as they take on a role that is different from their 'real' life and communicate using their emotions, body language, vocal expression, symbols and gestures.

Drama involves exploration, inquiry and experience based on developed drama knowledge, skills and understandings. It also allows children who are not necessarily

MMADD about the arts

Drama involves exploration of emotions through movement.

confident and proficient at reading and writing to be involved in valuable literacy activities in which they can achieve and even excel. Through this active engagement with drama, children can develop their literacy skills and become more confident in reading, writing, talking and listening. Through involvement in drama, children will also learn teamwork and cooperative skills, and develop independent learning and self-control; as well as learning how to express themselves through movement, body language and speaking, and how to empathise with others. It gives them the confidence to voice an opinion and teaches them to listen to and value the opinions of others.

Drama may be used as a response to a stimulus such as a text, a piece of music, a question, a problem or an artwork and can provide opportunities for enriching learning for all children across the curriculum. Drama can be central to a variety of classroom activities and may provide a means for the development of other skills in other areas such as writing, reading, listening, singing, speaking, moving, creating and constructing. The three main areas of drama education are making, performing and appreciating drama. Children are involved in these through participating in a variety of drama activities which include drama games, improvisation, role-playing, mime, storytelling, Readers' Theatre, play building, rehearsed and scripted drama, video drama and work with masks and puppets. Through these experiences, children will develop their knowledge, understanding and skills in relation to the unique language, techniques and elements of drama, such as space, tension, focus, context, symbols, contrast, mood and dramatic presentation. Understanding and manipulating these elements allows them to explore other roles, issues, problems and situations within the dramatic context.

Learning *through* drama

Although drama elements and techniques should be primarily used to develop dramatic learning experiences, they can also be very effectively used as an integral part of the learning process to help children learn about other subjects across the curriculum. Children with bodily-kinaesthetic and intrapersonal intelligences often find that they can develop a deeper understanding of the content and skills being taught if they can learn content and express what they know about the subject through drama. The following are examples of how drama can be used to extend learning in each of the art forms. These can be used and adapted to suit your subject, topic, outcomes and class.

Music
- Move in response to soft and loud, high and low, and fast and slow music.
- Listen to a short piece of descriptive music, for example an excerpt from the *Carnival of the Animals* by Saint-Saëns, *Pictures from an Exhibition* by Mussorgsky

or 'In the Hall of the Mountain King' by Grieg, and then in groups discuss their interpretation of the music and develop a drama in response to the music.
- Read through the lyrics of a song to be learned and add vocal expression to enhance the children's understanding of the meaning and content, prior to learning to sing the song expressively and with understanding.
- Use body movements and vocal sounds to show the meanings of different musical elements, such as dynamics (loud and soft), pitch (high and low), tempo (fast and slow), duration (beat, rhythm and accent) and tone colour (the different sounds made by different instruments).
- Create a puppet play that can be the stimulus for a musical composition to be played as an accompaniment to the play.

Visual arts
- Design and create masks or puppets based on characters from a story or creative dramatisation and then use them in a puppet play or drama.
- When drawing from direct observation or remembered images, have children mime the object, what it looks and feels like, what shape it is, how big or small it is and so on prior to drawing it.
- In pairs, have one child instruct another child verbally to form a shape or sculpture, specifically telling them where and how to move and place their body parts, and then have them each create this artwork using clay or playdough.
- Have each child create a vocal collage on a certain topic (e.g. my favourite things) and then create a collaged artwork using magazine pictures, drawings, computer-generated photos and so on on, the same theme.

Dance
- Have small groups perform a created dance and then, using freeze frames, have them freeze every few seconds or minutes, and have the dancers explain to the rest of the class why they are each in the position in which they are frozen; continue the dance and then freeze again and repeat the explanations.
- Dramatise a village scene from another culture where the local people are celebrating and dancing their traditional dance; include characterisation and movements to convey the culture and context of the dance.

Media
- Create a still image with a group of children, photograph it and print out three copies of it. Frame it to show only one child, a small group and the whole group; and discuss how effective each framing is and why.
- Create a series of freeze frames to tell a story; photograph these and use the photos as a storyboard in the development of a video.
- Prepare and present a Readers' Theatre presentation for radio, record and edit it, and then share it with others for feedback.
- Dramatise a production meeting as the directors decide on the creation of a new children's program; discuss the appropriate timeslot for the program, what advertisements should be allowed during the show, what is the targeted age group

and what will be the key message of the program; ensure each board member is encouraged to give reasons for their answers to each of these questions.

Learning *in* drama: The elements of drama

The following elements need to be considered as children make, perform and appreciate drama.

Tension

Tension is the creation and controlled use of energy throughout a dramatic experience that culminates in a climax and resolution. Tension can be created in drama by the use of the unexpected, mystery, unresolved conflict, mime instead of words, contrasting music, lighting and actions, and by the constricting of parameters, such as space, pace or time.

Focus

As makers of drama children need to learn how to create a focus to draw specific attention to certain themes, issues, characters or actions as portrayed in the drama. This can be done through the use of body language, words, actions, vocal expression, careful staging and use of lighting, props or costumes and so on. If there is an audience, the performers need to consider how to direct the focus of that audience to specific themes, issues, characters, action, plot and so on being portrayed in the drama.

Mood

Through drama people can be touched emotionally. Encourage children to consider the mood of their drama and how they can change or enhance the mood they are portraying, through vocal expression, body language, pace, actions, staging, use of space, sound effects, lighting, costumes and so on.

Time

Time sets the drama in its context so the audience knows if it is portraying the past, present or future. This can be conveyed through costumes, staging, props, actions, words, and so on. The pace of the dramatic context is also an important aspect of time.

Contrast

Dramatic meaning and enjoyment can be enhanced through the use of the juxtaposition of contrasting opposites such as stillness after movement; sound followed by silence; contrasting size, shapes and levels of movement; and contrasting emotions portrayed through gestures, facial and vocal expressions, posture and so on.

Symbol

The use of symbols and metaphors can be a powerful tool in drama. Children need to understand how objects or people can be used to represent meaning beyond the literal, that an object can be given a specific meaning, a symbol can give different messages in different cultures and contexts, and the use of certain gestures and movements can be symbolic. It is important for children to understand also that although some objects have shared meaning, others may have personal meaning that could be different for each child.

Space

The effective use of space is an important aspect of creative drama. Space can enhance or limit what occurs in the drama and it can significantly shape a performance. In considering their use of space, children need to make informed choices about the size and shape of the space in which they are working, the use of different levels within the space, the relationships with the audiences within the context of the space, and their use of common and personal space.

Audience skills

Part of learning drama is the ability to be part of a respectful audience, whether in the classroom, the school hall or a drama theatre. Children should be taught how to be an actively engaged audience through modelling, observation, discussion and specific instruction. Being part of an audience involves listening carefully, analysing what is being performed in relation to the language of drama, observing their peers and others share themselves through drama, enjoying the performance, and encouraging the performers through clapping and positive, constructive comments and feedback.

Performance aspects of drama

Although most classroom drama is focused on the process and not so much the product, there may be a time in the year that the class can work towards presenting a performance. Putting on a play can be a valuable educational learning experience and enhance the self-esteem of children, as well as being good public relations for the school and part of the school's tradition, bringing prestige and finance to the school, or building positive social interactions and pleasure to those involved. It can also disrupt the normal school timetable; cause major stress to a small group of teachers; place major demands on time, space and energy for the staff; and can sometimes take the place of developmental, sequential and effective classroom drama programs throughout the school! However, once the school has decided to put on a production, staff will need to consider the use of staging, lighting, costumes, make-up, props, sound effects, music and so on.

Part of learning drama is the ability to be part of a respectful audience.

Staging and sets
Staging is the physical placing of a piece of drama for a performance. It includes the shape and size of the performance space — whether it is to be theatre in the round, at the front of a classroom or on a stage in the school hall. It also includes the design of the sets, the use of props, if relevant, and the movement of actors.

Lighting
Simple lighting can be very effective in a drama performance; lighting can focus attention onto an object or person, and can assist with creating contrast, mood and tension through the effective use of levels, spotlights, floodlights and colours.

Costumes and make-up
The effective use of costumes can give characters credibility, power and status or group identity and can help to set the context and culture of the drama. Bright or coloured lighting can change the actor's appearance, so make-up to give the actor a natural look should be used. Character make-up can be added to transform the look of the actor into the desired role he/she is playing. Keep costumes and make-up simple.

Costumes and make-up can give characters credibility.

Masks and props
Masks and props can be used in a performance to disguise, identify, conceal or protect an actor or to act as a symbol. Masks can cover the whole or part of the face. Using commercial masks can be limiting as they are generally character and emotion specific; so children should be encouraged to create their own masks, whether simple brown-bag or paper-plate masks, photographs pasted onto a sheet of card or more complicated papier-mâché or gypsona masks. (See Chapter 5, 'Introduction to visual arts education' for specific procedures and ideas for doing this activity.) When they have a mask to wear, children should explore the character portrayed and match their body movements and gestures to the role or character portrayed by the mask.

Sound effects
These can be prerecorded, computer-generated, made by the actors on the stage or created by helpers off stage, using found objects, junk materials or percussion instruments. It is important that sound effects are heard at the correct time to match the appropriate action or words and are loud enough to be heard by the audience.

Music
Think about how music can be used effectively in the production; if there is a school orchestra or band, work with its conductor to find suitable music for the children to play for the overture (beginning music before the start of the performance), during the performance and at the end of the presentation. If the production is a musical, children will need to practice the solo, ensemble (group) and chorus items carefully so that all words are heard clearly and the singing is in time and in tune. Prerecorded

or computer-generated music can be used but ensure that it does not drown out what is happening on stage. With all music being played in the public arena, check the copyright restrictions through the Australasian Performing Right Association Limited (APRA) before you start practising or writing it into the program, as some companies charge quite a lot for the performance of their music, whether live or recorded.

Types of drama

Early learning experiences in drama can involve children in dramatic play where they improvise and create roles using their imagination to develop foundation drama skills, techniques and understandings to assist them in later years. Drama learning experiences should encourage children to manipulate the elements of drama to make their own drama or to interpret and re-create the drama of others. They can be used to learn and develop skills or as part of the process of making drama about a selected topic. Types of drama can include drama games, spontaneous improvisation, improvisation in role, movement and mime, choral reading or speaking, story telling, Readers' Theatre, using puppets and masks, scripted drama and play building. These are explained briefly below; for more in-depth information refer to the suggested readings at the end of the chapter.

Drama games

Sociodrama games often find their beginnings in schoolyard children's games and can then be adapted for the drama classroom so that they include both sexes and all children, who learn to interact positively with those with whom they may not normally play. These games can be used for warm-ups at the start of the lesson to assist children in focusing their minds and bodies on the theme or learning experiences of the lesson and can also be used to introduce specific skills. For example, working in pairs, Child A makes a slow, simple action on one plane and Child B mirrors the action. Extend this into two planes (i.e. forwards and backwards, and up and down). Move the lesson into children mirroring movements associated with the theme or issue to be developed through the lesson.

Drama games can help develop self-control, initiative, trust, spatial awareness, teamwork and confidence in children as well as being a fun and enjoyable start or end to the lesson. Warm-ups and drama games should be used productively and not just as time fillers, as they can introduce and reinforce one or more of the elements of drama or the theme of the lesson; however, teachers need to be clear about how these games will be used and not use them just as an end in themselves. Many of the warm-ups described in Chapter 6, 'Introduction to dance education' can be thoughtfully adapted for use in relevant drama lessons.

Improvisation

Spontaneous improvisation

Children can use improvisation to respond spontaneously to real or imagined situations or stimuli through drama to explore issues, ideas, characters, texts, stories, events and so on. Improvisations

MMADD about the arts

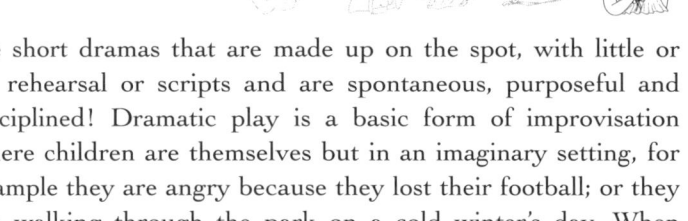

Walking through the park on a cold winter's day.

are short dramas that are made up on the spot, with little or no rehearsal or scripts and are spontaneous, purposeful and disciplined! Dramatic play is a basic form of improvisation where children are themselves but in an imaginary setting, for example they are angry because they lost their football; or they are walking through the park on a cold winter's day. When doing improvisation children need to consider:

- Where is the scene set?
- What is happening?
- When did it happen?
- How did it happen?
- Who is involved?
- What are they doing?
- What are they feeling?
- What motivates them?
- What is at stake?
- How will it start?
- How will it end?

Role improvisation

In another form of improvisation, role improvisation, children can portray real or imagined people in specific circumstances and are encouraged to 'become' another character, whether known, unknown or imagined, from books, real life or fantasy. They act, talk, move and think like this other person, taking on their values, attitudes and actions, and they learn how to 'step into another's shoes' and live, walk and talk as another person in another context, exploring their real-life issues and attitudes using the elements, skills and techniques of drama. Improvisation can extend further into characterisation and then acting, as children learn to live the life of the different characters. This may lead to a performance to an audience of some friends, the class or a larger group.

Children should be encouraged to participate in improvisation situations that could include:

- inventing make-believe roles;
- exploring roles that children know;
- exploring roles from different countries and cultures;
- sustaining a chosen character over a sequence of scenes to create depth and credibility;
- using movement, body language, vocal expression, props and costumes to establish the identity of a character or role, and to enhance that role within the given context;
- exploring and challenging stereotypes, and exploring current news events, current issues in school, topics covered in other subject areas, broader events and issues around the world and so on.

Developing improvisational skills

Improvisational skills and techniques can be developed through the following drama activities:

- **Barrier games.** This can be played in groups of three, with one child (C) standing behind a barrier of some sort, or standing with her back to the other two children (A and B). Child B moves and freezes into his own unique creative position, or into a position to portray a character or object in a text or picture. Child A describes to Child C how to move into this position, using only words. When they are finished, the barrier is removed and Child C compares her position with that of Child B. This is an effective activity for young children when working on learning different body parts, directions and positions and for developing verbal skills. It can also be used to lead into exploring a text, picture, issue or theme within the drama lesson.

- **Sculptures.** In this activity children work in pairs or small groups and cooperatively create a human sculpture. It involves one or more children being the 'living clay' and one child being the sculptor who moulds the other children into the shape, movement and expression of a character or object in a story or picture without any verbal discussion between sculptor and clay. At a later stage, the sculptor may explain why she created her living artwork in the way that she did, and the 'living clay' may describe how she felt as that particular person or object. This can also be a device used in the development of a theme, issue or characterisation within a drama lesson.

- **Still images/Freeze frames.** In using this device, children create a still image with their bodies to portray a picture or scene, or freeze to show a selected moment in the drama they are creating, and then discuss how they felt about their role in the still image, their attitudes and feelings, how their role relates to the other children's parts, and how the whole still image was developed. Still images can help children focus on their role in relation to others and deepen their learning about what they are doing.

- **Hot seating/Questioning in role.** This activity can help children understand and 'walk in the shoes' of the characters in texts, stories pictures or events. It helps them identify implicit meanings that may not initially be clear in literacy texts they are studying by thinking through what is actually written and why the characters act and say what they do in the text. It can also be used to assist children in developing a drama as it is being rehearsed. In hot seating, children are selected to take on the role of different characters from a story, picture or the drama in which they are involved; then the rest of the class, or a group of questioners, ask all the children questions about who they are and why they think, feel and act as they do. Children need to be familiar with the text, picture or drama context and the 'hot seating' characters may do extra research and discussion about their particular roles. If working from a picture or text as a stimulus, or when developing a drama, children should discuss in small groups

One child moulds her friends into a sculpture.

who they think each of the characters are in relation to the others, what their personalities are like, what they are doing, how they are feeling, what they are thinking, where they have come from and what they will be doing next. They then clarify in their own minds who they are in role and identify when they are ready to be questioned. This can lead to creative story writing or play building in response to the picture or issue being developed.

- **Teacher-in-role.** This process encourages the teacher to step out of her 'normal' classroom role of instructing and directing and take on a role within the drama that allows the teacher to direct the development of the drama from within instead of imposing it from without. She becomes one of the characters and relates on the same level within the drama as the children who discuss and develop the characters and action without constantly referring to a teacher who is outside the dramatic context. It is preferable for the teacher not to be an important character or a leader, as this is similar to her out-of-role teacher persona. Teacher-in-role gives the teacher the opportunity to extend, empower and challenge the children's thinking, language, actions, knowledge and attitudes, alter the structure and action, and customise the drama activities from within the dramatic context, to achieve the desired outcomes. The teacher may wear some identifying feature such as a hat or scarf so children remember that she is in role, but when she steps out of role to become a spectator, teacher or facilitator she should remove the identifying feature and state that she is now out of role.

    For further information about teacher-in-role see *Beyond the script* by Ewing and Simons (2004) and *Pretending to learn* by O'Toole and Dunn (2002).

- *Vocal collage.* Groups of children choose a theme or issue and brainstorm words related to it. Based on this they prepare and present a collage of vocal and instrumental sounds, words and phrases, and so on to describe this topic, using contrasting high and low voices (pitch), soft and loud voices (dynamics), fast and slow voices (tempo) and smooth and sharp voices to create an aural collage of sounds describing the topic. Vocal collages can be used to set the scene for a drama (i.e. a hot, dry desert or a cool rainforest), or to encourage the children to verbalise their feelings within an improvised role.

Storytelling

Telling a story can be a means in itself or used as a springboard for drama, artwork, musical composition or creative writing. Since the beginning of time, stories have been used to entertain; pass on information, values and culture; and nourish the spirit. In the classroom, children can tell real or imagined stories in a circle, with one child telling one or more sentences and then another child following on the story with some further sentences, and so on around the circle until the story is completed, with all children exploring the roles, characterisations and situations they have created. Alternatively, children can use picture cards, a graphic score, a storyboard or photos as a stimulus to telling a story, either individually or with others.

When telling stories, encourage the children to use appropriate gestures, facial and vocal expression, body movements and so on to add expression and context to the story. Storytelling can lead into creating a drama to show a different ending to the story; it could be based on a 'hot issue' in the classroom or school such as racism or bullying and allow children to work through different endings to a given scenario.

Readers' Theatre

This activity allows hesitant readers to practise text and read it aloud with confidence as well as providing all readers with the opportunity to explore the meaning and content of the text and  present it using gestures, facial and vocal expression, simple movements and sound effects. Readers' Theatre can provide links with the elements of music as children alter their vocal expression in relation to pitch (high and low), tempo (fast and slow) and dynamics (loud and soft) to portray the different characters, emotions and actions in the script. The Readers' Theatre script needs to be written clearly so that the different roles of narrator and characters are plainly seen by the children. Children need to decide where and how they will stand (i.e. in a line, in a circle, in the same or different levels), and if they need any simple props, movement or sound effects to make the presentation more effective. They should be given time to practise their parts individually and as a group and then present it to an audience for feedback. Their performance could also be videoed for reflection so those in role can see how effective the presentation was and make any changes if required.

Choral reading and speaking

If children are studying a poem or a picture book, it might be appropriate to have the class or a small group read or say the poem or text together, using vocal and facial expression and gestures to convey the message effectively. Choral speaking requires very little space; can enhance the children's diction, enunciation and the creative use of their voices; provides positive social interaction; and is suitable for any age level. Techniques that can be used in choral speaking include speaking in unison (all together); in two groups with different parts, creating a cumulative reading with one child starting and each line adding another child's voice, including solo passages to contrast the unison speaking (e.g. solo/chorus); and having each child say one line followed by everyone speaking together.

Movement and mime

Children can develop spatial and body awareness through moving in different ways and exploring drama without speech or sound effects. There are clear links between movement in drama and movement in music and dance, and so movements can create authentic integration experiences across the arts, achieving outcomes in each of the three art forms. When miming, children should make exaggerated movements so the audience can understand clearly the message or dramatic action being conveyed. The emphasis of mime should be upon clarity of detail and accuracy in depicting the desired message, action or emotion.

Movement and mime allow children to focus on their body movements, gestures,

MMADD about the arts

facial expressions and use of space to non-verbally portray expression, emotions, characterisation, actions, movements, a message, interaction with objects and so on. As such, movement and mime can be used to allow the children to express themselves, communicate with their bodies and explore their environment and relationships in response to a narrated story, poem, piece of music or theme being explored.

Play building

When play building, children work together to create a dramatic work about a selected topic or issue which generally develops over several weeks. Children should have already learned a series of sound dramatic techniques, skills and understandings which they can use in this valuable learning experience. They work on their topic with the teacher scaffolding their learning through planned frameworks; build the play through discussion, negotiation, improvisation, rehearsal, reflection and refining; and then create a finished product that they can share with the rest of the class or another audience.

By being involved together with the teacher in this dramatic learning process children can begin to explore their own and others' belief systems, identify if they need to have power and control others and, in some cases, change their behaviours and attitudes to other people and circumstances. Through their involvement in play building children may develop popularity and leadership skills that they may not normally experience. By watching carefully how each child engages with each other and with the material being explored, teachers will also gain knowledge which will help them respond to the individual needs of each child.

For further information about play building see *Beyond the script* by Ewing and Simons (2004).

Scripted drama

When using scripted drama, ensure that the plays chosen are appropriate for their purpose and will achieve the desired drama outcomes for the class. Scripts can be commercial ones or children may create and present their own scripted plays for others to share and comment on. Children will need time to plan, rehearse and present their plays to an audience. In this activity, as with all arts learning experiences, the process and integral learning undertaken while children are working on the script is as important as the final product.

Puppets and masks

Making puppets or masks to be used in a drama activity can be a valuable way to have children focus on a character and understand who it is, what it is thinking, why it acts as it does and so on. As they explore the characterisation of their character, they can show what they know about it through the creation of different features, costumes, expressions and so forth on their puppet or mask. It may work best if children design their mask or puppet first on a piece of paper to ensure they include all the relevant features and identify what they want it to communicate to the audience.

If possible, allow children to watch a video or a live performance featuring the use of masks or puppets as well as seeing a variety of different types of masks or puppets such as appear on the website www.masks.org. Different kinds of puppets to use in drama could include string, glove, sock, finger, shadow and rod puppets, and masks may be commercial or made ones and can be half-masks or full-face masks. When using masks, actions and words need to be exaggerated to express the meaning without facial expressions.

For practical suggestions for different puppets and masks that can be made by children, see the relevant section in Chapter 5, 'Introduction to visual arts education'.

Video/Audio drama

This process is used when plays or other dramatic works are created for the specific intention of being recorded on video or audio tape. See suggestions in Chapter 4, 'Introduction to media education', for practical suggestions for using videos in the classroom.

Practical considerations

Drama lessons need space and will most likely create some noise! As a teacher, don't be afraid of on-task, constructive noise but ensure that all children know the signal to freeze or to move back on-task. Establish routines and expectations so children know what noise and actions are acceptable within the drama classroom and what are not. Discuss these, remind children about them at the start of the drama lesson and be consistent with your expectations throughout the lesson. Self-control is vital to the drama lesson as often the value of the learning experience will be lost when there is little self-discipline. Encourage and expect a full commitment and focused concentration from the children and they will reap the rewards of deep and relevant learning, the satisfaction of achievement, the development of self-confidence and self-esteem, as well as great enjoyment from the activities. For suggestions about developing behaviour management strategies in the arts classroom, see the section in Chapter 2, 'The creative arts classroom'.

Preparation

When you prepare the classroom for drama, ensure you have a safe, clear space free from obstacles. You may decide to use the school hall or playground; if you do, establish the physical boundaries to let the children know what areas are out of bounds. Decide beforehand if you want children to take off their shoes; consider comments discussed in Chapter 6, 'Introduction to dance education'.

As with dance, establish clear signals to give instructions such as freeze, finish up the activity, make less noise and so on. Know what activities children have done, what skills they have developed and what stage and indicators they are working towards (this could be different for different children). Teach the elements, techniques and structures for drama before expecting children to create their own drama artworks. Refer also to the practical considerations and safety issues for dance lessons in Chapter 6, 'Introduction to dance education', as most of these also apply to drama lessons.

Structure

When first teaching drama, teachers should be sensitive to children's need for structure and routine, and scaffold the children's learning and experiences with clear

demonstrations and instructions as well as simple activities based on known stories and characters, thus providing them with a wide variety of ideas and suggestions for their movements and drama making. As children become more confident in sustained, creative drama experiences and develop a sound vocabulary of drama tools, techniques and skills, they will require less structure and fewer parameters in their drama making, performing and appreciating.

Improvisation in role

Drama lessons also need the children and the teacher to agree that they are entering a 'make-believe' or 'pretend' situation and to continue within this role for a stated period of time. Children need to be encouraged to develop their imagination and creativity, to appreciate and respect each other's personal space, to obey instructions such as 'freeze' or 'find a space', and to know the purpose of the drama. At the end of the experience a debriefing time should be included as children step out of role and discuss issues, emotions and actions relating to their experiences in role.

Purpose

Teachers need to know why they are teaching this particular drama lesson or program to their specific class of children. They need to clearly establish the purpose in their minds before they start to plan. Sometimes this will mean identifying a key question to be explored throughout the lesson through role-play, improvisation or play building; it may be determining what skills, techniques, elements or types of drama the children need to learn or reinforce; or it may be establishing a problem, issue or topic that the children will explore and interrogate using drama. The lesson needs to build on what children have experienced previously and build from the known to the unknown.

Motivation

Children often need to be motivated to join in the drama activities by the teacher providing a thought-provoking question, issue for discussion or point of interest to be followed throughout the lesson. The teacher may start with a picture and ask the children why the people are doing the actions portrayed in the picture; start with a literature text and provide children with a problem to solve from the story; discuss a recent event from the schoolyard or newspaper, asking children to suggest reasons and possible solutions to certain events or incidents; or become a teacher-in-role and set up the drama activities using this point of view to challenge and extend the children's thinking, actions and imagination.

Lesson planning

Teachers should plan their drama program carefully as children need to be assisted to develop as confident drama makers, appreciators and performers through carefully developed and sequenced non-threatening learning experiences and processes which cover a range of activity areas within drama. Lessons should start with a brief warm-up, followed by introductory activities and skill development, leading to the main section of the lesson, and also include time for debriefing, reflection and relaxation.

Warm-ups, discussion and games

Starting the lesson with warm-ups, which can include drama games, can motivate the children, introduce or reinforce the lesson's content, give the children a single focus and help to increase the blood supply and circulation of blood to the muscles to help prevent injuries. These may also include some vocal as well as physical warm-ups as it is important for children to exercise their jaw muscles, explore the different sounds they can make with their voices and bodies, and develop clarity in their enunciation. Lessons may also start with a motivating discussion and introductory activity based on the theme or issue to be investigated in the main part of the lesson.

Focused learning experiences

Follow the warm-ups with some introductory learning experiences to teach or reinforce one or more of the drama techniques, such as mime, use of puppets or improvisation, and the elements of drama such as focus, tension, mood or symbol, which will then lead in to the main drama-making activity for the lesson. This section is where most of the learning and creativity will take place, where the children will be exploring a topic, theme or issue and using the relevant elements, techniques, devices and language of drama to create their own dramatic context, action and meaning. This may take several lessons, or it can remain within the one drama lesson if it involves shorter learning experiences.

Closure activities

Complete the lesson with a summary closing activity, a debrief if necessary to ensure children are comfortable in being out of their role, and a cool-down period of reflection, relaxation and stillness. The reflection can include consideration of how effective the use of language and actions was in the context of the drama, how authentic the children felt their role-playing was, how they felt at different moments throughout the drama, or what they have learned in relation to drama skills, elements and techniques as well as in relation to the content and context of the topic or issue explored.

Springboards for drama

Stimuli for drama activities and lessons can come from a variety of areas, including themes, drama skills to be learned, learning in other subjects or key learning areas, music, artworks, videos, literacy texts, writing, objects or television programs.

Using themes

Relate drama activities to your classroom theme; for example, if you are exploring the theme of the gold rush in social studies you could use or adapt the following ideas:

- **Freeze frames/Hot seating.** View the artwork *Bailed up* by Tom Roberts (www.artgallery.nsw.gov.au/collection) and have children create a freeze frame representing the scene. Each character in the scene could then be questioned (hot seating) as to their involvement in the hold-up, their feelings, where they have come from, where they are going and so on. Have children improvise a similar situation from the 21st century (e.g. an armoured guard van being held up on its way from the bank).

- **Hot seating.** Have one child as the chief gold digger and encourage the rest of the children to ask that child questions about the conditions of the goldmine camp, how they staked their claim, what they had to pay to keep their portion of land, how gold is found, what happens to it after it has been discovered, how much they have found, what their hopes and aspirations are and so on.
- **Storytelling.** Seat the children in a circle and create and tell a story about (say) a day in the life of a gold digger, bailed up on the way to the bank or finding a large nugget of gold. Have each child create and tell a short section of the class story and then indicate when the next person should continue with his/her version of the story.
- **Readers' Theatre.** Select a relevant text about life in the gold rush and adapt a section of it for Readers' Theatre. Have a group of children practise and then perform it using vocal and facial expression, body language and sound effects.
- **Performance.** Based on their knowledge of the life and times in the gold rush and these lead-up experiences, have the children create a drama showing the lives, feelings, actions and experiences of the gold diggers and then present this to another class.

Developing a skill or activity

You may spend several lessons focusing on the skill of (say) miming before using it as a device within the broader context of drama. Activities to develop children's skills in this area could include:

- Watch a video of a celebrated mime artist and identity key aspects of mime observed in the video.
- Develop these aspects through a variety of short activities using exaggerated but detailed and accurate movements without speaking, such as showing different emotions with the whole body, running home from school to tell Mum some exciting news, getting into a car, bus or train, and opening up a beautifully wrapped present.
- Narrate a story and have children mime what is happening throughout the story using the concepts and understandings they have learned about mime previously.
- Create a group still image of an artwork and mime what has happened before and after the picture was taken.
- Develop a drama which tells a created story using only body movements and no speech to convey the action, characters, events and context.

Music

Music can be used as a stimulus for drama in several ways, such as:

- After listening to a piece of music that tells a story or describes an event, discuss possible stories arising from the music, who is involved, what is happening and so on, and then create an improvisation or tell the story of the children's interpretation of the music.
- Use percussion instruments to create sound effects for a Readers' Theatre or a storytelling presentation.
- Use the words of a song as a poem for choral reading or Readers' Theatre.

Artworks

Use artworks (photos, paintings, drawings, collages, sculptures and so on — check out www.theartgallery.com.au, www.artgallery.nsw.gov.au/collection, www.art.com or http://gallery.euroweb.hu for examples of artworks) as a stimulus for creating drama, for example:

- Examine one of Brueghel the Younger's paintings, for example *Children's Games* or *Village Feast*, and identify what each of the people is doing. Have children take on roles of the different people in the picture and create a drama based on what is happening in the picture. Show through the drama who the people are, what has led up to this picture, what is happening and what will happen next.

- Using the two pictures *Manly Beach — Summer is Here** by Ethel Carrick Fox (1913) and *Manly Beach — Five Girls on Longboards** by Ray Leighton (1940), discuss the differences between these beach scenes and what one would see today at the beach. Create a group still image of each of the artworks. As the teacher taps different children on the shoulder, have them tell what they are thinking, doing and feeling. Improvise a third beach scene depicting a beach this year, and repeat the activity.

- Using the colour photograph *Something More, No. 1** by Tracey Moffat (1989) create a small group sculpture and use hot seating to find out what each character is thinking, doing and saying. Develop an improvisation by discussing and exploring the characters of each of the people in the photo and portraying a story showing what happened before, during and after what is seen in the photo.

- From the stimulus print *Off Visiting** by Kevin Mortensen (1994) discuss the use of the mask and costume to create a fantasy person. Have children design and make their own fantasy masks and then use them to explore different ideas for stories that they can improvise and share with the other children.

Literacy texts

- Find a narrative poem, discuss and demonstrate the characterisation, events and story, and then improvise actions in role to the reading of the poem.

- Use a picture book, such as *Shutting the Chooks in* by Libby Gleeson (Scholastic Press) to explore improvisation and Readers' Theatre. From the story, have different groups of children act out the role of the boy whose task it is to shut the chooks in from each part of the setting; for example, when he leaves the house and goes 'out the door, down the steps and across the yard'. The short, succinct lines in the text evoke the different feelings the boy experiences as he sets out to feed the chooks and shut them in for the night. Have the children use the text as a script for Readers' Theatre. Encourage them to use their voices, faces and gestures expressively and to use body posture and sound effects carefully to portray the feelings evoked in the text. For further ideas for using literature, see 'Drama activities based on literature texts' further on in this chapter.

---

* These prints are part of the art resource package *Beyond the Frame* published by the NSW Department of Education and Training Curriculum Support Directorate, Sydney, 2000.

Objects

- Bring in a selection of interesting objects, one for each child, and have children feel them and hold them, discussing their shape, feel, colour, possible use, aesthetics and so on. In pairs, have the children explore and develop different characters for each object and then create an improvised dialogue between the two objects using dramatic voices and moving the object expressively as it 'speaks'. Bring two pairs together and have the four objects interact with each other using expressive voices and gestures. Create a problem for them to solve, and include a beginning, a building of tension, climax and resolution.

- Have children use an object, such as a chair or a pencil, as if it were a variety of other items or symbols and show with movement how these items could be used. For example, the chair, in their imagination, could become a bed for a cat, an umbrella, the seat in a bus, a surfboard, a lion and so on; and the pencil could symbolise or become a hairclip, a toothbrush, a worm, a snake, a magic wand, a hockey stick and so on. Extend this activity by telling a story around the circle and include the different interpretations of the object in the story.

Activities to introduce the elements of drama

Here are some sample activities to introduce the different elements of drama so children become confident using them within the drama learning experiences. See the list of references at the end of the chapter for the publishing details of the texts mentioned. Develop your own activities based on your children's interests and experiences, the theme with which you are working, the focus of the drama lesson and your anticipated outcomes.

Drama games

- **Name games.** Have the children sit in a circle. All the children individually then say their name and mime what they enjoy doing; for example, 'My name is Simone and I enjoy (*mime what they enjoy doing*)'. The rest of the class guess what they are miming. Adapt the mime to relate to the themes to be explored in the lesson.

- **What feeling is that?** As different 'feelings flashcards' are shown, children display the pictured emotion with their whole bodies, including their faces. This could lead into a lesson focused on exploring the theme of emotions.

Improvisation games

- **Community roles.** As a class, make a list of community members who help us (e.g. firefighter, nurse, teacher and shopkeeper). Brainstorm what they do, who and how they help, where they work, when you need them and so on. In small groups improvise situations where these community members are at work. This could lead into a drama lesson that is based on a particular occupation.

Improvising roles based on stories, songs and poems

We're going on a bear hunt by Rosen and Oxenbury

- **Class discussion.** Discuss with the children what frightens them and why they think they are frightened. Would they be frightened of large animals, such as bears? Why? Why not? Show pictures of different types of bear. What would you do if you saw one?
- **Mime.** Have children identify possible places for bears to live, and then mime walking through these environments, looking for different types of bear, for example:
  — black bear in long wavy grass;
  — polar bear in a deep cold river;
  — brown bear near the river, in thick oozy mud;
  — big black bear in a big dark forest;
  — polar bear in a swirling, whirling snowstorm;
  — big brown bear in a narrow, gloomy cave.
- **Introduce story.** Read the story through with the children using contrasting vocal expression for the chorus and walking through the different environments.
- **Choral speaking.** Read through the story again with creative vocal expression, this time having the children repeat each phrase after you have read it, for example:
  — We're going on a bear hunt (We're going on a bear hunt)
  — We're going to catch a big one! (We're going to catch a big one!) and so on.
- **Miming and choral speaking.** Divide the class in half and have one half speak the echo part of the story, while the other half mimes the actions from the text. Finish by having the miming children snuggling under the covers and pretending to be asleep. Repeat and swap parts so everyone has a turn at both miming and choral speaking.

Walking through long wavy grass.

Still images

Having a wonderful time, wish you were here!

Divide the class into two groups and let each group choose a scene from a selection of postcards, pictures or photos of Australian landscapes. Group A stand at the back of the room and cooperatively decide on a scene from a picture postcard they sent home from their holidays, for example:

- at the beach;
- sunset at Uluru;
- skiing at Thredbo;
- at a Barrier Reef resort.

One by one, children from Group A move to the front of the room and take up a position which represents the shape of any object from the picture postcard and freeze into that shape until the whole group have taken up their positions.

Group B have the chance now to guess where the picture postcard is from and what it is depicting; if they cannot guess, the teacher asks Group A to bring the picture to life with relevant movements and sounds. When Group B have guessed the picture, it is then their turn to present a picture postcard to Group A.

Choral speaking/reading

There was an old lady who swallowed a fly

- **Class discussion.** Show a picture of a fly and a spider and ask which creature would eat the other? Imagine eating a fly yourself. What would you think about that? How would you feel after you had swallowed it? Imagine if it were still alive in your stomach and wiggled and jiggled around there. How would you feel? Show children pictures of a bird, a cat, a dog, a goat, a cow and a horse and have them arrange them in order of size. Discuss which animal could catch another of the animals. Imagine eating these animals whole. How would it feel?

- **Improvisation.** Have children demonstrate how they might go about catching and then eating each of the animals. Show the effort and feelings involved in this activity and include any relevant speech to show these emotions.

- **Reading the poem.** Read the poem through and discuss the cumulative structure of the poem. Read it through again, with different children improvising the lady swallowing the different animals.

- **Choral reading and mime.** Choose one person to mime the old lady and then divide the rest of the class into two groups, A and B. Have the two groups read or say the poem in two parts with expression while the 'old lady' mimes to the narrative.

Group A: There was an old lady who swallowed a spider,
Group B: How absurd to swallow a spider . . .
Together: She swallowed the spider, to catch the fly . . .

Storytelling

In groups, create a new story based on the structure of *There was an old lady* and share this with the rest of the class, using vocal expression and improvisation.

Movement and mime

Chinese whisper mimes

Select a group of about six children to go outside while the rest of the class work out a dramatic scenario which can be acted out by one person, for example: cycling to a friend's place, knocking on a friend's door, talking to the friend, and going out into the garden and playing ball with the friend.

One person from the outside group is called in and the dramatic scenario is verbally explained to them. The second person from the outside group comes in and the first person mimes the scenario as carefully as he can, for the second person. The third person from the outside group is called in and the second person has to mime the scenario as she understood it to the third person. The first person is not allowed to communicate with any of the outside group members. Continue this with the fourth, the fifth and then the sixth person from the outside group. The six children then line up and, starting from the sixth person, explain what they thought they were acting out. Have the first person act out his version of the scenario again, and then tell them the verbal version of the drama.

Shoes from Grandpa by Mem Fox

- **Drama game.** Seat children in a circle and have the first child say and mime, 'I got up in the morning and put on my socks'. The second child says and mimes, 'I got up in the morning and put on my socks and shoes'. The third child repeats the words and mime of the previous children and adds her own piece of clothing. Continue this around the circle.

- **Class discussion.** Show some different types of clothing and discuss what clothes children put on when they get out of bed on different days — school uniform on school days, casual clothes for Saturdays, smart clothes for going out somewhere special, warm clothes for winter and cool clothes for summer and so on.
- **Improvisation.** Have children mime putting on each set of clothes as they discuss them and then improvise what they might do in each set of clothes.
- **Introduce the story.** Read through the story and show the children the pictures.
- **Mime to narration.** As the story is read again, have children create different movements for each line, and repeat the movements cumulatively to the end of the story. A small group of children may like to add appropriate instruments and vocals to create sound effects to accompany the mimed story.

Drama activities based on literature texts

Rain May and Captain Daniel by Catherine Bateson

One of the themes in this book is that of children being unpleasant to others and how this was resolved.

- **Freeze frames.** Have children find a space by themselves, close their eyes and imagine a time when someone was unkind to them. When the tambourine plays have them show with their bodies how they felt when this happened; when the tambourine stops, have them relax and open their eyes. Repeat the activity but have them think of a time when they were unkind to someone else and have them show with their bodies stopping doing this (stop playing the tambourine), pause for thinking time, and then play the tambourine so children can show how they felt when this happened. Discuss how they felt in each situation and what they could have done to change the situation.

- **Improvisation from the text.** Read through the sections of the book about the other children being unpleasant to Rain and Daniel. In small groups, explore this scene with improvisations and complete it by showing how Rain made them all like Daniel.
- **Improvisation from life.** In groups, create a real or imagined story-line about unpopular children at school and show how they are treated by the other children. Devise a way to show how they can become popular so that everyone

will want to play with them and how they react to this. Decide on the characters required for this play and work out the following:
- When does the situation take place?
- Who are they?
- Where are they?
- Why do they act that way?
- What are they thinking?
- What do they say to each other?
- What do they do to each other?
- How is the situation resolved?

Have the children practise the dramatisation of their story and present it to the rest of the class. Comment on how effectively each group resolved the bullying situation.

A different sort of real: The diary of Charlotte McKenzie, Melbourne 1918–1919 by Kerry Greenwood

- **Class discussion: Diary writing.** Show children a diary and discuss the different types of diary, (electronic diaries, diaries for dates and times, diaries for writing private thoughts in and so on). Ask the children if they have kept a diary. Suggest they keep a diary of what they did over one week, and then share one entry with a friend.

- **Improvisation: Different viewpoints.** Charlotte's gift from her Uncle Donald was a blank book from France, made of very beautiful paper and bound in elegant blue leather. She used it to write a diary of her thoughts, feelings and actions as she lived through the end of World War I and the influenza pandemic. In it, she mentioned several important people in her life. Identify these and discuss each character and how they were important in Charlotte's life. Divide the children into groups of seven and ask each child in the group to role-play one of the characters in Charlotte's family. Include:
  - Charlotte;
  - her mother;
  - her father;
  - Amelia (12 years old);
  - Lily (10 years old);
  - Albert (6 years old);
  - Uncle Donald.

  Have them write down in their 'diary' about how they saw the war, the influenza pandemic, Charlotte's work as an assistant nurse and other parts of the story from their viewpoint. Have children read aloud their diary and have another person role-play the character as the diary is read aloud.

- **Improvisation: Historical changes.** From the text and from interviews with older people in the community, brainstorm all the differences that children notice between the way people lived in Charlotte's time and the way they live today in relation to:

- cars;
- washing clothes;
- ironing clothes;
- getting hot and cold water;
- trains;
- food;
- music;
- leisure activities;
- jobs for girls;
- christmas presents and celebrations;
- possessions and so on.

Record the differences using words and pictures. Divide the class into pairs and have one child take on the role of living in the early 20th century and the other the role of living in today's society. Have them discuss day-to-day happenings and try to explain to the other children how they live/d their lives and what they do/did each day.

- **Storytelling.** Have four or five children take on the roles of Charlotte at different stages of her life: as a child, as the young girl in the book, as the young woman she becomes after the book finishes, as an older woman perhaps with her own family, and as an elderly lady looking back over her long life. Have them tell the rest of the class about their experiences as Charlotte in each stage of her life.
- **Hot seating.** Encourage the rest of the class to ask the different Charlottes questions about their life, work, current world news, living conditions, changes they have seen and what they have learned from their experiences.

Jamil's shadow by Christine Harris

- **Miming emotions.** Using pictures, masks or flashcards showing different emotions, have children portray each emotion with their bodies. In pairs, have them choose an emotion and make up a sentence that includes this emotion.
One child reads the sentence expressively and the other one mimes the action and expression; for example, 'Startled by the noise, the boy sprinted from the room'.
- **Choral reading.** Select paragraphs from throughout the story that show a variety of actions and emotions. Photocopy these and give them to small groups of children. Examples of paragraphs could include those beginning:

  (page 9)   Impulsively, Jamil stood . . .
  (page 9)   Suddenly Jamil stopped . . .
  (page 17) That was the last story . . .
  (page 18) Hot tears prickled at Jamil's eyelids . . .
  (page 21) 'Is something stuck in your paw? . . .
  (page 23) 'I only have a little . . .
  (page 23) 'You have no manners . . .
  (page 25) He straightened . . .
  (page 32) The door of Jamil's hut slammed shut . . .
  (page 42) Jamil opened the door . . .

(page 48) Jamil tried to grab the table . . .
(page 62) The earth was hard and damp.

Have each group of children practise reading through their paragraph with expression. Encourage them to think about who is in the text, what they are feeling, why they are feeling that way, how they would act and so on. Share the paragraphs with the rest of the class.

- **Improvisation.** Using the same groups with the same paragraphs, have some children read the text with expression, while others role-play what is happening in the text. Encourage them to show the feelings and actions that they discussed in the previous activity.

The Potato People by Pamela Allen

- **Class discussion.** Bring to class some new and old potatoes, pins, toothpicks and scraps of fabric. Discuss with the class the differences between the new and old potatoes.
- **Mime.** Have the children show with their bodies the round, plump new potato, and then slowly crinkle up, start to grow roots and turn into an old potato. Dress up one potato using the materials you have brought. Each time a piece is attached to the potato have children respond as though they are having a pin or toothpick stuck into that part of their potato body!
- **Improvisation.** As a class, have children discuss what the Potato People might have talked about when Grandma and Jack were not around. Have children discuss the following questions about the Potato People:
  — How did they feel about being dressed up with pins and having toothpicks stuck into them?
  — What sort of people are they: happy, grumpy, old, young, anxious, carefree and so on?
  — How did they feel when they were left alone for so long and started to grow horns?
  — How did they feel when it rained and the storms came?
  — What did they say to each other?
  — How did they feel when they were buried in the compost heap?
  — Did they call out for help, or realise it was for the best?
  — Then what happened in the dark, under the compost?
  — How did they feel when they heard Grandma and Jack digging them up?
  — What did they say to each other?

  In small groups have children work on an improvisation to show their representation of what the Potato People were like and how they reacted to the events in the story. Compare the different interpretations from the different groups. Reflect on the presentations and discuss why they were different and how effectively they were presented.

A year on our farm by Penny Matthews

- **Class discussion.** Show pictures of trees and landscapes in different seasons. Discuss the differences and what times of the year the different seasons happen.

Ask children which season they prefer and why. Discuss what activities they do in the different seasons.

- **Drama game.** Have all the children find a space by themselves and, as the tambourine is shaken, pretend they are in a particular season, and then freeze as the tambourine stops playing. As the teacher taps all the children in turn on the shoulder they say what they are doing and what season they are in, and then they relax.
- **Reading the book.** Read the book through, showing the pictures as you read the text. Discuss the different activities done on the farm in the different seasons. List these on the blackboard or whiteboard, for example:

  Summer: Picking fruit, spreading hay, checking water troughs;
  Autumn: Planting vegetables, milking cows, looking after lambs;
  Winter: Mending fences, planting trees, crutching sheep;
  Spring: Shearing sheep, baling hay, watering trees.

  Read through the text again and improvise each of these activities as the text is read.
- **Group sculptures.** In groups, select one picture from the book to present as a still image. Work out who will be which person, object or animal. Have one person sculpt the rest of the children to form a still representation of the picture.
- **Hot seating.** Have the sculptor then touch the children on the shoulder, one at a time, and have them tell what they are doing and what they are thinking.
- **Reflection.** Take a photo of each still representation either digitally or on a 35-millimetre camera. Print the photos and show them to the children; then have them discuss the effectiveness of their representations. Display the photos alongside each of the pictures on which they were based and include a short caption explaining what the photo is about.

Bear and Chook by Lisa Shanahan

- **Readers' Theatre.** The text of *Bear and Chook* is ideal for Readers' Theatre as it is mainly dialogue. Groups of children could take on the following roles: Narrator, Bear 1, Bear 2, Chook 1 and Chook 2. Break up the text for each of the roles and present it as a Readers' Theatre, as suggested below:

Narrator:	One morning Bear and Chook . . .
Bear 1:	What do you want to be . . .
Chook 1:	An old chook.
Bear 2:	Oh!' (wrinkles his nose)
Chook 2:	What about you, Bear?
Bear 1:	I think . . .
All:	CRICKETY — CROCK SPLODGE!

If needed, demonstrate how to give different emphasis to different words to emphasise the meaning; discuss how different parts of the story can be read, using vocal expression, body language and sound effects. Work out how and where the different readers should stand, thinking about the effective use of levels and space.

MMADD about the arts

Snap! Went Chester by Tania Cox

- **Drama game.** Identify the different animals in the story and have children discuss and demonstrate how each animal would stand, move slowly and move quickly. Select one child to be Chester and have the other children choose to be one of the other animals in the story. All the children take up their positions in the shape of their animals around the room. As Chester approaches each child and snaps he/she runs, flies, jumps or swims in character away to the side of the room. If Chester snaps at a pelican, the pelican chases him to the side of the room; he becomes Chester and continues the game.

- **Choral reading.** Select a narrator and seat the children so they can all read the text of the book. The narrator reads the main part of the text, and the rest of the class read together the words 'Snap! went Chester' and 'Snap!' Have them emphasise the loud sound by clapping their hands together at the word 'Snap!'.

- **Readers' Theatre.** Write a simple Readers' Theatre adaptation of the text of *Snap! Went Chester*. Read it through several times in small groups with half the group being the narrator and the other half being Chester. Share their work with the other groups and reflect on how effectively certain groups used vocal expression, gestures and sound effects to create clarity of meaning in the text.

Two Summers by John Heffernan

- **Class discussion and choral reading.** Using stimulus pictures of the dry Australian landscape, brainstorm words describing the drought-stricken farmlands and the feelings of those living there. Encourage the use of a thesaurus to extend the children's vocabulary. Have children read through the words listed using expressive voices to show the despair, dryness and devastation that a drought brings to the countryside. Show other pictures of lush, green Australian countryside and create another list of words to describe a well-watered farm and surrounding countryside. Read through the words expressively showing the hope, freshness and vitality of the green environment.

- **Vocal collage.** Divide the class into small groups and have each group choose one aspect of the dry landscape (trees, dry creek beds, native animals or birds, empty tanks, starving sheep and cattle, farmers and their families and so on). Have them create a vocal collage of sounds, words, phrases and so on to describe their chosen aspect, using contrasting high and low voices (pitch), soft and loud voices (dynamics), fast and slow voices (tempo) and smooth and sharp voices, as well as instruments and other sound effects to create an aural collage of sounds describing the topic. The teacher, or selected child, can then orchestrate this vocal collage to create an aural depiction of the drought-stricken landscape. Remind the children of the pictures and words created that describe the lush green countryside and farmlands. Create a contrasting vocal collage depicting the countryside which has had a lot of rain. Tape both vocal collages and reflect on the effectiveness of the different sounds used to describe the two different landscapes.

- **Improvisation.** Brainstorm how the two friends in the story may interact when they meet up again this summer. Discuss the differences in the farm and how this may affect what they do together. Identify issues that might make or break the boys' friendship over the summer and decide on a theme or message about which they can build a play. Create one symbol that can be used to represent the grass-covered farm and another symbol to represent the drought-stricken farm and use these in the development of the play as the friends reflect on the previous summer and compare it with this summer. Explore the different characters and events happening on the farm through the use of activities such as mime, movement, still images, hot seating, teacher in role, music, improvisation and role-plays. Work out the story-line and structure for the play. Develop the dialogue and action, and then rehearse, reflect and refine the process and content of the play several times until the class are satisfied that they have created a play that effectively presents the message which they set out to convey.

Milli, Jack and the dancing cat by Stephen Michael King

- **Hot seating.** After several readings of the story, ask children who their favourite character is in the story. Encourage them to look at the pictures and read the text to find out as much about that character as possible. Select children to role-play Milli, Jack, the dancing cat and the villagers. Have the class ask each of them questions about their thoughts, feelings, actions and dreams to build up a picture of the whole character. Change over roles and see if other children can add extra information to what the class have learned about the characters.

- **Puppets and masks.** Discuss the different personalities and characteristics of each of the key people in the story and examine the pictures to identify what are their physical attributes. In groups, make some simple masks or puppets for the characters of Milli, Jack, the dancing cat and the villagers. Each group practises and then presents their version of the story using the puppets or masks. Examples could include:
  — Milli making creative artworks;
  — the villagers doing ordinary things;
  — Milli making ordinary boots and shoes;
  — Jack and the dancing cat coming to town;
  — the villagers and Jack talking;
  — Jack meeting Milli;
  — Jack and the dancing cat teaching Milli how to dance;
  — Milli making them wonderful shoes, clothes and musical instruments;
  — Milli making wonderful creative things for herself;
  — Jack saying goodbye to Milli;
  — the villagers interacting with (the new outwardly creative) Milli;
  — Jack and the dancing cat returning for a nice cup of tea and meeting the villagers and Milli.

Share these with the rest of the class; discuss how effective the different characters were in each presentation. (For suggestions of how to make different kinds of puppet, see Chapter 5, 'Introduction to visual arts education'.)

SPRINGBOARDS FOR DISCUSSION AND APPLICATION

1. Create a series of learning experiences based on at least three types of drama and include the use of several elements of drama that develop children's ability to use these conventions in the process of making drama.

2. Select a key learning area and brainstorm ways that the skills and knowledge relevant to this key learning area can be learned and expressed through drama activities.

3. Develop a drama program based on a literature text, showing how the three areas of making, performing and appreciating can be developed and implemented in a selected primary classroom through exploring one of the themes in the text.

FURTHER READING

Baldwin, P. (2002), *Teaching literacy through drama*, Routledge Falmer, London.
Bolton, G. (1992), *New perspectives on classroom drama*, Simon & Schuster, England.
Bowell, P. & Heap, B.S. (2001), *Planning process drama*, David Fulton Publishers, London.
Burton, B. (2003), *Living drama*, Longman, Melbourne.
Burton, B. (2004), *Creating drama*, Pearson Education, Melbourne.
Cheirt, J. & Hunsberger, B. (2004), *All you need to teach drama, ages 5–8*, Macmillan Teacher Resources, Melbourne.
Cheirt, J. & Hunsberger, B. (2004), *All you need to teach drama, ages 8–10*, Macmillan Teacher Resources, Melbourne.
Colwell, E. (1992), *Storytelling*, Thimble Press, Stroud, UK.
Engblom, L. (1993), *Dramarama*, Australian Teacher Network, Sydney.
Ewing, R. & Simons, J. (2004), *Beyond the script: Drama in the classroom*, Primary English Teachers Association, Sydney.
Fox, M. (1988), *How to teach drama to infants without trying*, Ashton Scholastic, Sydney.
Heathcote, D. & Bolton G. (1995), *Drama for learning*, Heinemann, London.
Hughes, J. (Ed) (1991), *Drama in education: The state of the art*, NSW: Educational Drama Association, Sydney.
Mooney, M. & Nicholls, J. (eds) (2004), *Drama journeys*, Currency Press, Sydney.
Neelands, J. (1987), *Making sense of drama*, Heinemann, London.
NSW Department of Education and Training (1998), *Exploring the worlds of K–6 drama: From ancient Anna to the cloth of dreams*, Author, Sydney.
O Neill C. (1995), *Drama worlds: A framework for process drama*, Heinemann, Portsmouth, UK.
O'Toole, J. & Dunn, J. (2002), *Pretending to learn*, Longman, Sydney.
Stinson, M. & Wall, D. (2003), *Drama active, Book 1*, McGraw-Hill, Sydney.
Warren, K. (1999), *Hooked on drama*, 2nd edn, Social Science Press, Katoomba, NSW.

REFERENCES

Allen, P. (2003), *The Potato People*, Penguin Books, Camberwell, Vic.
Bateson, C. (2003), *Rain May and Captain Daniel*, University of Queensland Press, Brisbane.
Cox, T. (2004), *Snap! Went Chester*, Hodder Headline, Sydney.

Fox, M. (1992), *Shoes from Grandpa*, Ashton Scholastic, Gosford, NSW.
Gleeson, L. (2004) *Shutting the chooks in*, Scholastic Press, Lindfield, Sydney.
Greenwood, K. (2002), *A different sort of real: The diary of Charlotte McKenzie, Melbourne 1918–1919*, Sholastic Press, Gosford, NSW.
Harris, C. (2002), *Jamil's Shadow*, Penguin Books, Camberwell, Vic.
Heffernan, J. (2004), *Two summers*, Scholastic Press, Gosford, NSW.
King, S.M. (2004), *Milli, Jack and the dancing cat*, Allen & Unwin, Melbourne, Vic.
Matthews, P. (2003), *A year on our farm*, Omnibus Books, Gosford, NSW.
Rosen, M. & Oxenbury, H. (1989), *We're going on a bear hunt*, Walker Books, Newtown, NSW.
Shanahan, L. (2003), *Bear and chook*, Hodder Headline, Sydney.

chapter eight
Integration and the arts

An integrated learning environment will contribute to meaningful and long-lasting educational experiences for children.
(Anderson & Lawrence, 2001)

Learning outcomes
By the end of this chapter, students will be able to:
- show their understanding of different levels of integration by planning learning experiences showing service connections, symmetric correlations and *syntegration*;
- plan a series of integrated arts learning experiences that include the Multiple Intelligences.

Introduction

'So much to teach — so little time!' is the cry from many classrooms. The crowded curriculum has led to teachers finding different ways of teaching all they need to teach within the given time period, and this has sometimes led to their integrating the learning experiences. For many years academics and practitioners have advocated the use of integration in the educational classroom to provide children with holistic and meaningful learning experiences from which they can generalise understandings and then apply these to other situations.

The whole-language movement emphasised holistic rather than fragmented learning and often used a theme as a focus, suggesting teachers integrate learning across the curriculum to enhance children's ability to read, write, talk and listen.

The increasing diversity within classrooms and schools has given rise to integrated programs which aim to develop harmonious living within and without the school community, taking advantage of the differences and using cross-curriculum approaches to explore diversity and harmony issues.

As the knowledge base explodes through the use of mass media and technology, the emphasis of education is changing from learning and remembering facts, which will soon be out of date, to understanding the underlying concepts, applying them to new situations, and being able to develop generic skills such as research, analysis, synthesis, evaluation, problem solving, teamwork, leadership and critical thinking to live and work in tomorrow's world. For many teachers this has led to their exploring different ways of engaging children in learning experiences, with integration being a key aspect of this process.

To integrate or not to integrate, that is the question!

However, in investigating how to integrate the curriculum effectively, practitioners and researchers have found that, in many cases, *integration* has become a meaningless and overworked word! Everyone seems to have a different understanding and explanation of the word; some are ardent proponents for their interpretation of integration and others are just as wholeheartedly against it, seeing integration as a diluting of important outcomes within discrete key learning areas.

For some teachers, integration means developing learning experiences based on a theme; for others it is using the same song or artwork in two different key learning areas. One set of teachers may use the word 'integration' when they have children colour in a stencil about a science experiment, and another set of teachers may ask their children to complete an integrated project exploring a theme and then have them present their work using some type of technology.

Adding to the confusion of definitions, there are distinct connotations for the word 'integration' within the context of special education, where children with disabilities are schooled alongside 'regular' children in the classroom. Although integration of special-needs children is an important aspect of schooling, this chapter refers to integration within the context of curriculum and not special education.

To find out what integration is, we can begin by examining its opposite. In a non-integrated environment, children move from one subject or key learning area to another, making no links or connections between the two and learning the skills, knowledge and understandings of each key learning area within the closed doors of that particular key learning area. Then they pack up their books, take out new ones, sometimes move to another room, and become involved in learning experiences within another key learning area, totally unrelated to what they were engaged in several minutes before. This can lead to the curriculum being moulded into boxes of learning with little external context, links or explanations as to how what was learned in one key learning area can relate to what they are learning in another key learning area.

However, in realising that this type of learning environment may not be meaningful to many children, some teachers respond by moving to the other end of the continuum and planning 'integrated' programs that lose all integrity within the individual key learning areas and end up being superficial activities loosely based on a theme, but with little depth or meaningful outcomes.

Either approach rarely gives children holistic and authentic learning experiences using their preferred intelligences and providing the opportunity for in-depth understanding, development of generic skills and the ability to generalise and apply what they have learned to other situations. Therefore, there needs to be a balance between the two extremes so that children are achieving discrete indicators and outcomes in each of the key learning areas but are also engaging in authentic learning within a meaningful, holistic context, and being given the opportunity to develop generic skills as well.

Various models of integration

Integration can occur across different key learning areas or it can occur within one key learning area and across subjects, such as within the arts. Learning experiences that involve music, media, visual arts, dance or drama can achieve outcomes within the specific art form, across art forms and/or across other key learning areas. There are at least three models or levels of integration where key learning areas or subjects can work together to achieve outcomes. Each is valid in itself when used by a creative and resourceful teacher to promote the children's understanding and application of their learning, and each can also be used alongside the other models within the context of a program of work.

Because the word 'integration' had so many positive and negative connotations and understandings in education, this book uses it in a broad sense and includes the following three models of integration. They are *service connections* (one key learning area servicing learning in another key learning area), *symmetric correlations* (two key learning areas using the same material to achieve their own outcomes) and what we will call *syntegration* (a created word which indicates that key learning areas are working together synergistically to explore a theme, concept or focus question and achieving their own outcomes as well as generic outcomes).

Service connections

Service connections within key learning areas or subjects occur when concepts and outcomes are learned and reinforced in one key learning area by using material or resources from another key learning area with no specific outcomes from the servicing key learning area. Examples of the arts servicing other key learning areas include:

- singing '*Botany Bay*' to reinforce learning about the British colonisation of Australia;
- viewing a Balinese dance video when learning about the culture of Bali;
- presenting a choral reading of a poem in a literacy lesson;
- drawing the life cycle of the butterfly to document what children have learned in science.

> **Service connections:** One key learning area or art form servicing learning and outcomes in another key learning area or art form.
>
> **Symmetric correlations:** Two key learning areas or art forms using the same material to achieve their own individual outcomes.
>
> **Syntegration:** Several key learning areas or art forms working synergistically together to explore a theme, concept or focus question and achieving their own outcomes as well as generic outcomes.

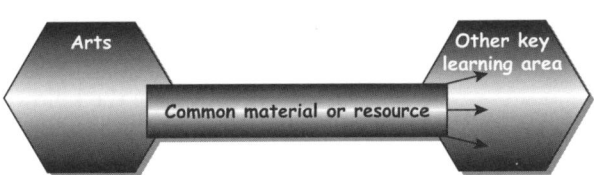

Service connection

Another example of the arts being used to achieve outcomes in other key learning areas is the use of counting songs to assist in learning to count in mathematics although this will often achieve no music outcomes. Making up a rap to help children remember the steps for procedural text writing uses the children's musical and kinaesthetic intelligences to achieve literacy but few musical outcomes. Learning to sing 'The Alphabet Song' assists in memorising the letters of the alphabet; and singing the 'Little Red Caboose', colouring in red balloons, dramatising the story 'Little Red Riding Hood' and dancing with red scarves to music may help reinforce the concept of the colour 'red' but may achieve little in the way of creative arts outcomes. Although these and other instances of service connections can be important teaching and learning tools, they should not be viewed as valid arts lessons. Instead, they should be seen as using arts resources or materials to achieve outcomes from the key learning area that is serviced by the arts.

Using the arts to connect with other key learning areas may certainly enhance the learning experiences of children who learn kinaesthetically, visually or musically; may help them achieve outcomes in key learning areas where previously they have failed; and may also provide all children with enjoyment and motivation. Using service connections within the curriculum is a valid way of achieving certain outcomes but should not be confused with symmetric correlation or *syntegration*. However with a little extra thought and preparation, service connections can become symmetric correlations and outcomes in both key learning areas can be achieved.

Symmetric correlations

Symmetric correlations centre around common or shared resources, materials or ideas being used within two or more key learning areas or art forms to achieve authentic outcomes in both key learning areas or art forms. The figure illustrates how this is

Symmetric correlation

a more symmetrical approach than the previous model of service correlations as both key learning areas or art forms benefit from the learning experiences. Unlike service connections, symmetric correlations view achieving outcomes in both key learning areas as equally important; one does not service the other. For example, if exploring the concept of the colour 'red' by singing the song 'Little Red Caboose', dancing with red scarves, creating artworks using the colour red and dramatising the story of *Little Red Riding Hood* is seen as achieving valid outcomes for literacy, teachers could then examine their arts program and develop stage-appropriate activities which involve the colour 'red' and these materials and activities. If these activities are appropriate to each art form, they could then include them in their developmental program as they introduce and reinforce relevant skills, knowledge and understandings in each of the art forms. Thus outcomes and indicators can be achieved in both key learning areas which can both retain their integrity.

Other examples of symmetric correlation between the arts and other key learning areas could include the following:

- singing *'Botany Bay'* in a music lesson and learning about structure (verses and chorus) as well as dynamics (loud and soft) *and* listening to or singing the song in a social studies lesson and using it to explore the feelings, experiences and reasons for convicts coming to Australia;

- learning a Balinese dance in a dance lesson and exploring ways of using hand gestures, movements and space to create a similar dance of their own *and* viewing a video of Balinese dance as part of an exploration of Balinese culture in social studies;

- exploring different ways of presenting a choral reading of a poem in a drama lesson to develop the use of vocal expression *and* reading the poem through together analysing the poem for its literary value;

- drawing a caterpillar, cocoon and butterfly from observation or photos, focusing on line, cross-hatching and positive/negative space in a visual arts lesson *and* using these drawings to create a display about the life cycle of a butterfly with written annotations to reinforce and present what they have learned in a science lesson.

Through symmetric correlations, teachers can begin to break down the barriers between the key learning areas and recognise that learning can occur effectively and discrete outcomes can be achieved within two or more key learning areas using common resources or material.

Syntegration

Synergy occurs when the sum of the whole is greater than the sum of the individual parts. When used in this context, synergy occurs when the outcomes achieved through *syntegration* are greater than those achieved if each key learning area was taught by itself or connected or correlated with other key learning areas. *Syntegration* occurs when teachers plan purposefully to use broad themes or

Syntegration

concepts that move across key learning areas so that the theme or concept is explored in a meaningful way by and within different key learning areas. Each key learning area's indicators and outcomes remain discrete and the integrity of each key learning area is maintained. *Syntegration* also achieves outcomes that transcend those in each key learning area such as the development of generic skills (observation, research, problem solving, teamwork and so on). Through *syntegration*, a higher level of learning and critical thinking is stimulated as children are encouraged to apply, compare, analyse, synthesise and evaluate ideas and concepts across the key learning areas or art forms.

As children explore learning experiences across the key learning areas they can see their learning as authentic and meaningful. Within a broader context, learning is relevant to their lives, interests, intelligences, learning styles, needs and abilities, and it draws from multifaceted sources. *Syntegration* can break down the barriers between different key learning areas and encourage children to extend their thinking. It provides them with real-life experiences that are holistic and not segregated into separate boxes. When planning a *syntegrated* theme, teachers should ensure that the outcomes are authentic and have integrity within each relevant key learning area, that artificial relationships are not created between the key learning areas or art forms, and that the discrete knowledge, skills and understandings of each key learning area are not blurred for the sake of the theme. Rather, a theme or concept should be explored using the many facets or windows of different key learning areas and so a deeper, more holistic understanding of the theme or concept is achieved. It is important to ensure that learning experiences are selected on the basis of promoting and enhancing children's learning and not just because the activities include other key learning areas.

An example of *syntegration* within the arts could be a unit based on impressionism. Learning experiences could include learning about the cultural context of this period through appreciating art, music, dance, media and drama artworks created in this style, and then making their own artworks within the impressionistic style in each of the art forms. A researched and analysed exploration of the historical events surrounding and producing the impressionistic period could be undertaken in social studies and children could write an impressionistic poem or create a narrative text that explains their understanding of the concept of impressionism from a variety of viewpoints and then illustrate it with relevant scanned and photographed images to achieve English outcomes.

Another theme could encourage children to focus on patterns in each of the art forms as they make and appreciate music, media, visual arts dance and drama artworks. Through this *syntegration* approach children could develop teamworking, leadership, cooperative, listening and problem-solving skills. The program could then be expanded across key learning areas as they explore patterns in maths, literature, nature and science. When implementing *syntegrated* programs, teachers should ask themselves three questions:
- Are these learning experiences enhancing and extending children's understandings of the theme, concept or focus question?
- Are these learning experiences achieving authentic outcomes in the relevant key learning areas?
- Are children developing generic skills through involvement in this unit?

If these questions can be answered in the affirmative then *syntegration* should be occurring in the program.

An example of the generic skills that can be developed and extended through a *syntegrated* program can be seen in the box: Community Harmony Project: Real-life *syntegrated* creative arts project.

Integrated arts programs, multiliteracies and Multiple Intelligences

A *syntegrated* program can be based on a theme or concept, and use the arts to develop multiliteracies or utilise the Multiple Intelligences across the curriculum to enhance and deepen understandings and learning experiences.

Thematic programs

When considering a theme, concept or focus question to explore using service connections, symmetric correlations and/or *syntegration* it is important that it is broad enough to cover several selected key learning areas or art forms with integrity. At times it will be difficult to cover all key learning areas or art forms, so don't force the correlations or *syntegration* as it is better to have a cohesive, well-thought out unit which only covers (say) four key learning areas than one which includes all key learning areas superficially. Themes should be meaningful to the children, be based

Community Harmony Project: Real-life *syntegrated* creative arts project

Children from Greentree Public School* were given the unique opportunity to explore their role in the community through the creative arts and learn how they could use the arts to promote harmony within that community. The school is located in a low socioeconomic area with 87% of children coming from a non-English speaking (mainly Arabic) background. Through engaging in a variety of integrated creative arts experiences the children examined how their backgrounds play a major role in their view of themselves and their community. The project was also seen as an important vehicle in which children could develop their leadership and artistic skills.

Eighteen children from Years 4–6 were chosen to work on this project; they were selected mainly on the basis of their artistic ability and some of the children also had basic leadership skills. Over a period of two terms, during lunchtimes and after school, the 18 children worked with their teacher and a university lecturer to develop and curate an innovative art exhibition of their works on the theme of 'My Community: The Power of Story'. To prepare for this, the children were involved in a series of integrated arts activities which focused on the theme of community harmony and children were encouraged to talk, learn, research and think about what community harmony meant to them, how they could bring about harmony within their own community (whether in the classroom, at school, at home or in the wider local community) and how they could express their understanding of this theme in a variety of media and art forms.

As part of the Community Harmony Project, the children visited art galleries to learn about conceptual art, practised sketching in the city, took black-and-white photographs of their community, visited the Brett Whiteley Studio, enjoyed drawing with pastels as taught by a visiting artist, learned about curating an exhibition and created a series of artworks that were then exhibited for six weeks at the university's Margot Hardy art gallery.

Whiteley gallery.

In the lead-up to the exhibition, the children were involved in a series of music and visual arts learning experiences during their lunchtimes and also developed a rap, a Readers' Theatre presentation, a multimedia presentation and a puppet play for the launch of the exhibition, all of which focused on community harmony. Each student was responsible for different aspects of the preparation of the exhibition and, before the launch, they spent a full day hanging and labelling all the artworks.

Following the successful launch of their art exhibition, the young artists practised how to teach a selection of arts activities, and then taught the rest of their school how to create visual arts and music artworks. During the two days after the exhibition launch, three classes at a time were bussed onto the university campus where every class of children walked through the exhibition, and were encouraged by two of the 18 children to talk about what they saw and then write or draw their responses to the displayed artworks.

Each class then rotated around the music and visual arts activities where pairs of the 18 children taught small groups how to make up pieces of music on tuned and untuned percussion instruments and how to create visual artworks using silk painting, marbling, clay and glass painting. Over 300 children aged 5 to 13 were involved in this exciting and innovative project to bring the whole school community onto a university campus and to expose all the children to peer-taught art and music activities. For most of the 300 children this was their first experience working with clay, silk, marbling, glass painting, and tuned and untuned percussion instruments, and visiting an art gallery.

Teaching music.

Over the few months that these 18 children worked together on this project, they achieved discrete outcomes in each of the art forms of music, media, dance, drama and visual arts and showed a significant development in the area of self-confidence, self-esteem and leadership. When they took on the role of teacher in the workshops they showed that they understood the need to be prepared, the need to keep their students engaged as well as the need to build the relationship with the students by welcoming them into the room, explaining the rules and consequences, demonstrating skills and praising the children who did well. Their teachers, the university lecturers and the preservice student teachers who observed these lessons were amazed at the children's teaching

Learning marbling.

MMADD about the arts

Whiteley gallery.

ability as they showed outstanding initiative, leadership and organisational skills in this environment.

Involvement in this project made the children aware of their own behaviour as students and as a result some of them have made very positive changes in their own behaviour. They were given responsibility and, knowing that people were depending on them and that the success of the exhibition depended on their carrying out their jobs, they became accountable and rose to the occasion. Being part of this select group, they developed a sense of being special and they felt they had to live up to the important role for which they had been chosen. Although the children were unused to these sorts of social situation where a lot of self-control is required, and in class were often impulsive and easily distracted with short attention spans, it was amazing to see them modify their behaviour to suit each situation because they were the leaders of an important project and this was their event for which they were responsible. They took total ownership of the event. Taking them outside their normal school environment was very important because it brought them out of their comfort zone, it exposed them to experiences that they would never have had otherwise and it broadened their horizons, opening up to them previously unknown possibilities in the area of future study and careers as well as artistic experiences.

Practising Readers' Theatre.

The children flourished in an environment that allowed them to create and express themselves freely. They learned that art could be free from rules and that they could express themselves in a way that they couldn't in any other learning area. The project also provided children with a reason for learning, gave meaning, depth and understanding to their learning and put it in a real-life context. They could see why they were doing activities — they were not just time fillers but there was a purpose to their learning and it was up to them to ensure the success of the project and the exhibition. The children also learned to appreciate different art forms and to see the art in their surroundings that previously they had taken for granted.

Apart from achieving outcomes in a variety of art forms and key learning areas, one of the major successes achieved by the project was giving these particular children an opportunity to experience the arts in a way that they would never have had otherwise. The majority of children had never been to an art gallery and had little experience in arts education within their schooling, so this was a life-changing experience that will affect them for many years to come. As they embraced the opportunities the project gave them, they opened a door that had been shut by circumstances, by the poverty of their arts experiences in home and in school, and the lack of any similar experiences in their lives.

Practising teaching music.

For such children as Ahmed, the project has been a platform for developing and extending his confidence, maturity and leadership skills and has allowed him to express himself through art and dance. It gave him the opportunity to prove to himself, his teachers and his family what he was capable of doing.

Iman grew up in a family of six girls and often struggled in academic areas. She felt her identity was in her appearance and focused on this as being the most important aspect of her life. This project has given her a new identity: that of teacher and artist. She even surprised herself as well as others with her artistic ability, initiative, leadership and teaching skills. It has been a wonderful opportunity to inform her parents and teachers about what she is capable of achieving. She initially had no idea what she wanted out of life, and had no affirmation about her artistic and leadership skills; after this experience she is determined to go to university and become an art teacher!

Mary is a dominant twin and involvement in the project has increased her maturity and understanding of what a responsibility it is to be so capable. It has helped her deal with jealousy and learn to be dependable. She has also seen the benefit of being responsible and has learned how to develop trust, respect and admiration in others, and through the project she has developed significant leadership and organisational skills.

These vignettes of changed lives show only the tip of the iceberg — it is hard to predict just how much this project has influenced the lives of each of these 18 children. Now that they have had these opportunities and have had their eyes opened to artistic and broader life possibilities, they have more choices in life and in their future. They have learned that there can be other futures for them that they had not previously considered, their horizons are so much broader, they have developed personal tools to help them meet the challenges of life and they know that they 'can do anything'.

*Names and details have been changed for privacy reasons.

Introducing the art exhibition.

Learning music.

Wrapping artworks.

Teaching art

on their interests, and be age-appropriate and flexible enough to allow the children to explore their interests, as well as covering key learning experiences, processes, understandings and skills. It may be possible to combine a theme with an underlying concept or focus question to bring further depth to the learning experiences. For example, if the theme is 'Rainforests' the underlying focus question may be 'Why are rainforests important and how should we protect them?'. Themes may arise from the syllabus, a special event such as the Olympic Games, a current news item, a book that children have enjoyed reading, generic skills such as cooperation or research,

specific skills common to several key learning areas, key concepts or processes, or a school issue that needs to be addressed such as bullying or community harmony.

Some important questions to ask before beginning to plan for a *syntegrated* unit include:

- Why am I doing this theme?
- Who will I be teaching in this theme?
- How do they learn best?
- Why is it important for these children to complete this unit?
- What do I want the children to learn from completing this unit both generally and specifically?
- How can I use the different key learning areas to enhance and extend their understanding of the theme and underlying concepts?
- As well as achieving certain key learning area outcomes, will they be achieving any generic skills (observation, analysis, research, communication, evaluation, problem solving, group-work skills and so on)?
- How will children demonstrate what they have learned in this unit?
- How will I assess their learning in this unit?

Then within each relevant key learning area, begin to plan learning experiences to enhance and extend children's understanding of the theme or concept, while achieving authentic and stage-appropriate indicators and outcomes for that key learning area.

All programs and key learning areas do not have to be totally *syntegrated* or, indeed, totally separate from any other key learning area; rather, there should be a balance across the year of discrete, focused programs in key learning areas, as well as service-connected, symmetric-correlated and *syntegrated* programs of work. At times a particular piece of content, understanding or skill needs to be taught as such within one key learning area; another time a resource or material from one key learning area can be used to teach some skills, knowledge or understanding within another key learning area. At other times, two key learning areas may use the same resource or material to achieve outcomes for their own particular skills, knowledge and understandings. And, finally, a theme may be explored using a focus question or concept that can use each of the key learning areas to bring a multifaceted depth of understanding about the theme, can achieve authentic indicators and outcomes from each of the discrete key learning areas which maintain their own integrity, and are stage-appropriate and can develop generic skills and attitudes within the children.

Multiliteracies and the arts

Literacy used to mean the ability to read and write a language. If one considers words as symbols which can be coded as one writes and decoded as one reads the language, the definition of literacy can be broadened to include the ability to code, decode and understand any system of symbols. This expanded definition of literacy can then encompass the coding, decoding and understanding of visual, musical, kinaesthetic, computer, multimedia, multicultural, critical, written and oral literacies. A well-rounded education should develop each of these literacies in our children so that they can make meaning from, and interact effectively with, the world around them. Therefore, it is imperative that schools make this focus on a broader education a vital component of their learning programs. They can do this by using the arts as key factors in developing many, if not all, of these multiliteracies.

Teaching each art form by itself, as well as integrating the arts across the curriculum, can help children develop confidence in using each of these literacies within a variety of meaningful learning experiences. Within the arts, children can learn musical literacy by engaging in sequential music and dance learning experiences; they can develop kinaesthetic literacy through involvement in dance, drama, music and, in some cases, visual arts; visual literacy can be developed through visual arts and media learning experiences; computer and multimedia literacy can be learned through engaging in media programs and reinforced through using computers and technology as tools in music, dance, drama and visual arts lessons; as children deconstruct text to understand each character and event in drama, or analyse and evaluate an artwork, dance or piece of music, they are developing critical literacy skills; and as they learn about and appreciate music, dance, visual arts, media or drama artworks from different cultures and contexts they are developing their multicultural literacy. Oral literacy is central to each of the art forms as children work together in planning, creating, sharing and reflecting on their drama, dances, musical compositions, media presentations and cooperative artworks.

The development of these multiliteracies can also be used as the central focus of a unit of work that integrates learning across subjects and/or key learning areas. They can also be developed through a program of work which recognises the importance of the Multiple Intelligences. For example, as children are involved in visual-spatial learning experiences they can be developing their visual literacy; as they engage in activities aimed at developing musical intelligences, they are learning musical literacy; and they extend their oral literacy by participating in verbal-linguistic activities. The following section gives further information about using the Multiple Intelligences in the arts classroom.

Brief overview of the Multiple Intelligences

As teachers use the arts to learn more about each art form, as well as being vehicles for learning in other key learning areas, they are most probably implementing learning experiences that utilise a variety of intelligences. Howard Gardner in his book *Frames of mind* (1993) first challenged the traditional view of intelligences, and then advocated the theory of human intellectual competences that he called *Multiple Intelligences*. He believes that every child is 100% intelligent in his/her own way and that if teachers plan learning experiences based on the child's preferred intelligence, the child will learn and succeed in school. The Multiple Intelligences were initially presented by Gardner as another way of describing intelligence apart from the traditional IQ testing. Gardner defines intelligence as 'the ability to solve problems or fashion products that are of consequence in a particular cultural setting or community'. He believes that children may have different intelligence profiles when they are born, and these intelligences or potentials can either be developed or left

Do not ask, 'How smart are you?'. Rather ask, 'How are you smart?'.

MMADD about the arts

Gardner's Multiple Intelligences

Musical

Visual-Spatial

Bodily-Kinaesthetic

Verbal-Linguistic

Logical-Mathematical

Naturalistic

Intrapersonal

Interpersonal

in their neophyte state, depending on the experiences children are given the opportunity to engage in at home and at school.

The intelligences with which children end up, and which they use to learn about the world and to solve problems, are different for every child. When working with Multiple Intelligences we do not ask the child 'How smart are you?' but rather 'How are you smart?' It is really important that children understand their strengths and weaknesses in relation to the Multiple Intelligences so that they and their teachers can use their strengths to learn and understand new material and concepts and develop their weaker intelligences. There are numerous 'tests' in the books and websites listed at the end of the chapter, to help children and their teachers determine their personal intelligence profile.

A brief overview of each intelligence is included below.

Musical intelligence (music smart)

Children with a strong musical intelligence love to sing, hum, rap and chant, and find it easy to remember melodies, songs and rhythms and keep the beat in music. They are often tapping their fingers or feet in class as they work and enjoy listening to and playing music. When learning, they prefer to put the information to be learned into chants, songs and raps; create new words about the content to familiar tunes; learn songs that teach the knowledge; and use music as a background.

Visual-Spatial intelligence (art smart)

Children with a strong visual-spatial intelligence enjoy doing art and craft activities, acting in plays, completing jigsaws and mazes, taking photos and videos, playing video games, reading maps, drawing and creating three-dimensional artworks. They find it easier to remember faces than names, like to draw or sketch their ideas, enjoy building things, like looking at photos and talking about them, and take special notice of people's clothes, cars, hairstyles and so on. They learn best when they can see the content in charts, graphs, maps and diagrams; when visualisations or PowerPoint presentations are used; when they do mind-mapping; when words are accompanied by pictures or graphic symbols; and when they can make models, videos, photos or diagrams about what they are learning and draw, paint or make collages to express themselves and their understandings.

Bodily-Kinaesthetic intelligence (body smart)

Children who have a strong bodily-kinaesthetic intelligence enjoy dancing, gymnastics and athletics. They use their bodies to send messages, and they like to be active and to touch objects around them. They learn physical activities quickly, enjoy acting and improvisations, and are good at fixing things. To learn best, they need to be involved in creative movement, dance and mime; hands-on, tactile experiences; physical and relaxation exercises; and cooperative or competitive games which use the whole body.

Verbal-Linguistic intelligence (word smart)

Children with a strong verbal-linguistic intelligence spend much time reading, and they can spell easily and enjoy doing crosswords. They can read, write and talk confidently; have a good vocabulary; learn other languages easily; and love stories, riddles, word games and jokes. They learn best when involved in talking, reading and writing, telling stories, listening to radio shows, group discussions, brainstorming, listening to audio tapes or CDs, and debates.

Logical-Mathematical intelligence (logic smart)

Children who have a strong logical-mathematical intelligence are fascinated with numbers, love to solve mathematical problems and brain teasers, are good at estimating, and enjoy computer games and playing with numbers. They are keen to create experiments to test things out, and enjoy putting information into lists and diagrams and working with patterns, as well as collecting and categorising objects. They prefer a learning environment that includes a logical and sequential presentation of the content; scientific demonstrations; challenges in estimating and measuring distances, height and weight, using a calculator or computer; mathematical ideas and concepts; and organisation and exploration of patterns and numbers.

Intrapersonal intelligence (self smart)

Children who enjoy being by themselves often have a strong intrapersonal intelligence. They are good with their imagination and have a strong opinion or feeling about things as they have spent time thinking them through carefully. They will often keep a journal of personal reflections and thoughts and are generally self-motivated. They enjoy setting and meeting their own goals, they don't seem to worry about what others think of them as much as other children do, and they stand up for their beliefs. To create an effective learning environment for these children, ensure that they have the opportunity to work by themselves in an independent study or project with self-paced learning, that their instruction is personalised and individualised, and that they have time for study and reflection by themselves. Organise a quiet corner in the classroom for individual reading, encourage children to set their own goals and formulate strategies to achieve these, and give them contract work to complete within a given time.

Interpersonal intelligence (people smart)

Children who have a strong interpersonal intelligence are outgoing, make friends easily and like to be with other children. They enjoy working in groups to solve problems, often feel empathy for others and love playing cooperative games. They are often leaders, organising others to work together amicably, and feel confident when meeting new people. To create a supportive learning environment for these children, give them the opportunity to work with others and play team sports, organise a class event, and be involved in group or peer teaching, simulations, improvisations and group projects.

Naturalistic intelligence (nature smart)

Children with a strong naturalistic intelligence are observant and enjoy identifying and classifying the flora and fauna around them. They enjoy being outdoors, gardening, bushwalking and looking after animals, and are often interested in recycling and other environmental causes. They tend to use the natural world as a means to view the rest of the world and to use it to help them organise their personal world. When catering for these children, give them the opportunity to be involved in field trips and to work outdoors, in categorising activities to find connections, and in recognising and devising patterns in their work and that of others. Organise a nature table in the classroom where children can learn more about the natural world and bring their own information and findings to share with other children.

How do the Multiple Intelligences relate to the classroom?

In his discussion about Multiple Intelligences, Gardner notes that the linguistic-verbal and the mathematical-logical intelligences are generally given priority in schools through emphasis and testing. However, Gardner is convinced that all the intelligences have equal claim to priority and that every child is 100% intelligent.

When considering each of these intelligences individually, it is clear that involvement in the art forms of music, media, dance, drama and visual arts allows children to learn through the full range of the eight intelligences. For example, within the art form of music, the reading and writing of music involves logical and mathematical intelligences; moving to music uses the bodily-kinaesthetic and spatial intelligences; seeing patterns in music and creating music using the stimulus of natural flora and fauna relates to the naturalistic intelligence; working cooperatively in groups, making music together in ensembles and performing with friends develops the interpersonal and verbal-linguistic intelligences; composing and practising music by oneself, showing one's feelings through the music and reflecting individually on music heard develops the intrapersonal intelligence; and creating, performing and appreciating music develops the musical intelligence.

Every child is 100% intelligent.

Therefore, it would seem that if teachers developed integrated programs which emphasised the five art forms and, as a result, gave children the opportunity to be involved in some or all of the eight intelligences, all children would be given the opportunity to learn and develop skills effectively using their individual intelligence profile.

If we see each child in the class as having different intelligence profiles, this has significant repercussions on our teaching as we have to look at children as individuals, each with different strengths and weaknesses in the ways that they learn skills, solve problems and understand knowledge. Instead of teaching using one set approach (which is usually based on the teacher's preferred intelligence) and expecting all children to respond and learn using this approach, teachers would work out each of their children's particular intelligence profiles and design activities to help them learn using their individual strengths as well as working on developing their weaker intelligences.

Teachers have found that, by using the creative arts and the Multiple Intelligences in the classroom, all the children are given opportunities to express themselves and learn effectively within their particular intelligence profile. Learning experiences covering the Multiple Intelligences can help all children learn: the English as a second language (ESL) child, the gifted pupil, the one who has difficulty reading, the shy child and the student with special needs — all may find success and enjoyment in the challenge of learning through their preferred intelligence. In the light of the theory of Multiple Intelligences, children should not be labelled as 'failures' or 'low-achievers'; rather, one could suggest that the teaching methods have failed to connect with the child. If such children are taught using learning methods based on their preferred intelligences they are more likely to succeed and achieve beyond initial expectations.

Four approaches using the Multiple Intelligences in the classroom

So how can we integrate the Multiple Intelligences into the classroom so that every child is given the opportunity to learn through their preferred intelligence profile? Four approaches are suggested and these include the use of learning centres, project work, integrating the intelligences within a lesson or program, and inviting an expert to extend children's learning in an intelligence-specific lesson. These approaches can provide children with authentic and meaningful learning experiences so that their understanding is enhanced within each relevant key learning area.

Learning centres

Developing learning centres in the classroom can encourage the use of different intelligences. (See Chapter 2, 'The creative arts classroom' for more details about setting up learning centres.) The activities within the learning centres can be intelligence-specific and provide children with ways of learning that might have been previously excluded from the classroom not based on Multiple Intelligences. For example, one learning centre might have a musical focus, another one might use kinaesthetic activities to enhance learning and a third might have a visual-spatial emphasis. Children could be encouraged to spend time at these learning centres when they have completed their work or as a part of contract work. As well as engaging in activities in the learning centres which focus on their own preferred intelligences, they should also complete work from learning centres featuring activities based on their weaker intelligences so they can work on strengthening these.

Projects

Project work is *not* about sending the children to the library or Internet to find three books or websites about a topic, copying or cutting and pasting the information, drawing or pasting pretty pictures around the project, printing it and putting it in a professional-looking binder for marking. This approach does little to provide

children with in-depth meaningful learning experiences to help them understand the concept, theme or set of knowledge. However, student-focused projects encourage children to explore an issue or question that is important and meaningful to them; create their own data set by interviewing or surveying people, brainstorming with friends or recording observations; and research relevant information which they can rewrite in their own words. They should be encouraged to use their preferred intelligences to complete and present the project and be given the opportunity to work individually, with a partner or in groups. In project work, the teacher becomes the facilitator: guiding the children to identify questions, problems and processes; helping them find the appropriate resources; challenging them about different ways of doing this; and encouraging them to use different ways of presenting the collected information, by using a combination of multimedia, dance, drama, music and visual arts as well as written work.

Lessons and programs using the Multiple Intelligences

Using this approach the intelligences can be integrated throughout lessons and programs of work. Look for ways to bring the Multiple Intelligences into each set of learning experiences across the curriculum as intelligences are rarely used in isolation and children usually use them in combinations to learn effectively. For example, if listening to a piece of music as part of a music lesson, children could do the following:

- Tap the beat and learn to sing or hum the main theme or tune (musical intelligence).
- Close their eyes, listen to it and visualise what is happening in the music and how they feel about it (intrapersonal intelligence).
- Draw their feelings and/or what they visualised as the music plays again (visual-spatial intelligence).
- Share with a friend or the class about what they felt or visualised and how this was represented in their artwork and then write a summary of this below the picture (verbal-linguistic intelligence).
- Identify the structure of the music in relation to patterns, sequences or sections in the music (logical-mathematical).
- Work in groups to create a dance to show the structure of the music (bodily-kinaesthetic and interpersonal intelligences).
- Collect natural objects, name and categorise them and then create a representation of the music using these as instruments (naturalistic intelligence).

Intelligence-specific lessons by an expert

Another approach to developing children's understanding through the Multiple Intelligences could be to bring in 'experts' who are strong in a particular intelligence to work with the children in their field of interest or expertise. For example, a local musician, actor, singer, naturalist, social worker, engineer, artist or a sportsperson could be used to teach intelligence-specific lessons that would add meaning and motivation to the children's learning. An extension to this would be to work out a program where those children who have strengths in the expert's particular intelligence be given the opportunity to be mentored by the expert throughout the rest of the year or even longer. This mentoring experience can make a significant difference to a child's self-esteem, life and future.

The arts, multiple intelligences and literacy

Of all the key learning areas in Australian primary schools, numeracy and English literacy are expected to take significant priority, and therefore classrooms often focus only on the verbal-linguistic and mathematical-logical intelligences. However, despite the importance and priority given to these subjects, there are still constant references in the community, media and educational institutions that literacy standards are falling and that many children entering secondary schools cannot read and write effectively.

Methods used to teach English literacy, as defined by reading, writing, talking and listening, are many and varied and are often seen as creating controversy in some teaching circles. At times, one approach gains precedence for a few years and then is condemned and replaced by another approach, until this is thought not to work and another method is advocated, and so the cycle continues. Literacy methods can be confusing to parents and sometimes to teachers and children, as arguments go back and forward about the best way of teaching children to read and write, talk and listen.

Integrating the arts and the Multiple Intelligences across the curriculum can enhance literacy teaching and understanding. This approach can help children who learn best through music or through movement as they sing or chant grammar rules or spelling words or show a story through movement before committing it to paper. It can help the children who may fail a spelling test after reading through a list of words and trying to memorise them, but who would do much better if the words were coloured and of different textures, or if they could draw them in the sand so they could feel them and learn to spell kinaesthetically. It can also help those children who learn best through interaction with others, by self-reflection, by involvement with nature, or by drawing, singing, moving and other hands-on activities. This approach can assist the teacher when assessing the children; instead of always asking them to write what they have learned, their learning and understanding of a particular concept can be shown through drawings, movement, drama or multimedia presentations. For example, after an excursion to the zoo, instead of having children write about it and then, if time permits, illustrate their story, give them the choice of drawing about their experiences first and then writing about what they have drawn. If children have strong visual-spatial intelligence, they will often produce much better written work after they have explored and expressed visually what they have learned.

Give children the choice of drawing about their experiences first and then writing about what they have drawn.

When programming for English literacy learning, as well as for other subjects, teachers should challenge themselves to include a variety of intelligences in each set of learning experiences. This will give all children the opportunity to learn by using their preferred intelligence. Here are some ideas to get you started — read them through and then create your own intelligence-focused learning experiences relevant to your program or unit of work.

Musical intelligence

- Write new words to familiar tunes expressing the content of the lesson in the lyrics.
- Create a rap to learn a sequence of procedures or explain a concept.
- Clap the rhythm of words or create a rhyme about how to spell a word, to help with children's spelling.
- Create a soundscape or graphic score with musical instruments to accompany the reading of a story.
- Listen to music from different countries or styles and discuss their similarities and differences.
- Read the verses and chorus of songs as a poem before learning to sing them.

Bodily-Kinaesthetic intelligence

- Present a story using mime, improvisation or dance.
- Spell words by tracing them in sand, walking the shape of the letters on the floor or in the playground, using body shapes to show letters, cutting letters out of sandpaper and using their fingers on the rough surface to draw the shape of the letters.
- Show the meanings of words through improvisation or mime.
- Create a Readers' Theatre presentation of a story using gestures and vocal expression.

Visual-Spatial intelligence

- Create a storyboard using photos, collages or drawings of a story to show children's understandings about the sequence, characters and events.
- Model, make a collage, paint or draw the significant sections of a story.
- Cut out words from a magazine and use them to form the basis of a story.
- Read and write poems that have the shape of the content; for example, if the poem is about autumn leaves, it would be written in the shape of a leaf.
- Use mind-mapping to document the procedures of an experiment, the outline of a story, the personality traits and actions of characters in a story, and important aspects of an information report.
- Draw words to show their meaning visually.
- Draw the outline of the shape of different words to help with word recognition.

Verbal-Linguistic intelligence

- Retell the story to a group of friends.
- Retell the story from a different point of view (i.e. let the wolf tell his version of *The Three Little Pigs*).
- Write a summary of the story.
- Answer verbal or written comprehension questions about the text.
- Involve children in hot seating to find out more about the characters in the text.
- Debate issues raised in the text.
- As a group create a different ending to a familiar story.
- Write a newspaper report of what happened in the text.
- Write a procedural or factual recount of a previous learning experience or school event.

Logical-Mathematical intelligence

- List the steps required for a recipe or a science experiment, or how to create a graphic score, use the digital video and still cameras, travel from home to school and so on.
- Identify logical structures or sequences in pieces of music or in stories (i.e. the beginning or introduction, building tension, character or theme development, repetition of theme, tension, climax, resolution and conclusion).
- Count repetitions of phrases, pictures or words in a story.
- Write messages in secret codes.
- Talk about concepts such as speed, distance, height, length and volume. For example: How fast were the hare and tortoise travelling? How far did Goldilocks have to run to hide from the three bears? How tall was the beanstalk Jack climbed? How much water would the dingo's billy have to hold to boil the wombat? How long was Pinocchio's nose?
- Create a timeline of events in a story, historical event, growth of a plant, life cycle of a butterfly and so on.

Intrapersonal intelligence

- Reflect on how the three little pigs felt about leaving home and what they felt when the wolf came knocking at their door.
- Keep a journal of activities they have enjoyed in class.
- Document what they have learned and how they felt after a performance.
- Compare literacy examples from their portfolio over the year and reflect on how they have developed in this area.
- Listen to a piece of music or examine an artwork, and then visualise what could be happening in the music or artwork and use this to write a story based on the music or artwork.
- Write an argument expressing their personal feelings for or against an issue raised in a text.

Interpersonal intelligence

- Work together to create a Readers' Theatre presentation, choral reading or improvisation based on a favourite book.
- Use peer tutoring, matching competent with less competent children.
- Work together to create a musical picture or visual arts mural to depict the characters and events in a story.
- In pairs, take turns in reading alternate paragraphs of a text to each other, using vocal expression.
- Tell a story around the circle about an object or person, with one child starting and the next child continuing the story.
- In groups or as a class, talk about the illustrations of the text and how the artist has used line, colour, space and form effectively.
- In pairs, take it in turns to spell words aloud to each other.

Naturalistic intelligence

- Plant a garden or grow pot plants and document the changes; take photos, print them out and write in all the different parts of the plant.
- Draw pictures or take photos of favourite animals or pets and use these as the basis for creative story writing.
- Discuss ways of recycling rubbish in the playground and classroom.
- Read aloud to your dog. (Yes, it does help — check out *READ: Reading Education Assistance Dogs* on the Internet for more information!)
- Write down the procedures for looking after a pet.
- Tell the rest of the class about your pet and why it is so special.
- Have children take time to look at the day sky and the night sky, and then discuss and document what they see and feel.
- Visit a zoo, farm, aquarium or nature park and then draw, write, dance, create music or model responses to the visit.

Syntegrating the arts and Multiple Intelligences to explore colour

The above examples have been suggested to help the creative teacher begin to explore how to teach English literacy using the eight intelligences. The following is an example of a *syntegrated* program using the arts and Multiple Intelligences to explore mixing and using colour, as well as the concept and symbolism of colour. These learning experiences can be used and adapted across the primary school, with some being simplified and others made more challenging to suit the experiences, interests and abilities of the target children.

1. Visual arts: Colour your world with rainbows

Indicators: Children will show their understanding of primary and secondary colours by creating their own and examining the use of them in artworks.

Introduction activities

(*Spatial-Visual*)

Read together the book *Mouse paint* by Ellen Stoll Walsh (see reference at the end of the chapter for publishing details) as an introduction to colour mixing.

Experiment with mixing red with blue, red with yellow, and yellow with blue to create secondary colours.

Developing the theme

(*Spatial-Visual; Logical-Mathematical*)

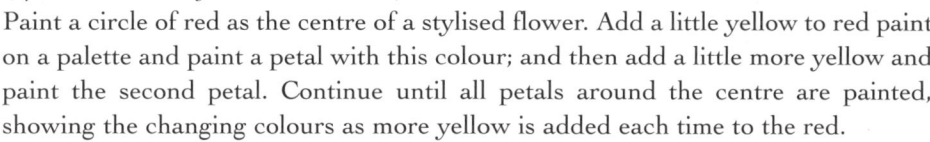
Picture using cool colours.

Paint a circle of red as the centre of a stylised flower. Add a little yellow to red paint on a palette and paint a petal with this colour; and then add a little more yellow and paint the second petal. Continue until all petals around the centre are painted, showing the changing colours as more yellow is added each time to the red.

Repeat using blue as the centre and adding a little more red for each petal, and then use yellow as the centre of a third flower and progressively add more blue.

Extension: Create a colour wheel and show primary and secondary colours, warm and cool colours, and harmonious and contrasting colours (see Stoikovich, 1993, pp. 1–2). Create artworks using one or more of these sets of colours. Identify which of these colours are found in the rainbow.

Closure activities

(*Interpersonal*)

Share your work with each other, ask questions, comment and reflect on the effective use of colours.

Examine artworks by famous artists who use mainly primary colours, for example:

- *Diamond Painting in Red, Yellow and Blue* (Piet Mondrian);
- *Woman Seated in an Armchair* (Henri Matisse);
- *Dance at Bougival* (Pierre August Renoir);
- *Yellow Sweater* (Amedeo Modigliani).

Picture using warm colours.

Discuss how effectively they have used primary colours in these artworks.

2. Visual arts: Colour your world with rainbows

Indicators: Children will demonstrate how tints and shades are produced and will create two- and three-dimensional artworks to show their understanding of this concept.

Introductory activities

(*Visual-Spatial*)

Select a favourite colour from the rainbow. Look at pictures, magazines and artworks; identify how many different shades and tints of this colour can be found. Discuss the difference between shades and tints, for example:

MMADD about the arts

- Shades are created when *black* is added to a colour.
- Tints are created when *white* is added to a colour.

Developing the theme
(*Visual-Spatial*; *Logical-Mathematical*)

Have each child select one primary colour and either black or white and, using only these paints, create an artwork. Place a blank piece of paper in landscape format. Place a small amount of the selected colour in a palette. Paint a strong stripe of this colour in the centre from the top to the bottom of the page. Add a small amount of white to it and use this new colour to paint a stripe to the right of the centre stripe. Add another small amount of white to the mixed colour and paint another stripe to the right of the previous stripe. Continue adding more white and painting a stripe to the right of the previous stripe until the right side of the paper is reached. Repeat this activity, but add black to the initial primary colour and paint the stripe to the left of the centre stripe and so on.

Experiment with creating tints and shades.

Extension: Use the different shades and tints of a selected colour to create a headdress, mask and/or costume in this colour. Use collage materials, feathers, sequins, and so on to add texture, patterns, line and variety.

Closure activities
(*Interpersonal*)

Share the striped painted papers children have created and have them match the created colours with colours used in the costumes, masks and/or headdresses. Reflect together on the effectiveness of using one primary colour with its tints and shades to create an artwork.

3. Drama: Colour your world with rainbows

Indicators: Children will explore elements of movement in relation to a poem and will perform the poem using choral narration, improvisation and costumes.

Introductory activities
(*Musical*; *Bodily-Kinaesthetic*)

Experiment with body and vocal sounds that can be used to create the sounds of a storm. Start with soft sounds, build up to a climax, and then gradually decrease the sound. Ask:
- What often happens at the end of a storm? (Rainbow)
- What causes a rainbow? (Sun shining through raindrops)

Developing the theme
(*Linguistic-Verbal*; *Bodily-Kinaesthetic, Naturalistic*)

Read through the poem *The Rainbow Fairies* (Anon.) below.

How does this reflect your knowledge about how rainbows are formed? Have children give an explanation of the cycle of water.

Select children to role-play the poem as it is narrated. Have children show how Father Sun would move. How would the two little clouds move? Are they young or old, happy or sad? Would they move fast or slowly? How would each coloured fairy move? Would they each move the same way? Or could each colour represent a different emotion (e.g. red = anger, yellow = excitement, blue = serenity)? Brainstorm what emotion each colour could stand for and have children move to represent each colour fairy and a corresponding emotion. Interview each colour fairy to find out more about their characters and feelings (hot seating).

Closure activities
(*Interpersonal*)

Have a small group prepare and present a choral reading of the poem, while selected children act out the different parts, using elements of movement as explored in the above activities. Add other props, sound effects and costumes as necessary. (Suggestion: The rainbow fairies could wear the headdresses as created in one of the previous visual arts activities in this unit.) Reflect on how effective the visual and aural representation was of the poem.

The blue fairy.

> **The Rainbow Fairies (Anon.)**
> 1. Two little clouds, one Summer's day,
>   Went flying through the sky,
>   They went so fast, they bumped their heads,
>   And soon began to cry.
> 2. Old Father Sun looked out and said,
>   'Well never mind, my dear!
>   I'll send my little fairy folk
>   To dry your falling tears!'.
> 3. One fairy came in Violet,
>   And one in Indigo.
>   In Blue, Green, Yellow, Orange, Red,
>   They made a pretty row!

4. Dance: Colour your world with rainbows

Indicators: Children will explore the different elements of dance and use these to portray the content of a poem on colour.

Introductory activities
(*Bodily-Kinaesthetic*)

Identify the seven colours of the rainbow. Divide the class into small groups, each group taking a colour of the rainbow. Brainstorm objects that are each of these colours. Creating a voice and movement collage, have each person in the group show movements to represent one or more of the listed objects, using contrasting levels, dynamics, space, energy, time and flow.

MMADD about the arts

Representations of the colour purple.

Developing the theme
(*Linguistic-Verbal*; *Interpersonal*)

Give each group a different poem from the book *A song of colours* by J. Hindley or another similar book with colour poems, for example *Hailstones and halibut bones* by Mary O'Neil (see the references at the end of the chapter for publishing details). Use only those colours that are rainbow colours. Have each group examine the illustrations and discuss how these relate to the poem. Then have each group read through their poem and work out creative dance movements that could represent each phrase. Focus on using contrasting levels, dynamics, energy, time and flow of movements.

Closure activities
Have each group present their poem to the rest of the class with one person narrating the poem and others responding with improvised creative dance movements to portray the content of the poem. Relax and then reflect on the effectiveness of the use of different elements in each group's dance in portraying the poem visually.

5. Visual arts: Colour your world with rainbows

Indicators: Children will examine illustrations in relation to the use of shades and tints; children will create an artwork with single or mixed media to portray objects and feelings as related to a selected colour, using only this basic colour, its shades and tints.

Introductory activities
(*Logical-Mathematical*; *Linguistic-Verbal*)

Divide the class into six groups, with each group taking one of the poems from the selected book. Examine the illustrations for the selected poem. Note how different shades and tones of the primary colour have been used to create depth, life and movement to the illustrations. Have children list words that relate to this colour of the rainbow. These words can include objects, people, plants and animals, places and emotions.

Developing the theme
(*Interpersonal*; *Intrapersonal*; *Visual-Spatial*, *Naturalistic*)

Individually, in pairs or as a group, create an artwork based on this list of words using paint (acrylic or watercolour), collage materials, crayons, pencils or charcoal, or mixed media to create different effects. Encourage children to experiment with the use of shades and tints, lines, patterns, cross-hatching and textures in their artworks. These artworks may be realistic or abstract to effectively portray feelings, the natural and constructed world, and objects related to the selected colour.

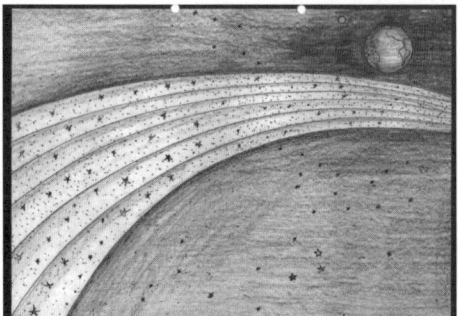

Representations of the colours indigo.

Closure activities
(*Linguistic-Verbal*)

Share and discuss the completed artworks with the artists discussing the reasons they used the different media, shades and tints. The rest of the class can respond regarding the effectiveness of the artworks and what they liked about them.

6. Music: Colour your world with rainbows

Indicators: Students will explore different ways of playing instruments, use them to represent the content and emotion of the poem, and then create a sound picture to represent a selected colour.

Introductory activities
(*Interpersonal; Bodily-Kinaesthetic*)
Divide the class into small groups with each group taking one of the poems from the selected poetry book. Read the poem aloud and explore its meaning through movements and vocal sound effects to represent each movement.

Developing the theme
(*Musical*)

Representations of the colour blue.

Discuss how different percussion instruments could be used to represent each colour, concept, object and/or phrase within the poem. Experiment with adding different instruments throughout the poem; identify if instruments should be played loudly or softly, fast or slowly, high or low, at regular or irregular intervals, and so on to effectively represent the sounds in the poem. Play the instruments to the reading of the poem, and then create a piece of music (sound picture) using the same instruments played in a similar way, but without any words, to describe the colour.

Closure activities
(*Verbal-Linguistic*)
Share these pieces of created music with the rest of the class and discuss how effectively the instruments portrayed the colour.
Extension: Have each poem narrated and add the dance movements, vocal sounds and instruments to the poem.

7. Drama: Colour your world with rainbows

Indicators: Children will individually create and expressively present a poem or prose passage in response to artwork stimuli; in groups, they will present a debate confidently and will practise and present in groups a Readers' Theatre story based on *The story of the rainbow* (see below).

Introductory activities
(*Intrapersonal; Verbal-Linguistic*)
Examine the artworks prepared in the previous visual arts activity and have all the children write some sentences or a poem about one of the artworks (not their own). Have the children read these out to the class with expression, using their voices to portray the feelings in the poem and so on.

Representations of the colour green.

MMADD about the arts

Developing the theme
(*Verbal-Linguistic, Naturalistic*)
Have the children form groups around each colour of the rainbow and then prepare and present a debate in which each group declares that their colour is the best and most important colour in this world. Include references to the importance of colour in nature.

Distribute copies of *The story of the rainbow: An Indian legend*. Have different children read each paragraph out loud. Discuss how the story's ideas about the importance of each colour were the same or different from those the children had presented. Have each group, based on a different colour of the rainbow, practise reading their paragraph from the story as a Readers' Theatre presentation. Two extra people or groups will also be needed for Readers 1 and 9.

Closure activities
(*Verbal-Linguistic*)
Put the story together as a Readers' Theatre presentation with a narrator being Reader 1 and each group holding up the artworks based on their colour and reading their paragraph from the story together expressively at the appropriate time.

Reflect on the effectiveness of this presentation and if any changes need to be made.

The story of the rainbow: An Indian legend (Anon.)
Reader 1: A time long ago, all the colours in the world started to argue; each claimed that she was the best, the most important, the most useful, the most powerful.

Reader 2: *Green* said, 'Of course I am the most important. I am the sign of new life and of hope. I was chosen to paint the grass, the trees, the leaves — without me all the animals would die. Look out over the countryside and you will see that I cover the earth with a carpet of vitality, beauty and life'.

Reader 3: *Blue* interrupted: 'You only think about the earth, but look up and see the sky and the sea; water is the basis of life and this is drawn up by the clouds from the blue sea. The expanse of sea and sky gives space and peace and security. Without my life-giving force and calming influence you would all burn out or die of thirst'.

Reader 4: *Yellow* chuckled: 'You are all so serious. I bring laughter, fun and warmth into the world. The sun shines a brilliant yellow, the moon gleams a peaceful yellow and the stars sparkle bright yellow. Every time you look at a sunflower, a daffodil or a cob of corn the whole world starts to smile. Without me there would be no fun or laughter'.

Representations of the colour yellow.

Reader 5: *Orange* snorted in derision: 'I am the colour of nutrition, health and strength. I may be scarce but I am precious for I serve the inner needs of human life. I carry all the most important vitamins in my carrots and pumpkins, oranges, mangoes, persimmons and pawpaws. I don't hang around all the time, but when I fill the sky at sunrise or sunset, my beauty is spellbinding so no one gives another thought to any of you'.

282

Reader 6: *Red* shouted impatiently: 'I am the blood that courses through your veins, the ruler of you all, blood, life's blood. I am the colour of danger and of bravery, of fire and of safety. I am fire in the blood and am willing to fight for a cause. Without me earth would be as dull and empty as the desert. I am the colour of passion and of love; the red, red rose, the coral tree, the poinsettia and the poppy'.

Reader 7: *Purple* drew himself regally to his full height. He was very tall and he spoke with great pomp and strength: 'I am the colour of royalty and power; kings, chiefs and bishops have always chosen to wear me for I am a sign of authority and wisdom. People do not question me, they hasten to obey'.

Reader 8: There was a pause, then *Indigo* spoke up, much more quietly than all the others, but just as determinedly: 'Think of me. I am the colour of depth and silence. You hardly notice me, but without me, you all become superficial. I represent thought and reflection, twilight, outer space and deep waters. You need me for balance and contrast, for prayer and inner peace'.

Reader 9: The *mighty rain* had been listening as the colours argued and he called them to listen: 'You foolish colours, fighting among yourselves, each trying to dominate the others. Look at yourselves, each one of you is unique and different. Come together and celebrate these differences. Join hands with one another and come with me. I will stretch you across the sky in a great rainbow of colour, as a reminder that you can all live in peace together.'

Reader 1: And so whenever a good rain has washed the earth, we can see a rainbow in the sky and remember that we are each important and unique and together we can create beauty.

8. Dance: Colour your world with rainbows

Indicators: Children will use the elements of dance to explore ways of representing colours in movement; and create a speech rhyme and related dance.

Introductory activities
(*Interpersonal; Bodily-Kinaesthetic*)
Divide the class into seven groups. Have each group select a colour of the rainbow and brainstorm nouns that are this selected colour. Explore different movements to represent each of these nouns using different levels, dynamics, speed, patterns and so on.

Developing the theme
(*Verbal-Linguistic; Musical*)
Create a speech rhyme using four of the above nouns, each with the colour as the adjective, for example:

> Red rooster, red rooster,
> Red danger, red danger,
> Red soldiers, red soldiers,
> Red berries, red berries.

Representations of the colour red.

MMADD about the arts

Create a simple repeated movement for each line, for example:
- Squat down and flap bent arms quickly.
- Jump up with arms outstretched.
- March on the spot.
- Pick berries carefully from small and tall trees.

Develop this into a simple dance with four or eight beats for each line of the speech rhyme. Repeat it several times to music that has a strong beat and so create a dance sequence. Add appropriate coloured scarves or ribbons to emphasise the colour relating to the dance. Join with another group and prepare a two-colour dance sequence.

Closure activities
(*Intrapersonal, interpersonal*)
Have each group share their dance sequences, firstly as they say the speech rhyme, and then without any words, just movements. Line up the groups in the order of the rainbow, and one by one have them perform their dance without words, flowing from one group to the next. Reflect on how effective they were in using elements of dance to represent their colour.

9. Music: Colour your world with rainbows

Indicators: Children will learn to sing the song and will show their understanding of rhythm, beat, dynamics, pitch, structure and tone colour through a variety of song-based activities.

Representations of the colour orange.

Introductory activities
(*Musical; Verbal-Linguistic*)
Listen to the song 'I Can Sing a Rainbow' by Arthur Hamilton, *ABC Sing Along!* 1984. Show the two different sections by clicking fingers in the first one ('Red and yellow' . . .) and clapping the beat in the second section ('Listen with' . . .). Explore the rhythm of the song by clapping it or tapping the rhythm on desks with pencils as the song is sung. Read through the words together. Discuss which colour of the rainbow is missing from the song and which colour in the song is not in a rainbow. Substitute 'indigo' for 'and pink'.

Developing the theme
(*Bodily-Kinaesthetic*)
Work out which lines could be sung loudly, medium or softly to convey the lyrics more clearly and experiment with using different dynamics. Add appropriate instruments for the loud, medium and soft sections. Decide on actions to represent the words in the song. In the written music, find the highest and the lowest notes; show the pitch contour of the song with hands in the air. Add instruments to represent each colour.

Extension: Learn the appropriate sign language for the song.

Closure activities
(*Interpersonal*)
Put the above music activities together as the song is sung (i.e. have different groups clap the beat and rhythm); add actions, add instruments, draw the pitch contour and play instruments for the dynamics.

10. Media: Colour your world with rainbows
Indicators: Children will analyse and evaluate what they have learned and how they have learned it; then they will use a variety of media techniques to plan and present a creative portrayal of what they have learned about colour throughout the program.

Introductory activities
(*Interpersonal, verbal-linguistic*)
Examine all the artworks created in this program and discuss the connotations and symbolic use of the different colours of the rainbow. Have the children brainstorm in groups the different ways they have learned about colour and which ways each child enjoyed and found the most effective. Discuss how different forms of media could be used to portray what they have learned about their own learning and about colour. (Children could be told at the start of the program that this will be expected of them on the completion of the program, so, if they wanted to create (say) a video, they might take video clips or photos of work being done throughout the program.)

Developing the theme
(*Interpersonal, verbal-linguistic, visual-spatial, musical, bodily-kinaesthetic, logical-mathematical*)
In groups have children decide on a form of media to express what they have enjoyed and learned about colour throughout the program. Media presentations could include creating a PowerPoint presentation, a sequence of annotated creative photos, a video and radio interviews. Have children create a storyboard of the content of the media presentation of their learning, share it with another group and the teacher for feedback, and then prepare their presentation. Include relevant music to accompany the presentation.

Closure activities
(*Intrapersonal, verbal-linguistic*)
View the different media presentations and reflect on how effectively they portrayed what the children had learned about colour throughout the program.

SPRINGBOARDS FOR DISCUSSION AND APPLICATION

1. Develop a series of learning experiences in dot point form listing how you could use an artwork or song to achieve:
   (a) outcomes in another key learning area (service connection);
   (b) outcomes in art or music and in another key learning area (symmetric correlation);
   (c) outcomes in several key learning areas, to enhance learning about a theme or concept and to develop generic skills (*syntegration*).
2. Identify the eight Multiple Intelligences and list ways of including them in the arts classroom.
3. Plan a unit of work based on a theme or concept to include all art forms, other key learning areas if relevant and the eight Multiple Intelligences.

FURTHER READING

Anderson, W. & Lawrence, J. (2001), *Integrating music into the elementary classroom*, 5th edn, Wadsworth/Thomson Learning, Stanford, California.
Creative Educational Systems (2000), *Teaching curriculum through the arts*, Dovehaven Press, East Brunswick, New Jersey.
Gardner, H. (1993), *Frames of mind: The theory of Multiple Intelligences*, 2nd edn, Basic Books, New York.
Gardner, H. (1993), *Multiple Intelligences: The theory in practice*, Basic Books, New York.
Gardner, H. (1999), *Intelligence reframed: Multiple Intelligences for the 21st century*. Basic Books: New York.
Jensen, E. (1993), *Super-Teaching: Master strategies for building student success*, Excellence in Teaching, Sydney.
Jensen, E. (1995), *The learning brain*, The Brain Store, San Diego, California.
Jensen, E. (2001), *Arts with the brain in mind*, Association for Supervision and Curriculum Development, Alexandria, Virginia.

Jensen, E. (2002), *Brain compatible strategies*, Focus Education Australia, Adelaide.
McGrath, H. & Noble, T. (1995), *Seven ways at once: Books 1 and 2*, Longman Australia, Melbourne.
Russell-Bowie, D. & Thistleton-Martin, J. (2005), *Literacy and creative arts activities for Bookweek 2005,* Karibuni Press, Sydney.
Russell-Bowie, D., Madsen, V., Graham, N., Norman, N. & Trevisan, T. (2002), *The New Extended Creative Arts Handbook.* Karibuni Press, Sydney.
Veenema, S., Hetland, L. & Chalfen, K. (eds) (1997), *The Project Zero classroom: New approaches to thinking and understanding*, Project Zero, Harvard, Cambridge, Massachusetts.

USEFUL WEBSITES
Multiple intelligences checklists
http://www.cortland.edu/psych/mi/measure.html
http://members.shaw.ca/rjbiebrich5/MyWeb5/Self-Awareness/MultipleIntelligences.htm
http://www.kn.sbc.com/wired/fil/pages/listmultiplega.html
Teaching using Multiple Intelligences
http://www.newhorizons.org/strategies/mi/front_mi.htm
http://ali.apple.com/ali_sites/ali/exhibits/1000328/Multiple_Intelligences.html

http://www.cookps.act.edu.au/mi.htm
http://www.uwsp.edu/education/lwilson/learning/3mides.htm
http://pareonline.net/getvn.asp?v=5&n=10
Arts integration
http://www.learner.org/channel/workshops/artsineveryclassroom/artsroles.html
http://www.greenville.k12.sc.us/district/support/tandl/arts.asp
http://www.newhorizons.org/strategies/arts/front_arts.htm

REFERENCES

Hindley, J. (1998), *A song of colours*, Walker Books, Sydney.
O'Neil, M. (1961), *Hailstones and halibut bones*, TheWindmill Press, Alexandria, Virginia, available from Amazon.com.
Stoikovich, V. (1993), *Visual arts for teachers*, Holding Education Aids, Sydney.
Walsh, S.E. (1995), *Mouse paint*, Red Wagon Books, available from Amazon.com.

chapter nine
Putting it all together: An introduction to programming in the arts

Only you will be able to determine how you can best meet the needs of a particular group of students.
(Groundwater-Smith, Cusworth & Dobbins, 2001)

Learning outcomes
By the end of this chapter, students will be able to:
- show their understanding of the content and elements of each art form by writing an integrated arts program for a selected class of children;
- analyse how the Multiple Intelligences can be utilised in an integrated program;
- adapt a sample program for a selected class.

Introduction

Are you ready to teach the arts? So far, we have looked at the background to arts education for Australian primary schools, learned some teaching strategies for implementing the arts in the primary classroom, explored introductory content and teaching ideas for each of the art forms (music, media, visual arts, dance and drama) and discussed the practicalities of integrating these art forms within the arts key learning area as well as across the curriculum using the framework of the Multiple Intelligences theory. This final chapter will help you synthesise all of this information by discussing programming in arts education and then presenting several sample integrated arts programs which are relevant to other key learning areas, but which also achieve discrete arts learning outcomes. Use these programs as springboards to developing your own programs, adapting and customising them to suit your own children and your relevant state or territory syllabus framework.

Programming in arts education

When programming for the arts, children's learning experiences should be sequential and developmental, building on past experiences in a variety of ways, integrating the children's overall learning experiences and achieving generalised outcomes as well as specific indicators that provide a focus for learning which can be assessed.

An effective arts program needs to cater for all the children in the class, so the teacher needs to know each child's prior learning experiences, abilities, skills and interests in relation to each of the art forms as well as his/her cultural and home background. In the one class there may be children with special needs either physically or mentally, and there may be others who have had several years of learning to play an instrument or have enjoyed dance classes inside or outside school. Some children may not understand or speak much English, some may be able to read and write English really well, while others could be struggling in this area. Some children may work well in groups while others, for various reasons, work best by themselves. Some children will be natural leaders while others will be happy to follow. All children will have different combinations of preferred learning styles and different intelligence profiles. Learning experiences in the arts program offered in the primary classroom need to cater for all of these needs, interests, backgrounds, intelligences and ability levels. Each year teachers should identify what outcomes were achieved in the previous year, what stage their children are at in relation to each art form and then build on this information, extending children's skills, understandings and processes at a more challenging level.

Making, performing and appreciating

Within a comprehensive program for the creative arts, children should be given the opportunity to experience the creative arts through:

- making, designing, composing and creating;
- performing (not applicable in visual arts and media);
- appreciating and analysing.

Children should experience exploring, making and performing the music, dance and drama that has been created by other people. Performing does not necessarily mean putting on a formal presentation to an audience; rather, it can be learning to sing a song, dancing expressively to music or their sharing drama with others. Through this they learn basic skills, ideas and concepts related to each of the different art forms within the creative arts.

These experiences can form a firm foundation for the children to experiment, explore and develop their own individual pieces, making, composing, designing and creating a variety of different artworks whether in dance, drama, media, music or visual arts. Children also need to be able to analyse and reflect on their own and others' work and to appreciate the skills, techniques, terminology, elements, media and processes involved, and how each artwork communicates to an audience (whether this be one person, their own class, a whole school or a concert hall full of people) within each art form.

When programming, these areas need to be included and developed throughout each year of the primary school, both in each individual art form and when the creative arts are integrated with each other and across the curriculum.

Music

Children's musical experiences should be organised to ensure they are programmed sequentially, building on past experiences in a variety of ways and achieving outcomes that can be assessed. When teaching within the framework of the musical concepts of duration, dynamics, pitch, structure and tone colour, using the activity areas of making, performing and appreciating, the above needs can be met creatively with meaningful learning experiences which include songs, raps, chants, instrumental music and movement.

Media

When involved in media learning experiences, children are exploring and deepening their understanding of the concepts and constructs of media and how they work together to convey messages to selected audiences. In designing media, children research content and use relevant resources, codes and conventions which they then utilise to create media texts using a range of technologies. They need to develop skills to analyse, interpret and evaluate the meanings in the media around them, both their own and that of others. Different schools have differing qualities and quantities of technology available for the children to use in this art form, so teachers need to identify what is available and program media learning experiences based on the available resources.

Visual arts

A stimulating environment that encourages learning, as well as adequate time, resources and facilities, is important in the programming and teaching of visual arts. Resources need not be expensive or extensive and facilities can be basic (e.g. two buckets for water can be used if no taps are available). Programming should include the opportunity for children to develop their skills, processes and techniques in making artworks based on a variety of subject matter, such as people, other living things, objects, places and events. Different types of media such as drawing, painting, printmaking, collage, sculpture, masks, puppets, textiles and digital forms should be used throughout the program so children are given the opportunity to develop their skills in each of these two- and three-dimensional forms.

Dance

Within the framework of making, performing and appreciating, children need to experience a variety of types of dance, such as folk and modern dances, teacher-directed dances, improvised dances and composed dances. Through these different types of dance, the elements of action, time, dynamics, space, structure and relationships need to be explored through a wide variety of experiences. Building on a foundation of performing dances, dance sequences can be created and developed, stimulated by music, pictures, stories, events, feelings or poems, and then children can be encouraged to produce original dances to share with others. Their critical analysis skills need to be focused and developed as they view their own dances and those of others.

Drama

Drama may be used as a response to a stimulus such as a text, a piece of music or a painting and can provide opportunities for enriching learning for all children. Drama can be central to a variety of classroom activities and may provide a focus for the development of other skills already programmed (e.g. writing, reading, listening, singing, speaking, moving and constructing). Drama learning experiences could include improvisation, role-playing, movement and mime, storytelling, Readers' Theatre, choral speaking, storytelling, rehearsed and scripted drama, and work with masks and puppets. Through these experiences, children will develop their knowledge, understanding and skills in relation to the elements of drama, such as tension, focus, mood, time, contrast, symbol and space.

Purpose, content and teaching strategies

The above overview indicates the general skills, knowledge and understandings to be covered each year in creative arts programs. However, when focusing on one program (e.g. a term's work), it is important to be more specific and to know why you are going to teach this program to these particular children. Is it to develop children's understanding, knowledge and skills in making, performing or appreciating? Is it to develop their understanding of a specific element or group of elements within an art form? Or is it to develop further their critical appreciation and analysis skills? The purpose of the unit and how it relates to the children's understandings and skills needs to be clear before programming begins.

When starting to program, identify which syllabus outcomes you will be working towards throughout this unit in each of the art forms. Then write down several

specific indicators in each art form that will let you know that children have achieved the purpose of the unit of work in each art form, for example: the children will be able to sing the song 'John Brown's Holden' confidently and in tune using appropriate dynamics; the children will demonstrate that they can move to the beat and rhythm of the music; the children will create a collage as a response to Jeannie Baker's work, showing their understandings of line, colour and texture; the children will create a PowerPoint presentation on the theme of relationships; or the children will perform a Readers' Theatre script confidently using appropriate gestures and vocal expression.

Once you are clear about the general and specific purpose of the program, then you need to decide the content, identify the steps needed to present this content sequentially and developmentally, and determine how the children's learning will be assessed. In this planning stage, you will need to think about the following points; these may not all appear in your written program but they certainly need to be considered. Refer to Chapter 2, 'The creative arts classroom' for further details on these topics.

Contextual description

- Who are you teaching?
- What are their prior experiences, interests, needs and abilities in this art form?
- At what stage are they in relation to each art form? (Remember that in one class, there may be different children at several stages in each art form and you will need to cater for these differences.)
- Why are you teaching this content to these particular children?

Outcomes and indicators

- What general outcomes are you working towards in this unit?
- What specific indicators do you want the children to be able to achieve by the end of the unit in each art form?

Introductory activities

- How will you begin the program and motivate the children (e.g. with a song, a piece of music, an activity, a story, a game, an artwork or a video)?
- How will you keep this motivation high throughout the rest of the program?

Developing the theme

- What songs, music, stories, activities and so on will you use to achieve the purpose of the unit?
- What content will you include to ensure all the children in your class are engaged in activities that they are able to complete and which also have some challenges for them?
- How will this content be developed (from the known to the unknown; from the simple to the more challenging and so on)? List the steps clearly to show how children's learning will progress through the unit.

- What will you do to encourage all children to be engaged in learning throughout the unit?
- How will the Multiple Intelligences be covered in this program?
- What activities can be included that will stimulate the children's enjoyment, enthusiasm, development and confidence in each art form?

Closure activities

- How will you include a time of reflection, analysis and feedback for the children to think about and discuss their learning; that is, what they think they have learned, what they enjoyed, what they found challenging and what they would like to learn next in this art form?
- How will you bring closure to the end of the program?
- Although the process of learning is the most important aspect of a program, if there is an identifiable product at the end, this may be shared with the rest of the class, across the stage level or with the whole school. This can incorporate a feeling of closure, achievement and purpose for the children. However, avoid making the main purpose of the unit a final production, although this can be an important part of some programs.

Assessment of learning

In the programming format that you decide to use, include a section where an overall assessment of the children's achievement within each section of the unit, as related to the specific indicators for that art form, can be noted, as well as their achievements by the end of the unit. A variety of assessment techniques need to be used so all children are given the opportunity to display what they have learned. This evidence needs to be documented in some way so the next program can build on what they have learned in this program.

Questions to consider:
- How will you assess to what extent children have achieved the indicators set out at the start of the program?
- How will you assess how effectively children are working towards the anticipated syllabus outcomes for the program?
- How will you collect evidence for this (i.e. observation, checklists of names against indicators or skills, audio or video taping work samples, worksheets, self or peer reviews, portfolios and so on)?

Resources

Identify what resources are available to you and what resources you will need when teaching the program. Hopefully these are very similar! If there are some resources that will ensure your program's indicators and outcomes are achieved successfully, but that are not available, you may have to think creatively about how you can improvise, lobby your principal for some funds to purchase them or change the activities to fit within the available resources.

It may be worthwhile to investigate what resources are available throughout the school. Maybe there are some percussion scores, instruments, art or drama equipment

MMADD about the arts

that you can discover hidden in the sports storeroom or in the art resource room. Check out the library for CDs and cassettes of music, books, teaching resources and percussion scores. You may be surprised at what you find! Check with your principal and/or creative arts committee to see if there are any funds you could use to purchase specific resources that you will use regularly. You may even volunteer to show some of the rest of the staff how you are using them in your classroom, and encourage them to do the same! Once you have identified all the resources required for the program write them down and think through how you will use the resources in each lesson.

Summary of content in music, media, art, dance and drama

Content in music

Making, performing and appreciating

Making
Performing
   Singing
     Playing instruments
     Moving
Appreciating

Elements of music

Duration
Pitch
Tone colour
Dynamics
Structure

Types of music

Vocal music (songs, rhymes and raps)
Instrumental music
Student compositions
Music for movement

Content in media

Designing, making and appreciating

Skills and processes

Framing
Lighting
Focal point
Cropping
Displaying
Designing
Layout
Formatting
Interviewing

Sequencing
Scripting
Writing
Storyboarding
Shooting
Special effects
Recording
Editing
Adapting
Distributing
Publishing
Transmitting

Forms of media

Television
Film
Photography
Print
Radio
Computer and electronic media

Content in visual arts

Designing, making and appreciating

Subject matter

People
Emotions
Other living things
Objects
Places and spaces
Events

Elements

Line
Tone
Colour
Texture
Shape
Form
Space
Pattern

Forms

Two-dimensional forms
   Drawing
   Painting
   Printmaking
   Photography
Three-dimensional forms
   Sculpture
   Collage
   Ceramics
   Textiles
   Digital forms

Content in dance

Making, performing and appreciating

Elements of dance

Action (what we move)
Time (when we move)
Dynamics (how we move)
Space (where we move)
   Personal and common space
   Patterns

Body shapes
Size
Extension
Levels
Simple directions
Relationships (with whom we move)
Structure (How dance is organised)

Contexts

Teacher-directed dances
Students' compositions
Cultural and historical dances

Content in drama

Making, performing and appreciating

Elements of drama

Tension
Focus
Mood
Time
Contrast
Symbol
Space
Performance elements of drama

Types of drama

Drama games
Improvisation
Storytelling
Readers' Theatre
Movement and mime
Play building
Scripted drama
Puppets and masks
Video-audio drama

MMADD about the arts

Sample integrated arts programs for four stages: Introduction

Six sample integrated programmed units of work have been included which can be used in conjunction with integrated learning experiences from other key learning areas. For example, when studying *Wombat stew* by Marcia Vaughan in English, literacy outcomes would be explored and worked towards within the context of the English program. To enhance these learning experiences, adapt and implement the integrated arts program based on the text and this will achieve indicators and outcomes for each of the art forms as well as deepen the children's understanding of the text and enhance their literacy outcomes. The programmed activities should be adapted to make them more simple or challenging depending on the age, stage, prior experiences and abilities of the children.

The units of work are set out in two different programmed formats to give examples of different ways of programming. It would be anticipated that they would cover several lessons in each of the art forms, depending on the children's age, stage, prior experiences and abilities in the art form. Remember to include motivating introductions, effective behaviour management strategies, sequenced and developmental learning experiences, and cool-down and reflection periods for feedback in each lesson. (See Chapter 2, 'The creative arts classroom' for further lesson planning ideas.) Outcomes will need to be filled in as relevant to the state or territory syllabus and assessment comments should be completed after the unit has been implemented.

1. **I Am Me!** This program is suitable for younger children as it uses the art forms to explore science, social studies and personal development themes covering different parts of the body, how the body can move and the different emotions we can feel.

2. **Wombat Stew.** Based on a favourite children's book *Wombat stew* by Marcia Vaughan (see the reference at the end of the chapter for publishing details), this program develops children's understanding of the text using the five art forms, explores the different movements and attributes of the Australian animals mentioned in the text, and works towards an integrated presentation of the story.

3. **Transport.** In this program, children develop their understanding of different means of transport, both real and imagined, through exploring integrated movement, music, media and art learning experiences.

4. **The Sea.** Based on the text *The rainbow fish* by Marcus Pfister (see the reference at the end of the chapter for publishing details), children learn about how sea creatures live and move, and explore different aspects of the sea and how these can be represented through the art forms.

5. **Sounds Great!** Based on a science theme of how sounds are made, this program uses the arts to explore the making of musical instruments and how sounds can be created, categorised and used.

6. **'Advance Australia Fair!'** Using the national anthem as the starting point, this program uses the different art forms to help children understand the meaning of the verses and then examines both natural and built features in different environments throughout Australia. It relates to the social studies theme of natural and constructed environments, patterns of place and location.

MMADD about the arts

1. Programming proforma for dance: I Am Me

Specific indicators: Students will explore different ways of moving body parts focusing on different levels, speeds and use of space; learn to sing and dance the hokey-pokey at different speeds using different body parts and levels; reflect on the effective use of different elements of dance.

Activity areas			Contexts of dance	Learning experiences	Elements						Outcomes from syllabus
Perf	Mak	App			Act	Time	Dyn	Spc	Rel	Str	
	✧			**Introductory activities** • Explore different ways of moving different parts of the body to music with a strong beat. • In pairs (A and B), Child A explores different ways of slowly moving (e.g. the right arm).	✧				✧		(Teacher to insert relevant outcomes from state or territory syllabus)
	✧		Students' compositions	• Child B mirrors this movement. Change over so that Child B leads with another body part and Child A mirrors this movement. • Repeat, using different levels, speeds and space. **Developing the theme** • Learn to sing and dance the hokey-pokey. • Sing and dance it at different speeds using a variety of body parts. • Make up new verses for different parts of the body. • Create a simple dance using only one part of the body (e.g. just arms, just legs, just top half).	✧	✧	✧	✧	✧	✧	
✧		✧	Cultural and historical dances	**Closure activities** • Sing and dance the song and the new dances through again. • Reflect on what body parts were used and what levels they moved in (i.e. head: high; arms: medium; feet: low). • Have children demonstrate different parts of the body moving, and talk about which parts are moving and how they are moving.	✧			✧			

Resources: • Copy of hokey-pokey on cassette/CD • Cassette player/CD • Instructions for hokey-pokey • Room to move
Assessment, based on specific indicators: (Teacher to complete at end of activity)

Activity areas = *Performing, Making, Appreciating*; **Contexts of dance** = *Students' compositions, Teacher-directed dances, Cultural and historic dances*;
Elements = *Action, Time, Dynamics, Space, Relationships, Structure*

Putting it all together: An introduction to programming in the arts — Chapter 9

2. Programming proforma for music: I Am Me

Specific indicators: Children will experiment with singing a variety of songs about the body; learn to sing and add appropriate actions to the song 'I Am Me'; identify the structure of the song (verse/chorus); reflect on the effectiveness of adding movements and instruments to song.

Activity areas					Repertoire	Learning experiences	Elements					Outcomes from syllabus
Performing			Mak	App			Du	Pi	Dy	TC	St	
S	M	Pl										
*				*	Vocal music: Songs	**Introductory activities** • Experiment with singing different songs about parts of the body and add actions to these, e.g. 'Clap, clap, clap your hands Heads and Shoulders; If You're Happy'; or 'This is the way we stamp our feet /shake our leg/nod our head', etc. to 'Here We Go Round the Mulberry Bush'.	*					(Teacher to insert relevant outcomes from state or territory syllabus)
		*		*		**Developing the theme** • Listen to the song 'I Am Me' and clap the beat to the verses and click fingers to the beat during the chorus.						
	*	*			Movement	• Learn to sing the chorus, adding appropriate actions; listen to the verses and make up actions to each verse as it is heard on the tape.			*	*		
	*	*				• Learn to sing each verse; add appropriate actions and instruments to the verses.					*	
		*				• Sing song through again, singing the verses softly and the chorus loudly. • Experiment with singing different lines at different dynamic levels. **Closure activities**			*	*		
*	*					• Sing the song again with movements and instruments and dynamic levels. • Discuss how effective these were in creating interest and adding meaning to the song.						

Resources: • Copies of song about body parts • Copy of 'I Am Me' • CD of 'I Am Me' • CD player
Assessment, based on specific indicators: (Teacher to complete at end of activity)

Activity areas = Performing (*Singing, Moving, Playing instruments*), *Making, Appreciating*; **Repertoire** = *Vocal music: Songs and rhymes, Instrumental music, Students' compositions, Movement*; **Elements** = *Duration, Pitch, Dynamics, Tone colour, Structure*

MMADD about the arts

3. Programming proforma for drama: I Am Me

Specific indicators: Children will explore different whole body movements which reflect different emotions, focusing on effective use of space, levels and dynamics; use these to dramatise excerpts about emotions from a book; create their own sentences about emotions to dramatise; reflect on the effectiveness of each child's dramatisations.

Activity areas			Type	Learning experiences	Elements							Outcomes from syllabus
Perf	Mak	App			Te	F	M	Ti	C	Sy	Sp	P	
	✶		Improvisation	**Introductory activities** • Discuss and explore different whole body movements that reflect different emotions. • Include emotions such as happy, sad, angry, worried, excited and surprised. • Experiment with using different levels, dynamics and use of space to communicate these emotions. **Developing the theme** • Read excerpts from a book, (e.g. *Bob the builder and the elves* by Emily Rodda) which shows one or more characters going through a range of different emotions.									(Teacher to insert relevant outcomes from state or territory syllabus)
	✶		Movement and mime	• Read out a sentence describing one emotion and have children improvise movements based on the text. • Repeat with different sentences from the text. • Create a vocal collage of these sentences accompanied by body movements to reflect the content of the text. **Closure activities** • Continue with this activity, having individual children creating their own sentences and dramatising the emotions described in their sentences. • Reflect on the appropriateness of the movements.									

Resources: • Room to move • Copy of *Bob the builder and the elves* by Emily Rodda, or use appropriate excerpts from another book • Paper and pencils
Assessment, based on specific indicators: (Teacher to complete at end of activity)

Activity areas = *Performing, Making, Appreciating*; **Types of drama** = *Drama games, Improvisation, Storytelling, Readers' Theatre, Movement and mime, Puppets and masks, Video/audio drama, Play building*; **Elements** = *Tension, Focus, Mood, Time, Contrast, Symbol, Space, Performance*

300

Chapter 9 — Putting it all together: An introduction to programming in the arts

4. Programming proforma for visual arts: I Am Me

Specific indicators: Children will experiment with different media and techniques to represent different parts of the body; create a representation of themselves using a variety of media and techniques; share their artworks with others and appreciate the work of other children; sing 'I Am Me' using their created person to show the different body parts.

Activity areas			Forms	Learning experiences	Subject matter						Outcomes from syllabus
Des	Mak	App			Pe	Em	LT	Obj	P/S	Ev	
✻				**Introductory activities** • Experiment with different media and techniques for making representations of different parts of the body, e.g. paper plates for heads, collage materials for features. • Draw around hands on cardboard, cut out, staple to concertina strip of paper for arms; step in paint and create two footprints, dry, cut out and staple to concertina strip of paper for legs; cut out a shape for the torso, write words or make a collage of magazine pictures on it to indicate why child is special and his/her likes and interests; a photo of the child may also be glued onto the torso. **Developing the theme** • Create a person using the above techniques; staple arms to sides of torso; staple the legs to the bottom of the torso; staple the plate to the top of the torso. **Closure activities** • Share artworks with each other; comment on similarities and differences. Take photos of the artworks and display these with the artworks (see media activity). • Sing the song 'I Am Me' pointing to the body parts of the artworks when these are mentioned in the song. • Display each child's artwork with the name clearly seen, and caption the artwork with the first and last lines of the song: 'I am me and I'm very glad' . . . . 'There's no one else like me!'							(Teacher to insert relevant outcomes from state or territory syllabus)
	✻		Painting Drawing 3D						✻		

Assessment, based on specific indicators: (Teacher to complete at end of activity)

Resources: • Paper plates • Collage materials • Felt pens • Cardboard • Scissors • Stapler and staples • Glue • Paint

Activity areas = *Designing, Making, Appreciating*; **Forms** = 2D: *Drawing, Painting, Printmaking, Photography*; 3D: *Sculpture, Collage, Ceramics, Textiles, Digital Forms*; **Subject matter** = *People, Emotions, Living things, Objects, Places and spaces, Events*

MMADD about the arts

5. Programming proforma for media: I Am Me

Specific indicators: Children will photograph their partners; learn more about each other through preparing and recording a radio interview with the partner; and create a display to show what they have learned about their partner.

Activity areas			Skills and processes	Learning experiences	Form of media						Outcomes from syllabus
Des	Mak	App			TV	Fi	Ph	Pr	Ra	C/E	
	✻		Shooting	**Introductory activities** • In pairs, have each child take several photos of their partner showing different emotions, and then print them out. • Talk with each other about what they like about their partner and what makes their partner feel happy, sad, angry, surprised and so on. Relate this to the photos. **Developing the theme** • Prepare simple interview questions to ask their partner as a radio interview. Find their partner's favourite song to play at the start and end of the interview.			✻				(Teacher to insert relevant outcomes from state or territory syllabus)
			Interviewing								
	✻		Recording	• Record the interview and then swap around so each child has the opportunity to interview the other child. • Questions could include topics such as likes and dislikes, hobbies, favourite sports, favourite music, films and television shows, pets, home and family life. • Play back the recorded interview and reflect on how effective the questions and answers were in portraying the character of the child. **Closure activity**					✻		
✻			Displaying	• Create a display of the photos; write a description of their partner with information gained from interview and display this under the relevant photos.				✻			

Resources: • Camera • Printer • Recorder (audio/electronic) • Paper • Felt pens • Computer
Assessment, based on specific indicators: (Teacher to complete at end of activity)

Activity areas = Designing, Making, Appreciating; **Skills and processes** *= Write in what skills and processes are being learned;*
Forms of media *= Television, Film, Photography, Print, Radio, Computers and electronic media*

Putting it all together: An introduction to programming in the arts   Chapter 9

1. Programming proforma for drama: Wombat Stew

Specific indicators: Students will explore ways of moving like the different animals in the story; develop a Readers' Theatre presentation of the story with some children reading it and others miming the animals; reflect on the effectiveness of the presentation in relation to the different dramatic elements.

Activity areas			Type	Learning experiences	Elements								Outcomes from syllabus
Perf	Mak	App			Te	F	M	Ti	C	Sy	Sp	P	
	✽		Improvisation	**Introductory activities** • Read through *Wombat stew* by Marcia Vaughan. • Explore ways of moving like each of the animals, e.g. — koala: slow and sleepy; — echidna: short, sharp movements; — emu: graceful movements. • Experiment with speaking like the different animals.				✽					(Teacher to insert relevant outcomes from state or territory syllabus)
			Storytelling	**Developing the theme** • Tell the story of *Wombat stew* around the circle, with children being the different animals in the story. • Use the voice and expression of each of the animals as they tell part of the story from their point of view.	✽								
✽		✽	Scripted dramas	• Develop a Readers' Theatre-type presentation of the story, using vocal expression, sound effects and gestures; use a mask or puppet or other symbol to represent each character in the story. **Closure activities** • Reflect on how effective the children's animal gestures and voices were in representing each character. • Repeat the presentation, making changes based on these reflections.					✽	✽	✽	✽	

Resources: • Copies of *Wombat stew* by Marcia Vaughan   • Room to move
Assessment, based on specific indicators: (Teacher to complete at end of activity)

Activity areas = *Performing, Making, Appreciating*; **Types of drama** = *Drama games, Improvisation, Storytelling, Readers' Theatre, Movement and mime, Puppets and masks, Video/audio drama, Play building*; **Elements** = *Tension, Focus, Mood, Time, Contrast, Symbol, Space, Performance*

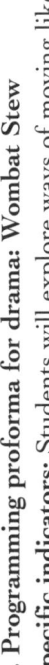

303

MMADD about the arts

2. Programming proforma for dance: Wombat Stew

Specific indicators: Students will learn to sing the song 'Wombat Stew' from the text; experiment with movements to represent the lyrics; create and share a movement sequence to accompany the singing of the song; reflect on the effectiveness of the movement sequence in relation to the story and characters.

Activity areas			Contexts of dance	Learning experiences	Elements						Outcomes from syllabus
Perf	Mak	App			Act	Time	Dyn	Spc	Rel	Str	
				Introductory activities							(Teacher to insert relevant outcomes from state or territory syllabus)
	*			• Chant the song 'Wombat Stew' that is repeated throughout the text; learn to sing it as a song (see the music at the back of the book).	*						
				• Experiment with different movements which could represent a dingo stirring the billy and dancing around it, looking forward to eating the fat, tasty wombat.	*	*	*	*			
			Students' compositions	**Developing the theme**							
	*			• Create an eight-beat movement sequence which incorporates some of the above movements and matches the words of the song; use different levels to create contrast and interest.							
				• All repeat these as the song is sung, and then repeat the song and the movements.				*	*		
	*			• Create a similar set of movements, but incorporate some different ones to reflect each version of the song as it is repeated throughout the text.							
				Closure activities							
				• Refine and rehearse the dance until it flows smoothly as the different verses of the song are sung. Repeat it twice each time the song appears in the book.	*		*	*	*	*	
*		*		• Reflect on how appropriate it is to the text and make changes where necessary.							

Resources: • Copy of the song from *Wombat stew*. • Room to move
Assessment, based on specific indicators: (Teacher to complete at end of activity)

Activity areas = Performing, Making, Appreciating; **Contexts of dance** = Students' compositions, Teacher-directed dances, Cultural and historic dances;
Elements = Action, Time, Dynamics, Space, Relationships, Structure

Chapter 9
Putting it all together: An introduction to programming in the arts

3. Programming proforma for music: Wombat Stew

Specific indicators: Students will experiment with untuned instruments to represent the different characters in the story and use these instruments as the story is read; accompany the song 'Wombat Stew' with tuned instruments; reflect on the effectiveness of the instruments.

Activity area					Type	Learning experiences	Elements					Outcomes from syllabus
Performing			Mak	App			Du	Pi	Dy	TC	St	
S	M	Pl										
						Introductory activities						(Teacher to insert relevant outcomes from state or territory syllabus)
✻					Movement	• Identify the different characters in the text; show how they move and discuss what sounds they might make.						
		✻	✻		Students' compositions	• Experiment with different loud and soft untuned percussion instruments to create sounds to represent each of the characters from the story in relation to how they move and what they say.						
						Developing the theme						
		✻	✻	✻	Vocal music; Songs; Instrumental music	• Using tuned instruments, have a small group learn to play the melody of the song 'Wombat Stew'. Have some other children play bass line notes to the beat as indicated by the guitar chords (C, F, G) as an accompaniment to the song.		✻				
						• Sing the song, as the small groups play the melody and the accompaniment to the song.		✻	✻	✻	✻	
						Closure activities						
		✻	✻			• Read through the story, with children playing untuned percussion instruments to represent the different characters each time the characters are mentioned.	✻	✻	✻	✻	✻	
	✻					• Have the tuned instrument groups play the melody and accompaniment of the song each time it is played.						
						• Reflect on how appropriate the use of the instruments is throughout the story.						

Resources: • Tuned percussion instruments • Non-tuned percussion instruments • Melody and guitar chords of song • Copy of the song 'Wombat Stew'

Assessment, based on specific indicators: (Teacher to complete at end of activity)

Activity areas = Performing (Singing, Moving, Playing instruments), Making, Appreciating; **Repertoire** = *Vocal music: Songs and rhymes, Instrumental music, Students' compositions, Movement;* **Elements** = *Duration, Pitch, Dynamics, Tone colour, Structure*

MMADD about the arts

4. Programming proforma for visual arts: Wombat Stew

Specific indicators: Students will observe pictures and photos of animals and experiment with drawing techniques to draw one of the characters from the story; create masks to represent a character; use the masks when presenting the story with music, drama and dance; reflect thoughtfully on the presentation.

Activity areas			Forms	Learning experiences	Subject matter						Outcomes from syllabus
Des	Mak	App			Pe	Em	LT	Obj	P/S	Ev	
				Introductory activities • Examine pictures of the animals mentioned in *Wombat stew*. • Discuss what techniques have been used to make each animal look different; look at photos of these animals and compare these with the drawings; how are they different/the same?			✱				(Teacher to insert relevant outcomes from state or territory syllabus)
	✱		Drawing	• Experiment with drawing different animals' faces from observation of these pictures; use shading, colour and line to create depth and character in the animals' faces.							
	✱		3D: Masks Collage	**Developing the theme** • Have small groups each design and then create a paper-plate mask (or use other medium if available, e.g. gypsona, papier-mâché) of one of the animals mentioned in the story. • Features on the masks can be drawn on, or paint may be used; collaged materials may also be glued onto the faces to create a 3D effect. **Closure activities** • Have the text narrated while some children, wearing the masks, dramatise the story; have a music group which plays the non-tuned and tuned percussion instruments from the music activity and a dance group which presents the created movement sequence from the dance activity at the appropriate time in the narration.							
✱				• Reflect on the appropriateness and effectiveness of the masks in representing the different characters in the story.							

Resources: • Pictures and photos of animals mentioned in the story • Art paper • Felt pens • Coloured pencils • Paper plates (or other medium for masks) • Collage materials • Glue • Paint • Brushes • Water • Newspaper to cover tables • Elastic for masks
Assessment, based on specific indicators: (Teacher to complete at end of activity)

Activity areas = *Designing, Making, Appreciating*; **Forms** = 2D: *Drawing, Painting, Printmaking, Photography*; 3D: *Sculpture, Collage, Ceramics, Textiles, Digital forms*; **Subject matter** = *People, Emotions, Living things, Objects, Places and spaces, Events*

Chapter 9
Putting it all together: An introduction to programming in the arts

5. Programming proforma for media: Wombat Stew

Specific indicators: Children will record the Readers' Theatre presentation, as well as the song and musical accompaniments to the story; create a storyboard and dramatised version of the text including the dances to the audio recording; video the integrated presentation and reflect on its effectiveness.

Activity areas			Skills and processes	Learning experiences	Form of media						Outcomes from syllabus
Des	Mak	App			TV	Fi	Ph	Pr	Ra	C/E	
	*		Recording	**Introductory activities** • Audio record the Readers' Theatre presentation of the story; include the singing of the song, the tuned percussion bass line and melody, and the untuned instruments playing when each character is mentioned.					*		(Teacher to insert relevant outcomes from state or territory syllabus)
*			Sequencing Storyboarding	**Developing the theme** • Create a simple storyboard based on the text to show the sequence of the story as it could be dramatised. • Create a dramatised version of the story using masks; include the dance created previously to the song.				*			
			Shooting Recording	• Practise the drama and dance to the recorded Readers' Theatre presentation and musical accompaniment. • Video the drama and dance presentation.			*				
		*	Transmitting	**Closure activity** • View the videoed presentation and discuss the effectiveness of the dance, drama, masks and music working together to help them learn about the animals and the story. • Discuss and then draw or write what they enjoyed and learned about the series of activities based on the text.							

Resources: • Audio and video recording and playback equipment • Felt pens • Paper • Tuned and untuned musical instruments • Masks • Room to move

Assessment, based on specific indicators: (Teacher to complete at end of activity)

Activity areas = *Designing, Making, Appreciating*; **Skills and processes** = *Write in what skills and processes are being learned*;
Forms of media = *Television, Film, Photography, Print, Radio, Computers and electronic media*

MMADD about the arts

1. Programming proforma for media: Transport

Specific indicators: Children will share their knowledge about different methods of transport; select one method and use the Internet to find out more about it; create a poster summarising this information; share their new knowledge with the rest of the class; and display their posters creatively.

Activity areas			Skills and processes	Learning experiences	Form of media						Outcomes from syllabus
Des	Mak	App			TV	Fi	Ph	Pr	Ra	C/E	
				Introductory activities • Discuss how each child came to school. Ask them: How would you get to the nearest city? To the Gold Coast? To London, Lebanon, China and so on? To the moon? To the bottom of the ocean? • Show pictures of different methods of transport and have children share what they know about these modes of transport.							(Teacher to insert relevant outcomes from state or territory syllabus)
	✧		Design Layout Writing Publishing	**Developing the theme** • Using various search engines to find pictures and information about different forms of transport on the Internet (e.g. www.google.com or www.pictureaustralia.org), have small groups each investigate a different mode of transport. • Design and create a poster on the computer or with felt pens, about their selected mode of transport, using downloaded pictures, magazine pictures or photographs taken by the children. Include short, succinct sentences to tell about the mode of transport.			✧			✧	
✧		✧	Displaying	**Closure activity** • Have each group present to the rest of the class their poster and information about their mode of transport. Have the rest of the class give feedback on the posters and how they display the information. • Display these posters creatively.							

Resources: • Pictures of different modes of transport • Paper • Felt pens • Computer • Internet access • Printer • Magazines
Assessment, based on specific indicators: (Teacher to complete at end of activity)

Activity areas = *Designing, Making, Appreciating;* **Skills and processes** = *Write in what skills and processes are being learned;*
Forms of media = *Television, Film, Photography, Print, Radio, Computers and electronic media*

Putting it all together: An introduction to programming in the arts — Chapter 9

2. Programming proforma for visual arts: Transport

Specific indicators: Students will examine different artworks depicting transport, discuss the various styles and media used and select one of these to create their own representation of a mode of transport; discuss the various styles and media used and select one of the class about the inspiration and creation of their artwork; reflect on the effectiveness of the different styles and media used.

Activity areas			Forms	Learning experiences	Subject matter						Outcomes from syllabus
Des	Mak	App			Pe	Em	LT	Obj	P/S	Ev	
		✴		**Introductory activities** • Look at different pictures of ways of travelling (e.g. see the Art Pack called *Travelling* from S&S Supplies, PO Box 81, Thornleigh, NSW, 2120 ph (02) 8975 1155 or search for *Transport* at www.pictureaustralia.org). • Discuss similarities and differences in styles, techniques and media used.							(Teacher to insert relevant outcomes from state or territory syllabus)
	✴		Painting Drawing	• Experiment with designing and creating a representation of a selected mode of transport using one of these styles and media. When dry, cut out each of the transport artworks. **Developing the theme**							
	✴		Painting 3D collage	• Design and create a class or group mural of a landscape that includes roads, sky and sea, using a variety of techniques (torn tissue paper, paint applied with scrunched-up newspaper, paint spread with a comb, collage using similar colours cut from magazine pictures and so on). • Add the children's created modes of transport to this mural.				✴			
		✴		**Closure activities** • Have each child report on the style and media they used to produce their part of the completed mural and their artwork. • Discuss how effective it was in depicting the chosen mode of transport and the mural.							

Resources: • *Travelling:* Art Pack W1 • Coloured tissue paper • Paint • Brushes • Water • Newspaper • Comb • Magazines • Scissors • Glue • Large sheets of paper or cardboard • Felt pens • Art paper • Pencils
Assessment, based on specific indicators: (Teacher to complete at end of activity)

Activity areas = *Designing, Making, Appreciating*; **Forms** = 2D: *Drawing, Painting, Printmaking, Photography*; 3D: *Sculpture, Collage, Ceramics, Textiles, Digital forms*; **Subject matter** = *People, Emotions, Living things, Objects, Places and spaces, Events*

MMADD about the arts

3. Programming proforma for drama: Transport

Specific indicators: Students will learn to sing the song 'How Did You Travel?'; explore different ways of dramatising using various modes of transport; dramatise each verse of the song; create and dramatise a new form of transport, and then create a third line to the song about this form; share the new verses with movement and reflect on the use of dramatic elements to effectively represent each mode of transport.

Activity areas			Type	Learning experiences	Elements									Outcomes from syllabus
Perf	Mak	App			Te	F	M	Ti	C	Sy	Sp	P		
	✧		Choral speaking	**Introductory activities** • Chant the words together to the song, 'How Did You Travel to School?' and then learn to sing the song.	✧									(Teacher to insert relevant outcomes from state or territory syllabus)
			Improvisation	• Explore different ways of dramatising using the modes of transport mentioned in the song, step by step (e.g. Car: find keys, unlock door; open door; sit down; close door; put on seat belt; put key in ignition; check passengers have seat belts on; put foot on clutch/accelerator, hands on wheel, and slowly drive off and so on. • Include the use of tension, symbol and contrast in the improvisation. **Developing the theme** • Divide class into eight groups; give each group one verse of the song to create an improvisation of travelling in the mode of transport for that verse, as the song is sung.		✧			✧	✧	✧	✧		
	✧		Movement and mime	• Have each group then create and improvise their own imagined form of transport to school, and make up a third line to the song using appropriate elements. **Closure activities** • Share the new verses and movements with the rest of the class. • Discuss the effectiveness of the movements to reflect the new mode of transport in relation to the elements of drama.		✧			✧	✧				
✧		✧										✧		

Resources: • Copy and words of the song 'How Did You Travel to School?' • CD of song
Assessment, based on specific indicators: (Teacher to complete at end of activity)

Activity areas = *Performing, Making, Appreciating*; **Types of drama** = *Drama games, Improvisation, Storytelling, Readers' Theatre, Movement and mime, Puppets and masks, Video/audio drama, Play building*; **Elements** = *Tension, Focus, Mood, Time, Contrast, Symbol, Space, Performance*

Putting it all together: An introduction to programming in the arts   Chapter 9

4. Programming proforma for music: Transport

Specific indicators: Students will experiment with different instruments to represent the modes of transport in 'How Did You Travel?' and in 'John Brown's Holden'; use body percussion to show the structure and dynamics in the song; show the tempo through movement and add tuned percussion to the song 'This Train'; reflect on how effective the use of the different concepts can be to create contrast and interest to a song.

Activity area					Type	Learning experiences	Elements					Outcomes from syllabus
Performing			Mak	App			Du	Pi	Dy	TC	St	
S	M	Pl										
					Vocal music: Songs	**Introductory activities**						(Teacher to insert relevant outcomes from state or territory syllabus)
✻		✻	✻			• Sing the song 'How Did You Travel to School?'						
						• Experiment with different instruments which could represent the different modes of transport mentioned in the song. Play the instruments as the song is sung.				✻		
						• Select instruments to represent a car, and make it sound as though a crash, a puncture and so on is happening.			✻	✻		
					Vocal music: Songs	**Developing the theme**						
✻		✻	✻			• Learn to sing the song 'John Brown's Holden'.						
						• Add appropriate instruments to represent what happens in each verse (e.g. prang and puncture).				✻		
		✻		✻		• Click fingers to beat of verse, clap beat of chorus.	✻					
		✻		✻		• Use flashcards to indicate dynamics (large = loud, small = soft sounds).			✻			
		✻	✻	✻		• Learn song 'This Train' while clicking fingers to beat. Walk around room to beat showing changing tempo.	✻	✻				
		✻				• Add tuned percussion instruments to the beat, to create a bass line, following the guitar chords above the music.					✻	
					Movement	**Closure activities**						
✻	✻	✻	✻	✻		• Sing through songs again, with instruments and movements.						
						• Identify how changing tempo, dynamics and use of different instruments can add interest and contrast to songs.						

Resources: • Copies of 'How Did You Travel to School'; 'John Brown's Holden'; and 'This Train' • Untuned instruments • Flashcards • Tuned instruments
Assessment, based on specific indicators: (Teacher to complete at end of activity)

Activity areas = *Performing (Singing, Moving, Playing instruments), Making, Appreciating;* **Repertoire** = *Vocal music: Songs and rhymes, Instrumental music, Students' compositions, Movement;* **Elements** = *Duration, Pitch, Dynamics, Tone colour, Structure*

311

MMADD about the arts

5. Programming proforma for dance: Transport

Specific indicators: Students will learn to sing the song 'My Paddle' and add appropriate movements to the song; choose a different mode of transport and create a movement sequence to represent it; share their movement sequences with others and discuss use of elements.

Activity areas			Contexts of dance	Learning experiences	Elements						Outcomes from syllabus
Perf	Mak	App			Act	Time	Dyn	Spc	Rel	Str	
				Introductory activities • Learn to sing the song 'My Paddle'. • Experiment with four appropriate movements, one to represent each line of the song (e.g. paddling canoe, clap hands and raise arms like ray of sunshine, flying like a large bird, paddle on other side of canoe).	✽						(Teacher to insert relevant outcomes from state or territory syllabus)
	✽			• In groups explore four different movements to represent a selected mode of transport (a different mode for each group) showing an understanding of the different elements of dance.	✽	✽	✽	✽	✽	✽	
			Students' compositions	**Developing the theme** • Develop each of the four movements to last for four beats. Using these movements, create a 16-beat movement sequence based on these basic four movements (e.g. repeat each basic movement four times, change levels, change direction, change tempo or change floor patterns). • Basic movements may be stylised to create a smooth flowing sequence. • Add music with strong beat to assist movements.	✽	✽	✽	✽	✽	✽	
				Closure activities • Have each group share their movement sequence, one after the other, to the music to create a continual dance sequence to the music. • Reflect on their effective use of dance elements.	✽	✽	✽	✽	✽	✽	
✽		✽									

Resources: • Copy of song 'My Paddle' • Room to move • Music with a strong beat • CD of song and CD player
Assessment, based on specific indicators: (Teacher to complete at end of activity)

Activity areas = *Performing, Making, Appreciating;* **Contexts of dance** = *Students' compositions, Teacher-directed dances, Cultural and historic dances;*
Elements = *Action, Time, Dynamics, Space, Relationships, Structure*

Putting it all together: An introduction to programming in the arts   Chapter 9

1. **Programming proforma for visual arts: The Sea**
Specific indicators: Students will discuss and compare the different styles, techniques and media used in a variety of artworks to depict the sea; create a seascape using media, techniques and styles explored; read the story and discuss pictures and real objects which relate to the sea; design and create a puppet based on the story; create an outline drawing of a sea creature; create a mural using these outlines on the seascape; reflect on the effectiveness of the use of different styles, techniques and media to create art.

Activity areas			Forms	Learning experiences	Subject matter						Outcomes from syllabus
Des	Mak	App			Pe	Em	LT	Obj	P/S	Ev	
✽		✽		**Introductory activities** • Observe different artworks of the sea. Discuss and compare how different colours, techniques and styles are used to depict movement and atmosphere in a seascape.							(Teacher to insert relevant outcomes from state or territory syllabus)
	✽		Drawing Painting	• Explore ways of expressing this using a variety of media. • Design and create a large mural of a seascape using some of the styles, techniques and media observed and discussed in the artworks.					✽		
		✽		**Developing the theme** • Read *The rainbow fish* together. • Discuss the illustrations and the sights, sounds, smells and textures of the seascape described visually and verbally in the book.			✽				
	✽			• Feel real shells, seaweed and so on and from this and from observing pictures, draw a variety of the sea creatures mentioned in the text.							
	✽		Drawing Painting	• Use a black felt pen to draw the outline, and then colour in with paints or felt pens using patterns and colours seen in the pictures of the observed fish and objects. • Using skills learned from the drawing activity, design and create puppets for the characters in the story.							
✽	✽	✽		**Closure activities** • Glue the created sea creatures onto the background mural of the sea. • Share the completed puppets and discuss how they were designed and created.							
✽	✽	✽		• Compare artworks with another child or small group; discuss and identify similarities and differences in the techniques, styles and media used.							

Resources: • Collection of artworks depicting the sea • *The rainbow fish* by Marcus Pfister • Shells and other sea objects • Paint • Felt pens • Art paper • Brushes • Water • Glue • Scissors • Large sheets of paper or cardboard for mural • Materials for puppet making
Assessment, based on specific indicators: (Teacher to complete at end of activity)

Activity areas = *Designing, Making, Appreciating;* **Forms** = 2D: *Drawing, Painting, Printmaking, Photography;* 3D: *Sculpture, Collage, Ceramics, Textiles, Digital forms;* **Subject matter** = *People, Emotions, Living things, Objects, Places and spaces, Events*

313

MMADD about the arts

2. Programming proforma for music: The Sea

Specific indicators: Students will explore and identify which instruments could be used to represent different parts of the mural developed in the visual arts lessons; use the mural as a graphic score; learn to sing 'The Sea' and add body percussion to the beat; add appropriate instruments, dynamic levels and movements to represent each verse; reflect on the effectiveness of adding instruments and dynamics to the song.

Activity area					Type	Learning experiences	Elements					Outcomes from syllabus
Performing			Mak	App			Du	Pi	Dy	TC	St	
S	M	Pl										
		✱	✱		Students' compositions	**Introductory activities** • Experiment with instruments that could be used to represent each sea creature or object in the mural. • Use the completed mural as a graphic score to create a sea soundscape (i.e. use a pointer and move it from left to right across the mural; when it touches a fish, stone, waves, beach and so on, the instrument which represents it is played, and then stops when the pointer moves on).	✱			✱	✱	(Teacher to insert relevant outcomes from state or territory syllabus)
	✱	✱	✱		Vocal music: Songs	**Developing the theme** • Listen to the song 'The Sea' and use different body percussion to the beat for each verse. Learn to sing the song. • Use flashcards to show different dynamic levels for each verse to represent the lyrics appropriately. • Add instruments and movements to each verse to represent the lyrics (e.g. drums for waves crashing).			✱			
	✱	✱	✱	✱	Movement	**Closure activities** • Sing the song through with the different dynamic levels, the instruments and the movements. • Discuss which parts of the song sung this way worked well and which could be done better. • Sing the song through again with these changes.				✱		
✱	✱	✱										

Resources:
- See artworks from visual arts activity
- Untuned percussion instruments
- Copy of 'The Sea'
- Flashcards showing content for each verse
- Dynamic flashcards (i.e. with 'loud', 'medium', 'soft' written on them or with large, medium and small pictures of fish drawn on them)

Assessment, based on specific indicators: (Teacher to complete at end of activity)

Activity areas = *Performing* (Singing, Moving, Playing instruments), *Making, Appreciating;* **Repertoire** = *Vocal music:* Songs and rhymes, Instrumental music, Students' compositions, Movement; **Elements** = *Duration, Pitch, Dynamics, Tone colour, Structure*

Chapter 9
Putting it all together: An introduction to programming in the arts

3. Programming proforma for dance: The Sea

Specific indicators: Students will improvise movements to represent different sea creatures, using a variety of levels, dynamics, directions and speeds; choreograph their movements simply; create a dance based on these movements; share dances and reflect on each other's work.

Activity areas			Contexts of dance	Learning experiences	Elements						Outcomes from syllabus
Perf	Mak	App			Act	Time	Dyn	Spc	Rel	Str	
			Teacher-directed dance	**Introductory activities** • Using flashcards of sea creatures (or objects representing them) call out, for example, 'fish'. Children move across the room, exploring different ways of moving as a fish, using different levels, dynamics and speeds. As the cymbals clash, children change direction. • Repeat using a different sea creature, and ensure children explore different levels, speeds and directions appropriately in the given space. **Developing the theme** • In groups, select a sea creature and brainstorm verbally and with movements how it might move around its sea environment. Share movements with another group. • In groups, make up a 'map' to show how each sea creature could move as part of a 'sea dance'. • Add appropriate movements to represent each sea creature based on these maps. Ensure a variety of dance elements are included in each dance sequence. **Closure activities** • Share the dance/movement sequence with each other, and the contrasting elements used in each dance.	✽	✽	✽	✽			(Teacher to insert relevant outcomes from state or territory syllabus)
	✽										
			Students' compositions		✽	✽	✽	✽	✽	✽	
✽		✽			✽						

Resources: • Flashcards of sea creatures • Room to move • Cymbal • Art paper • Felt pens
Assessment, based on specific indicators: (Teacher to complete at end of activity)

Activity areas = *Performing, Making, Appreciating*; **Contexts of dance** = *Students' compositions, Teacher-directed dance, Cultural and historic dances*; **Elements** = *Action, Time, Dynamics, Space, Relationships, Structure*

MMADD about the arts

4. Programming proforma for drama: The Sea

Specific indicators: Students will mime a selected sea creature or object related to the sea, showing how it moves in the sea and on the land; explore moving like characters in *The rainbow fish*, and create and use puppets to dramatise the story, focusing on different dramatic elements to enhance the drama; reflect on their dramatic interpretations and make changes where applicable.

Activity areas			Type	Learning experiences	Elements								Outcomes from syllabus
Perf	Mak	App			Te	F	M	Ti	C	Sy	Sp	P	
				Introductory activities									(Teacher to insert relevant outcomes from state or territory syllabus)
	*		Improvisation	• Prepare a box of special objects found at the seaside. • One at a time, children select an object secretly and show through movements which one was selected. • Extend this with children selecting a sea creature and miming how it might move through the sea and then on the land. **Developing the theme** • Read *The rainbow fish*. Discuss the theme of friendship and how to make friends.									
	*			• Explore moving like the different characters in the story. Use hot seating and have children answer questions about what character they are, how they are feeling as that character, what is happening, what they think about various events in the story and so on.	*	*	*	*	*	*	*		
		*	Narrative forms	• Using the simple puppets made in the visual arts unit, dramatise the story as it is narrated expressively, using the different elements of drama to enhance the presentation. **Closure activities** • Video record the presentation, view it and then discuss how effective they felt their dramatic interpretation was, and make improvements where appropriate.									
*													

Resources: • Box of special seaside objects • *The rainbow fish* story • Rainbow fish puppets from visual arts unit • Room to move
Assessment, based on specific indicators: (Teacher to complete at end of activity)

Activity areas = Performing, Making, Appreciating; **Types of drama** = Drama games, Improvisation, Storytelling, Readers' Theatre, Movement and mime, Puppets and masks, Video/audio drama, Play building; **Elements** = Tension, Focus, Mood, Time, Contrast, Symbol, Space, Performance

5. Programming proforma for media: The Sea

Specific indicators: Children will design a storyboard of the video puppet play of *The rainbow fish*; develop a PowerPoint presentation using still photos of the puppets; add a narrative and music to complete the presentation and share this with another class, reflecting on the effective use of music, words and photos.

Activity areas			Skills and processes	Learning experiences	Form of media							Outcomes from syllabus
Des	Mak	App			TV	Fi	Ph	Pr	Ra	C/E		
				Introductory activities								(Teacher to insert relevant outcomes from state or territory syllabus)
✻			Sequencing Storyboarding	• View the video presentation of *The rainbow fish* puppet play and list the key scenes from the story.		✻						
	✻			• Create a simple storyboard of these and design a PowerPoint presentation based on the puppet play.						✻		
				Developing the theme								
				• Take still photos of puppets in position as indicated in the created storyboard. Print these and scan them or download them onto the computer.			✻					
	✻		Scripting Publishing	• Using PowerPoint, create a simple presentation with the photos. The narrative could be improvised and recorded into the PowerPoint presentation, or it could be typed onto each frame of the presentation.								
			Special effects	• Depending on the children's and teacher's expertise, add in commercial or created music and/or sound effects as an accompaniment to the narrative.						✻		
				Closure activity								
		✻	Transmitting	• Share the completed PowerPoint presentation with another class and reflect on how effectively it told the story using words, photos and music.								

Resources: • Video of *The rainbow fish* puppet play • Paper • Felt pens • Computer • PowerPoint software • Digital camera • CDs for background music

Assessment, based on specific indicators: (Teacher to complete at end of activity)

Activity areas = *Designing, Making, Appreciating*; **Skills and processes** =*Write in what skills and processes are being learned*;
Forms of media = *Television, Film, Photography, Print, Radio, Computers and electronic media*

MMADD about the arts

Sounds Great!

1. Visual arts: Sounds Great!

Outcomes from syllabus
(Teacher to insert relevant outcomes from state or territory syllabus)

Indicators
Children will identify different ways of making sounds, brainstorm how to make musical instruments, design and create their own musical instrument, categorise the sounds of the instruments into how they are played, and document both verbally and on paper how their instrument was made and how it is played.

Activities
Designing, making, appreciating

Form of visual arts
Three-dimensional art

Subject matter covered
Objects

Learning experiences

- **Introductory activities**
  — Watch a video or listen to a CD of people playing bush-band instruments. Identify ways of making sounds (e.g. hitting, scraping, shaking and blowing). Show examples of homemade instruments.
  — Brainstorm different ways of making musical instruments.
  — In groups or individually, have children design their own musical instruments made from found or junk materials and list the materials they will need to construct these instruments.

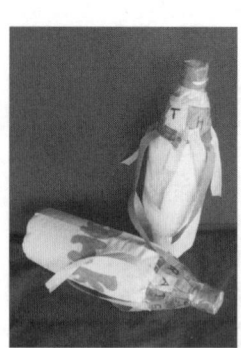

- **Developing the theme**
  — Collect a variety of materials and let children create their own musical instruments based on their initial designs. Encourage them to experiment with different ways of changing the sound their instrument can make (e.g. the pitch, whether it can be hit and shaken to create a sound, or blown and scraped to make a sound).
  — Check that created instruments are attractive, durable and safe when played; that is, make sure bottle tops don't come loose and fly off when the instrument is played. Ensure an adult supervises the use of hot glue guns or sharp knives.
  — Record all the children individually playing their completed instrument; play this recording back to the class and have them categorise the sounds into how they were produced (hit, blown, scraped, shaken, bowed and so on).

- **Closure activities**
  — Have the children each show their instrument and explain how they made it and demonstrate the different sounds that can be made from it.

Putting it all together: An introduction to programming in the arts — Chapter 9

Resources
Variety of materials for instrument making, for example plastic bottles with lids, tin cans, cardboard cylinders, metal bowls, rubber bands, jingle bells, ribbons, offcuts of wood, balloon, rubber gloves, rice, split peas, dowel rods, bottle tops, nails, hammer, paper plates, wire, scissors, wire cutters, wooden spoons, empty ice-cream container, bamboo and Stanley knife.

Assessment, based on specific indicators
(Teacher to complete at end of activity)

2. Music: Sounds Great!

Outcomes from syllabus
(Teacher to insert relevant outcomes from state or territory syllabus)

Indicators
Children will learn to sing and play the song 'Playing Our Instruments', using their homemade instruments, create and play a graphic score based on sounds they heard in a selected environment, compare the environmental sounds with their graphic score being played and discuss differences using musical language.

Activities
Making, performing (singing, playing instruments), appreciating

Type of music
Students' compositions

Elements covered
Duration, tone colour

Learning experiences
- **Introductory activities**
  — Have the children listen to the song 'Playing Our Instruments' and learn to clap the rhythm of the verse as they listen. Sing the chorus and clap the rhythm of the verse. Learn to sing the first verse and chorus of the song.
  — Categorise instruments created in the visual arts unit into instruments that can be hit, shaken, scraped or blown.
  — Sing the verse again; instead of 'ting, ting, ting, ting' just play their hit instruments to the rhythm, and then sing, 'go the hitting instruments' instead of 'goes the triangle'.
  — Repeat the verse for the different categories of instruments (e.g. 'go the blowing instruments', 'go the scraping instruments').
  — Sing the whole song through using only their created instruments and the new words to the song.
- **Developing the theme**
  — In groups, have children select an environment (e.g. library, playground, veranda or car park). Make an audio recoding of, and listen carefully to, the sounds in the environment for 30 seconds. Identify, count and categorise the

sounds heard during this time period into sounds that are loud/soft, fast/slow, high/low, regular/irregular, sharp/smooth, and so on. Check what they remembered with the recording. Write down the sounds they heard showing when and how they occurred within the 30-second interval, to create a symbolic graphic score.
— Using musical instruments created in the visual arts unit, explore how these instruments can be used to represent the different sounds heard in the selected environment.
— Play the graphic score with their own instruments. Record their composition.

- **Closure activities**
    — Replay the recording of the environmental sounds, and compare it with the recording of their composition based on the environmental sounds. Compare and contrast the two recordings, using musical language.

Resources
Audio recorder, homemade instruments from visual arts unit, felt pens, paper.

Assessment, based on specific indicators
(Teacher to complete at end of activity)

3. Dance: Sounds Great!

Outcomes from syllabus
(Teacher to insert relevant outcomes from state or territory syllabus)

Indicators
Children will move in response to different sounds made on instruments, create a movement-and-vocal sequence to show a pair of contrasting movements, create a movement sequence to the song 'Moving', share their dances and reflect on the effectiveness of the use of different elements of dance in the sequences.

Activities
Making, performing, appreciating

Contexts of dance
Students' compositions

Elements covered
Action, dynamics, time, space, structure, relationships

Learning experiences

- **Introductory activities**
    — Identify which of the homemade instruments could make sounds that are sharp, smooth, heavy, light, fast or slow. Play instruments from each of these six categories and have children move in response to the sharp, smooth, heavy, light, fast and slow sounds using different levels and directions.
    — In pairs, Child A makes (say) a sharp series of movements accompanied by vocal sounds and Child B mirrors the movements and sounds; then Child B makes a series of smooth movements and sounds and Child A mirrors these.

— In groups create a movement-and-vocal sequence to show a pair of these contrasting movements (i.e. fast and slow). Share these with the rest of the class.

- **Developing the theme**
  — Listen to the song 'Moving' and have children make non-locomotor movements in response to the lyrics (e.g. sharp, smooth, heavy, light, fast and slow movements).
  — Develop these into locomotor movements and include different levels and directions as indicated in the lyrics.
  — In groups, create a short dance sequence to the music of the song, with stylised movements to represent the sharp, smooth, heavy, light, fast and slow sounds. Add an accompaniment to the dance using the homemade instruments.
- **Closure activities**
  — Share the created dances with the rest of the class. Reflect on the effective use of the different elements of dance in the different performances.

Resources
CD and words of 'Moving', homemade instruments, room to move.

Assessment, based on specific indicators
(Teacher to complete at end of activity)

4. Drama: Sounds Great!

Outcomes from syllabus
(Teacher to insert relevant outcomes from state or territory syllabus)

Indicators
Children will mime to a narration using different levels and dynamics of movement, participate in choral reading with expression, use instruments as sound effects, create their own drama based on contrasting sound effects, and critically analyse their own and others' drama works.

Activities
Making, performing, appreciating

Type of drama
Improvisation, sound effects, choral reading, movement and mime

Elements covered
Tension, mood, contrast, space, performance

Learning experiences
- **Introductory activities.** Devise a narration based on a walk through different environments. As the narration is read or told expressively, play appropriate homemade instruments (from the visual arts unit) to create sound effects. Examples of different environments:
  — walking happily and lightly on a beautiful sunny day through the green countryside;

MMADD about the arts

- pushing your way through chest-high wavy grass that prickles and sticks in you;
- coming to a paddock and walking happily and lightly on a beautiful sunny day through the green countryside;
- wading waist deep through an icy cold, deep river, balancing on stones to keep from falling to the bottom of the river;
- climbing out and walking happily and lightly on a beautiful sunny day through the green countryside;
- squelching through thick, oozy mud that threatens to suck you in, step by step;
- clambering onto dry land and walking happily and lightly on a beautiful sunny day through the green countryside;
- creeping through a big, dark forest with scary sounds all around and trees reaching out to trap you with their spindly, gnarled branches;
- coming to the end of the forest and walking happily and lightly on a beautiful sunny day through the green countryside;
- battling your way through a whirling, swirling snowstorm, shivering with cold and being almost blinded by the snow;
- sheltering in a cave, feeling something soft and warm, realising it is a *bear* and running all the way back, through the snowstorm, through the big, dark forest, through the thick, oozy mud, through the icy, cold, deep river, through the thick wavy grass, back home up the stairs and into bed!

- **Developing the theme**
    - Read the story *Going on a bear hunt* (see 'Resources' below) with the children using contrasting vocal expression and instrumental accompaniment between the chorus and walking through the different environments.
    - Read through the story again with creative vocal expression and instruments, this time having the children repeat each phrase after you have read it, for example:

        We're going on a bear hunt (We're going on a bear hunt)
        We're going to catch a big one! (We're going to catch a big one!) and so on

    - Divide the class in four and have one-quarter read the first line, one-quarter read the echo part of the story, one-quarter play instruments as sound effects, while the final quarter mimes the actions from the text. Finish by the miming children snuggling under the covers and pretending to be asleep. Repeat and swap parts so everyone has a turn at both miming and choral speaking.
    - Have children create their own dramatised story based on the structure of *Going on a bear hunt*. Focus on including contrasting sounds that can be created by their homemade instruments as a key part of the drama and using these to convey emotions, characterisation, events and actions. Identify who is involved, what they are feeling, what is happening, why it is happening, how it starts, how tension is built up, what happens in the climax, how it is resolved and how it finishes.

- **Closure activities**
  — Share the dramas and reflect on the importance and effectiveness of the different sounds used to convey feelings, actions, events and characters.
  — Have children discuss and/or write about their experience, describing how they developed the drama, how they felt in the role, what part the music/sounds played in the drama, what they felt worked in the drama and why it worked, and how they felt the performance could be improved.

Resources
Going on a bear hunt by M. Rosen and H. Oxenbury (see reference at the end of the chapter for publishing details), homemade instruments (from visual arts unit), pens and paper.

Assessment, based on specific indicators
(Teacher to complete at end of activity)

5. Media: Sounds Great!

Outcomes from syllabus
(Teacher to insert relevant outcomes from state or territory syllabus)

Indicators
Children will describe one of the homemade instruments verbally, and create a poster showing a photo of their instrument, describing how it was made and played, and reflect on the effectiveness of the design and layout of the posters.

Activities
Designing, making, appreciating

Skills and processes
Designing, layout, formatting, shooting, writing, publishing, displaying

Form of media
Photography, print, computer

Learning experiences
- **Introductory activities**
  — Display all the homemade instruments in the centre of the circle. Have children select in their minds a homemade instrument that is not their own and have them describe it, for example: what it looks like; what was used to make it; how it was made; how it is played; and what sort of sounds it makes.
  — The rest of the children have to guess which instrument they are describing.
- **Developing the theme**
  — Have the children take a photo of their own homemade instrument, print and scan the photo, or download it onto the computer, and then create a poster on the computer. Include the photo and describe the procedures they went through to make the instrument, how it is played and what it sounds like.

- **Closure activities**
  - Display the posters around the room.
  - Reflect on the effectiveness of their design and layout.

Resources
Homemade instruments from visual arts unit, camera (scanner), computer, paper.

Assessment, based on specific indicators
(Teacher to complete at end of activity)

'Advance Australia Fair'
Written in association with Verity Madsen

1. Visual arts: 'Advance Australia Fair'

Purpose of program
Children will compare and contrast natural and built environments through each art form, in relation to the song 'Advance Australia Fair'.

Outcomes from syllabus
(Teacher to insert relevant outcomes from state or territory syllabus)

Indicators
Children will examine pictures of Australian landscapes and create their own 2D artwork to illustrate a line of 'Advance Australia Fair', create a natural feature from the Australian environment in clay, assist in creating a collaged mural featuring built environments and reflect on the visual arts techniques, media and skills used in the unit.

Activities
Designing, making, appreciating

Form of visual arts
2D: Drawing/painting; 3D: Ceramics, collage

Subject matter covered
Places and spaces

Learning experiences
- **Introductory activities: 'Advance Australia Fair'**
  - Using photos, travel brochures, pictures or calendars of Australian landscapes, discuss and identify the different types of natural features of Australia (desert, rainforest, mountains, beach and so on) and the composition of the pictures.
  - Categorise the pictures of the Australian landscapes and have children place each under one of the headings.
  - Discuss the bright, vibrant and bold colours found in the Australian landscape. Identify and record what colours children see in the pictures and how

the pictures make them feel. Create a word bank of these words to which the students can refer. Look at other artists' representations of Australian landscapes (e.g. those of Ken Done and Colin Lanceley). Compare and contrast photographs of actual scenes with an artist's representation of the same scene.
— Look through a book based on 'Advance Australia Fair' that illustrates each line of the song (see Resources for suggestions) and discuss why each picture was selected to illustrate the corresponding line of the song.
— Have each child select a line from the song and create his/her own two-dimensional artwork to represent the words, using appropriate colours and compositions. Mount and display each illustration with the corresponding line of the song below it. Display mounted artworks as a wall frieze, sequenced in the correct order.

- **Developing the theme: Natural environments**
  — Introduce and demonstrate the use of clay to children and the relevant vocabulary, for example:

Wedge	=	Method for removing the air bubbles
Slip	=	Mixture of water and a little clay for joining
Joining	=	Using slip to join pieces of clay together
Knead	=	Working the clay like bread dough
Roll	=	Using a rolling pin to make the clay flat
Slab	=	Flat piece of clay that has been rolled
Coil	=	Sausage-like shapes of clay
Pinch	=	Using the fingers to create a shape in the clay

  — Have children select a natural feature from the Australian environment and create a model of this in clay and then share their artworks with the other children, explaining how and why they created their artwork.

- **Closure activities: Built environments**
  — Discuss pictures and photographs of cities and other built environments (e.g. Sydney Opera House, Sydney Harbour Bridge and Parliament House). Look at examples of collage (e.g. Jeannie Baker's books) and discuss how collage can use a variety of media to create the desired representation.
  — Create a collaged class mural depicting a variety of built environments around Australia that feature in the new words to the song (written in the music lessons).
  — Discuss how each child used the different collage techniques and media to help create the class mural. Write the new words of the song under the mural.

Resources

Photos, pictures, travel brochures, calendars or Australian landscapes and built environments, Jeannie Baker books (e.g. *Window*, *Where the forest meets the sea*), clay, rolling pin, water, board, collage materials, large sheet of paper or cardboard for mural, paints, felt pens, book illustrating lines from 'Advance Australia Fair' (e.g. *Advance Australia Fair* by Peter Dodd McCormick uses Australian artworks; *Advance Australia Fair* by Peter Dodd McCormick, illustrated by John McIntosh, uses

MMADD about the arts

cartoon-style drawings; and *Sing! Australia* uses children's drawings). See the references at the end of the chapter for publishing details.

Assessment, based on specific indicators
(Teacher to complete at end of activity)

2. Music: 'Advance Australia Fair'

Outcomes from syllabus
(Teacher to insert relevant outcomes from state or territory syllabus)

Indicators
Children will learn to sing two verses of 'Advance Australia Fair', using beat, dynamics and pitch activities; create a rhythm rap about natural environments in Australia; add body and vocal percussion to the rap; create a simple melody to the rap; create a new verse to 'Advance Australia Fair' based on built environments; add appropriate dynamics and instruments; and discuss how effective this is.

Activities
Making, performing (singing, playing instruments), appreciating

Type of music
Vocal music: songs and raps; students' compositions

Elements covered
Duration, dynamics, pitch, tone colour, structure

Learning experiences
- **Introductory activities: 'Advance Australia Fair'**
  — Sing the first verse of 'Advance Australia Fair', keeping the beat using body percussion.
  — Using a book illustrating the song, discuss the meaning of the words of the second verse and learn to sing it.
  — Sing both verses of the song using body percussion to keep the beat.
  — Use hands to show the various changes in pitch of the song.
  — Using paper and felt pens have the children sing the song and graph the changes in pitch, showing the high and low parts of the song with lines.
  — Discuss which lines in each verse could be sung softly and which ones could be sung medium or loudly. Sing the two verses through again, clapping to the beat, singing lines softly, medium or loudly, as decided by the group. Discuss how effective this was and make any suggested changes.

- **Developing the theme: Natural environments**
  — List the different word pictures/descriptions in the song, for example:

    We are young and free
    Golden soil
    Wealth for toil
    Our home is girt by sea, and so on

- Select different percussion instruments to represent each description in the song. Experiment to see how the instruments can be played to create the best representation of these word pictures. Play these instruments to the song as it is sung. Discuss which sounds worked well and which ones could be modified to produce a better effect. Make necessary changes and sing the song again with the appropriate instruments.
- Decide on a symbol for each of the instruments used and how it was played. Write down a graphic score of the song, based on how and when each instrument was played. Play the graphic score back without the song, to create a piece of music about Australia.
- In groups, create a rhythm rap about the natural environments in Australia:

  > Deserts, farmlands, mountains high
  > Rainforests, Uluru, rivers dry
  > Waterfalls, rivers, golden sand
  > All together make up this land

- Chant the rap with body and vocal percussion.
- Select three notes (e.g. C, D, and E) on tuned percussion and experiment using the different notes to the rap, for example:

Des-	*ert*	*farm*	*lands,*	*Moun-*	*tains*	*high*
C	D	C	D	E	E	E

- Add notes to the whole rap, play it through and make changes to improve it.
- Sing and play the rap through confidently. Share it with the rest of the class.

- **Closure activities: Built environments**
  - Clap the rhythm of 'Advance Australia Fair' while singing the words. Discuss the metre of the song and how each line scans. Look at which words rhyme and which don't. Work out how many syllables are in each line.
  - Brainstorm built features around Australia (e.g. Opera House, Parliament House, Sydney Harbour Bridge, house in suburbia, high-rise apartments in the large cities, bridges and important buildings).
  - As a class, make up a new verse to the song, using these ideas, for example:

    > We've built our nation brick by brick,
    > Our buildings stand so fine,
    > Our bridges, towers and monuments,
    > Our heritage sublime.
    > Look east and west and north and south,
    > O'er landscapes rich or bare,
    > We've made our mark on history's page,
    > Advance, Australia fair!

  Mark in which lines could be sung loudly, which could be sung medium and which could be sung softly. Practise this and make necessary changes. Add appropriate instruments to represent the different words and objects in the new verse. Sing the new verse through with instruments and dynamics. Discuss if it could be made even better and, if so, how. Make necessary changes and practise.

MMADD about the arts

Resources
Words, music and CD of 'Advance Australia Fair', felt pens, paper, tuned and untuned percussion instruments, books illustrating 'Advance Australia Fair' (see visual arts resources).

Assessment, based on specific indicators
(Teacher to complete at end of activity)

3. Dance: 'Advance Australia Fair'

Outcomes from syllabus
(Teacher to insert relevant outcomes from state or territory syllabus)

Indicators
Children will move to illustrate phrases from 'Advance Australia Fair' showing considered use of different levels and directions, participate in a group sculpture/dance of a natural environment scene and then of a natural environment scene moving into a built environment scene, and reflect and comment on their work using the language of dance.

Activities
Making, performing, appreciating

Contexts of dance
Students' compositions

Elements covered
Action, time, dynamics, space, relationships, structure

Learning experiences
- **Introductory activities: 'Advance Australia Fair'**
  — Examine the artworks illustrating each line of 'Advance Australia Fair', either children's own artworks from the visual arts unit or those from commercial books (see visual arts resources). Call out different phrases of the song and have children create movements to represent the phrases (e.g. 'young and free', 'history's page', and 'joyful strains'). Repeat this activity and have children do the same movements but in a different direction. Repeat, and have children do the same movements but on a different level.
  — In groups have children create a dance to reflect the content of the lyrics of the national anthem using the elements of dance.
  — Share this with the rest of the class for comment and feedback, using the language of dance.
- **Developing the theme: Natural environments**
  — Examine pictures of natural environments throughout Australia; show and discuss the clay artworks created in the visual arts unit (i.e. what they represent, how the clay was moulded and how it felt when you kneaded it).
  — Move into small groups and designate one person in each group to be the potter. Start with the group as a 'lump of clay' and have the potter mould them into a natural environment scene.

- Put on music with a strong beat and have them create stylised movement sequences, as a group, starting from the low level of being a still lump of clay, and rising up to form parts of the completed sculpture of a natural environment scene.
- Develop a dance based on this activity. Practise it and improve it where necessary. Play through the complete dance sequence to music. If possible video the presentation and show it for feedback and discussion.

• **Closure activities: Built environments**
- In small groups, select one of the built features from the new verse made up in the music unit and the mural completed in the visual arts unit. Create a sculpture of it using the children's bodies and relevant props. Have the rest of the class guess which built feature it is.
- Put two groups together, and create a movement sequence starting with one sculpture and then move through a series of smooth movements to create the second sculpture (e.g. move from representing the Sydney Harbour Bridge to describing Parliament House with their bodies).
- Remain in this larger group and decide on one natural environment and one built environment. Discuss the steps that may be taken to change their bodies from representing a natural to a built environment.
- Create a series of movements which show, firstly, the natural environment, and then the beginning of buildings, the development of more built features and finally the built-up environment.
- Practise these and make the transitions smooth to create a single series of dance movements. Ensure that a variety of speeds, levels, contrasts, directions, locomotor and non-locomotor movements and so on are used to make it interesting.
- If possible, video this sequence and make changes after viewing it. If no video camera is available, use freeze frames or still photography, or have one person observe while the others move and have them offer suggestions for improvement and praise, as well as reflecting on the effective use of the different elements of dance.

Resources
Lyrics to 'Advance Australia Fair', pictures and artworks of natural and built environments around Australia, music with a strong beat, video camera.

Assessment, based on specific indicators
(Teacher to complete at end of activity)

4. Drama: 'Advance Australia Fair'

Outcomes from syllabus
(Teacher to insert relevant outcomes from state or territory syllabus)

Indicators
Children will improvise a scene from 'Advance Australia Fair', tell a story expressively with gestures about how a natural environment changes into a built

environment, create a drama based on a scenario about developing a natural environment, and comment and discuss the effective use of elements of drama in the children's shared performances.

Activities
Making, performing, appreciating

Type of drama
Improvisation, storytelling

Elements covered
Tension, focus, mood, time, contrast, symbol, space, performance

Learning experiences

- **Introductory activities: Advance Australia Fair**
  — Look again at the variety of artworks and photographs of Australian landscapes and at the children's own artwork illustrating the national anthem.
  — Have all the children or group select their own artwork and act out a description of the artwork and the relevant line in the song. Have them build a short improvisation about the people involved, the environment, how the people feel, what they are doing and so on. For example, for the line: 'Their home is girt by sea', children could act out a beach scene, with people swimming, surfing and sunbaking; or they could enact an under-the-sea picture, using fish, seaweed, dolphins and so on to tell a story. Encourage them to think about what is happening, why it is happening, who is involved, what they are feeling, why they are acting this way, how the improvisation starts, climaxes and ends, and so on.
  — Share the dramatisations of the song with the other children.

- **Developing the theme: Natural environments**
  — Look at the Jeannie Baker book *Window* and talk about each page and what is changing in the view out the window (i.e. countryside gradually changing to a cityscape).
  — Have the children take their artwork illustrating a line from 'Advance Australia Fair' and pretend they are looking out a window to this scene. Then have them describe verbally and with movements how the landscape could change over the years as the natural environment is gradually replaced by buildings and other built features. Encourage them to use the elements of drama, movement and voice skills to depict the changing landscape.
  — Have them sketch out the final picture they 'see' in their mind's eye of how their original landscape has changed into a built-up landscape.
  — Share these descriptions and sketches with the other children in the group.

- **Closure activities: Built environments**
  — Discuss 'hot issues' that could be raised when natural countryside is turned into a built-up environment (e.g. chopping down trees, pollution in the waterways and air, and loss of wildlife).
  — Create a drama based on one of these hot issues (e.g. a local council that has had an application from a wealthy businessman to build a large shopping centre in a parkland area).

- In creating the drama, think about the questions: Where is the scene set? What is happening? When did it happen? How did it happen? Who is involved? What are they doing? What are they feeling? What motivates them? What is at stake? How will it start? How will it end?
- Share the 'work in progress' dramas. Have the rest of the class comment and ask them questions such as: Where is the scene focused? How can contrasting movements be used to create clarity of message and interest? How can they use gesture more effectively? What is each person feeling and thinking? Do they need to add any props, costumes or sound effects to the drama? What is the mood of the scene and does it change?
- Continue to work on the dramas, make changes to improve them, rehearse and share performances.
- Video the performance and reflect on it using the language of drama.

Resources
Artworks and photographs of Australian landscapes, Jeannie Baker's book *Window*, paper, coloured pencils.

Assessment, based on specific indicators
(Teacher to complete at end of activity)

5. Media: 'Advance Australia Fair'

Outcomes from syllabus
(Teacher to insert relevant outcomes from state or territory syllabus)

Indicators
Children will photograph their 2D artworks, create a PowerPoint presentation based on the song 'Advance Australia Fair' using their digitised artworks and music, and video the dance and drama presentations.

Activities
Designing, making, appreciating

Skills and processes
Designing, layout, sequencing, writing, shooting, special effects, publishing

Form of media
Computer, video

Learning experiences
- **Introductory activities: 'Advance Australia Fair'**
  - Create a PowerPoint presentation of 'Advance Australia Fair' using digital photos taken of the artworks, type in the words for each line, and insert a recording of the song so the frames can be shown in sync with the song.
- **Developing the theme: Natural environments**
  - Video the dance presentation for feedback and discussion.

- **Closure activities: Built environments**
  — Video the drama presentations for feedback and discussion.

Resources
Video camera, computer, digital camera.

Assessment, based on specific indicators
(Teacher to complete at end of activity)

SPRINGBOARDS FOR DISCUSSION AND APPLICATION

1. Write an arts program for a selected class of children that includes discrete developmental learning activities and outcomes for each art form and that integrates across the arts and with at least one other key learning area.
2. Analyse what Multiple Intelligences have been included and what generic skills are being developed throughout the program.
3. Select one of the sample programs and adapt the ideas to suit a selected class, based on their previous experiences and their abilities, skills and understandings within each art form.

REFERENCES

Baker, J. (1987), *Where the forest meets the sea*, Walker Books, London.
Baker, J. (2002), *Window*, Walker Books, London.
Groundwater-Smith, S., Cusworth, R. & Dobbins, R. (2001), *Teaching: Challenges and dilemmas*, Harcourt, Sydney.
McCormick, P.D. (1991), *Advance Australia Fair*, Angus & Robertson, Sydney.
McCormick, P.D. (1996), *Advance Australia Fair*, illustrated by John McIntosh, Gap Publishing, Norman Park, Qld.
McCormick, P.D. (1996), *Sing! Australia*, Weldon Kids Publishing, Warriewood, NSW.
Pfister, M. (1992), *The rainbow fish*, North-South Books, New York.
Rosen, M. & Oxenbury, H. (1989), *We're going on a bear hunt*, Walker Books, London.
Vaughan, M. (1984), *Wombat stew*, Scholastic, Gosford, NSW.

Index

A is for Apple Pie (Greenaway) 182
A is for Aunty (Russell) 182–3
ABC 60
ABC Classic Kids 60, 76, 92
ABC (Pienkowski) 182
ABC Sing Along! 284
Aboriginal artwork 5, 181, 185
Aborigines 7
abstract expressionism 173
academic achievement 21
accent (music) 47, 70
Action: Education and the Arts 8
action, in dance 192, 205–7
adapting, of media 111
Advance Australia Fair (McCormick) 325
'Advance Australia Fair!' (song) 297, 324–32
advertisements 118, 120, 124, 132, 142, 143
aids *see* visual aids
Alice and Aldo (Lester) 182
Allen, Pamela 176, 179, 250
alphabet books 182
alphabet dance 222–3
'The Alphabet Song' 259
analogous colours 154
analytical skills 21
Anangu people 185
ancient art 171
Anderson, W. 256
Animal capers (Argent) 182
animal sounds 89
Animalia (Base) 182, 183, 222
animals 151, 186, 276
annotated work samples 41
anti-stress strategies 23
AppleWorks (software) 170
APRA 233
Argent, Kerry 182
arranging 65
art history 148, 149, 171–4
art software 142
arts
    appreciation of 182, 183–4, 186, 289–90

    art for art's sake 20
    definitions of 8
    exploration of colour 276–85
    importance of 20–4
    marginalisation of 9, 10
    relation to Multiple Intelligences 273–6
    in society 2–5
arts education
    approaches to 11–13
    economics of 4
    history of in Australia 5–11, 14
    national review of 10–11
    Senate inquiry into 10
    see also assessment; dance; drama; integration, and the arts; media; music education; programming, in arts education; visual arts education
assessment 38–41, 59, 293
attitudes, of teachers 17, 31
audiences 108, 114, 231
audio recordings 41
Australasian Performing Right Association Limited 233
Australia Council 7
'Australian Animals' (song) 81
Australian Education Council 9

Baby Bilby, Where Do You Sleep? (Oliver) 186
Baha Men 70
Bailed up (painting) 241
Baker, Alan 92
Baker, Jeannie 163, 292, 325, 330, 331
Bananas in Pyjamas Songbook 93
Baroque art 172
barrier games 235
The Barrumbi Kids (Norrington) 181
Base, Graeme 182, 222
bass lines 82–3
bass notes 51
Bastin, Henri 175
Bateson, Catherine 247
batik 169–70

beanbag beat 69
Bear and Chook (Shanahan) 251
beat 47, 49, 67, 68–70, 201, 223
Beat Wheels 72, 88
behaviour management strategies 29–33, 35
beliefs 3
Beyond Pink 74
Beyond the Script (Ewing and Simons) 236, 238
binary form 48, 194
'BINGO' (song) 70–1
bodily-kinaesthetic intelligence 268, 272, 278–9, 281, 283, 284–5
body language 25–6, 32
body percussion 73, 80, 90, 100–1, 136
Boku-Undo Company 159
'Botany Bay' (song) 74, 96, 259, 260
bottles, as musical instruments 85
'Bound for South Australia' (song) 97
Bowen, Wally 105
Boyd, Arthur 175
Breughel the Younger 243
bridge (music) 47
brochures 133–4, 135
A Burke and Wills Suite (Sculthorpe) 175
'Bydlo' 76

calendars 135
camera techniques 123, 127–31, 160
captions 133
card making 165
cardboard printing 158
cardboard puppets 162
Carmina Burana 75
Carnival of the Animals (Saint-Saëns) 92, 228
cartoons 133
Cat and Fish (Grant) 175
'Caterpillar' (song) 83
CD players 75
censorship classifications 121

ceramics 165–7, 177
Champions of Change... (Fiske) 21
chance, in dance 219–20
chants 48
character signs 132
characterisation, in films 124–5
children, getting to know 29–30, 198
Children's Games (painting) 243
chime bars 81, 82, 85, 98
Chinese whisper mimes 246–7
choral reading 237, 246, 249–50, 252, 279
choral speaking 237, 245, 246
chords 51
choruses 47, 48, 96
Christian, Erin 33
'Christmas Round' (song) 97
circus performers 221–2
clap sticks 181
Clark, V. 3
The Classic Kids Album 60, 92
classical art 171
classroom environments 31
classroom organisation 36
clay 165, 167
Clay, G. 3
'Click Go the Shears' (song) 74, 93, 96
clip art 171
close-ups 127
closed activities 11–12
codas 47
codes, in messages 113
collages
    to accompany text 180, 181, 182–3
    in drama education 229, 236, 253
    in media education 136
    using visual-spatial intelligence 274
    in visual arts education 157, 163–4
colour 132, 153–4, 276–85
Combs, M. 21
comedy, on television 120
comic strips 143
Common and Agreed National Goals for Australian Schooling 9
common space 211, 214
communication 2, 24–9
Community Harmony Project 262–5
complementary colours 154
composing 65, 98
compulsory education 6
computers 110, 114, 116, 138–45, 170
    see also electronic media; software

conducting 73, 80
consultation, in assessment 39
content analysis 112
contextual descriptions, in lesson plans 35
contrast, in drama 230
convention, in messages 113
cool colours 154
cooling down, in dance classes 207, 208, 211, 215, 220–1, 224
cooperative composing 98
copyright 233
costume 125, 232
Cox, Tania 252
craft, history of teaching of 7
creative writing 8, 111, 143
creativity 4, 20, 65, 191
Crees, Carol 70, 207
Crees, Gary 70, 207
crescendo 76
critical thinking skills 9, 21
cropping 111, 127
cross-hatching 179
crotchets 49, 51
Cubism 173
cultural context 114, 131, 191
cultural heritage 3, 29
curriculum development 6–7, 9
curriculum profiles 9
curriculum statements 9
Curtis, Neil 175
Cusworth, R. 288
cut-out cards 165
cut time 201
cyber kids 107

Dalcroze, Emile-Jacques 46
dance
    activities to teach elements of 203–24
    appreciating 196
    and bodily-kinaesthetic intelligence 274
    cooling down 207, 208, 211, 215, 220–1, 224
    dealing with refusal to join in 200
    developing dance lessons 202–3
    discipline in the dance class 199–200, 202
    in drama education 229
    elements of 192–3
    history of teaching of 6
    making dances 194–5
    organising the classroom for 198–9

performing 195–6
practical considerations 196–203
preparation for teaching 197
programming for 291, 295–8, 304, 312, 315, 320–1, 328–9
safety considerations 197–8
structured dances 195–6
student compositions 221–4
teacher confidence in teaching 197
teaching social dances 201–2
types of 196
using Multiple Intelligences 270, 279–80, 283–4
using music 55, 62–4, 88–9, 191, 200–1, 224
warm-ups for 197, 202–7, 209, 211–13, 216, 219, 221
ways of learning through 190–1
what to wear 199
working in groups 217
Dance at Bouvigal (painting) 277
Dawkins, John 9
debriefing, after drama activities 241
decision-making skills 21
definite pitch 47
Diamond Painting in Red, Yellow and Blue (painting) 277
Diary of a Wombat (French) 178–9
diary writing 248
didgeridoos 181
A Different Sort of Real... (Greenwood) 248–9
diminuendo 76
Dion, Celine 76
discipline, in the dance class 199–200
displaying, of artworks 111, 173
distribution, of media 111
Dobbins, R. 288
Done, Ken 325
'Doodah' (song) 74
drama
    activities to teach elements of 244–53
    based on literature texts 247–53
    in the classroom 227–8
    developing skills through 228
    drama games 233, 241, 244, 247, 251, 252
    elements of 230–3
    establishing a purpose 240
    history of teaching of 6, 7
    lesson planning 240–1
    lesson preparation 239
    as part of children's lives 227

Index

performance aspects 231–3
practical considerations in teaching 239–44
programming for 291, 295–7, 300, 303, 310, 316, 321–3, 329–31
rhythm dramas 74
stimuli for activities 241–2
types of 233–9
use of photography 131
using Multiple Intelligences 270, 278–9, 281–3
warm-ups for 233, 241
ways of learning through drama 228–30
see also Readers' Theatre
drawing 5–7, 156, 175–81, 185, 186, 274
Dry Weather (painting) 174
Drysdale, Russell 174, 175
Dunn, J. 236
duration, in music 45, 47, 67–9, 102
dyes, for silk painting 168
dynamics
  activities to teach 67, 75–80
  as an element of music 45, 47
  in dance 192, 209–11
  dynamic grids 78
  notation of 102

early finishers 31–2, 174
echo clapping 71
economic rationalism 4, 9
editing 111, 143
Education and the Arts 7–8
eighth notes 51
Eisner, E. 2
electronic media
  activities to teach elements of 138–45
  creating artworks with 170
  digital images to accompany text 179, 180, 182, 183, 184
  elements of 114
  genres of 110
  see also computers; Internet; software
Emerson, Ralph Waldo 24
emotions
  communication of through art 3
  expression of in dance 209, 210–11, 214
  expression of in drama 230, 244, 249
  expression of in media education 142

expression of in visual art 151
Emus in a Landscape (painting) 175
ensemble sounds 47
enthusiasm, of teachers 26, 32–3
environment, of the classroom 31
environmental sounds 74, 100
Escher, M.C. 185
etching 158
evaluation skills 21
events, in artworks 152
Everyday Kolor 157
Ewing, R. 226, 236, 238
exams 41
explanations 28, 31
Expressionism 173
eye contact 26, 28

The Farm Concert 79, 101
'The Farmer in the Dell' (song) 191
Fast Food Rockers 66
feedback 28–9, 36, 114
film
  activities to teach elements of 121–6, 143
  audio and visual aspects 123–4
  camera techniques 123
  characterisation in 124–5
  genres of 109, 122
  in media education 114
  use of light and dark 124
  see also photography; video
film plots 122–3, 124
film posters 121
finger puppets 162, 239
Finn report 9, 22
Fiske, E. 3, 5, 21, 44
flashcards
  in dance classes 201
  in drama classes 244
  in music classes 75, 76, 81, 83–4, 92, 95
flip books 134
focal points 111, 135
focus, in drama 230
Ford, R. 4
form 47–8, 67, 155, 194
formative assessment 39
formatting 111
Fowler, C. 1
Fox, Ethel Carrick 243
Fox, Mem 247
Frames of Mind (Gardner) 267
framing 110, 127, 129
free education 6
freeware 142

freeze frames 241, 247
French, Jackie 178–9
fruit and vegetable printing 158

game songs 48
Gardner, Howard 267, 268
generalist teachers 6, 11, 13–16
genres 113
gestures 26
Gill, S.T. 175
glass painting 157
Gleeson, Libby 185, 243
glove puppets 162, 239
Going on a Bear Hunt 93, 101, 322–3
Goldilocks and the Three Bears 85–6, 101
Graham, Bob 178
grammar 33
Grandpa and Thomas (Allen) 176
Grant, Joan 175
graphic scores
  features of 52
  and musical intelligence 274
  as stimuli for dance 221–2
  to teach dynamics 78, 79
  to teach musical structure 97–8, 99–100, 101–2
  to teach tone colour 95
Green Paper on education 9
Greenaway, Kate 182
Greentree Public School 262
Greenwood, Kerry 248
Grieg, Edvard 229
Groundwater-Smith, S. 288
gypsona masks 161

Hailstones and Halibut Bones (O'Neil) 280
half notes 51
Hamilton, Arthur 284
Hari, Mata 189
harmony 47, 83
Harris, Christine 249
Heffernan, John 174–5, 252
'Here We Go Looby Loo' (song) 218
'Hero' (song) 74
heroes 135, 219
Hertrich, J. 3
'He's Got the Whole World' (song) 93
Hi-5 63, 84
Hindley, J. 280
Hits for Kids 3 70
Hits for Kids 5 66

'Hokey-pokey' (song) 218
Hoodoo Gurus 76
hot seating 235, 242, 249, 251, 253
'How Did You Travel to School?' (song) 217, 310, 311

'I Am Me' (song) 96, 296, 298–302
'I Can Sing a Rainbow' (song) 284
'I Know an Old Lady Who Swallowed a Fly' (song) 99
I Thought I Heard (Baker) 92
identity 3
'If You're Happy and You Know It' (song) 75
illustrations, to text 183–4
iMovie (software) 126
implicit learning 21
impressionism 173
improvising
    in drama 233–6, 240, 244–9, 250, 253, 274
    in music 65, 68
'In the Hall of the Mountain King' (Grieg) 229
indefinite pitch 47
indicators, of effectiveness 35, 36, 40, 292
indigenous art 2, 5
    see also Aboriginal artwork
injuries, treatment of 198
inspectors 6
instrument grids 90
intaglio printmaking 158
integration, and the arts
    Community Harmony Project 262–5
    development of 257
    meaning of 257–8
    models of 258–62
    sample integrated programs 296–332
    thematic programs 262, 265–6
    see also Multiple Intelligences
intelligence quotient 21
intelligence-specific lessons 272–3
interactive activities 32
Internet 143, 150, 152, 170, 171
interpersonal intelligence 269, 272, 276–80, 283–5
interviews 41, 111, 137–8
intrapersonal intelligence 269, 272, 275, 280–1, 284–5
invitations 133–4
IQ 21
Italian terms, in music 53, 76

'It's All Coming Back to Me' (song) 76

'Jabbin, Jabbin' (song) 95
James, Ann 177
Jamil's Shadow (Harris) 249–50
Jensen, E. 21
Jethro Byrde (Graham) 178
jiggle puppets 162–3
jingles 120
'John Brown's Holden' (song) 75, 93, 96, 292, 311
Jones, P. 3
journalism 144–5
journals 41
Juniper, Robert 175
junk printing 158
'Just a Little Seed' (song) 83, 217

key competencies 9
key learning areas 10, 35
Kids Pix (software) 170
Kids Pix Studio (software) 170
King, Stephen Michael 253
knowledge 16
Kodaly, Zoltan 46
'Kookaburra' (song) 82–3
Kroeger, Chad 74

'L-O-V-E' (song) 84
'Lamb Stew' (song) 82
Lanceley, Colin 325
landscapes 175
language, in messages 113
Lawrence, J. 256
layout 111
Learning Centre Workcards 38
learning centres 37–8, 271
learning styles 29
Lee, Ann 74
Leighton, Ray 243
lesson evaluation 37
lesson planning
    in the arts generally 33
    in dance education 202–3
    in drama education 240–1
    elements of lesson plans 36
    importance of preparation 27
    in media education 115
    teacher's preparation 35
    in visual arts education 173–4
Lester, Alison 182
life skills 4
life training 22–3
lighting 111, 232

limbo 81
line, in visual art 153
The Lion, the Witch and the Wardrobe (film) 125
literacy 9, 33, 266–7, 273–6
    see also multiliteracies
literature, drama based on 247–53
lithography 158
Little Humpty (Wild) 177
'Little Red Caboose' (song) 259, 260
Little Red Riding Hood 259, 260
locomotor movements 55, 192, 206
logical-mathematical intelligence 269, 272–3, 275, 277–80, 285
logos 141
'Looby Lou' (song) 191
The Lost Thing (Tan) 183

Magritte, René 184
major scales 51
make-up 232
Manly Beach — Five Girls on Longboards (painting) 243
Manly Beach — Summer is Here (painting) 243
marbled cards 165
marbling 159–60, 186
marketing 108
masks 161–2, 232, 238–9, 253
Matisse, Henri 277
Matthews, Penny 179–80, 250
Mayali language 181
Mayer report 9, 22
McCormick, Peter Dodd 325
McIntosh, John 325
McLean, Andrew 179
McLuhan, Marshall 24
media
    analysing and appreciating 112–14
    in drama education 229–30
    forms of 106, 109–10
    influences of on children 106–7
    in marketing 108
    media-rich versus media-poor children 107
    media stereotypes 135
    violence in 109
    see also electronic media; media education
media education
    activities for teaching 117–45
    child-centred activities 116–17
    designing and making media 110–11, 117

Index

history of 6
lesson preparation 115
lesson structure 117
programming for 290, 294, 296–7, 307–8, 317, 323–4, 331–2
real-life activities 117
reasons for teaching 108–9
resources 115
using Multiple Intelligences 270, 285
see also computers; electronic media; film; photography; print media; radio
medieval art 171
melody 47, 67, 86, 98–9
messages 108, 113, 132
metaphors, in drama 231
Microsoft Fine Artist (software) 170
Microsoft Powerpoint (software) 138, 140–1, 143, 145, 285, 292, 317
Microsoft Word (software) 139–40, 170
migrants 7
Milli, Jack and the Dancing Cat (King) 253
Millicent (Baker) 163
Mills, J. 3, 23
mime 237–8, 244–7, 249–50, 274
mind-mapping 274
minims 49, 51
Minoeska (dance) 207–8
'Minoeskja' (song) 70
Miro, Joan 184
mixed media 179–80, 182
modelling 274
Modigliani, Amedeo 277
Moffat, Tracy 243
Mondrian, Piet 277
monochromatic colours 154
monoprinting 158
mood, in drama 230
Mortensen, Kevin 243
Mossalov, Alexander 218
motifs 47
motivation, to join in drama activities 240
Mouse Paint (Walsh) 277
Moussorgsky, Modest 76, 92
movement
 in mime 237–8, 246–7
 to music 55, 62–4, 88–9, 191, 200–1, 224
 see also dance
'Moving' (song) 70, 320–1

multicultural music 60
multiculturalism 7
multiliteracies 262, 266–7
multimedia *see* electronic media
Multiple Intelligences 262, 267–85
Murchison Sand Plain (painting) 175
Murray, Martine 180–1
music education
 activities to teach musical elements 66–102
 approaches to 45–6
 cultural context of music 61–2
 elements of music 45, 46–8
 explanations of musical terms 49–53
 history of 5–6, 7, 10
 listening to and appreciating music 55–6, 59–62, 92–3
 making music 54, 65–6
 moving to music 55, 62–4, 88–9, 191, 200–1, 224
 music software 142
 national review of 10–11
 performing music 54–5
 playing instruments 53–5, 63–5, 77, 88–9, 91–2
 practical considerations in class 56–7
 programming for 290, 294, 296–7, 299, 305, 311, 314, 319–20, 326–8
 reasons for teaching music 44–5
 repertoire in music 48
 United States 232–3
 using Multiple Intelligences 270
 using music in drama 228–9, 242
 ways of learning music 56–66
 see also duration, in music; dynamics; musical intelligence; pitch; singing; structure, in music; tone colour
music notation 102
musical instruments 53–5, 63–5, 77, 88–9, 91–2
musical intelligence 268, 272, 274, 278, 281, 283–5
musical notation 71
My Camp (painting) 175
'My Paddle's Keen and Bright' (song) 83, 84–5, 312

naïve art 183
Namatjira, Albert 185
narrative 118

national curriculum 9
naturalistic intelligence 270, 272, 276, 278–9, 280, 282
nature printing 158
neck-rolls 198
Nelson, Brendan 43
Neoclassicism 172
New South Wales, curriculum development 9–10
newspaper printing 158
newspapers 135–6, 145
'Noah's Ark' (song) 89–90
non-locomotor movements 55, 192, 206
Norrington, Leonie 181
notation (music) 102
notes (music) 50–1
'Nothing's Changing My Life' (song) 76
numeracy 9, 273
nursery rhymes 48

objects 152, 158, 244
observation 39
Off the wall dances 207
'Off the Wall' (song) 70
Off Visiting (print) 243
Office of Film and Literature Classification 121
'Old MacDonald' (song) 93, 96
Oliver, Narelle 186
'One Hand, One Heart' (song) 74
One hungry spider (Baker) 163
O'Neil, Mary 280
open-ended activities 12
opening shots, in films 122
Optical art 174
An Ordinary Day (Gleeson) 185
Orff, Carl 46, 75
ostinati 47, 52, 73, 93, 97
O'Toole, J. 236
'Our Family' (song) 91–2, 217
outcomes 40
 see also syllabus outcomes
The Overlanders (painting) 175
Oxenbury, H. 245, 323

packaging 133
paint blob printing 158–9
Paintbrush (software) 170
painting 5–7, 92, 156–7, 168, 176–8
paper making 164
paper-plate masks 161
paper tole cards 165, 166
papier-mâché masks 161–2

339

papier-mâché puppets 163
Papunya School Book of Country and History 185
Papunya School Publishing Committee 185
participation, by teachers 33, 236
partners, in dance classes 216
pattern, in visual art 155
peer assessment 40
peer tutoring 276
Penny, S. 4
pentatonic scales 52, 66, 85, 86, 87, 98–9
people, in art 151
percussion instruments 53, 201
    see also body percussion
performance 54–5, 195–6, 231–3, 242, 289–90
Perrin, S. 22
personal development 3–4, 20
personal space 25, 211–12, 214
pets 276
Pfister, Marcus 297, 313
photography
    activities to teach elements of 126–31, 143, 144
    camera techniques 127–31, 160
    creating artworks with 160
    genres of 109
    intensity and angle of light 131
    landscape versus portrait 130
    in media education 114
    use of light and dark 128
    see also film; video
phrases (music) 53, 95
physical fitness 190–1
physical reinforcement 30
Pictures at an Exhibition (Moussorgsky) 76, 92, 228
Pienkowski, Jan 182
'Pigs' (song) 82
pitch 45, 47, 50, 68, 80–7, 102
'Pizza Hut' (song) 66–8, 70, 75
places, in artworks 152
plaster of Paris 161
play building 238
'Playing Our Instruments' (song) 319
plots, in film 122–3, 124
poems 86, 94–5, 99, 243, 245–6, 281
pokare kare ana 69
'Pokare Kare Ana' (song) 216
polystyrene printing 159
Pop art 174
popular culture 108

popular songs 48, 76
portfolios 41
positioning 111
positive reinforcement 29, 30, 35
post-impressionism 173
postcards 133, 245–6
posters 133–4, 136, 143, 180
posture 25–6
The Potato People (Allen) 179, 250
poverty, and access to media 107
praise 30, 31, 41, 141, 199
preferred intelligences 27, 29
prehistoric art 171
preservice teachers 11, 33
Pretending to Learn (O'Toole and Dunn) 236
Price, L. 4
primary colours 153
principals 6, 15
print media 110, 114, 131–6
printmaking 158–9, 184, 186
problem-solving 21, 37, 195, 267
process-oriented activities 12–13
producers, of media 108, 113, 119
producing 143
product-oriented activities 12
professional development 11, 15, 139
programming, in arts education
    closure activities 293
    contextual description in 292
    for dance 291, 295–8, 304, 312, 315, 320–1, 328–9
    developing themes 292–3
    for drama 291, 295–7, 300, 303, 310, 316, 321–3, 329–31
    implementing programs 16–17
    for media 290, 294, 296–7, 307–8, 317, 323–4, 331–2
    for music 290, 294, 296–7, 299, 305, 311, 314, 319–20, 326–8
    overview 289
    programming in the curriculum 20
    sample integrated programs 296–332
    skills developed by 22–3
    for visual arts 290–1, 295–7, 301, 306, 309, 313, 318–19, 324–6
    see also assessment; indicators, of effectiveness; integration, and the arts; lesson planning; resources
project work 271–2
props, in drama 232
publishing 111

pulse 49
puppets 75, 162–3, 238–9, 253

quality of life 5
quarter notes 51
quavers 49, 51
questioning in role 235–6
questions, in class 39
QuickTime 141
quiet, in the classroom 31

The Rabbiters (painting) 174
radio 8, 110, 114, 136–8, 143
Rain May and Captain Daniel (Bateson) 247–8
Rain (Sculthorpe) 175
The Rainbow Fairies (Anon.) 278–9
The Rainbow Fish (Pfister) 297, 313, 316, 317
rainbows, exploring colour in 277–85
raps 48
READ: Reading Education Assistance Dogs 276
Readers' Theatre
    in drama education 242
    example texts 251, 252
    features of 237
    in programming 292
    for radio 229
    using literacy texts 243
    using Multiple Intelligences 274, 276, 281, 282
recording 111, 138
recreation, dance as 191
Red Landscape (Sculthorpe) 175
reflection 251
reflective journals 41
relationships, in dance 193, 216–19
relief printmaking 158
Renaissance 171
Renoir, Pierre August 277
repertoire 48
representations, in messages 113
resources
    for dance lessons 201
    importance of 26
    in learning centres 38
    in lesson planning 34–5, 36
    management of 31–2
    for media lessons 115
    paucity of 11
    in programming 293–4
    for visual arts lessons 170, 171–2
respect 22

rests (music) 51
Reverse Garbage 172
rewards 30, 199, 202
rhythm
    activities to teach 67–74
    elements comprising 49
    in musical intelligence 274
    as part of duration 47
    in songs 59
    to teach musical structure 95
    tone colour rhymes 90
rhythm dramas 74
rhythm grids 71, 72–3
rhythmic cards 72
ribbon sticks 75, 207–8
RICED model 198
Riddle, Tohby 182
Roberts, Tom 241
'Rock My Soul' (song) 76
Rococo art 172
rod puppets 239
role improvisation 234, 240
Romanticism 172
rondo form 48, 96–7, 194
Rose, J. 3
Rosen, M. 245, 323
routines 30–1, 199, 202, 239
rubber stamps 165
rubbings 158
rule of thirds 128–9
rules 30, 199, 202
Russell, Elaine 182–3

safety, in the classroom 172, 197
Saint-Saëns, Charles 92, 228
Sakura Innovative Marbling Dyes 159
scales 51, 52
Schools Commission 7
screen printing 159
scripted drama 238
scripting 111, 119–20
sculpture 160–1, 179, 184, 213, 235, 251
Sculthorpe, Peter 175
the sea, as a theme 297, 313–17
'The Sea' (song) 217, 314
secondary colours 153
self-assessment 40
self-confidence 24–5, 27
self-development 3–4, 20
self-expression 2, 4, 20, 23–4, 191
self-reflection 37
semibreves 49, 51
semiquavers 51

Senate inquiry, into arts education 10
sequencing 111
service connections 258, 259
sets, in drama 232
shadow puppets 163, 239
Shanahan, Lisa 251
shape, in visual art 155
shareware 142
'She'll Be Coming Round the Mountain' (song) 93
Shoes from Grandpa (Fox) 247
shooting (photography) 111, 143
Shutting the Chooks In (Gleeson) 243
signature tunes 136–7
signs 132, 134, 139
silk painting 168
SilkFix 168
Simons, J. 226, 236, 238
Sing! Australia 326
singing
    activities involving 54
    in dance classes 200, 217, 218
    in drama classes 245
    history of teaching of 5
    to learn musical structure 97
    to learn pitch 81–2
    with other activities 56
    silent singing to the beat 69
    in tone colour exercises 89, 93–4
    using songs to teach musical elements 66–8
    as a way of learning music 57–9
    see also names of specific songs
The Singing Hat (Riddle) 182
sixteenth notes 51
skills 16–17, 116, 117, 242
    see also life skills
'Skip to the Right' (song) 191, 218, 219
The Slightly True Story of Cedar B. Hartley... (Murray) 180–1
Snap! Went Chester (Cox) 252
social identity 3
social reinforcement 30
social skills 191
sociodrama games 233
sock puppets 239
software 142, 170
    see also specific software packages, e.g. *Microsoft Word*
Something More, No. 1 (photograph) 243
A Song of Colours (Hindley) 280
sound cards 182

sound effects 136, 138, 232
sounds, science of 297, 318–24
space 155, 193, 211–15, 231
special effects 111
specialist teachers 13–16
spelling 141
Spiderman sound track 74
spoken word 93
sponge marbling 160
spontaneous improvisation 233–4
staging 232
staves 50
The Steel Foundry 218
stencil printmaking 158
stereotypes, in media 135
stories *see* literature, drama based on; storytelling; words
The Story of the Rainbow: an Indian Legend 281–3
storyboarding 111, 119–20, 126, 143, 144, 274
storytelling 236–7, 242, 245, 246, 249
Strengthening Australia's schools (Green Paper) 9
string puppets 239
structure
    in dance 193, 219–21
    in drama 239–40
    in music 45, 47–8, 67, 68, 95–102
Stuart Little (film) 123
summative assessment 39
Sun Music (Sculthorpe) 175
surface printmaking 158
surrealism 173, 184
syllabus outcomes 35
symbols 2, 23, 132, 231, 266
symmetric correlations 258, 259–60
syntegration 258, 259, 260–5, 276–85
synthesising skills 21

Tailitnama Song (Sculthorpe) 175
Tan, Shaun 183
teacher-in-role 236
teachers 10, 11, 16–17, 33–4, 236
    see also generalist teachers; professional development; specialist teachers
technology, in arts education 8
    see also computers; media; software
television 109, 114, 118–21
tempo 47, 67, 70, 74–5, 201, 207
tension, in drama 230

ternary form 48, 194
tertiary colours 154
text analysis 112
textiles 167, 178, 179
  see also batik; tie-dyeing
texture, in visual art 154
thematic approach, to media analysis 112–13
thematic scores 79
themes, in drama 241–2
'Think Pink' (song) 74
The Three Billy Goats Gruff 79, 85, 101
Three Little Pigs 85, 101
tie-dyeing 169
time-filler activities 11
time, in dance 192, 207–8
time, in drama 230
time management 31–2
time-out, in dance classes 200
time signatures 47, 49–50, 72, 73–4, 208
title songs 136–7
To Town 101
token reinforcement 30
tone colour 45, 47, 68, 88–95, 102
tone, in visual art 153
toothbrush printing 159
traffic reports 138
training, for life 22–3
'Trains' (song) 76, 82
transmitting, of media 111
transport, as a theme 297, 308–12
Travelling (art pack) 309
'Treaty' 89
triads 51
tuned percussion instruments 53
'Twinkle, Twinkle Little Star' (song) 218
Two Summers (Heffernan) 174–5, 252–3
'Two Times' (song) 74

Ultan, L. 20
unison sounds 47
untuned percussion instruments 53
Upway Landscape (painting) 175

values 3
variety, in lessons 32

Vaughan, Marcia 296, 303
verbal-linguistic intelligence 269, 272, 273, 275, 278–85
verbal reinforcement 30
verses 47, 48, 96
Victoria, curriculum development 9
video 125–6, 143, 144, 145
video/audio drama 239
Village Feast (painting) 243
villains 135, 219
violence, in media 109
visual aids 26
visual arts education
  activities to teach forms of 174–86
  appreciating visual art 148–50
  designing and making art 148–9, 155–6
  elements of visual arts 153–5
  lesson planning 173–4
  lesson preparation 170–1
  practical considerations 170–3
  programming for 290–1, 295–7, 301, 306, 309, 313, 318–19, 324–6
  specific techniques 156–70
  subject matter in 150–1
  three-dimensional forms 160–1
  two-dimensional forms 156–7
  using Multiple Intelligences 270, 277–8, 280–1
  using visual arts in drama 229, 243
visual recordings 41
visual-spatial intelligence 268, 272, 273, 274, 277–8, 280, 285
visualisation, of stories 134
vocal collages 236, 253
vocal dynamics 78
vocal music 48
vocational training 4
voice 26, 32
volume *see* dynamics

walking excursions 144
Walsh, Ellen Stoll 277
'Waltzing Matilda' (song) 70, 74, 96
warm colours 154

warm-ups
  for dance 197, 202–7, 209, 211–13, 216, 219, 221
  for drama 233, 241
Warwick, Dene 74
watercolour painting 176
weather reports 121
We're Going on a Bear Hunt (Rosen and Oxenbury) 245
'The Wheels on the Bus' (song) 217
'When You Grow Up' (song) 92, 96
Where the forest meets the sea (Baker) 163, 325
Whitlam government 7
'Who Let the Dogs Out?' (song) 70, 71
whole-language movement 257
whole notes 51
The Wiggles 63
'Wild Colonial Boy' (song) 74
Wild, Margaret 177
Williams, Fred 175
Wimmera Landscape (painting) 175
Window (Baker) 163, 325, 330, 331
Woman Seated in an Armchair (painting) 277
Wombat Stew (Vaughan) 296, 303–7
woodcuts 158
words
  with dance 217–18, 220
  with drama 243, 245, 247–53
  with music 65–6, 80, 85–6, 92, 99–102, 134
  see also literature, drama based on; poems; storytelling
World sound matters 60
writing *see* creative writing
written tests 41

xylophones 98

A Year on Our Farm (Matthews) 179–80, 250–1
Yellow Sweater (painting) 277
Yothu Yindi 89
Young, Blamire 174
Young, S. 4